MAPS OF THE WORLD

Contents

	Page no.
THE WORLD	
Legend	2–3
World, political; population; time zones	4–5
NORTH AMERICA	
North America, political	6
Canada	7
Eastern Canada	8–9
Western Canada	10–11
USA	12–13
Eastern USA	14–15
Central USA	16–17
Western USA	18–19
Mexico	20–21
Central America and Caribbean	22
SOUTH AMERICA	
South America, political	23
South America	24–25
EUROPE	
Europe, political	26
British Isles	27
England and Wales	28–29
Scotland	30
Ireland	31
France	32
Spain and Portugal	33
Italy and The Balkans	34
Turkey	35

	Page no.
EUROPE (Ctd.)	
Central Europe	36–37
Scandinavia and The Baltic	38
ASIA	
Asia, political	39
Northern Russia	40–41
Eastern Russia	42–43
Asia, Southwestern	44–45
India and Southeast Asia	46–47
Central Asia and China	48–49
Japan and East Asia	50–51
East Indies	52–53
Japan	54
AFRICA	
Africa, political	55
Northern Africa	56–57
Southern Africa	58
AUSTRALIA	
Oceania	59
Australia	60–61
New Zealand	62
POLAR REGIONS	
Polar Regions	63
The World, Oceans	64
Index	65–112

Symbols for maps on pages:
8-22, 27-38, 40-54, 60-62

Inhabitants

More than 5 million — **New York**

1 000 000 - 5 000 000 — **Seattle**

250 000 - 1 000 000 — **Mexicali**

100 000 - 250 000 — **Tijuana**

25 000 - 100 000 — Sparks

Less than 25 000 — Monterey

National capital (UPPERCASE) — **OTTAWA**

State capital — **Boise**

International boundary

Disputed international boundary

State boundary

Disputed state boundary

Major road

Other road

Road under construction

Seasonal road

Railway

Canal

Highest peak in continent — McKinley

Highest peak in country — Logan

Height in feet — 17000ft

Depth in feet — 185ft

Coral reef

Dam — Kainji Dam

Waterfall — Niagara Falls

Pass —)(

International airport — ⊕

National airport — ✈

Historical site — ⌂

Scientific site — ⌂

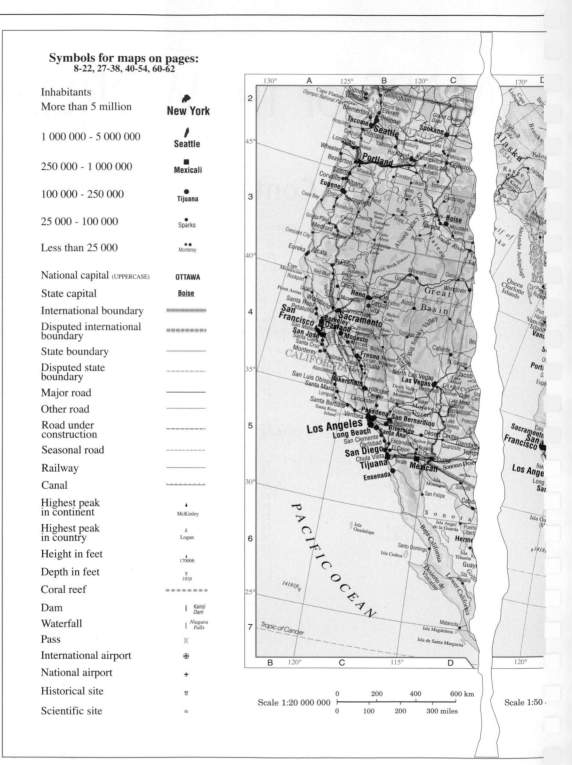

Scale 1:20 000 000

| 0 | 200 | 400 | 600 km |

| 0 | 100 | 200 | 300 miles |

Scale 1:50

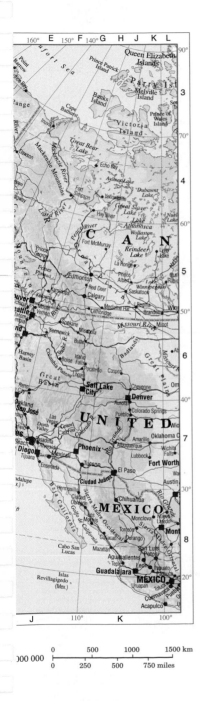

Symbols for maps on pages:
7, 24-25, 56-59

Inhabitants

More than 5 million

Chicago

Columbus   1 000 000 - 5 000 000

Quebec   250 000 - 1 000 000

Halifax   100 000 - 250 000

Anderson   Less than 100 000

NASSAU   National capital (UPPERCASE)

Sacramento   State capital

International boundary

Disputed international boundary

Major road

Road under construction

Major railway

Canal

McKinley   Highest peak in continent

Logan   Highest peak in country

17000ft   Heights in feet

185ft   Depths in feet

Coral reef

Scientific station

Territorial claims in Antarctica

Disputed territorial claims in Antarctica

Grand Coulee Dam   Dam

Virginia Falls   Waterfall

North Pole   Arctic Circle
Tropic of Cancer   Latitudes
Equator
Longitudes
Tropic of Capricorn   South Pole   Antarctic Circle

Colour Key for Contours

Glacier/ ice cap

6000m

5000m

4000m

3000m

2000m

1000m

500m

200m

0m

Marshland

Salt lake

Seasonal lake

Salt desert

Symbols for Political maps on pages:
5, 6, 23, 26, 39, 55

Inhabitants

Lagos   More than 5 million

Ibadan   1 000 000 - 5 000 000

Kano   250 000 - 1 000 000

Gashua   100 000 - 250 000

Maradi   25 000 - 100 000

National Capital

State Capital

International boundary

Disputed International boundary

State boundary

Railway

The letters and numbers in the map edges are there to help you find names. Look for London in the index **29** D4. Turn to page 29 and look top or bottom for number 4 and left or right for letter D. In this blue grid square you will find the city of London.

Scale 1:50 000 000 means that a distance on the map is 50 000 000 times longer on the Earth's surface e.g. 1 cm on the map represents 500 km on the surface and 1 inch on the map represents 800 miles.

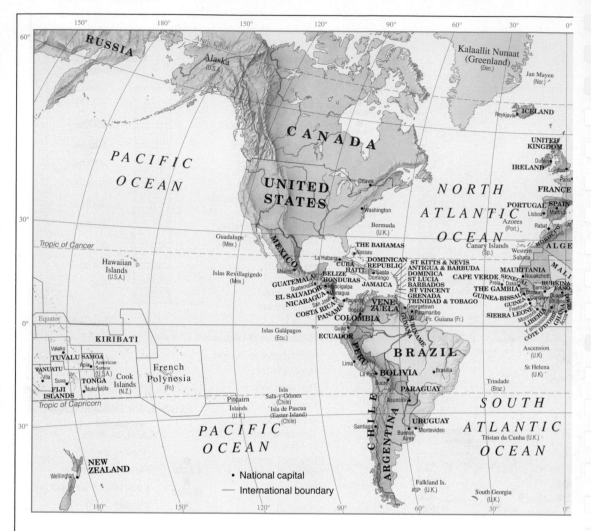

- National capital
— International boundary

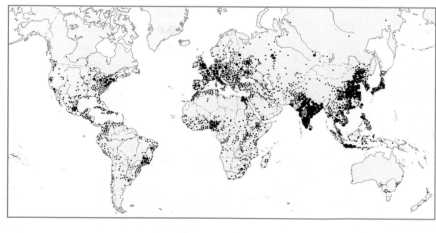

POPULATION

- 10 million inhabitants
- 1 million inhabitants

The density of population varies over the Earth's land surface. Some parts are sparsely populated because of geographical conditions; high mountains, hot deserts or cold tundra. Compare the maps on pages 8-9,10-11. Some parts are densely populated due to good living conditions, economically or physically convenient for the big cities, as well as other reasons such as religion or ethnic grouping. Population growth is mainly centred on the already densely populated areas.

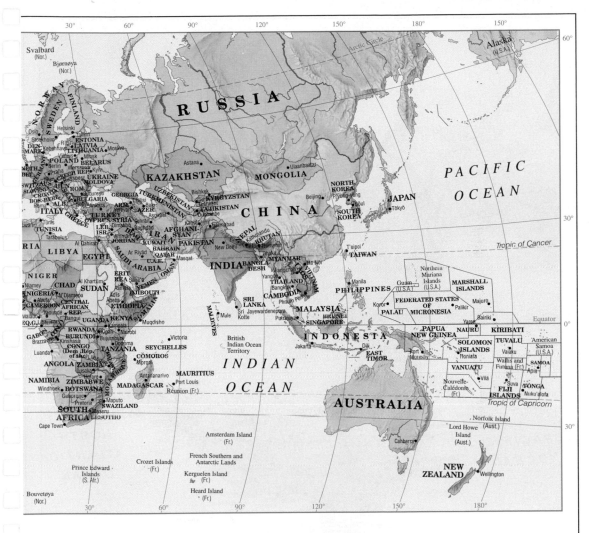

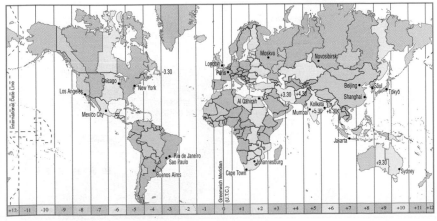

TIME ZONES

The Earth spins around its axis anticlockwise and completes one turn every 24 hours. As the world rotates it is day on the part facing the Sun and night on the side in shadow. As shown on this map, we have divided the Earth into 24 standard time zones. They are based upon lines of longitude at 15 degree intervals but mainly follow country or state boundaries. You can compare times around the world by using the map. For example; when it is 12 noon in London it is 5 hours earlier in New York or 7 am.

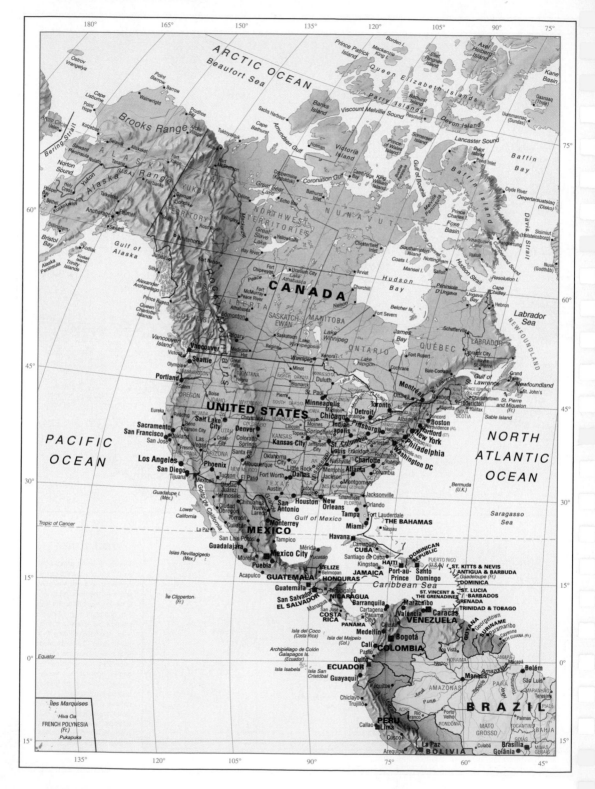

Scale 1: 31 250 000

0   500   1000km

0   300   600miles

© Geddes & Grosset

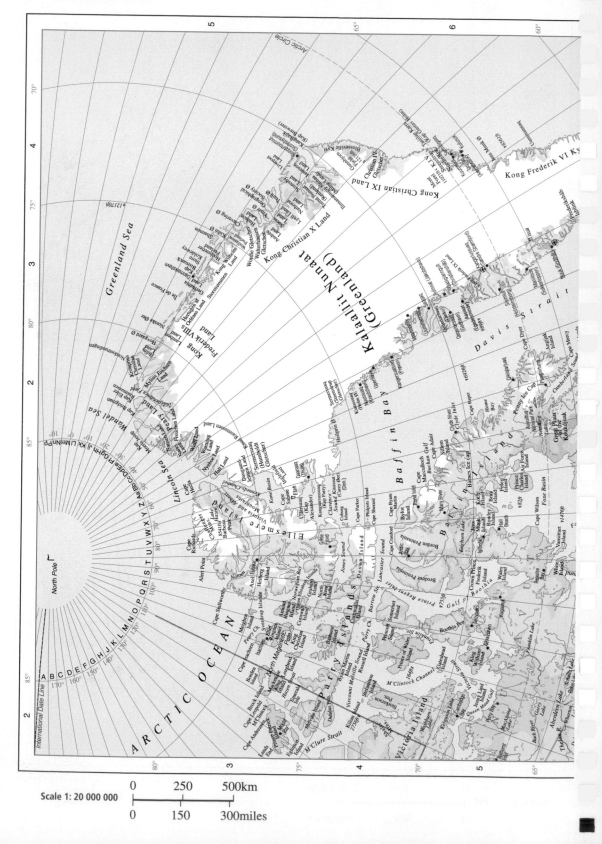

Scale 1: 20 000 000

| 0 | 250 | 500km |
| 0 | 150 | 300miles |

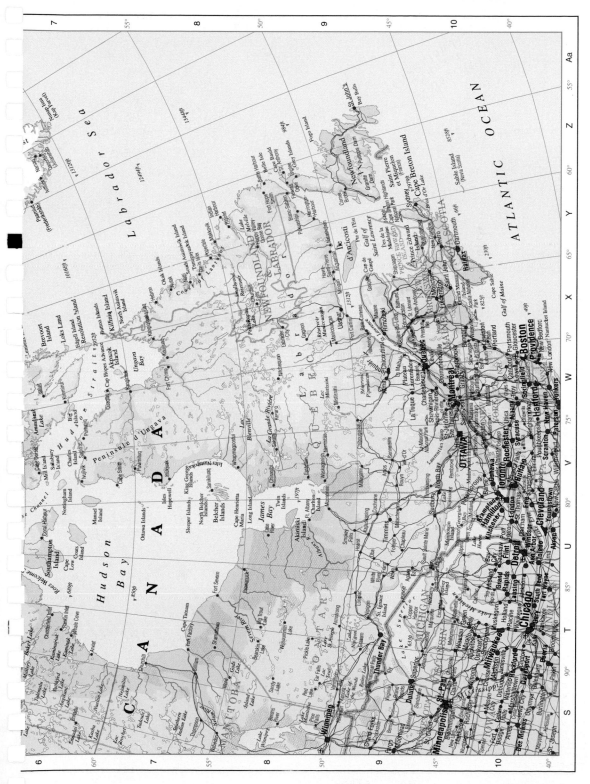

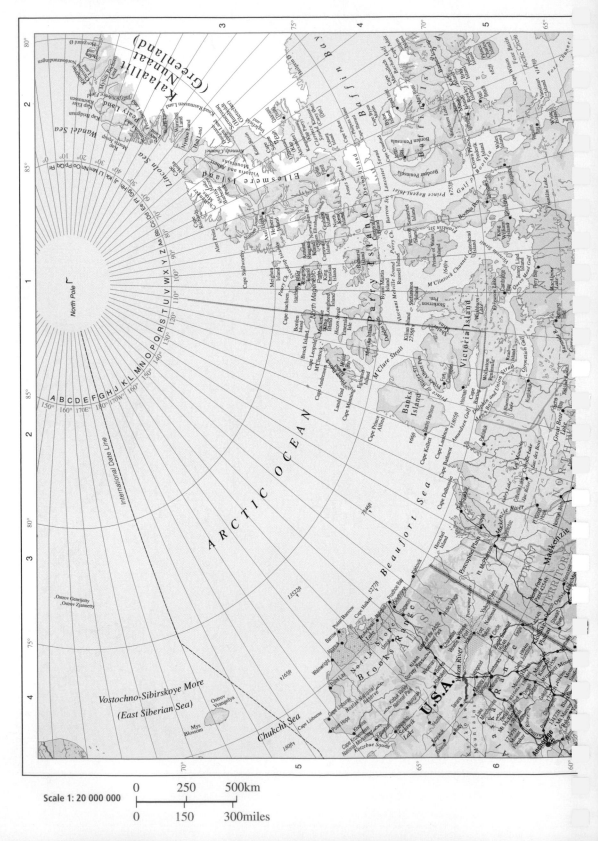

Scale 1: 20 000 000

0   250   500km

0   150   300miles

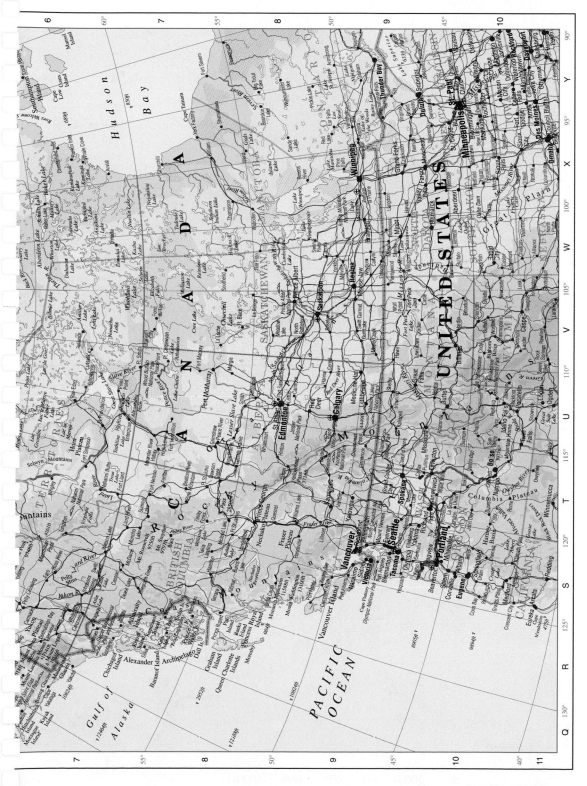

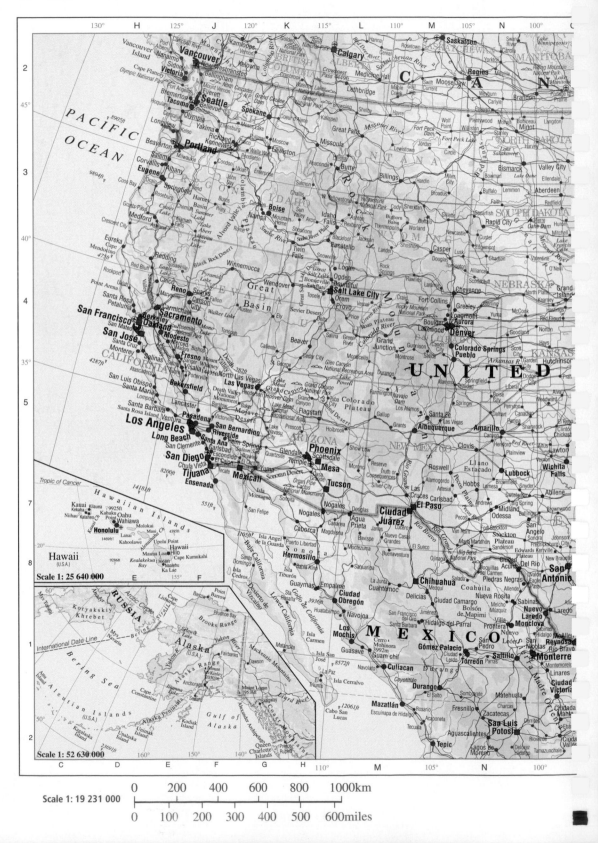

Scale 1: 19 231 000

0	200	400	600	800	1000km

0	100	200	300	400	500	600miles

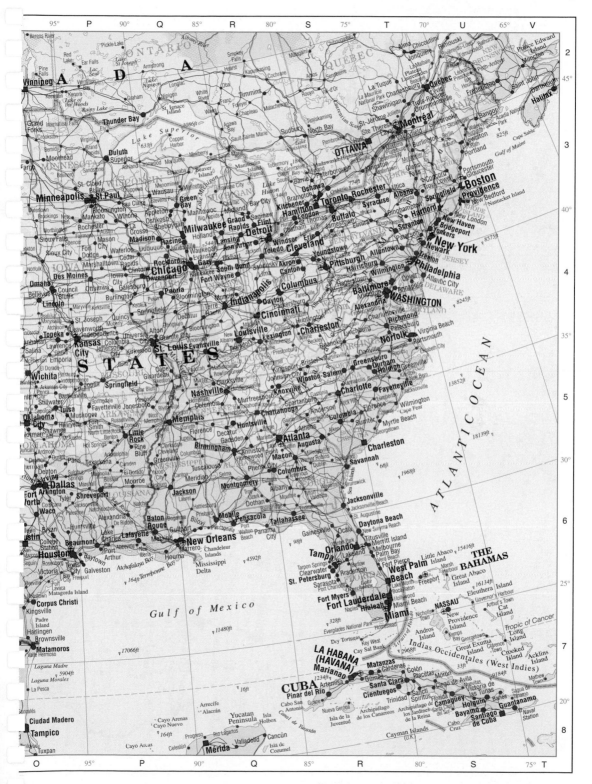

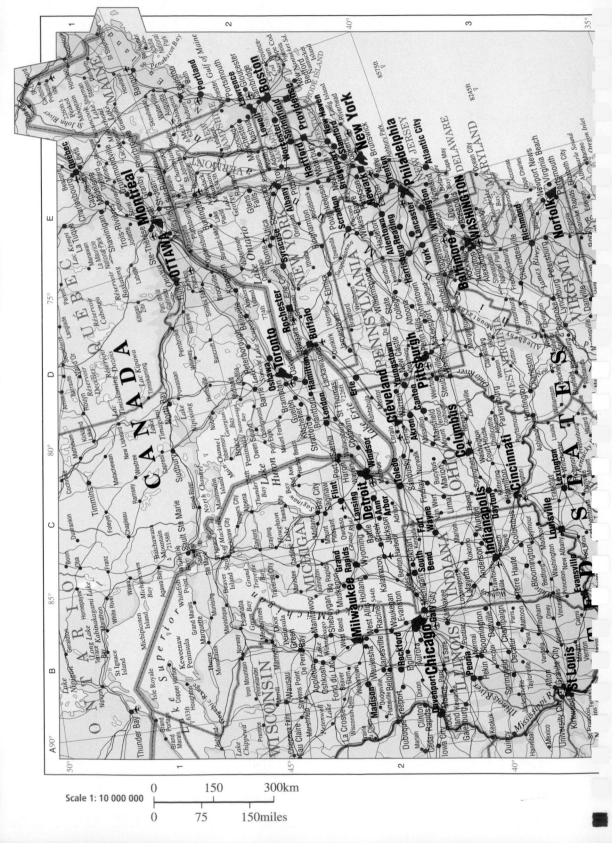

Scale 1: 10 000 000

| 0 | 150 | 300km |
| 0 | 75 | 150miles |

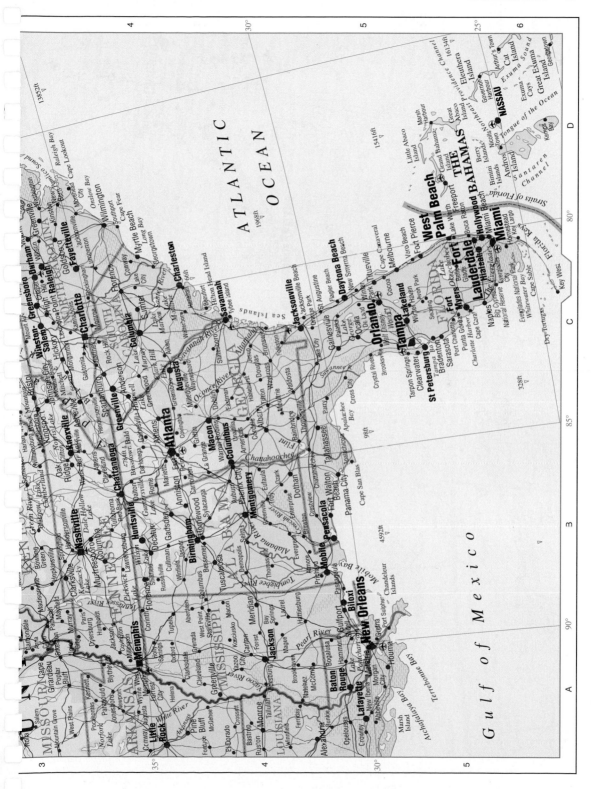

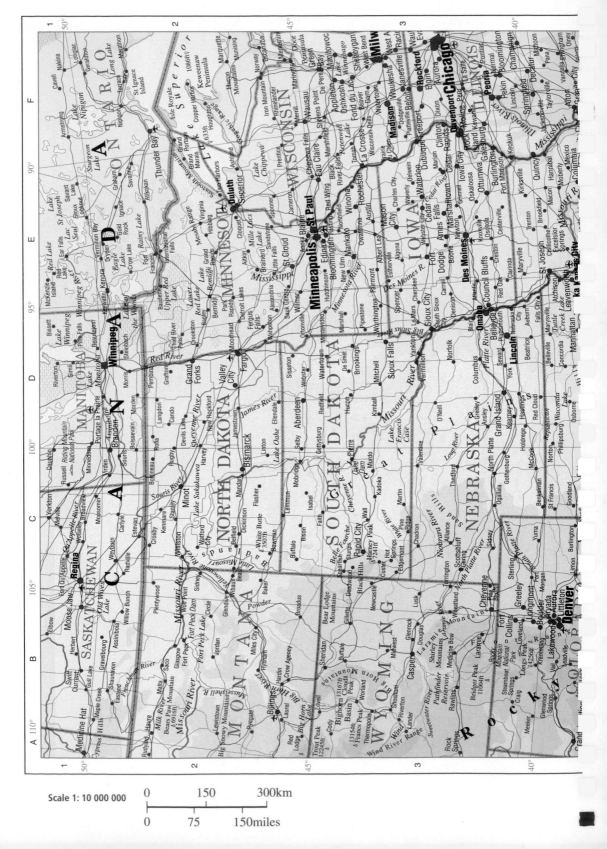

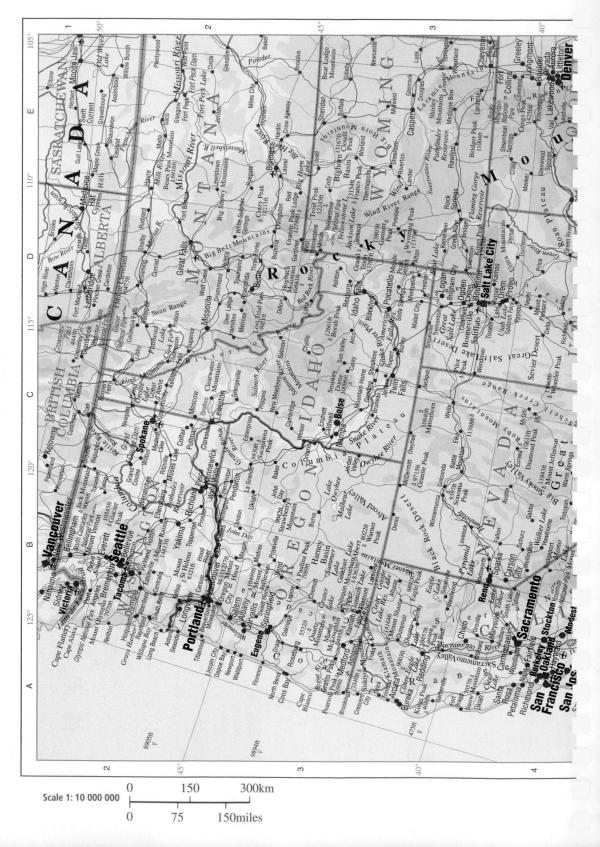

Scale 1: 10 000 000

0   150   300km

0   75   150miles

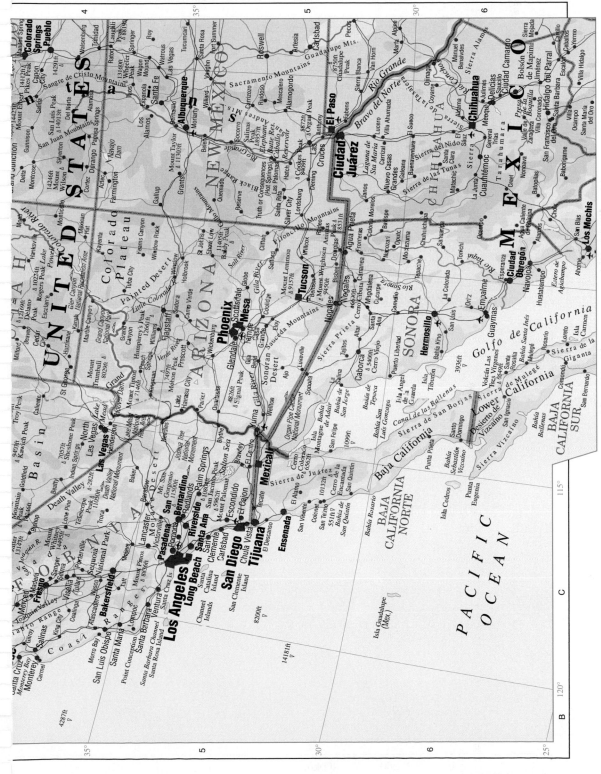

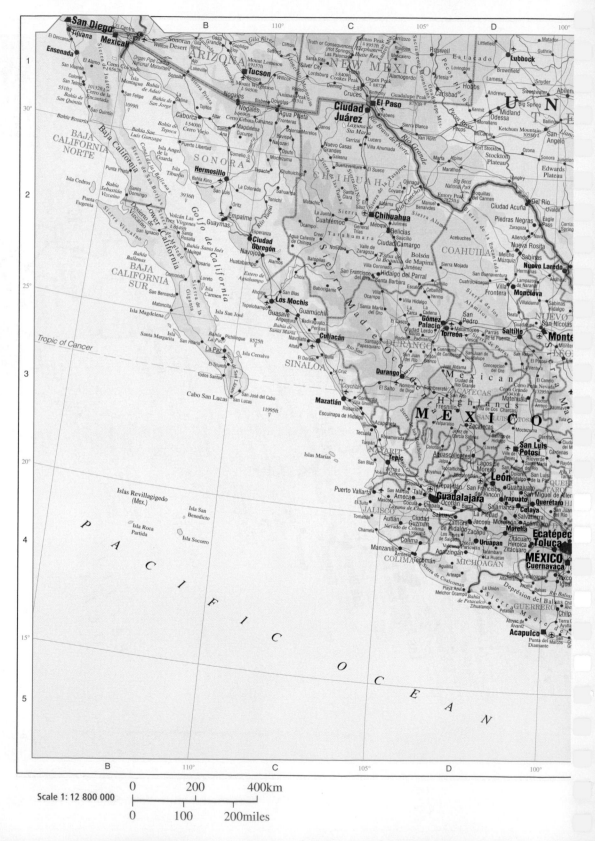

Scale 1: 12 800 000

0   200   400km

0   100   200miles

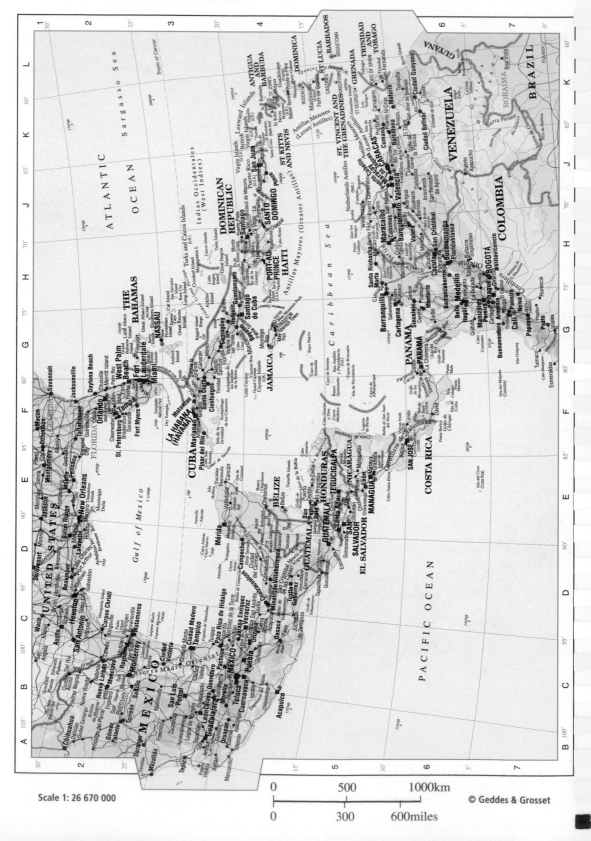

Scale 1: 26 670 000

| 0 | 500 | 1000km |

| 0 | 300 | 600miles |

© Geddes & Grosset

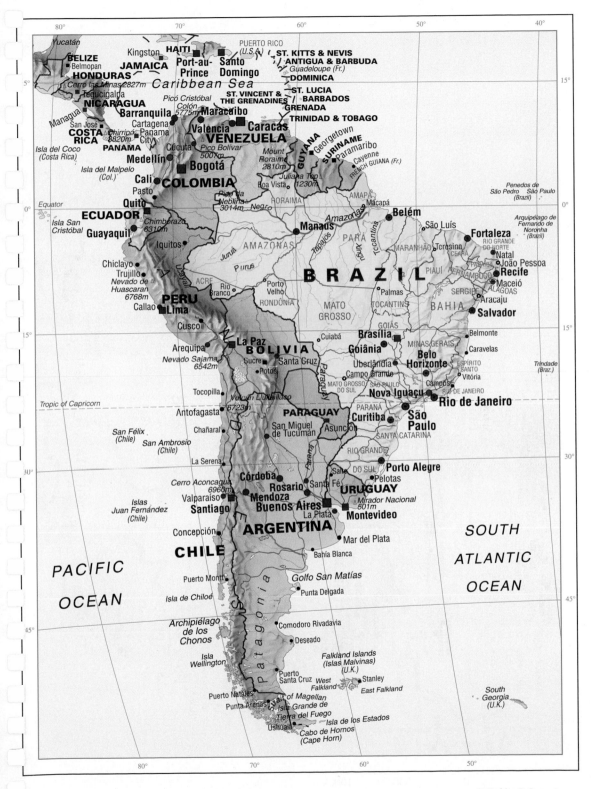

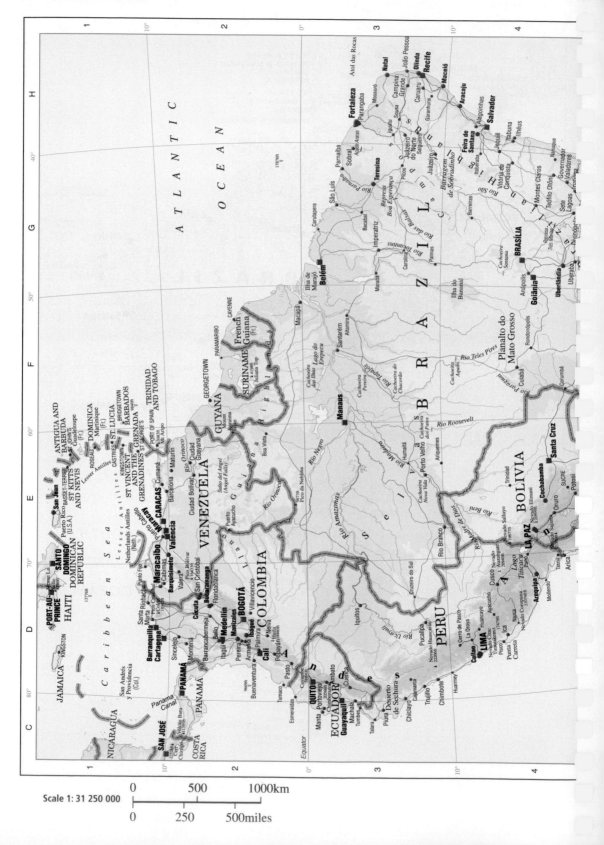

Scale 1: 31 250 000

| 0 | 500 | 1000km |

| 0 | 250 | 500miles |

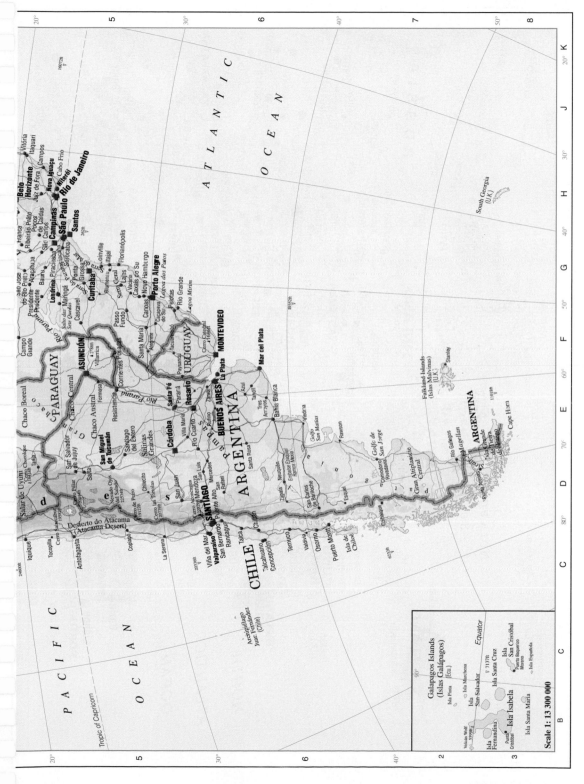

ATLANTIC OCEAN

PACIFIC OCEAN

Tropic of Capricorn

South Georgia (U.K.)

Falkland Islands (Islas Malvinas) (U.K.)
Stanley

PARAGUAY
ASUNCIÓN
Chaco Boreal
Campo Grande

URUGUAY
MONTEVIDEO
Mar del Plata

ARGENTINA

CHILE
SANTIAGO
Valparaíso
Viña del Mar

BUENOS AIRES
La Plata
Rosario
Santa Fé
Córdoba
San Miguel de Tucumán

Desierto de Atacama
(Atacama Desert)

Salar de Uyuni

Iquique
Tocopilla
Antofagasta
Copiapó
La Serena

Río de Janeiro
São Paulo
Santos
Campinas
Belo Horizonte
Vitória
Curitiba
Porto Alegre
Rio Grande
Pelotas

Cape Horn

Bahía Blanca
Viedma
Rawson
Golfo de San Jorge
Comodoro Rivadavia
Río Gallegos
Punta Arenas
Estrecho de Magallanes
Tierra del Fuego

Puerto Montt
Isla de Chiloé
Valdivia
Osorno
Temuco
Concepción
Talcahuano
Talca
Chillán

Galapagos Islands
(Islas Galápagos) (Ecu.)
Equator
Isla Marchena
Isla San Salvador
Isla Santa Cruz
Isla San Cristóbal
Puerto Baquerizo Moreno
Isla Isabela
Isla Fernandina
Isla Santa María
Isla Española
Volcán Wolf
Archipiélago Juan Fernández (Chile)

Scale 1: 13 300 000

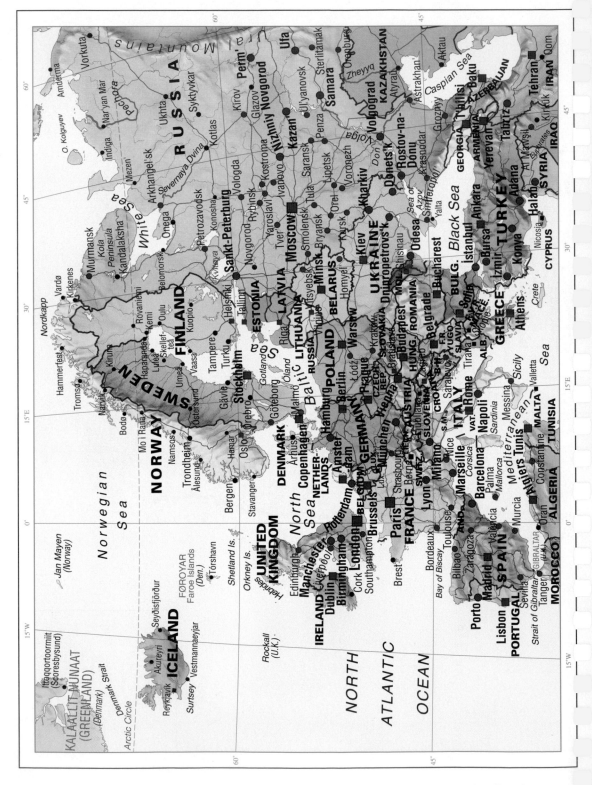

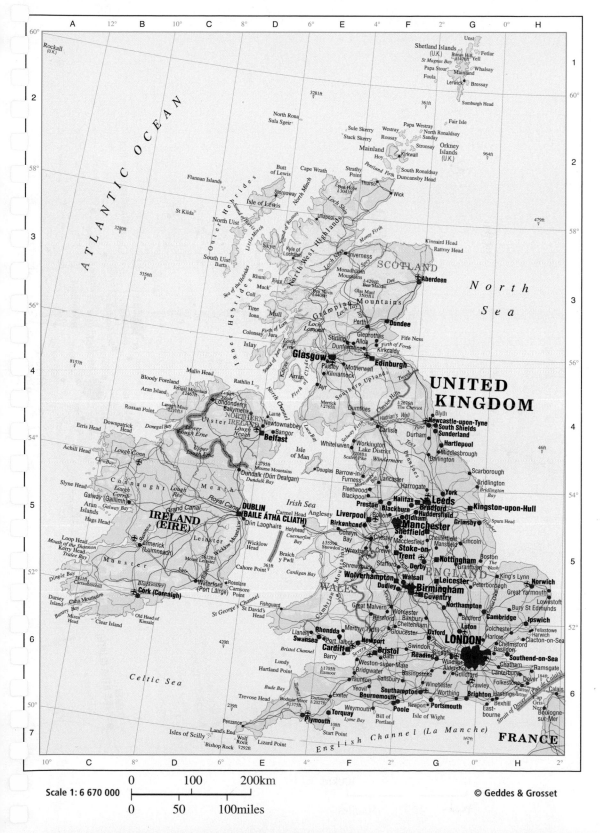

Scale 1: 6 670 000

0   100   200km

0   50   100miles

© Geddes & Grosset

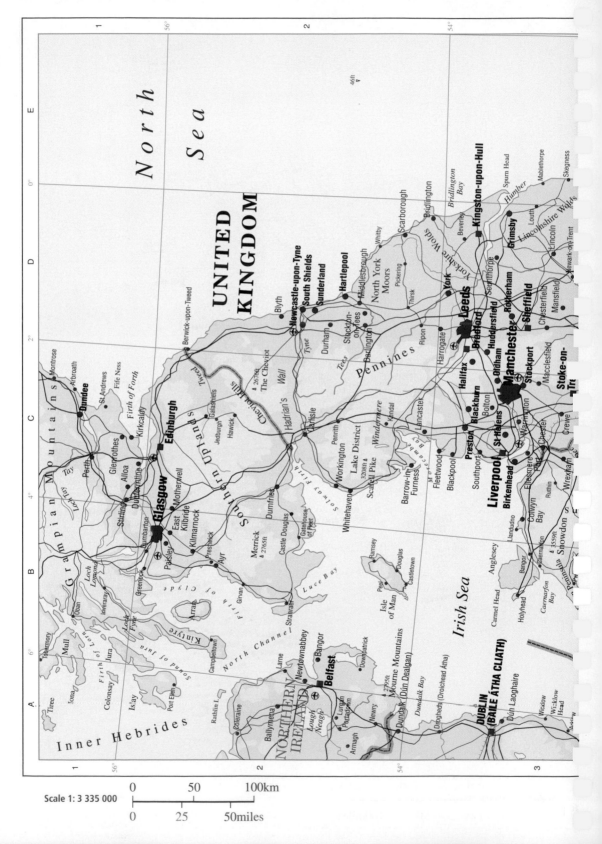

Scale 1: 3 335 000

0   50   100km
0   25   50miles

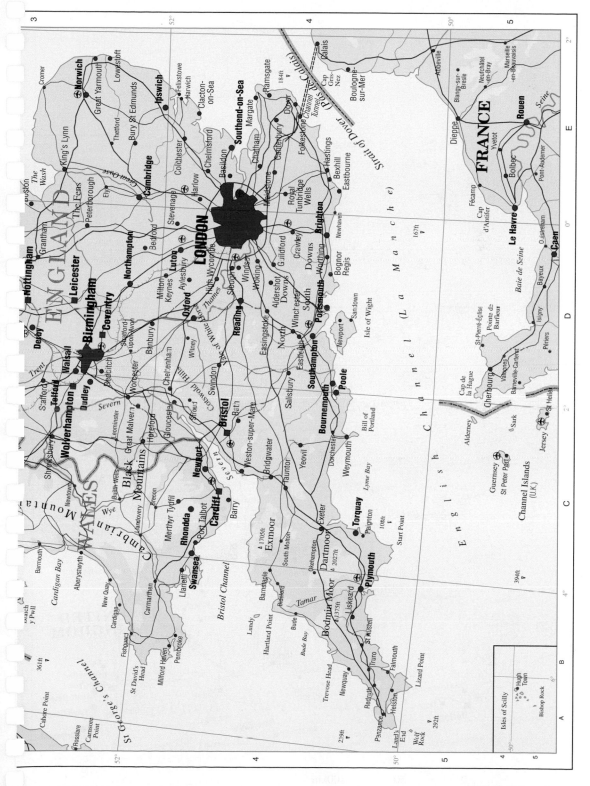

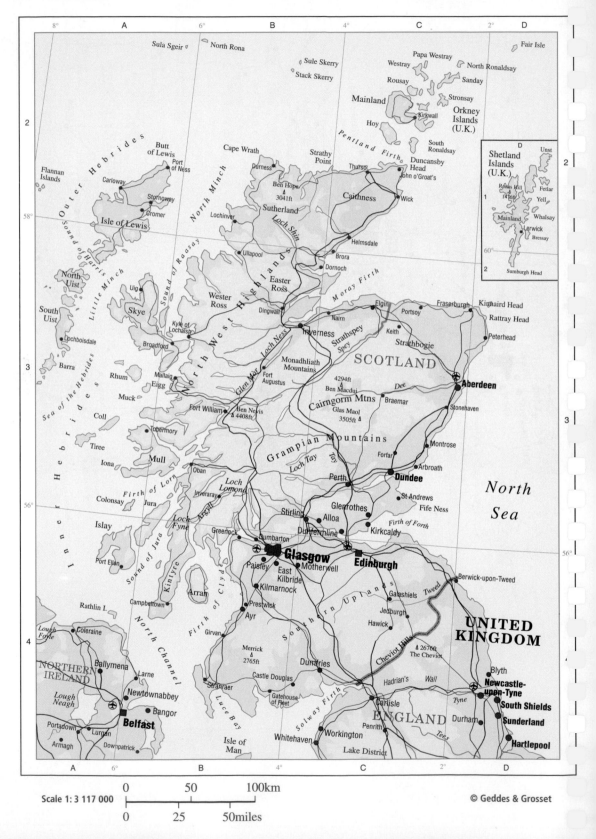

Scale 1: 3 117 000

0   50   100km

0   25   50miles

© Geddes & Grosset

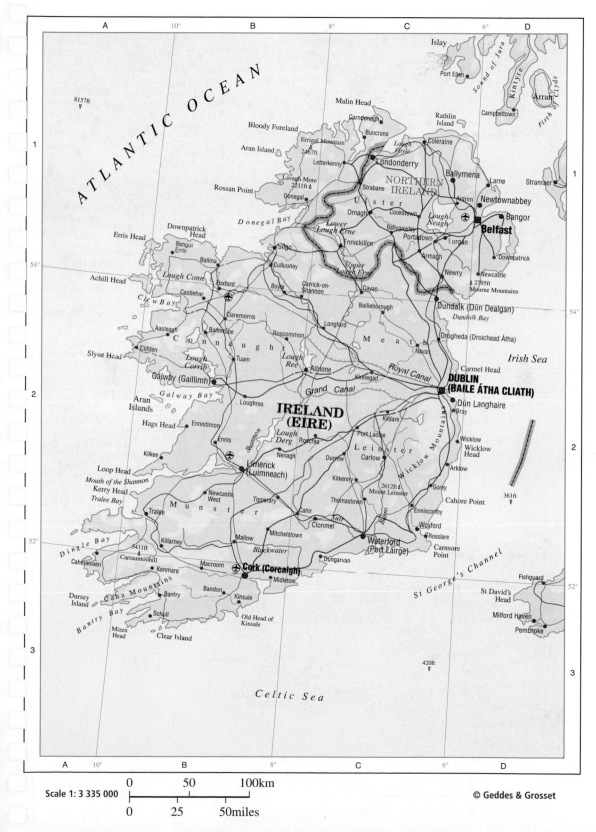

ATLANTIC OCEAN

8157ft

Malin Head

Islay

Port Ellen

Sound of Jura

Kintyre

Arran

Firth of Clyde

Carndonagh

Bloody Foreland

Buncrana

Rathlin Island

Aran Island

Errigal Mountain 2467ft

Lough Foyle

Coleraine

Campbeltown

Stranraer

Letterkenny

Londonderry

Ballymena

Larne

Rossan Point

Lavagh More 2211ft △

Donegal

Strabane

NORTHERN IRELAND

Antrim

Newtownabbey

Downpatrick Head

Donegal Bay

Omagh

U l s t e r

Cookstown

Lough Neagh

Belfast

Bangor

Erris Head

Bangor Erris

Sligo

Lower Lough Erne

Ballygawley

Portadown

Lurgan

Downpatrick

Achill Head

Ballina

Collooney

Enniskillen

Armagh

Newry

2795ft △ Mourne Mountains

Newcastle

Lough Conn

Foxford

Boyle

Carrick-on-Shannon

Cavan

Clew Bay

Castlebar

Bailieborough

Dundalk (Dún Dealgan)

Claremorris

Ballinrobe

Roscommon

Longford

Dundalk Bay

Aasleagh

C o n n a u g h t

Slyne Head

Clifden

Tuam

Lough Rec

Navan

Drogheda (Droichead Átha)

Lough Corrib

Allihone

Kinnegad

Royal Canal

Carmel Head

Irish Sea

Galway (Gaillimh)

Galway Bay

Loughrea

M e a t h

DUBLIN (BAILE ÁTHA CLIATH)

Aran Islands

Grand Canal

Dún Laoghaire

Hags Head

Ennistimon

IRELAND (EIRE)

Kildare

Bray

Ennis

Port Laoise

L e i n s t e r

Wicklow

Kilkee

Lough Derg

Roscrea

Carlow

Wicklow Head

Loop Head

Nenagh

Durrow

Wicklow Mountains

Arklow

Mouth of the Shannon

Limerick (Luimneach)

Kilkenny

Kerry Head

Newcastle West

Tipperary

Thomastown

2612ft △ Mount Leinster

Gorey

Cahore Point

Tralee Bay

M u n s t e r

Cahir

Enniscorthy

361ft

Tralee

Mallow

Mitchelstown

Clonmel

Barrow

Wexford

Rosslare

Killarney

Blackwater

Waterford (Port Láirge)

Carnsore Point

Dingle Bay

3411ft Carrauntoohill △

Macroom

Dungarvan

Cahersiveen

Kenmare

Cork (Corcaigh)

St George's Channel

Fishguard

Dursey Island

Caha Mountains

Bantry

Bandon

Kinsale

Midleton

St David's Head

Schull

Old Head of Kinsale

Milford Haven

Bantry Bay

Mizen Head

Clear Island

Pembroke

420ft

Celtic Sea

Scale 1: 3 335 000

0   50   100km

0   25   50miles

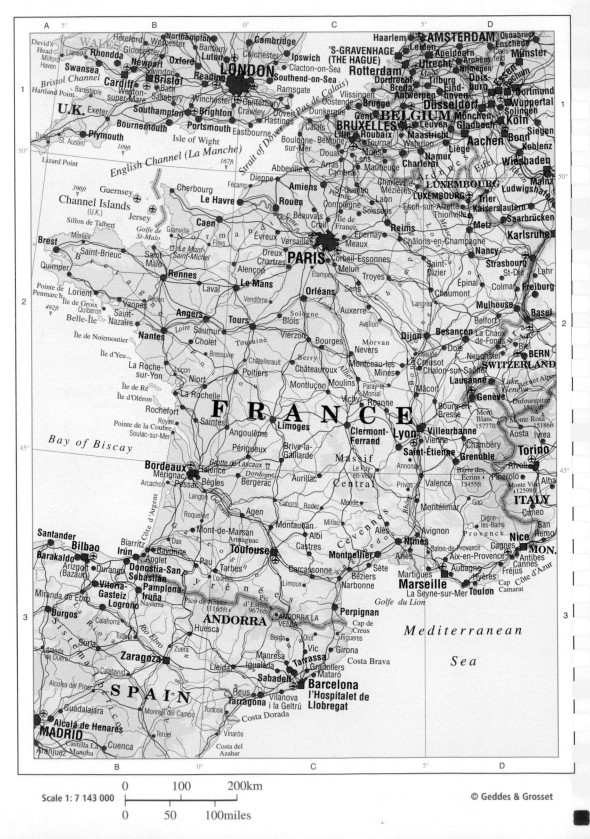

Scale 1: 7 143 000

0   100   200km

0   50   100miles

© Geddes & Grosset

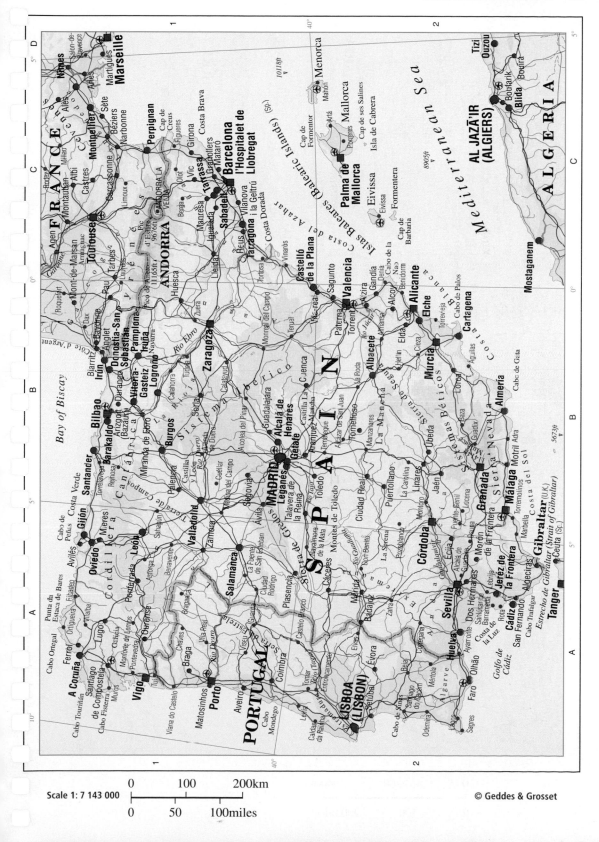

Scale 1: 7 143 000

0   100   200km

0   50   100miles

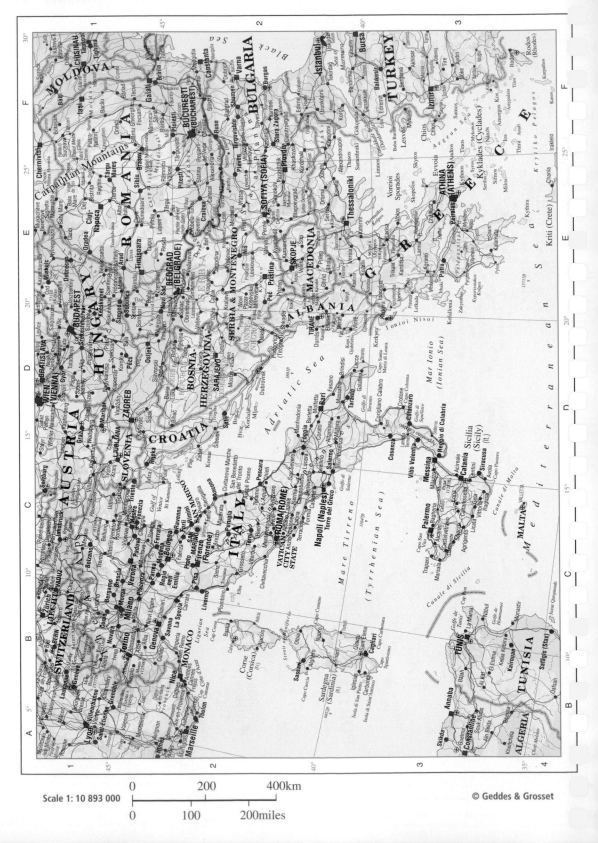

Scale 1: 10 893 000

© Geddes & Grosset

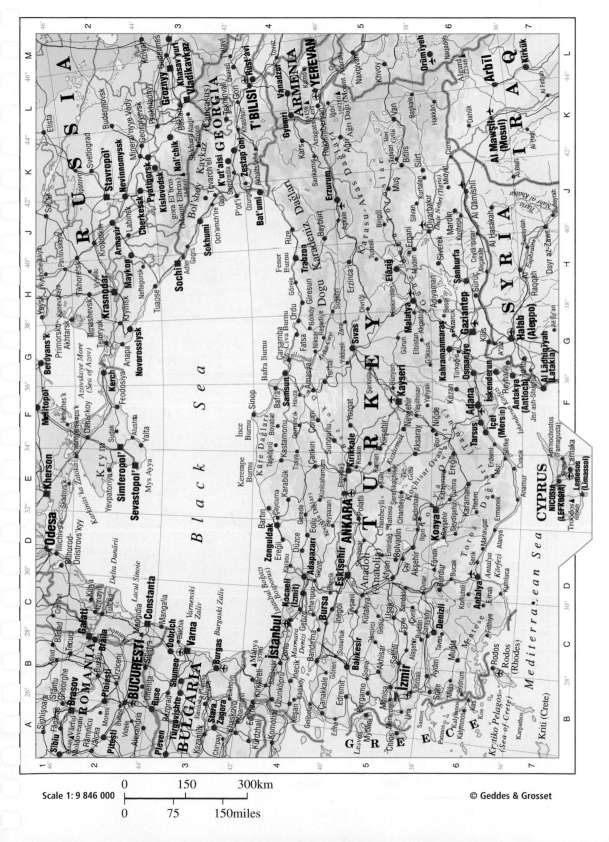

Scale 1: 9 846 000

0   150   300km

0   75   150miles

© Geddes & Grosset

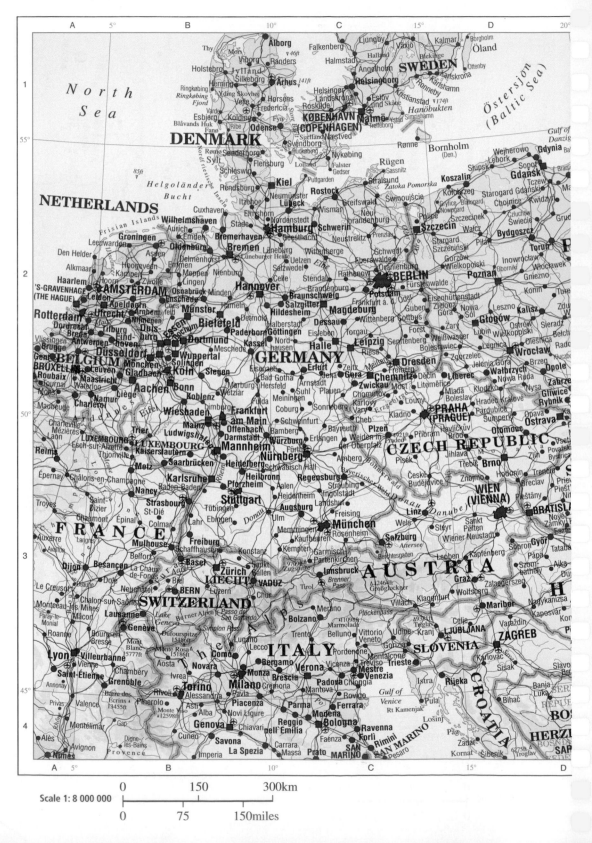

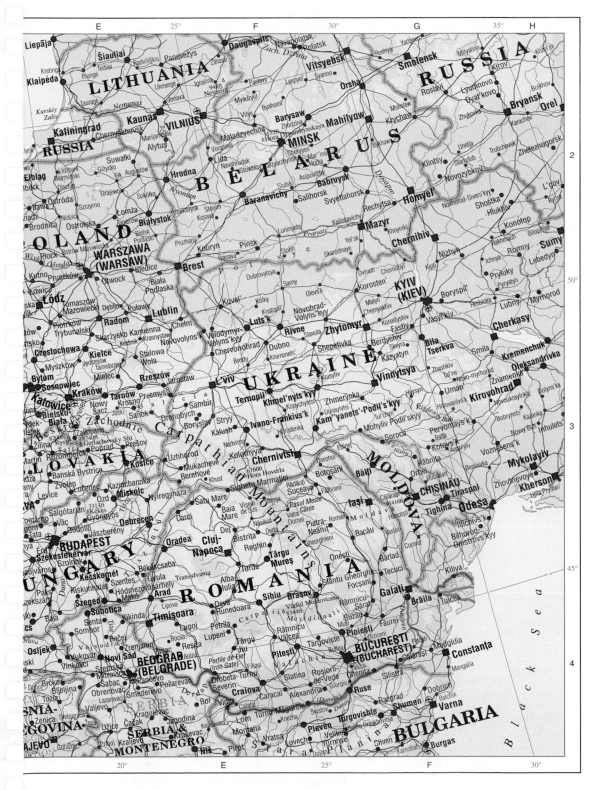

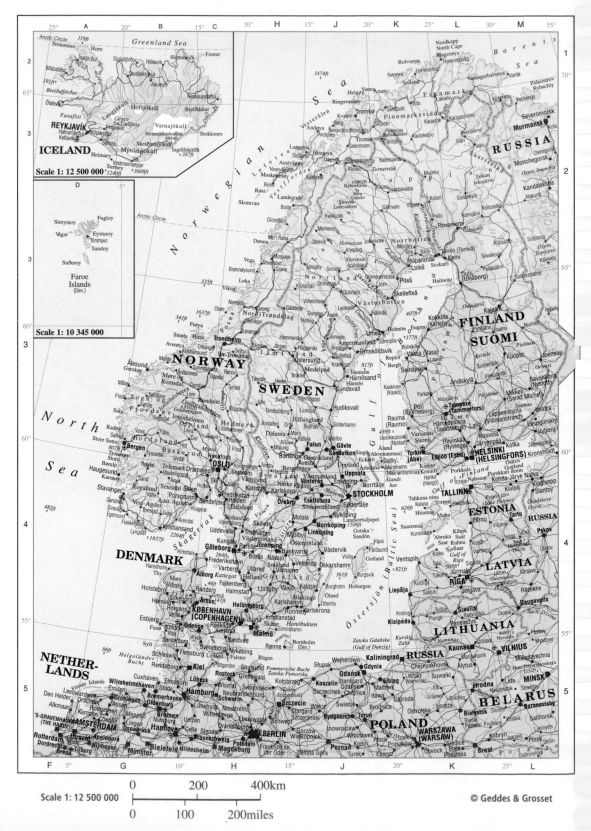

Scale 1: 12 500 000

Scale 1: 10 345 000

0   200   400km

Scale 1: 12 500 000

0   100   200miles

© Geddes & Grosset

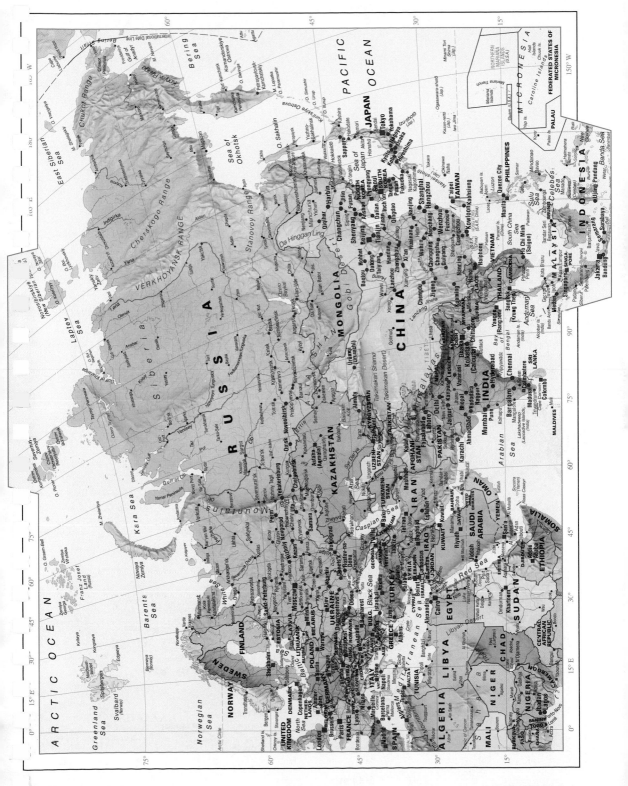

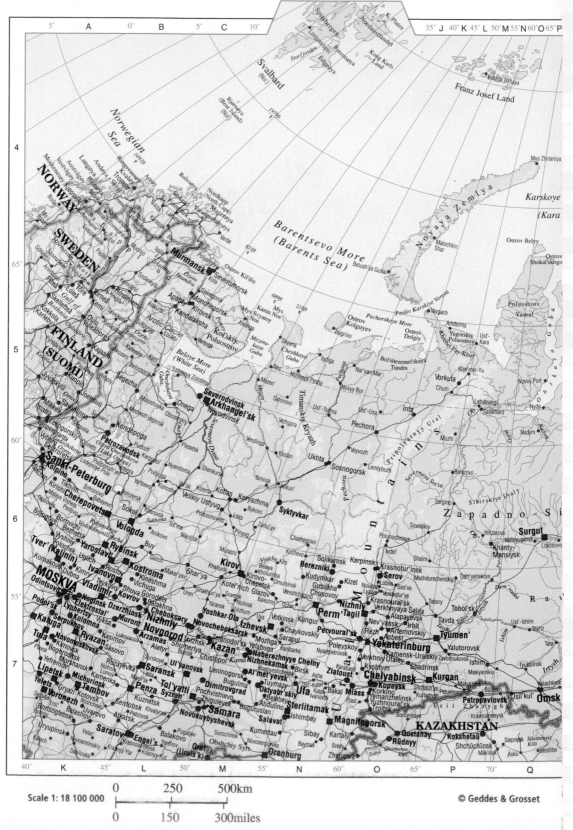

Scale 1: 18 100 000

```
0      250      500km
|---|---|---|
0    150    300miles
```

© Geddes & Grosset

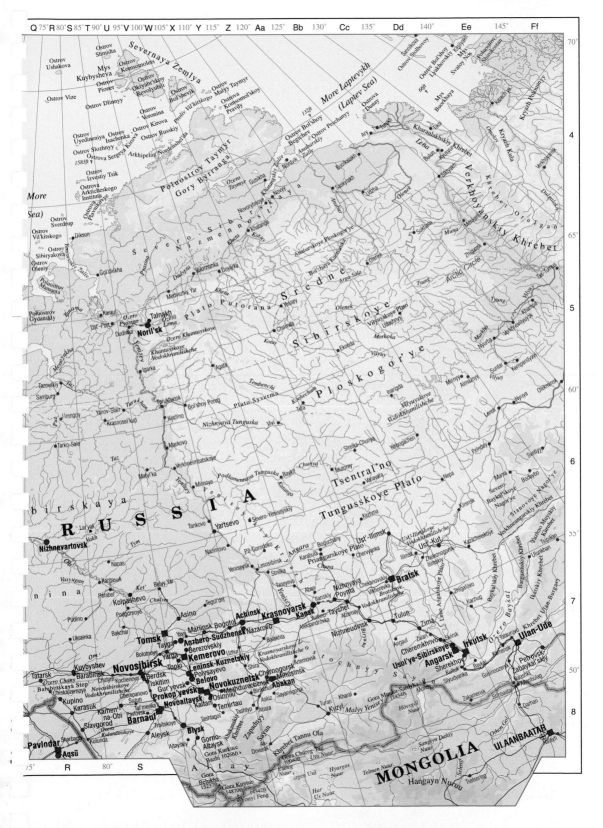

Q 75° R 80° S 85° T 90° U 95° V 100° W 105° X 110° Y 115° Z 120° Aa 125° Bb 130° Cc 135° Dd 140° Ee 145° Ff

70°

Ostrov Ushakova

Ostrov Stimidta
Mys Kuybysheva
Ostrov Pioner
Ostrov Komsomolets

Severnaya Zemlya

Ostrov Vize

Ostrov Oktyabr'skoy Revolyutsii

Ostrov Bol'shevik

Ostrov Dlinnyy

Ostrov Voronina
Ostrov Kirova
Ostrov Russkiy

Ostrov Uyedineniya
Ostrov Isachenka
Ostrova Sergeya Kirova

More Laptevykh
(Laptev Sea)

Ostrov Bol'shoy Begichev
Ostrov Peschanyy

Samkova
Ostrov Stolbovoy
Ostrov Bol'shoy Lyakhovskiy
Ostrov Svyatoy Nos

Poluostrov Shirokostan

Proliv Vil'kitskogo
Ostrov Bol'shevik
Malyy Taymyr
Ostrova Komsomol'skoy Pravdy

66ft

Mys Buorkhaya

Kryazh Polousnyy

Ostrov Slozhnyy
1583ft

Arkhipelag Nordenshel'da

Ostrov Izvestiy Tsik

Ostrov Arktichesogo Instituta

More
Sea)

Ostrov Sverdrup

Ostrov Vil'kitskogo

Dikson

Ostrov Sibiryakova

Ostrov Oleniy

Poluostrov Taymyr

Gory Byrranga

Ozero Taymyr

Kharaulakhskiy Khrebet

Lena

Verkhoyanskiy Khrebet

Khrebet Orulgan

Dulgalakh

4

Khatanga
Novyy
Khatanga

Buolkalakh

Novorybnaya

Khrebet

Balun

Tomtor

Verkhoyansk

65°

Poluostrov Mamonta

Yeniseyskiy Zaliv

More
(Kara Sea)

Karaul

Gol'chikha

Severo - Sibirskaya Nizmennosť a

Kotuy

Sybyakyakh

Ueba

Olenek

Muna

Zhigansk

Menkerekyan

Tyung

Poluostrov Gydanskiy

Tazovskiy

Samburg

Ust'-Port
Dudinka

Pyasino
Ozero
Lama

Talnakh

Noril'sk

Ozero Khantayskoye

Khantayskoye Vodokhranilishche

Plato Putorana

Khatanga

Kotuy

Tyung

Arctic Circle

Tyung

65°

Medvezhiy Yar

Khêta

Yessey

Olenek

Sredne

Vilyuyskoye Plato

Ushmun

Khamra

Verkhnevilyuysk

Nyurba

Suntar

Kempendyay

5

Igarka

Chirinda

Sibirskoye

Ekonda

Morkoka

Mirnyy

Almazny

Vilyuy

Vilyuy

Suntar

Olekminsk

60°

Prii
Irendgy

Krasnosel'kup

Yanov-Stan

Tura
Tembenchi

Agata

Plato Syverma

Kochechum
Tura

Ploskogor'ye

Inarigda
Yerbogachen

Vilyuyskoye Vodokhranilishche

Lensk

60°

Tarko-Sale

Taz

Bol'shoy Porog

Nizhnyaya Tunguska

Vivi

Strelka-Chunya

Nepa

Peleduy

6

Matyl'ka

Verkhneimbatskoye

Podkamennaya Tunguska
Baykit

Chunya

Mutoray

Varavara

Tsentral'no

Severo-Baykal'skoye Nagor'ye

Svetlyy

Bodaybo
Mama

Vanavara

Kezhma

Kirensk

Stanovoye Nagor'ye

b i r s k a y a

R U S S I A

Larʻyak

Severo-Yeniseyskiy

Tungusskoye Plato

Ust'-Ilimskoye Vodokhranilishche

Verkhneangarskiy Khrebet

Yuzhno Muyskiy Khrebet
Kaabe
Tsipikan

Nizhnevartovsk

Vakh

Tankovo

Angara
Boguchany

Ust'-Ilimsk
Ust'-Kut

Vitim

55°

Napas

Kargasok

Tym

Nazimovo

Pit-Gorodok

Karabula
Priangarskoye Plato
Chervyanka

Ust'-Ilimskoye Vodokhranilishche
Ilimsk

Zhigalovo

Baykal'sko-Lena

Kachug

Ozero Baykal

Barguzinskiy Khrebet

55°

Vasyugan

Parabel'

Belyy Yar

Yeniseysk
Lesosibirsk
Strelka

Chuna

Kr

Ilimsk
Zheleznogorsk

Ilimsk

Chekanovskiy

Khrebet Ulan-Burgasy

n i n a

Pudino

Kolpashevo

Tegul'det

Taseyevo

Aban

Nizhnyaya Poyma
Vikhorevka

Braisk

Zhipalovo

Baykal'skiy Khrebet

Gusinoozyorsk

7

Parabel'

Chulym

Asino

Mariinsk
Bogotol

Ilanskiy
Kuzhno-Tayshet

Nizhneudinsk
Tulun

Zima

Slyudyanka

Kyakhta

Tankhoy

Ukrainka

Bakchar

Yaya

Achinsk
Nazarovo

Krasnoyarsk
Kansk

Aleksandrovka

Tayshet

Tulun

Zima

Angarsk

Irkutsk

Ulan-Ude

Petrovsk-Zabaykal'skiy
Khilok

Pudino

Tomsk

Anzhero-Sudzhensk

Uzhur

Krasnoyarskoye Vodokhranilishche

Artemovsk

Cheremkhovo

Usol'ye-Sibirskoye
Angarsk
Sherekhov

Svirsk

Kultuk

Bichura
Mukhorshibir

Bolotnoye
Yurga
Topki

Kemerovo

Leninsk-Kuznetskiy

Chernogorsk

Minusinsk

Tulun

Selenduma

Novosibirsk
Berdsk
Iskitim

Polysayevo
Belovo

Novokuznetsk

Askiz
Sayanogorsk

Turan

Kharal

Zakamensk

Sukhbaatar
Bayangol
Darhan

50°

Tatarsk
Barabinsk

Kuybyshev

Gur'yevsk

Megndureobensk

Osinniki

Abakan

Kyzyl

Malyy Yenisey

Gora Munku-Sardyk
11456ft

8

Chistoozernoye
Novosibirskoye Vodokhranilishche

Prokop'yevsk
Novobaltaysk

Kaltan

Tashtagol

Tashtyp

Abaza

Sayan

Hövsgöl Nuur

Darhan

Kupino
Karasuk

Cherepanovo
Suzun

Tal'menka
Pavlovsk

Om'

Kamen-na-Obi

Novoaltaysk

Barnaul

Biysk

Gorno-Altaysk

Tashtagol

Zamdhyy

Turan

Kharal

Sanginyn Dalay

Mongolia

Orhon Gol

Slavgorod
Ozero Kulundinskoye

Skarbachu

Troitskoye

Aleysk

Altaysk

Kulunda

Altay

Gora Kurkute
Bazhi 10266ft

Khrebet Tannu Ola

100ft

Pürezh Nuur

Üvs Nuur

ULAANBAATAR
Baldyn

Pavlodar

Aqsü

Gora Belukha 15253ft

Altay

Dövurek

Gora Chürege Tag

Hyargas Nuur
Hüren Uul

Har Us Nuur

Telmen Nuur

MONGOLIA

Hangayn Nuruu

Tsetserleg

75° R 80° S

Gora Kuytun 14870ft
Youyi Feng

Gora Kuytun 14342ft
Youyi Feng

Hangayn Nuruu

1

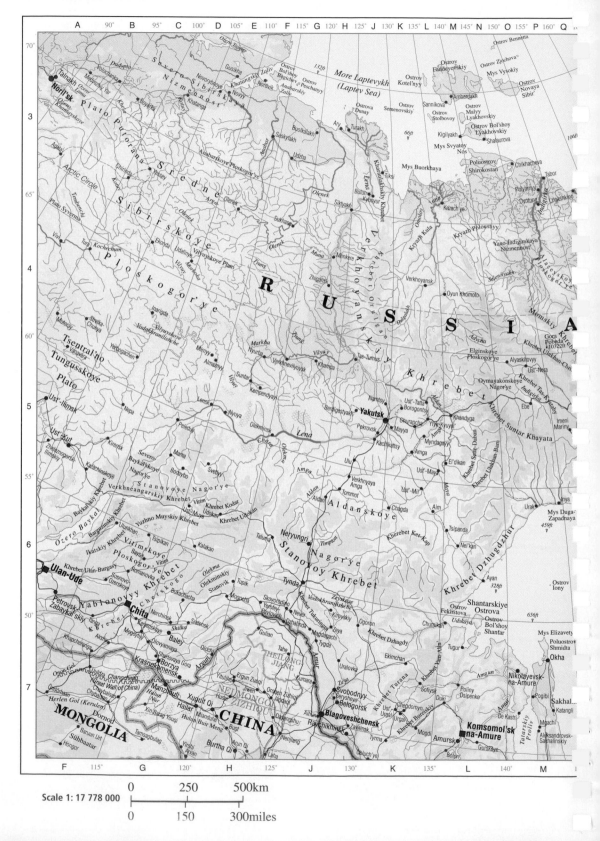

0   250   500km

0   150   300miles

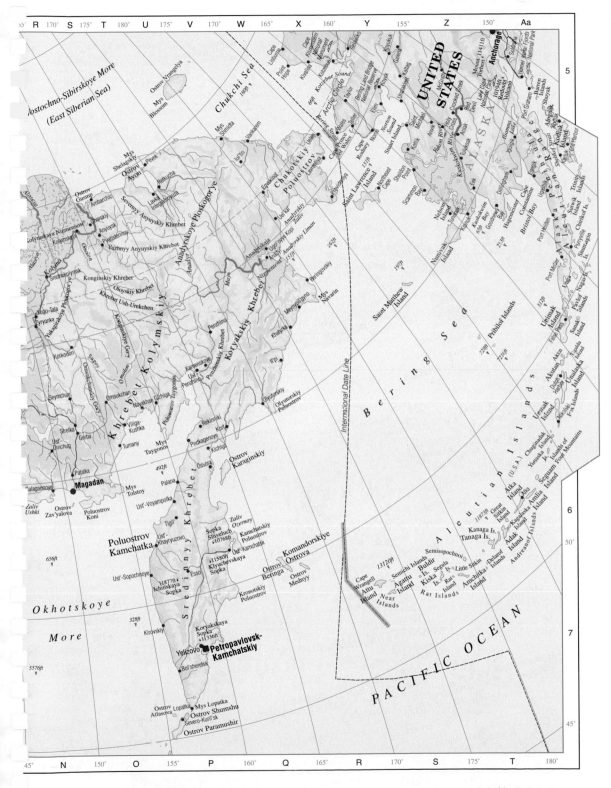

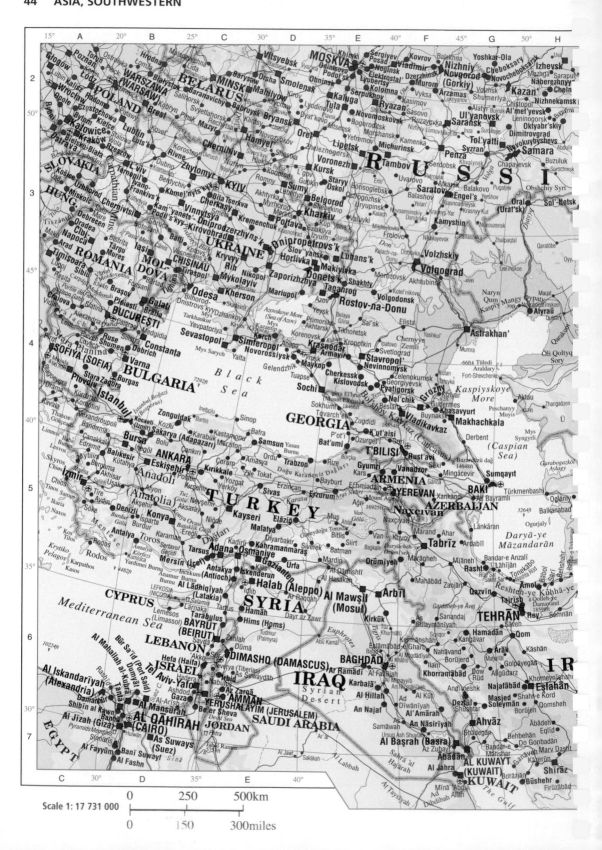

Scale 1: 17 731 000

0   250   500km

0   150   300miles

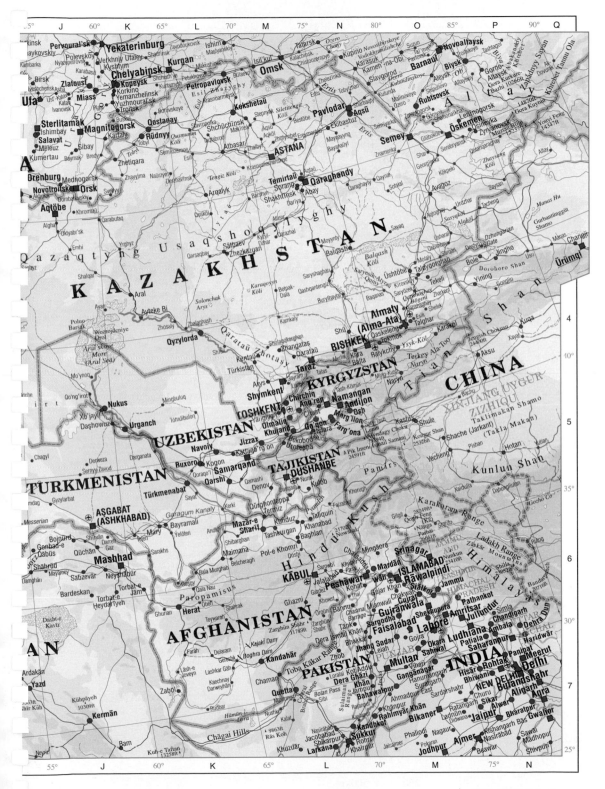

AFGHANISTAN
IRAN
PAKISTAN
NEPAL
KATHMANDU
ISLAMABAD
New Delhi
Delhi
INDIA
SRI LANKA
COLOMBO
SRI JAYAWARDENEPURA KOTTE
MALDIVES
MALE

Arabian Sea
INDIAN OCEAN
Tropic of Cancer

Karachi
Hyderabad
Ahmadabad
Surat
Mumbai (Bombay)
Pune (Poona)
Hyderabad
Bangalore
Chennai (Madras)
Mysore
Coimbatore
Madurai
Trivandrum
Cochin
Kolkata (Cal.)
Bhubaneshwar
Cuttack
Vishakhapatnam
Vijayawada
Nagpur
Bhopal
Jabalpur
Indore
Vadodara
Rajkot
Jaipur
Jodhpur
Bikaner
Lucknow
Kanpur
Varanasi (Benares)
Allahabad
Patna
Ranchi
Jamshedpur
Asansol
Dhanbad
Gaya
Agra
Gwalior
Kota
Ajmer
Amritsar
Ludhiana
Chandigarh
Dehra Dun
Meerut
Moradabad
Bareilly
Srinagar
Jammu
Rawalpindi
Peshawar
Quetta
Multan
Lahore
Faisalabad
Hyderabad (Sind)
Sukkur

Laccadive Islands
Amindivi Islands
LAKSHADWEEP
Kavaratti

Scale 1: 27 710 000
Scale 1: 19 245 000

0   250   500km
0   150   300miles

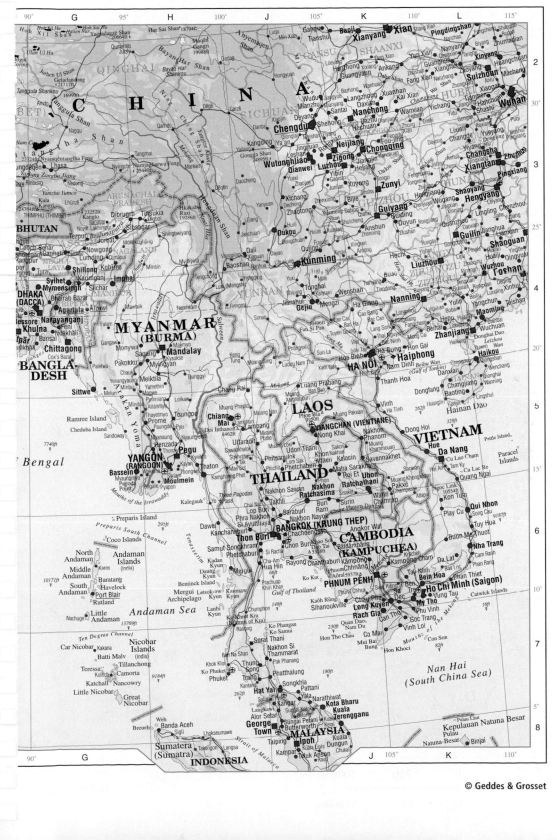

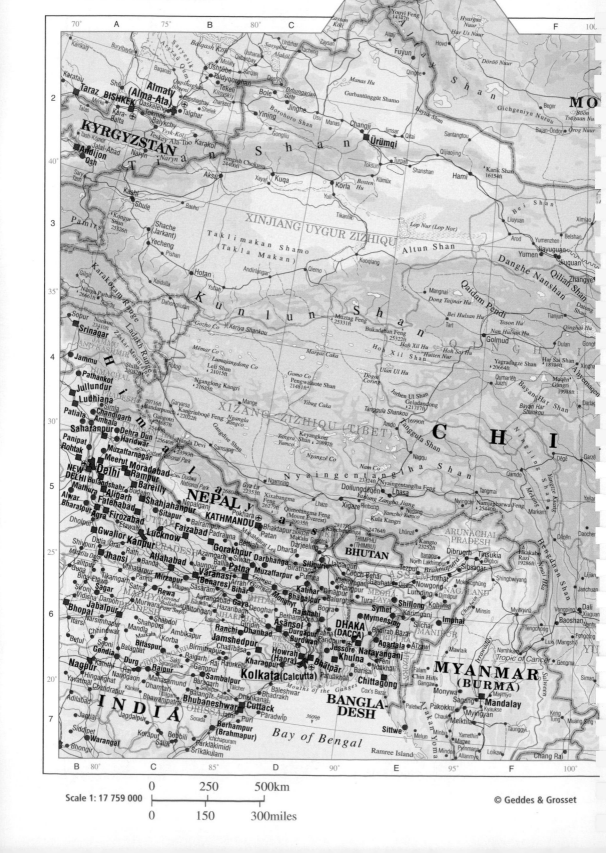

Scale 1: 17 759 000

| 0 | 250 | 500km |
| 0 | 150 | 300miles |

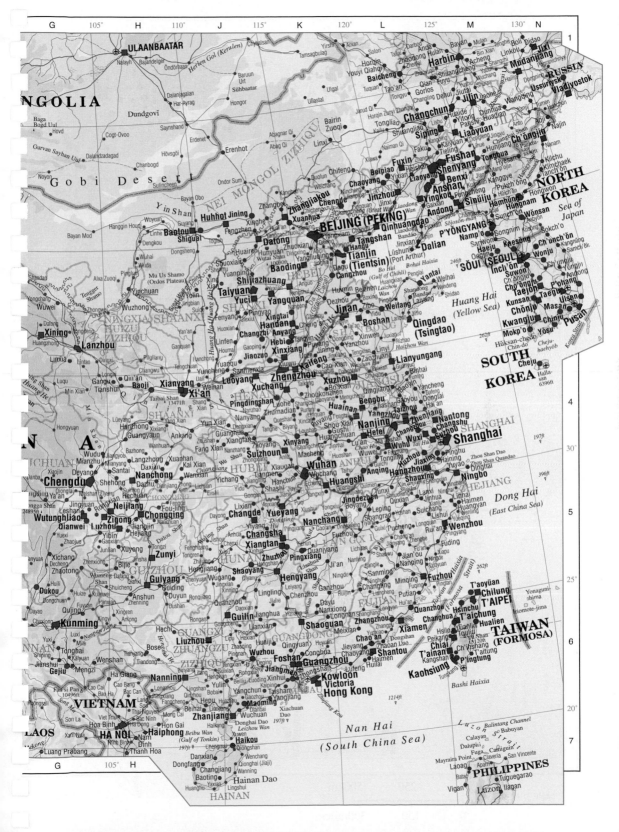

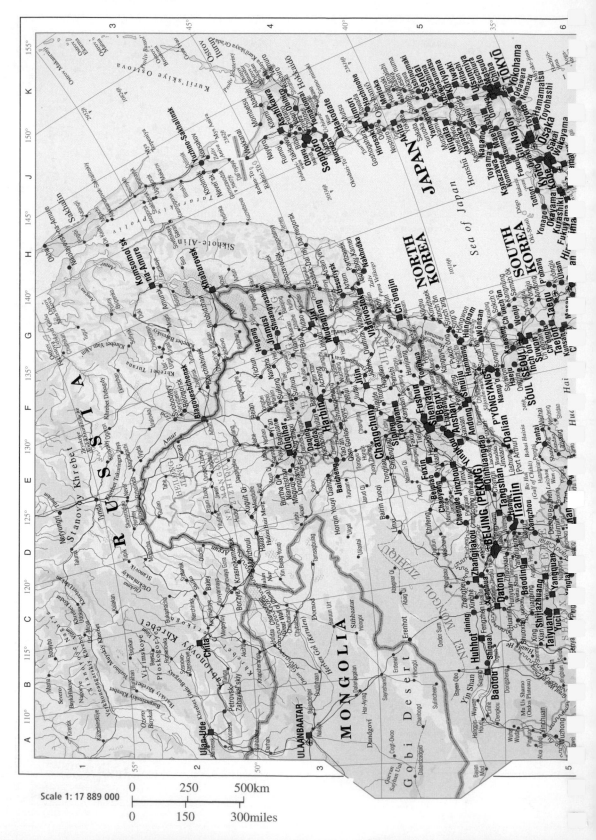

Scale 1: 17 889 000

| 0 | 250 | 500km |

| 0 | 150 | 300miles |

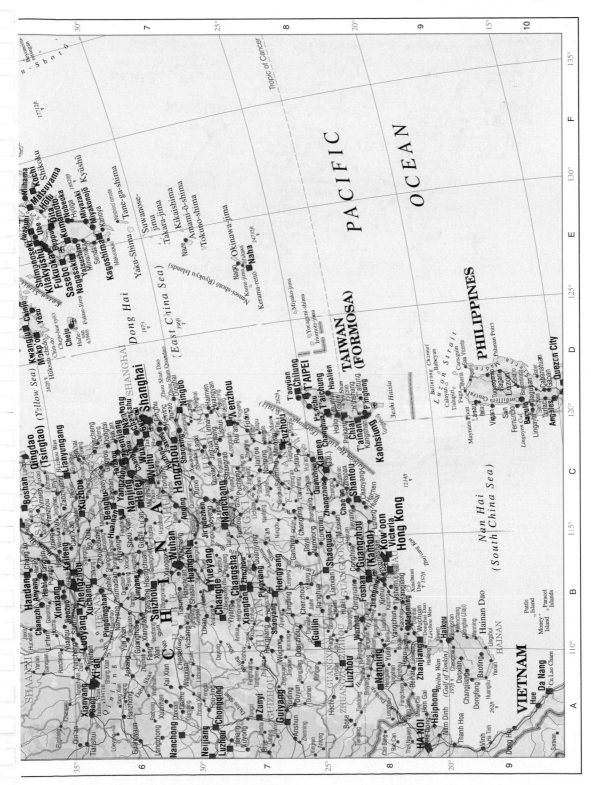

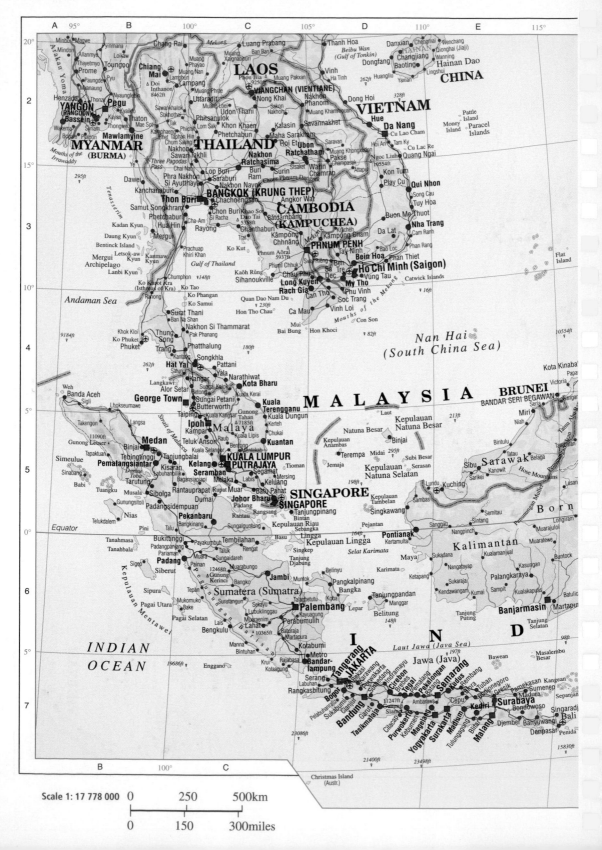

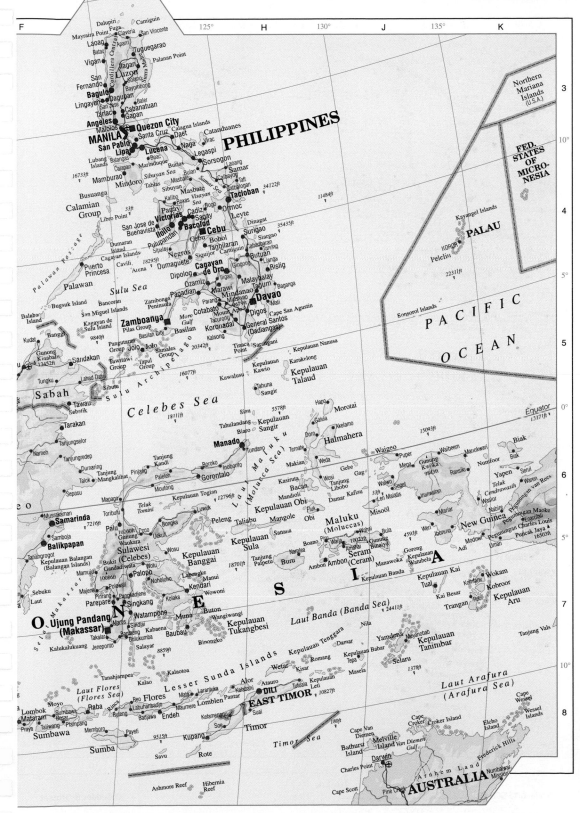

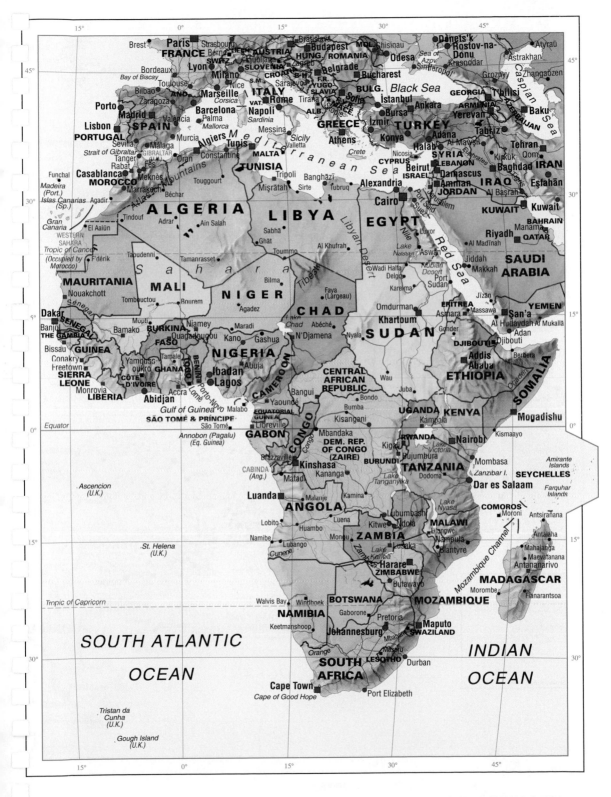

SOUTH ATLANTIC

OCEAN

INDIAN

OCEAN

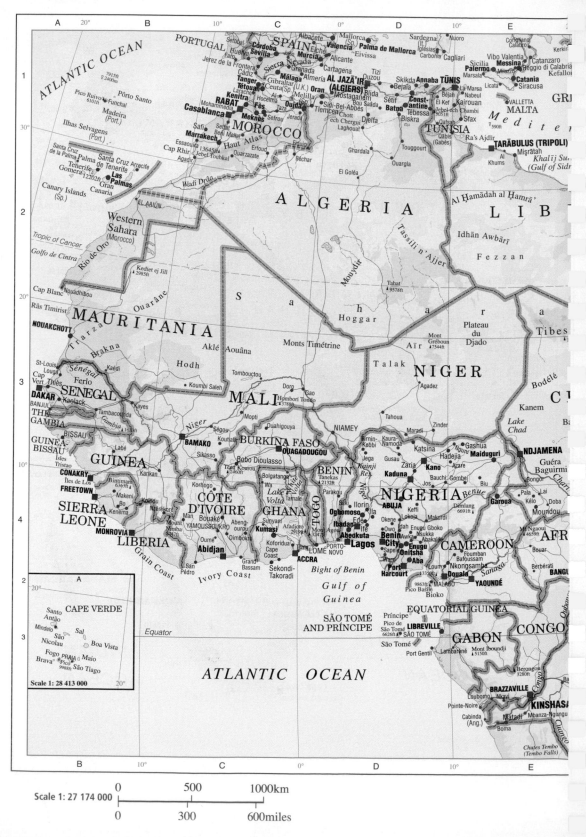

Scale 1: 27 174 000

0	500	1000km

| 0 | 300 | 600miles |

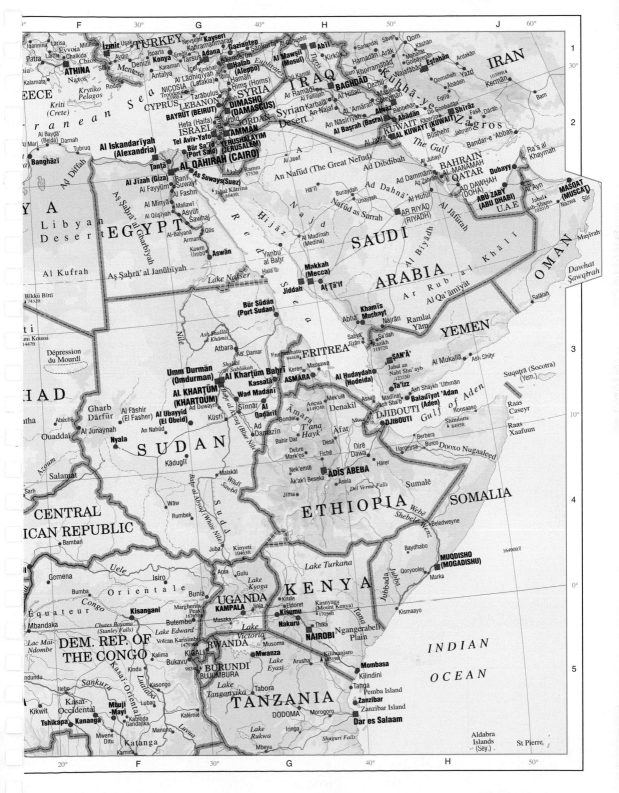

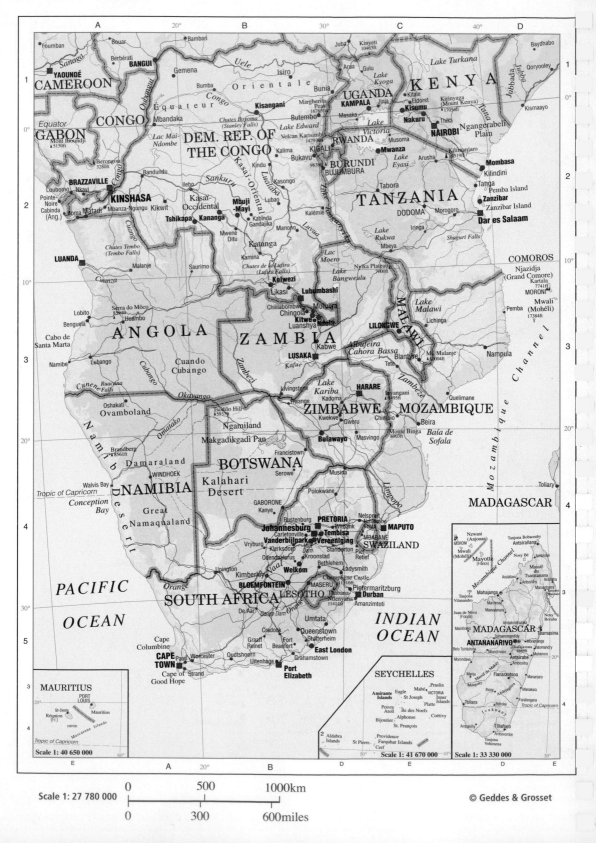

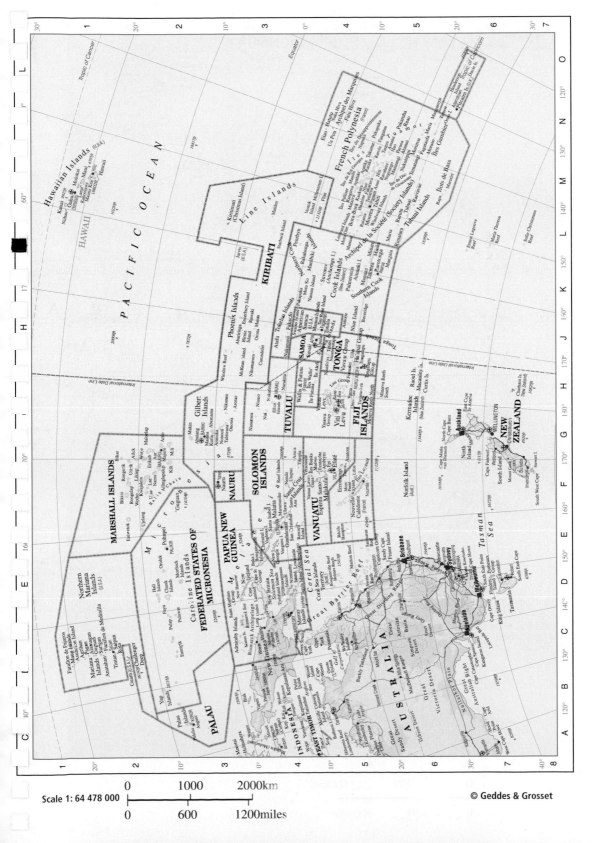

Scale 1: 64 478 000

| 0 | 1000 | 2000km |

| 0 | 600 | 1200miles |

© Geddes & Grosset

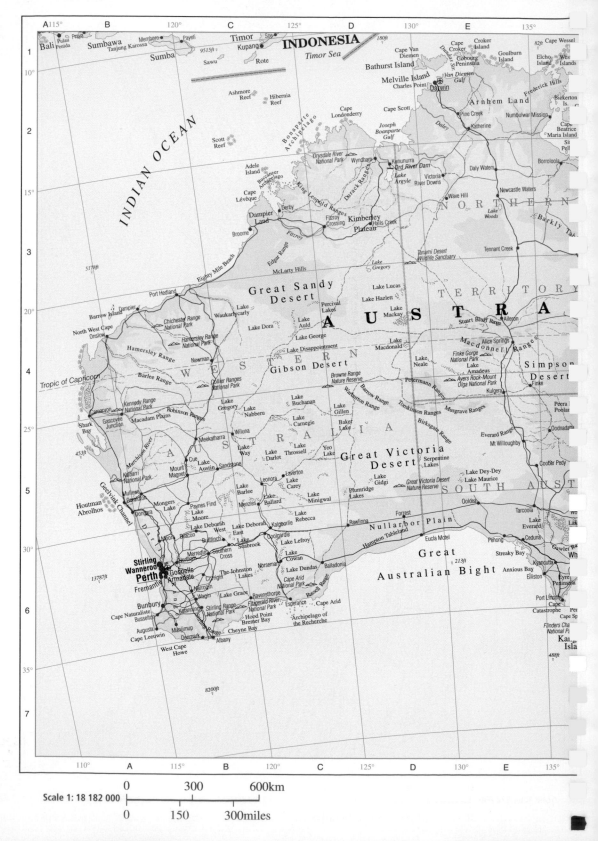

Scale 1: 18 182 000

| 0 | 300 | 600km |
| 0 | 150 | 300miles |

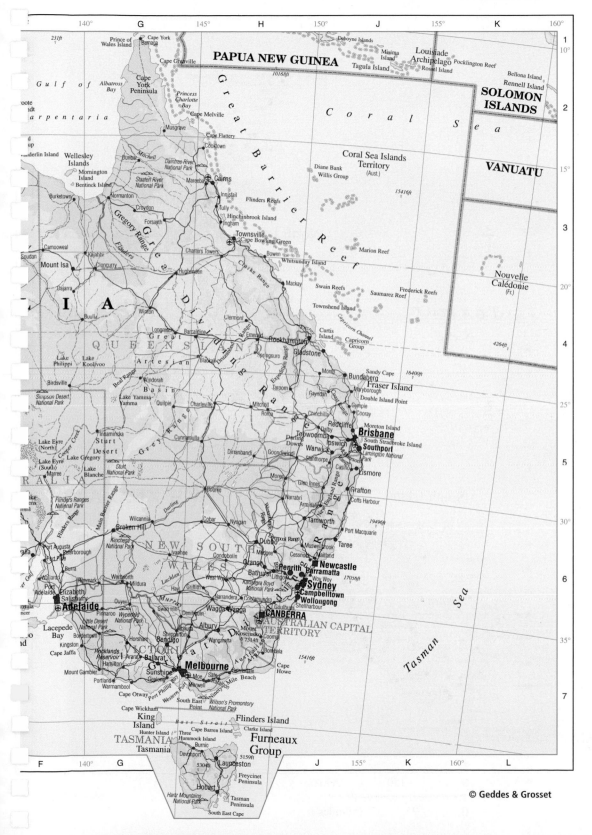

© Geddes & Grosset

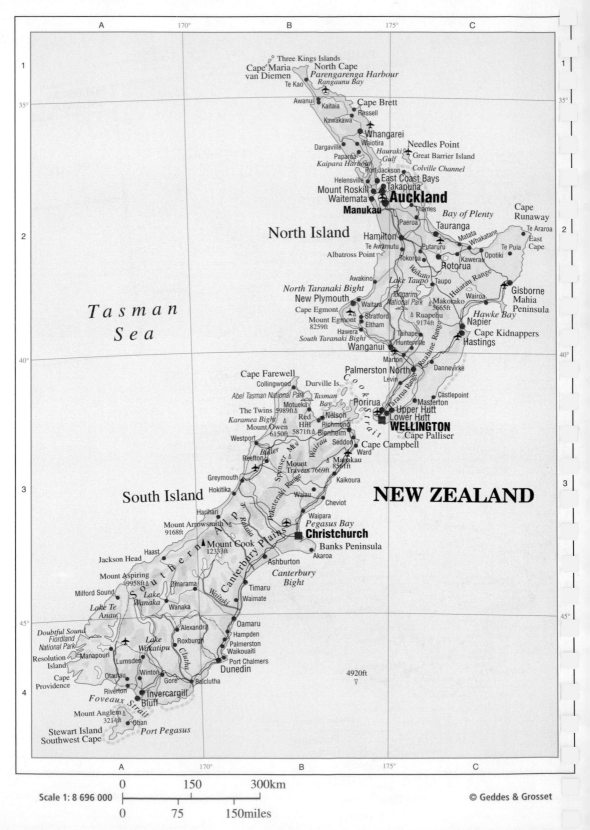

Scale 1: 8 696 000

0   150   300km

0   75   150miles

© Geddes & Grosset

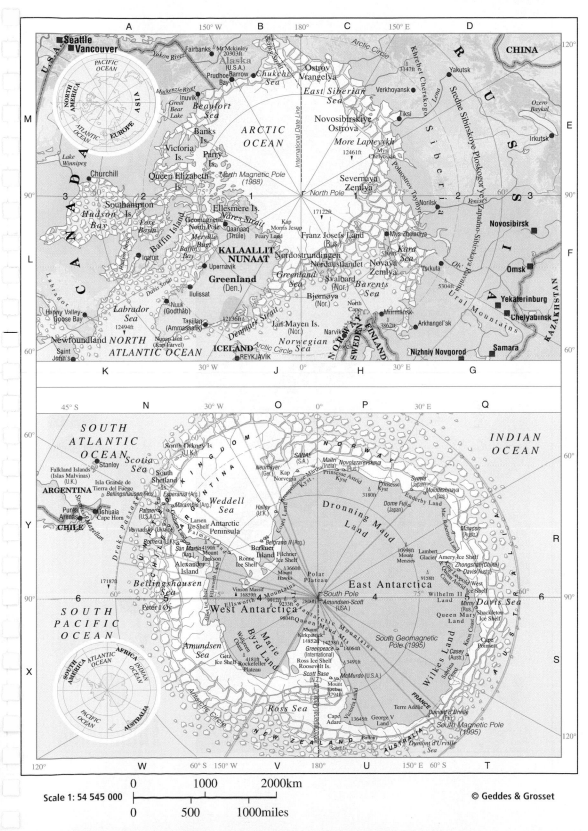

Scale 1: 54 545 000

```
0        1000      2000km
0      500     1000miles
```

© Geddes & Grosset

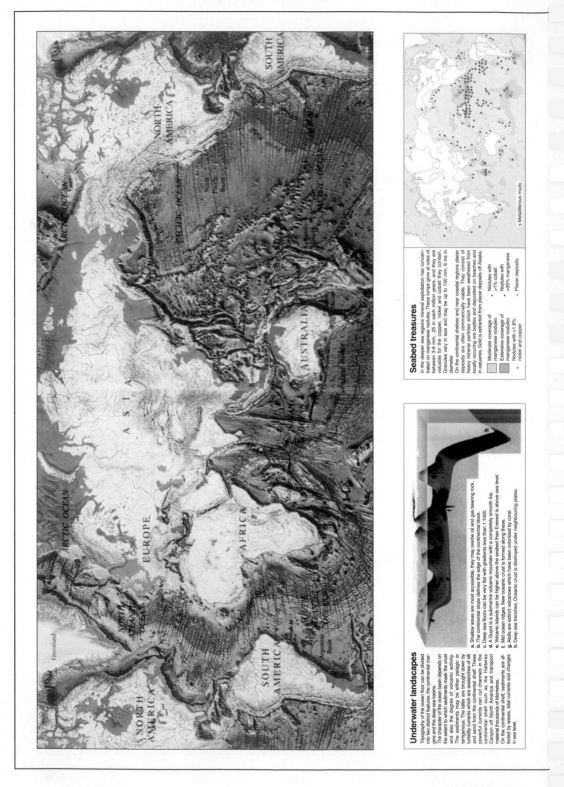

Underwater landscapes

Topography of the ocean floor can be divided into two distinct features: the continental margins and the deep sea basins.

The character of the ocean basin depends on the extent to which sediments mask the crust and also the degree of volcanic activity. The sediments may be either pelagic or terrigenous. The latter are brought down by turbidity currents which are avalanches of silt and sand from the continental shelf. These powerful currents can cut channels in the continental shelf such as the Hatteras Canyon off North America and transport material thousands of kilometres.

On the continental shelf, sediments are affected by waves, tidal currents and changes in sea level.

a. Shallow areas are most accessible, they may overlie oil and gas bearing rock.
b. The continental slope defines the edge of the continental block.
c. Deep sea floors can be very flat with gradients less than 1:1000.
d. A Guyot is a submarine volcanic mountain with a completely smooth top.
e. Volcanic islands can be higher above the seabed than Everest is above sea level.
f. Mid ocean ridges. New oceanic crust is formed along these.
g. Atolls are extinct volcanoes which have been colonized by coral.
h. Deep sea trenches. Oceanic crust is destroyed under neighbouring plates.

Seabed treasures

In the deeper sea regions mineral exploitation has concentrated on manganese nodules. These lumps grow at rates of between 3-8 mm, .25 in each million years, and they are valuable for the copper, nickel and cobalt they contain. Granules vary in size and may be up to 150 mm, 6 ins in diameter.

On the continental shelves and near coastal regions placer deposits are often commercially viable. They consist of heavy mineral particles which have been weathered from locally occuring ore bodies and deposited on beaches and in estuaries. Gold is extracted from placer deposits off Alaska.

☐ Moderate coverage of manganese nodules
  ▪ Nodules with >1% cobalt
■ Extensive coverage of manganese nodules
  ▪ Nodules with >35% manganese
  • Nodules with >1.8% nickel and copper
  ★ Placer deposits
  s Metalliferous muds

© Geddes & Grosset

Map Index

A Coruña 33 A 1
Aachen 36 B 2
Aalen 36 C 3
Aare 36 B 3
Aasiaat 8 Aa 5
Aasleagh 31 B 2
Aba 56 D 4
Ābādeh 44 H 6
Abag Qi 49 J 2
Abagnar Qi 50 C 4
Abaiang 59 H 4
Abakaliki 56 D 4
Abakan 41 U 7
Abakanskiy Khrebet 41 T 7
Aban 41 V 6
Abariringa 59 H 4
Abashiri 54 D 2
Abay 45 M 3
Abaza 41 U 7
Abbeville (U.S.) 20 F 2
Abdulino 44 H 2
Abéché 56 F 3
Abel Tasman National Park 62 B 3
Abemama 59 G 3
Abengourou 56 C 4
Abeokuta 56 D 4
Aberdeen (South Dakota, U.S.) 16 D 2
Aberdeen (U.K.) 30 C 3
Aberdeen (Washington, U.S.) 18 B 2
Aberdeen Lake 8 R 6
Abert, Lake 18 B 3
Aberystwyth 28 B 3
Abganerovo 44 F 3
Abidjan 56 C 4
Abilene 16 D 5
Abisko 38 J 2
Åbo 38 K 3
Abruka Saar 38 K 4
Abū Kamāl 44 F 6
Abu Road 46 C 4
Abuja 56 D 4
Acadia National Park 14 F 2
Acámbaro 20 D 3
Acaponeta 20 C 3
Acapulco 20 E 4
Acarigua 22 J 6
Acatlán de Osorio 20 E 4
Acayucan 20 F 4
Accomac 14 D 3
Accra 56 C 4
Acebuches 20 D 2
Acheng 50 E 3
Achill Head 31 A 2

Achinsk 41 U 6
Acireale 34 D 3
Acklins Island 22 H 3
Acri 34 D 3
Actopan 20 E 3
Açude Araras 24 G 3
Ad' Damar 56 G 3
Ad Damazīn 56 G 3
Aḑ Diffah 56 F 2
Ad Dīwānīyah 44 F 6
Ad Duwaym 56 G 3
Ada (U.S.) 16 D 5
Adair, Bahía de 18 D 5
Adair, Cape 8 W 4
Adak Island 43 U 6
Adamstown 59 M 6
Adana 35 F 6
Adapazarı 35 D 4
Addua Atoll 46 C 9
Adelaide 60 F 6
Adele Island 60 C 3
Adi 52 J 6
Adilabad 46 D 5
Adirondack Mountains 14 E 2
Ādīs Ābeba 56 G 4
Adıyaman 35 H 6
Adjud 35 B 1
Adler 35 H 3
Admiralty Island 10 Q 7
Admiralty Islands 59 D 4
Ādoni 46 D 5
Adra 33 B 2
Adrian 14 C 2
Adriatic Sea 34 D 2
Adycha 42 L 3
Adzhima 54 C 1
Aē Ēa'an 35 G 7
Aegean Sea 34 F 3
Āfar 56 G 3
Afghanistan 45 K 6
Afognak Island 43 Z 5
Afyon 35 D 5
Agadez 56 D 3
Agadir 56 C 1
Agalta, Sierra de 20 G 5
Agartala 47 G 4
Agata 41 U 4
Agattu Island 43 S 6
Agen 32 C 3
Agiabampo, Estero de 20 B 2
Agra 46 D 3
Ağrı 35 K 5

Ağrı Dağı 35 L 5
Agrigento 34 C 3
Agrihan 59 D 2
Agrinio 34 E 3
Agua Caliente de Chínipa 20 C 2
Agua Prieta 18 E 5
Aguascalientes (Mexico) 20 D 3
Aguascalientes (State, Mexico) 20 D 3
Águilas 33 B 2
Aguililla 20 D 4
Ahar 44 G 5
Ahe 59 L 5
Ahlat 44 F 5
Ahmadābād 46 C 4
Ahmadnagar 46 C 5
Ahmadpur East 46 C 3
Ahome 20 C 2
Ahunui 59 L 5
Ahvenanmaa 38 J 3
Aihun 50 E 2
Aiken 14 C 4
Aileron 60 E 4
Ailinglapalap 59 F 3
Ailuk 59 F 2
Aim 42 K 5
Aïn Beïda 34 B 3
Ainažl 38 K 4
Aïr 56 D 3
Aitutaki Island 59 K 5
Aix-en-Provence 34 B 2
Āīzawl 47 G 4
Aizuwakamatsu 54 C 3
Ajaccio 34 B 2
Ajanta Range 46 D 4
Ajigasawa 54 D 2
Ajka 36 D 3
Ajmer 46 C 3
Ajo 18 D 5
Āk'ak'i Beseka 56 G 4
Akaroa 62 B 3
Akashi 54 B 4
Akbaba Tepe 44 E 5
Akbulak 40 N 7
Akçadağ 35 G 5
Akçakale 35 H 6
Ak-Dovurak 41 U 7
Akelamo 52 H 5
Akhalts'ikhe 35 K 4
Akhisar 35 B 5
Akhtubinsk 44 G 3

Akimiski Island 8 U 8
Akita 54 D 3
Aklé Aouâna 56 C 3
Akola 46 D 4
Akpatok Island 8 X 6
Akron 14 C 2
Aksaray 35 F 5
Akşehir 35 D 5
Aksha 50 B 2
Aksu 48 C 2
Aktau 44 H 4
Aktobe 45 H 4
Akun Island 43 W 6
Akureyri 38 B 2
Akutan Island 43 W 6
Al' Amārah 44 G 6
Al Bādī 35 J 7
Al Başrah 44 G 6
Al Baydā (Beida) 56 F 1
Al Fallūjah 44 F 6
Al Fāshir (El Fasher) 56 F 3
Al Fashn 56 G 2
Al Fatḩah 35 K 7
Al Fayyūm 56 G 2
Al Hamādah al Ḩamrā 56 E 2
Al Ḩanīyah 44 G 7
Al Ḩaḑr 35 K 7
Al Ḩasakah 35 J 6
Al Ḩillah 44 F 6
Al Iskandarīyah (Alexandria) 56 F 1
Al Jahra 44 G 7
Al Jazā'ir (Algiers) 56 C 1
Al Jazīrah 44 F 6
Al Jīzah (Giza) 56 F 2
Al Junaynah 56 F 3
Al Kāf 34 B 3
Al Khālis 44 F 6
Al Kharṭūm (Khar Toum) 56 F 3
Al Kharṭūm Bahrī 56 G 3
Al Khums 56 E 1
Al Kufrah 56 F 2
Al Kūt 44 G 6
Al Kuwayt 44 G 7
Al Lādhiqīyah 35 F 7
Al Marj 56 F 1
Al Mawşil 35 K 6
Al Minyā 56 G 2
Al Miqdādīyah 44 F 6
Al Musayyib 44 F 6

Al Qaḑārif 56 G 3
Al Qāmishlī 35 J 6
Al Qūşīyah 56 G 2
Al Ubayyid (El Obeid) 56 F 3
Alabama 14 B 4
Alabama River 14 B 4
Alacrán, Arrecife 20 G 3
Alagir 35 L 3
Alagoinhas 24 H 4
Alajuela 22 F 5
Alaköl 45 O 3
Alakurtti 40 H 4
Alamagan 59 D 2
Alamogordo 18 E 5
Alamos 20 C 2
Alamos, Sierra 20 D 2
Alamosa 18 E 4
Åland 38 J 3
Ålands hav 38 K 4
Alanya 35 D 6
Alapaha River 14 C 4
Alapayevsk 40 O 6
Alaşehir 35 C 5
Alaska 10 K 5
Alaska Peninsula 43 X 5
Alaska Range 10 M 6
Alaska, Gulf of 10 N 7
Alatyr' 44 G 2
Alava, Cape 18 A 2
Alazeya 43 O 3
Alazeyskoye Ploskogor'ye 42 N 3
Alb 8 U 8
Alba 34 B 2
Albacete 33 B 2
Alba-Iulia 36 E 3
Al-Balyanā 56 G 2
Albania 34 D 2
Albano Laziale 34 C 2
Albany (Aust.) 60 B 7
Albany (Georgia, U.S.) 14 C 4
Albany (New York, U.S.) 14 E 2
Albany (Oregon, U.S.) 18 B 3
Albany River 8 U 9
Albatross Bay 60 G 2
Albatross Point 62 B 2
Albemarle Sound 14 D 3

Albert Lea 16 E 3
Alberta 10 T 7
Albi 32 C 3
Ålborg 38 G 4
Albufeira Cahora Bassa 58 C 3
Albuquerque 18 E 4
Albuquerque, Cayos de 22 F 5
Albury 60 H 7
Alcalá de Guadaira 33 A 2
Alcalá de Henares 32 B 3
Alcamo 34 C 3
Alcázar de San Juan 33 B 2
Alchevs'k 44 E 3
Alcolea del Pinar 32 B 3
Alcoy 33 B 2
Aldabra Islands 58 D 2
Aldama 20 C 2
Aldan 42 J 5
Aldan (River) 42 K 4
Aldanskoye Nagor'ye 42 J 5
Aldershot 28 D 4
Alegrete 24 F 6
Aleksandrov 40 J 6
Aleksandrov Gay 44 G 2
Aleksandrovsk-Sakhalinskiy 42 M 6
Alekseyevka 44 E 2
Alençon 32 C 2
Alenuihaha Channel 12 E 7
Aleppo 35 G 6
Aléria 34 B 2
Alert Point 8 T 2
Alès 32 C 3
Alessandria 34 B 2
Ålesund 38 G 3
Aleutian Islands 43 T 6
Aleutian Range 43 Y 5
Alexander Archipelago 10 P 7
Alexander Island 63 Y 5
Alexander, Kap 8 W 3
Alexandra 62 A 4
Alexandra Falls 10 T 6
Alexandria (Louisiana, U.S.) 16 E 5

Alexandria (Romania) 34 F 2
Alexandria (Virginia, U.S.) 14 D 3
Alexandroupoli 34 F 2
Aleysk 41 S 7
Algarve 33 A 2
Algeciras 33 A 2
Algeria 56 C 2
Algha 45 J 3
Alghero 34 B 2
Algona 16 E 3
Algurd 35 L 6
Al-Hoceima 56 C 1
Äli-Bayramlı 44 G 5
Alicante 33 B 2
Alice 20 E 2
Alice Springs 60 E 4
Aligarh 46 D 3
Alīgūdarz 44 G 6
Alim Island 59 D 4
Alitak, Cape 10 L 7
Allahabad 46 E 3
Allakaket 10 M 5
Allanmyo 47 H 5
Allegheny Mountains 14 C 3
Allegheny Plateau 14 C 3
Allegheny River 14 C 2
Allende 20 D 2
Allentown 14 D 2
Alleppey 46 D 7
Alliance 16 C 3
Alloa 30 C 3
Alma 8 W 9
Alma-Ata 45 N 4
Almansa 33 B 2
Almaty 45 N 4
Almaznyy 41 Y 5
Almer'a 33 B 2
Al'met'yevsk 44 H 2
Alofi, Île 59 H 5
Alor 52 G 7
Alor Setar 52 C 4
Alpena 8 U 9
Alphonse 58 E 2
Alpine 16 C 5
Alps, The 36 B 3
Alta 38 K 2
Altai Shan 48 D 1
Altamaha River 14 C 4
Altamira 24 F 3
Altamont 18 B 3
Altamura 34 D 2
Altanbulag 41 X 7
Altar 18 D 5
Altata 20 C 3
Altay 48 D 1
Altayskiy 41 T 7
Alton 16 E 4
Altoona 14 D 2

Altun Ha 20 G 4
Altun Shan 48 E 3
Alturas 18 B 3
Altus 16 D 5
Alushta 35 F 2
Alva 16 D 4
Alvarado 20 E 4
Älvdalen 38 H 3
Alvord Valley 18 C 3
Alwar 46 D 3
Alxa Zuoqi 49 H 3
Alyaskitovyy 42 M 4
Alytus 36 E 2
Alzamay 41 V 6
Alzira 33 B 2
Amadeus, Lake 60 E 5
Amadjuak Lake 8 W 6
Amahai 52 H 6
Amami-ō-shima 50 E 7
Amanu 59 L 5
Amanu-Runga 59 L 6
Amanzimtoti 58 C 5
Amapu-Raro 59 L 6
Āmara 56 G 3
Amarillo 16 C 4
Amasya 35 F 4
Amatique, Bahía de 20 G 4
Ambala 46 D 2
Ambarawa 52 E 7
Ambarchik 43 Q 3
Ambardakh 42 L 2
Ambato 24 D 3
Ambatondrazaka 58 D 3
Amberg 36 C 3
Ambikapur 46 E 4
Ambilobe 58 D 3
Ambon 52 H 6
Ambon (Island) 52 H 6
Ambositra 58 D 4
Ambovombe 58 D 4
Ambrym 59 F 5
Amderma 40 O 4
Amdo 48 E 4
Ameca 20 D 3
American Falls Reservoir 18 D 3
American Samoa 59 J 5
Americus 14 C 4
Ames 16 E 3
Amga 42 K 4
Amgu 54 C 1
Amgun' 42 L 6
Amherst Island 14 D 2
Amiens 32 C 2
Amīndīvi Islands 46 C 6

Amirante Islands 58 E 2
Amlia Island 43 V 6
Ammassalik 8 Dd 5
Ammochostos 35 E 7
Āmol 44 H 5
Amorgos 34 F 3
Amos 8 V 9
Åmot 38 G 4
Amoy 49 K 6
Ampanihy 58 D 4
Amravati 46 D 4
Amritsar 46 C 2
Amund Ringnes Island 8 R 3
Amundsen Gulf 10 R 4
Amur 42 J 6
An Nahūd 56 F 3
An Najaf 44 F 6
An Nāsirīyah 44 G 6
An Nu'mānīyah 44 G 6
Anaa 59 L 5
Anabar 41 Y 3
Anabarskiy Zaliv 41 Y 3
Anabarskoye Plosko-gor'ye 41 X 3
Anaco 22 K 6
Anaconda 18 D 2
Anadoli (Anatolia) 35 D 5
Anadyr' 43 T 4
Anadyrskaya Niz-mennost' 43 T 3
Anadyrskiy Liman 43 T 4
Anadyrskiy Zaliv 43 U 3
Anadyrskoye Plosko-gor'ye 43 R 3
Anafi 34 F 3
Anáhuac 20 D 2
Anakapalle 46 E 5
Analalava 58 D 3
Anambas, Kepulauan 52 D 5
Anamur 35 E 6
Anamur Burnu 44 D 5
Anantapur 46 D 6
Anan'yiv 36 F 3
Anapa 35 G 2
Anápolis 24 F 4
Anatahan 59 D 2
Anatom 59 F 6
Anby n 50 E 5
Anbyŏn 54 A 3
Anchorage 10 N 6
Anchorage Island 59 J 5
Ancona 34 C 2
Anda 50 E 3

Åndalsnes 38 G 3
Andaluc'a 33 A 2
Andaman Islands 47 G 6
Andaman Sea 47 G 6
Andenes 38 J 2
Anderson (Indiana, U.S.) 14 B 2
Anderson (South Carolina, U.S.) 14 C 4
Andhra Pradesh 46 E 6
Andijon 45 M 4
Andīmeshk 44 G 6
Andirlangar 48 C 3
Andkhui 45 L 5
Andong 50 D 4
Andong (South Korea) 54 A 3
Andorra 32 C 3
Andorra la Vella 32 C 3
Andøya 38 J 2
Andreanof Islands 43 U 6
Andreasen, Cape 10 T 3
Andrée Land 8 Ff 4
Andrews 16 C 5
Andringitra 58 D 4
Andros 34 E 3
Andros Island 14 D 5
Androth 46 C 6
Aneto, Pico de 32 C 3
Ang'angxi 50 D 3
Angara 41 U 6
Angarsk 41 W 7
Angaul 41 W 7
Angaur 59 C 3
Angel de la Guarda, Isla 20 B 2
Angel Falls 22 K 6
Angeles 52 G 2
Ångermanälven 38 J 3
Ångermanland 38 J 3
Angers 32 B 2
Angijak Island 8 Y 5
Angikuni Lake 8 R 6
Angkor Wat 47 J 6
Anglesey 28 B 3
Anglet 32 B 3
Angola 58 A 3
Angostura 20 C 2
Angoulême 32 C 2
Ang'ren 45 M 4
Anguilla 22 K 4
Anguo 49 K 3
Anhua 49 J 5
Anhui 49 K 4
Anikovo 40 K 6

Animas Peak 18 E 5
Anina 36 E 3
Aniva 54 D 1
Aniva, Mys 50 H 3
Aniva, Zaliv 50 H 3
Aniwa 59 F 5
Anju 50 E 5
Ankang 49 H 4
Ankara 35 E 5
Ankleshwar 46 C 4
Anlak 43 Y 4
Anlong 49 H 5
Anlu 49 J 4
Ann Arbor 14 C 2
Anna 44 F 2
Anna (U.S.) 14 B 3
Annaba 56 D 1
Annapolis 14 D 3
Annapurna 46 E 3
Anniston 14 B 4
Anoka 16 E 2
Anqing 49 K 4
Anshan 50 D 4
Anshun 49 H 5
Ansley 16 D 3
Antakya 35 G 6
Antalaha 58 D 3
Antalya 35 D 6
Antalya Körfezi 35 D 6
Antananarivo 58 D 3
Anthony 18 E 5
Antibes 34 B 2
Anticosti, Île d' 8 Y 9
Antigua 22 K 4
Antigua (Guatemala) 20 F 5
Antigua and Barbuda 22 K 4
Antillas Mayores 22 H 4
Antillas Menores 22 K 4
Antioch 35 G 6
Antiope Reef 59 J 5
Antofagasta 24 D 5
Antrim 31 C 1
Antsirabe 58 D 4
Antsirañana 58 D 3
Antsohihy 58 D 3
Antu 54 A 2
Antun' 54 C 1
Anugul 46 F 4
Anuradhapura 46 E 7
Anuta 59 F 5
Anvik 43 X 4
Anxiang 49 J 5
Anxious Bay 60 E 6
Anyang 49 J 3
A'nyemaqen Shan 48 F 3
An'yudin 40 N 5
Anyue 49 H 4
Anyuysk 43 Q 3

Anyuyskiy Khrebet 43 R 3
Anzhero-Sudzhensk 41 T 6
Anzio 34 C 2
Aoga-shima 54 C 4
Aoji 54 B 2
Aomori 54 D 2
Aosta 36 B 3
Apalachee Bay 14 C 5
Apalachicola 20 G 2
Apan 20 E 4
Aparri 52 G 2
Apataki 59 L 5
Apatzingán 20 D 4
Apeldoorn 36 B 2
Apennines 34 C 2
Apia 59 H 5
Apizaco 20 E 4
Apostolove 44 D 3
Appalachian Moun-tains 14 C 3
Appennino 34 C 2
Appennino Calabro 34 D 3
Appleton 14 B 2
Apsheronsk 44 E 4
Aqköl 45 M 2
Aqsay 44 H 2
Aqsū (Kazakhstan) 45 N 2
Aqtaū 45 M 2
Aqtöbe 40 N 7
Aqtoghay 45 N 3
Ar Ramādī 44 F 6
Ar Raqqah 35 H 7
Arabian Sea 46 B 5
Aracaju 24 H 4
Araçatuba 24 F 5
Arad 36 E 3
Arafura Sea 53 J 8
Arafura, Laut 52 J 7
Aragats Lerr 35 L 4
Aragón 32 B 3
Aräk 44 G 6
Arakan Yoma 47 G 4
Aral 45 N 3
Aral Sea 45 J 4
Aral'skoye More 45 J 4
Aran Island 31 B 1
Aran Islands 31 B 2
Aranda de Duero 32 B 3
Arani 46 D 6
Aranjuez 32 B 3
Aranuka 59 G 4
Ararat 60 G 7
Aras Nehri 44 F 5
Aratika 59 L 5
Arbīl 35 L 6
Arbroath 30 C 3
Arcachon 32 B 3
Arcas, Cayos 20 F 3

Arcata 18 B 3
Arcelia 20 D 4
Archipiélago Juan
  Fernández (Chile)
  24 C 6
Arco 18 D 3
Arctic Bay 8 U 4
Arctic Circle 8 Bb 5
Arctic Ocean 8 V 2
Arctic Village 10 N 5
Ardabīl 44 G 5
Ardakān 45 H 6
Ardmore 16 D 5
Arena Island 52 G 4
Arenas, Cayo 20 F 3
Arendal 38 G 4
Arequipa 24 D 4
Arezzo 34 C 2
Arga-Sala 41 Y 4
Argentina 24 E 6
Argos 34 E 3
Argun 50 C 2
Argyle, Lake 60 D 3
Argyll 30 B 3
Arholma 38 J 3
Århus 38 H 4
Ari Atoll 46 C 8
Arica 24 D 4
Arid, Cape 60 C 6
Ariquemes 24 E 3
Arismendi 22 J 6
Arizgoit 32 B 3
Arizona (U.S.) 18
  D 5
Arjeplog 38 J 2
Arjona 22 G 5
Arkadak 44 F 2
Arkadelphia 16 E 5
Arkansas 16 E 4
Arkansas City 16
  D 4
Arkansas River 16
  E 5
Arkhangel'sk 40 K 5
Arkhara 54 B 1
Arklow 31 C 2
Arkticheskogo Insti-
  tuta, Ostrova 41
  S 2
Arles 32 C 3
Arlington 18 B 2
Arlington (Texas,
  U.S.) 16 D 5
Arlington (Virginia,
  U.S.) 14 D 3
Armadale 60 B 6
Armagh 31 C 1
Armagnac 32 C 3
Armant 56 G 2
Armavir 35 J 2
Armenia 44 F 4
Armenia (Colombia)
  22 G 7
Armenia (Country) 35
  L 4

Armeria 20 D 4
Armidale 60 J 6
Armstrong 8 T 8
Arnhem 36 B 2
Arnhem Land 60
  E 2
Arno 59 G 3
Arnøy 38 K 1
Arnstadt 36 C 2
Arod 48 F 2
Arorae 59 G 4
Arqalyq 45 L 2
Arrah 46 E 3
Arran 28 B 2
Arrecife 56 B 2
Arriaga 20 F 4
Arsen'yev 54 B 2
Artá 33 C 2
Arta 34 E 3
Arteaga 20 D 4
Artem 54 B 2
Artemisa 20 H 3
Artemivs'k 44 E 3
Artemovsk 41 U 7
Artemovskiy 40 O 6
Artesia 16 C 5
Artillery Lake 10 V 6
Aru, Kepulauan 53
  K 7
Arua 58 C 1
Aruba 22 J 5
Arun Qi 50 D 3
Arunāchal Pradesh
  47 G 3
Arusha 58 C 2
Arvada 18 E 4
Arviat 8 S 6
Arvidsjaur 38 J 2
Arxan 50 C 3
Ary 42 H 2
Arys 45 L 4
Arzamas 40 K 6
Aş Sahrā' al
  Gharbīyah 56 F 2
Aş Sahrā' al
  Janūbīyah 56 F 2
As Samāwah 44 G 6
As Sulaymānīyah 44
  G 5
As Suwaydāh 44 E 6
As Suways (Suez) 56
  G 2
Asahikawa 54 D 2
Āsānsol 46 F 4
Asbest 40 O 6
Ascoli Piceno 34 C 2
Āsela 56 G 4
Åsele 38 J 3
Aşgabat 45 J 5
Ash Shallāl al
  Khāmis 56 G 3
Asha 40 N 7
Ashburton 62 B 3
Asheville 14 C 3
Ashkhabad 45 J 5

Ashland (Kentucky,
  U.S.) 14 C 3
Ashland (Oregon,
  U.S.) 18 B 3
Ashland (Wisconsin,
  U.S.) 16 E 2
Ashmore Reef 60
  C 2
Ashtabula 14 C 2
Ashton 18 D 3
Asino 41 T 6
Asipovichy 36 F 2
Aşkale 35 J 5
Askim 38 H 4
Askiz 41 U 7
Asmara 56 G 3
Aspen 18 E 4
Assab 56 H 3
Assam 47 G 3
Assen 36 B 2
Assiniboia 18 E 2
Assiniboine River 16
  D 2
Astana 45 M 2
Asti 34 B 2
Astorga 33 A 1
Astoria 18 B 2
Astrakhan' 44 G 3
Astrolabe, Récifs de
  59 F 5
Astypalaia 34 F 3
Asunción 24 F 5
Asuncion Island 59
  D 2
Aswān 56 G 2
Asyūt 56 G 2
Atafu 59 H 4
Atascadero 18 B 4
Atasu 45 M 3
Atauro 52 H 7
Atbara 56 G 3
Atbasar 45 L 2
Atchafalaya Bay 20
  F 2
Atchison 16 D 4
Athabasca 10 U 8
Athabasca, Lake 10
  V 7
Athens (Georgia,
  U.S.) 14 C 4
Athens (Greece) 34
  E 3
Athens (Ohio, U.S.)
  14 C 3
Athina 34 E 3
Athlone 31 C 2
Atikokan 16 E 2
Atka 43 V 6
Atka Island 43 U 6
Atkarsk 44 F 2
Atlanta 14 C 4
Atlantic 16 D 3
Atlantic City 14 E 3
Atlantic Ocean 24
  G 6

Atlasova, Ostrov 43
  P 6
Atlin Lake 10 Q 7
Atmore 14 B 4
Atoka 16 D 5
Atoyac de Alvarez 20
  D 4
Atqasuk 10 L 4
Attapu 47 K 6
Attersee 36 C 3
Attu Island 43 S 6
Atyraū 44 H 3
Aubagne 34 B 2
Aubry Lake 10 R 5
Auburn (California,
  U.S.) 18 B 4
Auburn (Maine, U.S.)
  14 E 2
Auburn (Nebraska,
  U.S.) 16 D 3
Auckland 62 B 2
Augsburg 36 C 3
Augusta (Arkansas,
  U.S.) 16 E 4
Augusta (Australia)
  60 B 6
Augusta (Georgia,
  U.S.) 14 C 4
Augusta (Maine,
  U.S.) 14 F 2
Augusta (Maine,
  U.S.A.) 8 X 10
Augustów 36 E 2
Auld, Lake 60 C 4
Aur 59 G 3
Aurangabad 46 D 5
Aurangābād 46 E 4
Aurich 36 B 2
Aurillac 32 C 3
Aurora (U.S.) 16 C 4
Aust-Agder 38 G 4
Austin (Minnesota,
  U.S.) 16 E 3
Austin (Nevada,
  U.S.) 18 C 4
Austin (Texas, U.S.)
  16 D 5
Austin, Lake 60 B 5
Australia 60 D 4
Australian Alps 60
  H 7
Australian Capital
  Territory 60 H 7
Austria 36 C 3
Austvågøy 38 H 2
Autlán 20 D 4
Auxerre 32 C 2
Auyuittuq National
  Park 8 X 5
Avallon 32 C 2
Avan 45 K 3
Avarua 59 K 6
Aveiro 33 A 1
Avellino 34 C 2
Averøya 38 G 3

Avesta 38 J 3
Avezzano 34 C 2
Avignon 32 C 3
Ávila 32 B 3
Avilés 33 A 1
Avola 34 D 3
Avon Park 14 C 5
Awakino 62 B 2
Awanui 62 B 2
Awka 56 D 4
Axel Heiberg Island 8
  S 3
Ayacucho 24 D 4
Ayagoz 45 O 3
Ayamonte 33 A 2
Ayan 42 L 5
Aydin 35 B 6
Ayers Rock-Mount
  Olga National Park
  60 E 5
Aylesbury 28 D 4
Aylmer Lake 10 V 6
Ayon, Ostrov 43 R 3
Ayr (U.K.) 28 B 2
Ayteke Bi 45 K 3
Ayutla 20 E 4
Ayya, Mys 35 E 2
Az Zubayr 44 G 6
Azamgarh 46 E 3
Azare 56 E 3
A'zāz 35 G 6
Azerbaijan 44 G 5
Azotum 56 E 3
Azov 44 E 3
Azovskoye More 44
  E 3
Azovskoye More
  (Sea of Azov) 35
  G 2
Azul 24 F 6
Baba Burun 34 F 3
Babaeski 35 B 4
Babar, Kepulauan 52
  H 7
Babayevo 40 J 6
Babi 52 B 5
Babine Lake 10 R 8
Bābol 44 H 5
Baborigame 20 C 2
Babruysk 36 F 2
Babuyan 49 L 7
Bac Can 47 K 4
Bac Ninh 47 K 4
Bacan 52 H 6
Bacabal 24 G 3
Bacău 36 F 3
Bachu 48 B 3
Bacolod 52 G 3
Bad Hersfeld 36 B 2
Badagara 46 D 6
Baden-Baden 36 B 3
Badin 46 B 4
Badiraguato 20 C 2

Badjawa 52 G 7
Badland 16 C 2
Badulla 46 E 7
Badzhal'skiy Khrebet
  54 B 1
Baffin Bay 8 W 4
Baffin Island 8 U 4
Bafoussam 56 E 4
Bafra 35 F 4
Bafra Burnu 35 F 4
Baga Bogd Uul 49 G
  2
Bagalkot 46 D 5
Baganga 52 H 4
Bagansiapiapi 52 C
  5
Baghdād 44 F 6
Bagheria 34 C 3
Baghlan 45 L 5
Bagley 16 D 2
Bagulo 52 G 2
Bahamas, The 14
  E 5
Bahawalpur 46 C 3
Bahía Blanca 24
  E 6
Bahía Kino 20 B 2
Bahía, Islas de la 20
  G 4
Bahir Dar 56 G 3
Bahral Abyad (White
  Nile) 56 F 4
Bahral Azraq (Blue
  Nile) 56 G 3
Baía de Sofala 58 C
  4
Baia Mare 36 E 3
Balcheng 50 D 3
Baie-Comeau 8 X 9
Baile Átha Cliath 31
  C 2
Bailieborough 31 C
  2
Bainbridge 14 C 4
Baiquan 50 E 3
Bairiki 59 G 3
Bairin Zuoqi 50 C 4
Bairnsdale 60 H 7
Baja 36 D 3
Baja California 20 B
  2
Baja California Norte
  18 C 6
Baja California Sur
  20 B 2
Bājah 34 B 3
Bajandelger 50 A 3
Bajan-Öndör 48 F 2
Bakal 40 N 7
Bakchar 41 S 6
Bake 52 C 6
Baker (California,
  U.S.) 18 C 4
Baker (Montana,
  U.S.) 16 C 2

Baker (Oregon, U.S.)
18 C 3
Baker Lake (Aus-
tralia) 60 D 5
Baker Lake (Canada)
8 R 6
Bakersfield 18 C 4
Bakhmach 36 G 2
Bakı 44 G 4
Bala Murghab 45
K 5
Balabac Island 52
F 4
Balad 44 F 6
Balagannoye 43 N 5
Balaghat 46 E 4
Bālāghāt Range 46
D 5
Balakhna 40 K 6
Balakhta 41 U 6
Balakliya 44 E 3
Balakovo 44 G 2
Balangan Islands 52
F 6
Balangan, Kepulauan
52 F 6
Bālangīr 46 E 4
Balashov 44 F 2
Balchik 34 F 2
Balclutha 62 A 4
Baldy Peak 18 E 5
Baleares, Islas 33
C 2
Balearic Islands 33
C 2
Baler 52 G 2
Bāleshwar 46 F 4
Baley 42 G 6
Balezino 40 M 6
Bali 52 F 7
Balıkesir 35 B 5
Balikpapan 52 F 6
Balintang Channel 49
L 7
Balkanabad 44 H 5
Balladonia 60 C 6
Ballarat 60 G 7
Ballard, Lake 60 C 5
Ballenas, Bahía 20
B 2
Ballia 46 E 3
Ballina (Ireland) 31
B 1
Ballinger 16 D 5
Ballinrobe 31 B 2
Ballygawley 31 C 1
Ballymena 31 C 1
Balotra 46 C 3
Balqash 45 M 3
Balqash Köli 45 N 3
Balrampur 46 E 3
Balsas 20 D 4
Balsas, Déprésion
del 20 D 4
Balsas, Río 20 D 4

Balta 36 F 3
Bălţi 36 F 3
Baltic Sea 38 J 4
Baltimore (U.S.) 14
D 3
Baltiysk 36 D 2
Balurghat 47 F 3
Balykchy 45 N 4
Bamaga 60 G 2
Bamako 56 C 3
Bambari 56 F 4
Bamberg 36 C 3
Ban Ban 47 J 5
Ban Na Shan 47
H 7
Banbury 28 D 3
Bancoran 52 F 4
Bancroft 14 D 1
Banda 46 E 3
Banda Aceh 52 B 4
Banda Sea 52 H 7
Banda, Kepulauan 52
H 6
Banda, Laut 52 H 7
Bandao 49 L 3
Bandar Seri Be-
gawan 52 E 5
Bandar-e Anzalī 44
G 5
Bandar-e Māhshar 44
G 6
Bandar-e Torkaman
44 H 5
Bandarlampung 52
D 7
Bandırma 35 B 4
Bandon 31 B 3
Bandundu 58 A 2
Bandung 52 D 7
Banes 22 G 3
Banff National Park
10 T 8
Bangalore 46 D 6
Bangar 52 F 5
Banggai, Kepulauan
52 G 6
Banggi 52 F 4
Banghāzī 56 F 1
Bangka 52 D 6
Bangkinang 52 C 5
Bangko 52 C 6
Bangkok 47 J 6
Bangladesh 47 F 4
Bangor (Northern Ire-
land, U.K.) 28 B 2
Bangor (U.S.) 14 F 2
Bangor (Wales, U.K.)
28 B 3
Bangor Erris 31 B 1
Bangui 56 E 4
Bangui Suwayf 56 C 2
Banihāl Pass 45 N 6
Banja Luka 34 D 2
Banjarmasin 52 E 6
Banjul 56 B 3

Banks Island (British
Columbia, Canada)
10 Q 8
Banks Island (North-
west Territories,
Canada) 10 S 4
Banks Peninsula 62
B 3
Banks, Îles 59 F 5
Bannu 45 M 6
Banská Bystrica 36
D 3
Bantaeng 52 F 7
Bantry 31 B 3
Bantry Bay 31 A 3
Banyuwangi 52 E 7
Bao Ha 47 J 4
Bao Loc 47 K 6
Baoding 49 K 3
Baoji 49 H 4
Baoqing 54 B 1
Baoshan 48 F 5
Baoting 47 K 5
Baotou 49 H 2
Baoying 49 K 4
Baqanas 45 N 4
Bar Harbor 14 F 2
Barabinsk 41 R 6
Barabinskaya Step'
41 R 7
Baragarh 46 E 4
Barahona 22 H 4
Barakaldo 32 B 3
Baranagar 46 F 4
Bāranavichy 36 F 2
Baranof Island 10
P 7
Barbados 22 L 5
Barbaria, Cap de 33
C 2
Barbuda 22 K 4
Barca 20 D 3
Barcaldine 60 H 4
Barcelona
(Venezuela) 22
K 5
Bardeskan 45 J 5
Bareilly 46 D 3
Barents Sea 40 J 3
Barentsevo More 40
J ·3
Barguzinskiy Khrebet
41 X 6
Bari 34 D 2
Barinas 22 H 6
Barisal 47 G 4
Barisan, Pegunungan
52 C 6
Barkly Tableland 60
F 3
Bârlad 36 F 3
Bârlad (Romania) 35
B 1
Barlee Range 60 B 4
Barlee, Lake 60 C 5

Barletta 34 D 2
Barmer 46 C 3
Barmouth 28 B 3
Barnaul 41 S 7
Barnes Icecap 8 W 4
Barnstaple 28 B 4
Barquisimeto 22 J 5
Barra (U.K.) 30 A 3
Barra Patuca 20 H 4
Barragem de Sobrad-
inho 24 G 4
Barrancabermeja 22
H 6
Barranquilla 22 H 5
Barraute 14 D 1
Barreiras 24 G 4
Barren Island, Cape
60 H 8
Barren Islands 43
Z 5
Barrie 14 D 2
Barro 31 C 2
Barrow 10 L 4
Barrow Island 60 B 4
Barrow Range 60
D 5
Barrow, Point 10 L 4
Barrow-in-Furness 28
C 2
Barry 28 C 4
Barsak, Poluo 45 J 3
Barshyn 45 L 3
Bārsi 46 D 5
Barstow 18 C 5
Bartın 35 E 4
Bartlesville 16 D 4
Baruun Urt 50 B 3
Barysaw 36 F 2
Basel 36 B 3
Bashi Haixia 49 L 6
Basilan 52 G 4
Basilan City 52 G 4
Basildon 28 E 4
Basingstoke 28 D 4
Başkale 35 L 5
Baskatong, Réservoir
14 D 1
Basmat 46 D 5
Baso 52 C 6
Basra 44 G 6
Bass Strait 60 G 8
Bass, Îlots de 59 L 6
Bassein 47 G 5
Basse-Terre (Guade-
loupe) 22 K 4
Basseterre (St. Kitts
and Nevis) 22 K 4
Bastia 34 B 2
Bastrop 16 E 5
Basuo 47 K 5
Batabanó, Golfo del
20 H 3
Batac 52 G 2
Bataklik Gölü 44 D 5
Batam 52 C 5

Batang 52 D 7
Batangas 52 G 3
Batchawana Moun-
tain 14 C 1
Bătdămbăng 47 J 6
Bath (U.K.) 28 C 4
Bath (U.S.) 14 F 2
Batha 56 E 3
Bathurst (Australia)
60 H 6
Bathurst (Canada) 8
X 9
Bathurst Inlet 10 V 5
Bathurst Island (Aus-
tralia) 60 E 2
Bathurst Island
(Canada) 8 R 3
Bathurst, Cape 10
R 4
Batman 44 F 5
Batna 56 D 1
Baton Rouge 16 E 5
Batopilas 20 C 2
Batti Malv 47 G 7
Batticaloa 46 E 7
Battle Creek 14 B 2
Battle Harbour 8 Z 8
Battle Mountain 18
C 3
Batu Pahat 52 C 5
Batulicin 52 F 6
Bat'umi 35 J 4
Baturaja 52 C 6
Baubau 52 G 7
Bauchi 56 D 3
Bauld, Cape 8 Z 8
Bauru 24 F 5
Bavispe 18 E 5
Bawean 52 E 7
Bay Bulls 8 Aa 9
Bay City (Michigan,
U.S.) 14 C 2
Bay City (Texas,
U.S.) 20 E 2
Bay Springs 14 B 4
Bayamo 22 G 3
Bayan 50 E 3
Bayan Har Shan 48 F
4
Bayan Har Shankou
48 F 4
Bayan Mod 49 G 2
Bayan Obo 49 H 2
Bayanaūyl 45 N 2
Bayburt 35 J 4
Baydhabo 58 D 1
Bayerischer Wald 36
C 3
Baykal 41 W 7
Baykal, Ozero 41
X 7
Baykal'skiy Khrebet
41 X 7
Baykit 41 V 5
Baymak 40 N 7

Bayo Nuevo 22 G 4
Bayombong 52 G 2
Bayonne 32 B 3
Bayramali 45 K 5
Bayreuth 36 C 3
Baysa 42 F 6
Baytik Shan 48 E 1
Baytown 20 F 2
Baza 33 B 2
Bazhi 45 P 2
Bazhong 49 H 4
Beach 16 C 2
Beacon 60 B 6
Beal Range 60 G 5
Bear Lake 18 D 3
Bear Lodge Moun-
tains 18 E 3
Bears Paw Mountain
18 E 2
Bearskin Lake 10
Y 8
Beata, Cabo 22 H 4
Beatrice 16 D 3
Beatrice, Cape 60
F 2
Beatton River 10 S 7
Beatty 18 C 4
Beaufort (U.S.) 14
C 4
Beaufort Sea 10 N 4
Beaumont 16 E 5
Beaune 32 C 2
Beaupré 8 W 9
Beausejour 16 D 1
Beauvais 32 C 2
Beaver (Utah, U.S.)
18 D 4
Beaver Dam 14 B 2
Beaver Island 8 T 9
Beaverton 18 B 2
Beawar 46 C 3
Becan 20 F 4
Bečej 36 E 3
Béchar 56 C 1
Becharof Lake 10
L 7
Beckley 14 C 3
Bedford (Indiana,
U.S.) 14 B 3
Bedford (Pennsylva-
nia, U.S.) 14 D 2
Bedford (U.K.) 28
D 3
Beech Grove 14 B 3
Beeville 20 E 2
Beger 48 F 1
Bégles 32 B 3
Behbehān 44 H 6
Behshahr 44 H 5
Bei Hulsan Hu 48
E 3
Bei Shan 48 F 2
Beian 50 E 3
Beibu Wan 47 K 4
Beihai 49 H 6

Beijing 49 K 3
Beiliu 49 J 6
Bein Hoa 47 K 6
Beipiao 50 D 4
Beira 58 C 3
Beirut 44 E 6
Beishan 48 F 2
Beizhen 50 D 4
Beja 33 A 2
Béjah 56 D 1
Bejaïa 56 D 1
Bekasi 52 D 7
Békéscsaba 36 E 3
Bekobod 45 L 4
Bela 46 B 3
Belaga 52 E 5
Belarus 36 E 2
Belaya 40 N 6
Belaya Glina 44 F 3
Belaya Kalitva 44
  F 3
Belaya Kholunitsa 40
  M 6
Bełchatów 36 D 2
Belcher Islands 8
  U 7
Belcheragh 45 L 5
Belebey 44 H 2
Beledweyne 56 H 4
Belém 24 G 3
Belen 18 E 5
Belfast 28 B 2
Belfield 16 C 2
Belfort 36 B 3
Belgaum 46 C 5
Belgorod 44 E 2
Belgrade 34 E 2
Belinyu 52 D 6
Belitung 52 D 6
Belize 20 G 4
Belize (Country) 20
  G 4
Belize (River, Belize)
  20 G 4
Bella Coola 10 R 8
Bellary 46 D 5
Belle Fourche River
  16 C 3
Belle Glade 14 C 5
Belle Isle 8 Z 8
Belle-Île 32 B 2
Belleville (Canada)
  14 D 2
Belleville (Kansas,
  U.S.) 16 D 4
Bellevue (Nebraska,
  U.S.) 16 D 3
Bellevue (Washing-
  ton, U.S.) 18 B 2
Bellingham 18 B 2
Bello 22 G 6
Bellona Island 61
  K 2
Belluno 36 C 3
Belmopan 20 G 4

Belmullet 31 B 1
Belo Horizonte 24
  G 5
Belo Tsiribihina 58
  D 3
Belogorsk 50 E 2
Beloit 14 B 2
Belomorsk 40 H 5
Belorechensk 44 E 4
Belot, Lac 10 R 5
Belovo 41 T 7
Beloye More 40 J 4
Beloye, Ozero 40
  J 5
Belozersk 40 J 5
Belsham 48 F 2
Belukha 45 P 2
Belush'ya Guba 40
  M 3
Belyy Yar 41 T 6
Belyy, Ostrov 40 Q 3
Bemidji 16 D 2
Bemidji, Lake 16 E 2
Ben Tre 47 K 6
Bonaroo 46 E 3
Benavente 33 A 1
Bend 18 B 3
Bendigo 60 G 7
Benevento 34 C 2
Bengal, Bay of 47
  F 5
Bengbu 49 K 4
Bengkulu 52 C 6
Benguela 58 A 3
Beni Mellal 56 C 1
Benidorm 33 C 2
Benin 56 D 3
Benin City 56 D 4
Benito Juarez 20 F 4
Benkelman 16 C 3
Benson 18 D 5
Bentinck Island 60
  F 3
Benton 16 E 5
Bentong 52 C 5
Benue 56 E 4
Benxi 50 D 4
Beograd 34 E 2
Beppu 54 B 4
Berat 34 D 2
Berbera 56 H 3
Berbérati 56 E 4
Berchtesgaden 36
  C 3
Berdigestyakh 42
  J 4
Berdsk 41 S 7
Berdyans'k 35 G 1
Berdychiv 36 F 3
Berehove 36 E 3
Berens River 10 X 8
Berezevo 40 P 5
Berezivka 44 D 3
Berezniki 40 N 6
Berezovo 40 O 5

Berezovskiy 41 T 6
Berg 38 J 2
Berga 32 C 3
Bergamo 35 B 5
Bergamo 36 B 3
Bergen 38 G 3
Bergerac 32 C 3
Bergö 38 K 3
Bergslagen 38 H 3
Berhampore 46 F 4
Berhampur 46 E 5
Bering Glacier 10
  O 6
Bering Land Bridge
  National Reserve
  43 X 3
Bering Sea 43 T 5
Beringa, Ostrov 43
  R 5
Beringovskiy 43 T 4
Berkeley 18 B 4
Berkner Island 63
  N 4
Berlin (Germany) 36
  C 2
Berlin (U.S.) 14 E 2
Bern 36 B 3
Bernalillo 18 E 4
Berner Alpen 36 B 3
Berry Islands 14 D 5
Berwick-upon-Tweed
  28 C 2
Besançon 36 B 3
Besancon 36 B 3
Beskidy Zachodnie
  36 D 3
Beslan 35 L 3
Besni 35 G 6
Bessemer 14 B 4
Bestöbe 45 M 2
Bethany 16 D 4
Bethlehem 58 B 4
Béticos, Sistemas 33
  B 2
Betong 47 J 7
Betpak-Dala 45 M 3
Betroka 58 D 4
Bettiah 46 E 3
Bettles 10 M 5
Betul 46 D 4
Beveridge Reef 59
  J 5
Beverley 28 D 3
Bexhill 28 E 4
Beyoneisu-retsugan
  54 D 4
Beypazarı 35 D 4
Beyşehir 35 D 6
Bezhetsk 40 J 6
Béziers 32 C 3
Bhadrakh 46 F 4
Bhadravāti 46 D 6
Bhagalpur 46 F 3
Bhairab Bāzār 47
  G 4
Bhakkar 46 C 2

Bhaktapur 46 F 3
Bharatpur 46 D 3
Bharuch 46 C 4
Bhātpāra 46 F 4
Bhawanipatna 46
  E 5
Bhilwara 46 C 3
Bhiwani 46 D 3
Bhongir 46 D 5
Bhopal 46 D 4
Bhubaneshwar 46
  F 4
Bhuj 46 B 4
Bhusawal 46 D 4
Bhutan 47 F 3
Biak 59 C 4
Biała Podlaska 36
  E 2
Białogard 36 D 2
Białystok 36 E 2
Biaora 46 D 4
Biaro 52 H 5
Biarritz 32 B 3
Bickerton Island 60
  F 2
Bĭd 46 D 5
Bĭdar 46 D 5
Biddeford 14 E 2
Bideford 28 B 4
Bidzhan 50 F 3
Biel 36 B 3
Bielefeld 36 B 2
Bielsk Podlaski 36
  E 2
Bielsko-Biała 36 D 3
Bienville, Lac 8 W 7
Big Belt Mountains
  18 D 2
Big Bend National
  Park 20 D 2
Big Cypress National
  Reserve 14 C 5
Big Horn Lake 18
  E 2
Big Horn Mountains
  18 E 3
Big Horn River 18
  E 2
Big Island 8 W 6
Big Rapids 14 B 2
Big Sioux River 16
  D 3
Big Smoky Valley 18
  C 4
Big Snowy Mountains
  18 E 2
Big Spring 16 C 5
Big Trout Lake 8 T 8
Bighorn Basin 18
  E 3
Bight of Benin 56
  D 4
Bihać 34 D 2
Bihār 46 F 3
Bihār (State) 46 F 3

Bijapur 46 D 5
Bijeljina 34 D 2
Bijelo Polje 34 D 2
Bijie 49 H 5
Bijoutier 58 E 2
Bikaner 46 C 3
Bikar 59 G 2
Bikin 50 F 3
Bikini 59 F 2
Bila Tserkva 44 D 3
Bilaspur 46 E 4
Bilauktaung Range
  47 H 6
Bilbao 32 B 3
Bilecik 35 C 4
Bilhorod-Dnistro-
  vs'kyy 35 D 1
Billings 18 E 2
Bilopillya 36 G 2
Biloxi 14 B 4
Bimini Islands 14
  D 5
Bin Xian 50 E 3
Bin Xian (Hei-
  longjiang, China)
  54 A 1
Bina-Etāwa 46 D 4
Binaiya, Gunung 52
  H 6
Binghampton 14 D 2
Bingöl 35 J 5
Binhai 49 K 4
Binjai (Indonesia) 52
  B 5
Binjai (Indonesia) 52
  D 5
Binongko 52 G 7
Bintan 52 C 5
Bintuhan 52 C 6
Bintulu 52 E 5
Binyang 49 H 6
Bioko 56 D 4
Bira 50 G 3
Bira (Russia) 54 B 1
Bira (Russia) 50
  G 3
Birakan 54 B 1
Biratnagar 46 F 3
Birch'ul' 41 T 7
Birkenhead 28 C 3
Birksgate Range 60
  D 5
Birmingham (U.K.) 28
  D 3
Birmingham (U.S.) 14
  B 4
Birmitrapur 46 E 4
Birnie Island 59 H 4
Birnin-Kebbi 56 D 3
Birobidzhan 50 F 3
Birsk 40 N 6
Biryusa 41 V 7
Bisbee 18 E 5

Biscay, Bay of 32
  B 2
Bishkek 45 M 4
Bishop 18 C 4
Bishop Rock 28 A 5
Biskra 56 D 1
Bislig 52 H 4
Bismarck 16 C 2
Bismarck Archipel-
  ago 59 D 4
Bismarck Range 59
  D 4
Bismarck Sea 59
  D 4
Bismarck, Kap 8
  Hh 3
Bison 16 C 2
Bissau 56 B 3
Bissett 16 D 1
Biatrița 36 E 3
Bitlis 35 K 5
Bitola 34 E 2
Bitterroot Range 18
  C 2
Biu 56 E 3
Biwa-ko 54 C 3
Biya 41 T 7
Biysk 41 T 7
Björkön 38 K 3
Björneborg 38 K 3
Black Hills 16 C 3
Black Mountain 14
  C 3
Black Mountains 28
  C 3
Black Range 18 E 5
Black River Falls 16
  E 3
Black Rock Desert 18
  C 3
Black Sea 35 E 3
Blackall 60 H 4
Blackburn 28 C 3
Blackfoot 18 D 3
Blackpool 28 C 3
Blackwater (U.K.) 31
  B 2
Blackwell 16 D 4
Blagodatnyy 50 G 3
Blagoevgrad 34 E 2
Blagoveshchensk
  (Russia) 40 N 6
Blagoveshchensk
  (Russia) 42 J 6
Blaine 16 E 2
Blair 16 D 3
Blanche, Lake 60
  F 5
Blanco, Cape 18 B 3
Blanc-Sablon 8 Z 8
Blantyre 58 C 3
B'Idudalur 38 A 2
Blekinge 38 J 4
Blenheim 62 B 3
Blida 56 D 1

Blind River 14 C 1
Blitar 52 E 7
Bloemfontein 58 B 4
Blois 32 C 2
Bloody Foreland 31 B 1
Bloomington (Illinois, U.S.) 14 B 2
Bloomington (Indiana, U.S.) 14 B 3
Bloomington (Minnesota, U.S.) 16 E 3
Blora 52 E 7
Blosseville Kyst 8 Ff 5
Blossom, Mys 43 T 2
Blue Mountain Lake 14 E 2
Blue Mountains 60 H 6
Blue Ridge 14 C 3
Bluefield 14 C 3
Bluenose Lake 10 S 5
Bluff 62 A 4
Blumenau 24 G 5
Blyth 28 D 2
Blythe 18 D 5
Blytheville 14 B 3
Bo 56 B 4
Bo Hai 49 K 3
Bo Xian 49 K 4
Boa Vista 56 A 3
Boa Vista (Brazil) 22 K 7
Boac 52 G 3
Boano 52 H 6
Bobai 49 H 6
Bobbili 46 E 5
Bobo Dioulasso 56 C 3
Bobrov 44 F 2
Bobrynets' 44 D 3
Boca Grande 22 K 6
Boca Raton 14 C 5
Bochum 36 B 2
Bocşa 36 E 3
Bodaybo 42 F 5
Bodélé 56 E 3
Bodhan 46 D 5
Bodjonegoro 52 E 7
Bodmin Moor 28 B 4
Bodø 38 H 2
Bodrum 35 B 6
Boeng Tonle Chhma 47 J 6
Bogale 47 H 5
Bogalusa 14 B 4
Boghra Dam 45 K 6
Bognor Regis 28 D 4
Bogo 52 G 3
Bogor 52 D 7
Bogoroditsk 44 E 2
Bogotá 22 H 7

Bogotol 41 T 6
Bogra 47 F 4
Boguchany 41 V 6
Bohai Haixia 49 L 3
Böhmerwald 36 C 3
Bohodukhiv 44 E 2
Bohol 52 G 4
Bohuslän 38 H 4
Bois, Lac des 10 R 5
Boise 18 C 3
Boise City 16 C 4
Boise River 18 C 3
Boissevain 16 C 2
Bojnürd 45 J 5
Bolan Pass 46 B 3
Bole (China) 48 C 2
Bolesławiec 36 D 2
Bolgatanga 56 C 3
Boli 50 F 3
Bolivia 24 E 4
Bolkhov 44 E 2
Bollnäs 38 J 3
Bologna 34 C 2
Bologoye 40 H 6
Bolon' 50 G 3
Bolotnoye 41 S 6
Bol'shaya Chernigovka 44 H 2
Bol'shaya Glushitsa 44 H 2
Bol'shaya Kuonamka 41 X 4
Bol'sheretsk 43 P 6
Bol'shevik, Ostrov 41 W 2
Bol'shezemel'skaya Tundra 40 N 4
Bol'shoy Begichev, Ostrov 41 Y 3
Bol'shoy Kamen' 54 B 2
Bol'shoy Kavkaz 35 J 3
Bol'shoy Lyakhovskiy, Ostrov 42 M 2
Bol'shoy Porog 41 U 4
Bol'shoy Shantar 42 L 6
Bolton 28 C 3
Bolu 35 D 4
Bolvadin 35 D 5
Bolzano 36 C 3
Boma 58 A 2
Bombala 60 H 7
Bombay 46 C 5
Bømlo 38 F 4
Bon, Cap 34 C 3
Bona, Mount 10 O 6
Bonaire 22 J 5
Bonampak 20 F 4
Bonanza 20 H 5
Bonaparte Archipelago 60 C 2

Bondowoso 52 E 7
Bongka 52 G 6
Bongor 56 E 3
Botoşani 36 F 3
Bonifacio, Strait of 34 B 2
Bonito, Pico 20 G 4
Bonn 36 B 2
Bonners Ferry 18 C 2
Bonneville Saltflats 18 D 3
Boon 14 C 1
Böön Tsagaan Nuur 48 F 1
Boone 16 E 3
Booneville 16 E 4
Boosaaso 56 H 3
Boothia, Gulf of 8 S 4
Boquillas del Carmen 20 D 2
Bor (Russia) 40 K 6
Bor (Turkey) 35 F 6
Bor (Yugoslavia) 34 E 2
Bora-Bora 59 K 5
Borås 38 H 4
Borçka 44 F 4
Bordeaux 32 B 3
Borden Island 10 U 3
Borden Peninsula 8 U 4
Bordertown 60 G 7
Borgholm 38 J 4
Borisoglebsk 44 F 2
Borlänge 38 J 3
Borneo 52 E 6
Bornholm 36 D 2
Borogontsy 42 K 4
Borohoro Shan 48 C 2
Boroko 52 G 5
Borovichi 40 H 6
Borovskoye 40 O 7
Borroloola 60 F 3
Borşa 36 E 3
Boryslav 36 E 3
Boryspil' 36 G 2
Borzya 42 G 6
Bose 49 H 6
Boshan 49 K 3
Boshnyakovo 54 D 1
Bosnia-Herzegovina 34 D 2
Bosnian-Croat Federation 34 D 2
Bosporus 35 C 4
Bossier City 16 E 5
Bosten Hu 48 D 2
Boston (U.K.) 28 D 3
Boston (U.S.) 14 E 2
Boston Mountains 16 E 4

Bothnia, Gulf of 38 J 3
Botoşani 36 F 3
Botswana 58 B 4
Bou Saâda 56 D 1
Bouaké 56 C 4
Bouar 56 E 4
Boufarik 33 C 2
Bougainville Island 59 E 4
Bougainville Reef 59 E 5
Bougainville Strait 59 E 4
Bouïra 33 C 2
Boulder (U.S.) 18 E 3
Boulia 60 F 4
Boulogne-sur-Mer 28 C 2
Bountiful 18 D 3
Bourg-en-Bresse 36 B 3
Bourges 32 C 2
Bourgogne 32 C 2
Bourke 60 H 6
Bournemouth 28 D 4
Bow River 18 D 1
Bowen 60 H 3
Bowling Green 14 B 3
Bowling Green, Cape 60 H 3
Bowman 16 C 2
Boxing 49 K 3
Boyabat 35 F 4
Boyang 49 K 5
Boyarka 41 V 3
Boyle 31 B 2
Bozashchy Tübegi 44 H 3
Bozema 18 D 2
Brač 34 D 2
Bräcke 38 J 3
Bradenton 14 C 5
Bradford (U.K.) 28 D 3
Bradford (U.S.) 14 D 2
Brady 16 D 5
Braemar 30 C 3
Braga 33 A 1
Bragança (Portugal) 33 A 1
Brahmapur 46 E 5
Brahmaputra 48 E 5
Braich y Pwll 28 B 3
Brăila 35 B 2
Brainerd 16 E 2
Brakna 56 B 3
Brampton 14 D 2
Brandenburg 36 C 2
Brandon 16 D 2
Braniewo 36 D 2
Brantford 14 C 2

Bras d'Or, Lake 8 Y 9
Brasília 24 G 4
Braşov 35 A 2
Bratislava 36 D 3
Bratsk 41 W 6
Bratskoye Vodokhranilishche 41 W 6
Brattleboro 14 E 2
Braunschweig 36 C 2
Brava 56 A 3
Bravo del Norte, Río 18 E 5
Brawley 18 C 5
Bray Island 8 V 5
Brazas River 16 D 5
Brazil 24 F 3
Brazilian Highlands 24 G 5
Brazzaville 58 A 2
Brčko 34 D 2
Brebes 52 D 7
Breckenridge 16 D 5
Břeclav 36 D 3
Brecon 28 C 4
Bredbyn 38 J 3
Bredy 45 K 2
Breiðafjörður 38 A 2
Breiðdalur 38 C 3
Bremen 36 B 2
Bremerhaven 36 B 2
Bremer Bay 60 B 6
Bremerton 18 B 2
Brenner Pass 36 C 3
Brescia 36 C 3
Bressay 30 D 1
Bressuire 32 B 2
Brest (Belarus) 36 E 2
Brest (France) 32 B 2
Bretagne 32 B 2
Brett, Cape 62 B 2
Breueh 47 G 7
Brevoort Island 8 Y 6
Brewster, Kap 8 Gg 4
Brewton 14 B 4
Bridgeport (California, U.S.) 18 C 4
Bridgeport (Connecticut, U.S.) 14 E 2
Bridger Peak 18 E 3
Bridgetown 22 L 5
Bridgwater 28 C 4
Bridlington 28 D 2
Bridlington Bay 28 D 3
Brigham City 18 D 3
Brighton 28 D 4
Brindisi 34 D 2
Brisbane 60 J 5
Bristol (U.K.) 28 C 4

Bristol (U.S.) 14 C 3
Bristol Bay 43 X 5
Bristol Channel 28 B 4
British Columbia 10 R 7
British Virgin Islands 22 K 4
Brive-la-Gaillarde 32 C 2
Brno 36 D 3
Broadford 30 B 3
Broadus 18 E 2
Broadview 16 C 1
Brochet, Lac 10 W 7
Brock Island 10 U 3
Brockville 14 D 2
Brodeur Peninsula 8 T 4
Brodnica 36 D 2
Brody 36 F 2
Broken Hill 60 G 6
Brønnøysund 38 H 2
Brookfield 16 E 4
Brookhaven 16 E 5
Brookings (Oregon, U.S.) 18 B 3
Brookings (South Dakota, U.S.) 16 D 3
Brooks 18 D 1
Brooks Range 10 L 5
Broome 60 C 3
Brora 30 C 2
Broutona, Ostrov 50 J 3
Browne Range Nature Reserve 60 C 4
Brownfield 16 C 5
Browning 18 D 2
Brownsville 20 E 2
Brownwood 16 D 5
Bruce Peninsula 14 C 1
Bruneau 18 C 3
Brunei 52 E 4
Brunswick 14 C 4
Bryan 16 D 5
Bryansk 36 G 2
Brzeg 36 D 2
Bucak 35 D 6
Bucaramanga 22 H 6
Buccaneer Archipelago 60 C 3
Buchanan, Lake (Australia) 60 C 5
Buchanan, Lake (U.S.) 16 D 5
Bucharest 34 F 2
Bucureşti 35 B 2
Bucyrus 14 C 2
Budapest 36 D 3

Budaun 46 D 3
Bude 28 B 4
Bude Bay 28 B 4
Budennovsk 35 L 2
Buēagra 35 J 7
Buenaventura 22
  G 7
Buenaventura (Mex-
  ico) 20 C 2
Buenos Aires 24 E 6
Buffalo (New York,
  U.S.) 14 D 2
Buffalo (South
  Dakota, U.S.) 16
  C 2
Buffalo (Wyoming,
  U.S.) 18 E 3
Buffalo Lake 10 T 6
Buftea 35 A 2
Buga 22 G 7
Bugrino 40 L 4
Bugsuk Island 52
  F 4
Bugt 50 D 3
Bugul'ma 44 H 2
Buguruslan 44 H 2
Builth Wells 28 C 3
Buinsk 44 G 2
Bujumbura 58 B 2
Buka Island 59 E 4
Bukachacha 42 G 6
Bukavu 58 B 2
Bukhta Tikhaya 40
  M 1
Bukit Gandadiwata
  52 F 6
Bukittinggi 52 C 6
Bula 52 J 6
Būlaevo 40 Q 7
Bulan 52 G 3
Bulandshahr 46 D 3
Bulawayo 58 B 4
Buldan 35 C 5
Buldir Island 43 T 6
Bulgaria 34 F 2
Bull Shoals Lake 16
  E 4
Buller 62 B 3
Bullfinch 60 B 6
Bulukumba 52 G 7
Bulun 42 J 2
Bumba 58 B 1
Bunbury 60 B 6
Buncrana 31 C 1
Bundaberg 60 J 4
Bungo-suido 54 B 4
Bunia 58 B 1
Bunkie 16 E 5
Buntok 52 E 6
Bünyan 35 F 5
Buolkalakh 42 G 2
Buon Me Thuot 47
  K 6
Buorkhaya, Mys 42
  K 2

Būr Sa'īd (Port Said)
  56 G 1
Būr Sūdān (Port
  Sudan) 56 G 2
Burco 56 H 4
Burdur 35 D 6
Burdur Gölü 44 C 5
Burdwan 46 F 4
Bureiskiy, Khrebet 42
  K 6
Burgas 35 B 3
Burgaski Zahiv 35 C
  3
Burgos 32 B 3
Burgos (Mexico) 20 C
  3
Burgsvik 38 J 4
Burhanpur 46 D 4
Buri Ram 47 J 5
Burias 52 G 3
Burica, Punta 22 F 6
Burketown 60 F 3
Burkina Faso 56 C
  3
Burley 18 D 3
Burlington (Colorado,
  U.S.) 16 C 4
Burlington (Iowa,
  U.S.) 16 E 3
Burlington (Vermont,
  U.S.) 14 E 2
Burma 47 G 4
Burney 18 B 3
Burnie 60 H 8
Burns 18 C 3
Burns Lake 10 R 8
Burra 60 F 6
Bursa 35 C 4
Burtha Qi 50 D 3
Buru 52 H 6
Burundi 58 B 2
Bury St Edmunds 28
  [3
Burylbaytal 45 M 3
Buskerud 38 G 3
Buskul 45 K 2
Busselton 60 B 6
Bussol', Proliv 50
  K 3
Busuanga 52 F 3
Butembo 58 B 2
Buton 52 G 6
Butt of Lewis 30 A 2
Butte 18 D 2
Butterworth 52 C 4
Button Islands 8 X 6
Butuan 52 H 4
Buturlinovka 44 F 2
Buxoro 45 K 5
Buy 40 K 6
Buynaksk 44 G 4
Buzău 36 F 3
Buzluk Dağ 35 F 4
Buzuluk 44 H 2
Byahoml' 36 F 2

Byam Martin Island
  10 W 3
Byam Martin, Cape 8
  V 4
Bydgoszcz 36 D 2
Bykhaw 36 G 2
Bykov 54 D 1
Bykovo 40 L 5
Bylot Island 8 V 4
Byrranga, Gory 41
  V 3
Bytom 36 D 2
Ca Mau 47 K 7
Cabadbaran 52 H 4
Caballo Reservoir 18
  E 5
Cabanatuan 52 G 2
Cabimas 22 H 5
Cabinda (Angola) 58
  A 2
Cabinet Mountains
  18 C 2
Cabo De Santa
  Marta 58 A 3
Cabo Frio 24 G 5
Cabonga, Réservoir
  14 D 1
Caborca 18 D 5
Cabrera, Isla de 33 C
  2
Čačak 34 E 2
Caçapava do Sul 24
  F 6
Caccia, Capo 34 B 2
Cáceres (Spain) 33
  A 2
Cachoeira Aquibi 24
  F 4
Cachoeira das Ilhas
  24 F 3
Cachoeira do Cha-
  corão 24 F 3
Cachoeira dos Patos
  24 E 3
Cachoeira Nova Vida
  24 E 3
Cachoeira Pereira 24
  F 3
Cachoeira Santana
  24 G 4
Cadillac 14 B 2
Cádiz 33 A 2
Cadiz 52 G 3
Cádiz, Golfo de 33
  A 2
Caen 32 B 2
Caernarfon 28 B 3
Caernarfon Bay 28 B
  3
Cagayan de Oro 52
  G 4
Cagayan Islands 52
  F 4
Cagliari 34 B 3
Cagnes 34 B 2

Caguas 22 J 4
Caha Mountains 31
  B 3
Cahersiveen 31 A 3
Cahir 31 C 2
Cahore Point 31 C 2
Cahors 32 C 3
Caibarién 22 G 3
Caicos Islands 22
  H 3
Cairngorm Mountains
  30 C 3
Cairns 60 H 3
Caithness 30 C 2
Cajamarca 24 D 3
Calabozo 22 J 6
Calafat 34 E 2
Calagua Islands 52
  G 3
Calahorra 32 B 3
Ćalā'ïb 56 G 2
Calais 28 E 4
Calais, Pas de 28
  E 4
Calakmul 20 G 4
Calamian Group 52
  F 3
Calapan 52 G 3
Calatayud 32 B 3
Calayan 49 L 7
Calbayog 52 G 3
Calcutta 46 F 4
Caldas da Rainha 33
  A 2
Caldwell 18 C 3
Calgary 10 U 8
Cali 22 G 7
Calicut 46 D 6
Caliente 18 D 4
California 18 B 4
California, Golfo de
  20 B 2
Callao 24 D 4
Caltanissetta 34 C 3
Calvi 34 B 2
Cam Ranh 47 K 6
Camagüey 22 G 3
Camarat, Cap 34
  B 2
Camarón, Cabo 20
  G 4
Cambodia 47 J 6
Cambrian Mountains
  28 B 4
Cambridge (Idaho,
  U.S.) 18 C 3
Cambridge (Mary-
  land, U.S.) 14 D 3
Cambridge (Massa-
  chusetts, U.S.) 14
  E 2
Cambridge (U.K.) 28
  E 3
Cambridge Bay 10
  V 5

Camden 16 E 5
Cameron 16 E 2
Cameroon 56 D 4
Camiguin 52 G 2
Camooweal 60 F 3
Camorta 47 G 7
Camp Verde 18 D 5
Campbell River 10
  R 8
Campbell, Cape 62
  B 3
Campbelltown 60 J 6
Campbeltown 28 B 2
Campeche (Mexico)
  20 F 4
Campeche (State,
  Mexico) 20 F 4
Campeche, Bahía de
  20 F 4
Campina Grande 24
  H 3
Campinas 24 G 5
Campo Grande 24
  F 5
Campobasso 34 C 2
Campos 24 G 4
Campos 24 G 5
Camrose 10 U 8
Can Tho 47 K 6
Canada 10 V 7
Canadian 16 C 4
Canadian River 16
  C 4
Çanakkale (Turkey)
  35 B 4
Çanakkale Boğazi 34
  F 3
Cananea 18 D 5
Canarreos, Archip-
  iélago de los 22
  F 3
Canary Islands
  (Spain) 56 B 2
Canaveral, Cape 14
  C 5
Canberra 60 H 7
Cancún 20 G 3
Candelaria 20 F 4
Cando 16 D 2
Cangzhou 49 K 3
Çankırı 35 E 4
Cannanore 46 D 6
Cannes 34 B 2
Canoas 24 F 5
Canon City 18 E 4
Canora 10 W 8
Cantábrica,
  Cordillera 33 A 1
Canterbury 28 E 4
Canterbury Bight 62
  B 3
Canterbury Plains 62
  B 3
Canton (China) 49
  J 6

Canton (Mississippi,
  U.S.) 16 E 5
Canton (Ohio, U.S.)
  14 C 2
Canyon 16 C 5
Cao Bang 47 K 4
Cao Xian 49 K 4
Cap Blanc 56 B 2
Cap de Formentor 33
  C 2
Cap Rhir 56 B 1
Cap Vert 56 B 3
Cap-de-la-Madeleine
  14 E 1
Cape Arid National
  Park 60 C 6
Cape Breton High-
  lands National Park
  8 Y 9
Cape Breton Island 8
  Y 9
Cape Charles 14 D 3
Cape Coast 56 C 4
Cape Cod Bay 14 E
  2
Cape Columbine 58
  A 5
Cape Coral 14 C 5
Cape Dorset 8 V 6
Cape Girardeau 14
  B 3
Cape Horn 24 E 8
Cape Krusenstern
  National Monument
  10 K 5
Cape May 14 E 3
Cape of Good Hope
  58 A 5
Cape Smith 8 V 6
Cape Town 58 A 5
Cape Verde 56 A 3
Cape Yakataga 10
  O 6
Cape York Peninsula
  60 G 2
Cap-Haïtien 22 H 4
Capreol 14 C 1
Capricorn Channel
  60 J 4
Capricorn Group 60
  J 4
Car Nicobar 47 G 7
Caracal 34 E 2
Caracas 22 J 5
Caratasca, Laguna
  de 20 H 4
Carbonara, Capo 34
  B 3
Carbonia 34 B 3
Carcassonne 32 C 3
Carcross 10 Q 6
Cárdenas 22 F 3
Cárdenas (Mexico)
  20 E 3
Cardiff 28 C 4

Cardigan 28 B 3
Cardigan Bay 28 B 3
Cardston 18 D 2
Carei 36 E 3
Carey Øer 8 W 3
Carey, Lake 60 C 5
Caribbean Sea 22 G 5
Caribou 14 F 1
Carleton Place 14 D 1
Carletonville 58 B 4
Carlisle 28 C 2
Carlow 31 C 2
Carloway 30 A 2
Carlsbad (California, U.S.) 18 C 5
Carlsbad (New Mexico, U.S.) 16 C 5
Carlyle 16 C 2
Carmacks 10 P 6
Carmarthen 28 B 4
Carmel 18 B 4
Carmel Head 28 B 3
Carmen, Isla 20 B 2
Carmi 14 B 3
Carmichael 18 B 4
Carnarvon (Australia) 60 A 4
Carndonagh 31 C 1
Carnegie, Lake 60 C 5
Carnsore Point 31 C 2
Carolina 24 G 3
Carolina Beach 14 D 4
Caroline Islands 59 D 3
Carondelet 59 H 4
Carora 22 H 5
Carozal 22 G 6
Carpathian Mountains 36 E 3
Carpaţii Meridionali 36 E 3
Carpentaria, Gulf of 60 F 2
Carrara 34 C 2
Carrick-on-Shannon 31 B 2
Carrillo 20 D 2
Carrizal 18 E 5
Carrizo Springs 20 E 2
Carrizozo 18 E 5
Carroll 16 E 3
Carrollton 14 B 4
Çarsamba 35 G 4
Carson 18 B 2
Carson City 18 C 4
Cartagena (Colombia) 22 G 5
Cartagena (Spain) 33 B 2

Carthage 16 E 4
Caruaru 24 H 3
Carupano 22 K 5
Carutapera 24 G 3
Casa Grande 18 D 5
Casablanca 56 C 1
Cascade Range 18 B 3
Cascavel 24 F 5
Caserta 34 C 2
Casino 60 J 5
Casper 18 E 3
Caspian Sea 44 H 4
Cassiar 10 R 7
Castelló de la Plana 33 B 1
Castelo Branco 33 A 2
Castelvetrano 34 C 3
Castilla La Mancha 32 B 3
Castilla y León 33 B 1
Castle Douglas 28 C 2
Castlebar 31 B 2
Castlegar 18 C 2
Castlepoint 62 C 3
Castletown 28 B 2
Castres 32 C 3
Castries 22 K 5
Cat Island 22 G 3
Cataluña 32 C 3
Catanduanes 52 G 3
Catania 34 D 3
Catanzaro 34 D 3
Catastrophe, Cape 60 F 6
Catbalogan 52 G 3
Catoche, Cabo 20 G 3
Catwick Islands 47 K 6
Caucasus 35 J 3
Cavan 31 C 1
Cavell 16 F 1
Cavili 52 F 4
Caxais do Sul 24 F 5
Çay 35 D 5
Çaycuma 35 E 4
Cayenne 24 F 2
Cayman Brac 22 G 4
Cayman Islands 22 F 4
Cebaco, Isla 22 F 6
Ceballos 20 D 2
Ceboruco,Volcán 20 D 3
Cebu 52 G 3
Cedar City 18 D 4
Cedar Creek Reservoir 16 D 5
Cedar Falls 16 E 3

Cedar Rapids 16 E 3
Cedar River 16 E 3
Cedros, Isla 18 C 6
Ceduna 60 E 6
Cefalù 34 C 3
Celaya 20 D 3
Celebes 52 F 6
Celebes Sea 52 G 5
Celestún 20 F 3
Celje 36 D 3
Celle 36 C 2
Celtic Sea 31 C 3
Cendrawasih, Teluk 59 C 4
Centerville 16 E 3
Central African Republic 56 E 4
Central Brahui Range 46 B 3
Central Makrān Range 46 A 3
Central Range 59 D 4
Central, Cordillera (Philippines) 52 G 2
Centralia 18 B 2
Cepu 52 E 7
Ceram 52 H 6
Cereal 10 U 8
Cereté 22 G 6
Cerf 58 E 2
Cerralvo, Isla 20 C 3
Cerritos 20 D 3
Cerro de Pasco 24 D 4
České Budějovice 36 C 3
Çeşme 34 F 3
Cessnock 60 J 6
Ceuta 33 A 2
Cevennes 32 C 3
Ceylânpinar 35 J 6
Cha-Am 47 H 6
Chachoengsao 47 J 6
Chaco Austral 24 E 5
Chaco Boreal 24 E 5
Chaco Central 24 E 5
Chad 56 E 3
Chadron 16 C 3
Chãgai Hills 45 K 7
Chagda 42 K 5
Chagyl 45 J 4
Chai Nat 47 J 5
Chãībãsa 46 F 4
Chakwal 46 C 2
Chalkida 34 E 3
Challenger Deep 59 D 2
Challis 18 D 3
Châlons-en-Champagne 32 C 2

Chalon-sur-Saône 32 C 2
Chaman 45 L 6
Chambéry 36 B 3
Chamela 20 C 4
Champagne 32 C 2
Champasak 47 K 6
Champlain, Lake 14 E 2
Champotón 20 F 4
Chanbogd 49 H 2
Chandalar 10 N 5
Chandeleur Islands 20 G 2
Chandigarh 46 D 2
Chandrapur 46 D 5
Chang Cheng 50 C 4
Chang Rai 47 H 5
Changbai Shan 50 E 4
Changchun 50 E 4
Changde 49 J 5
Chang-hua 49 L 6
Changji 48 D 2
Changjiang 47 K 5
Changjiang (River) 49 H 4
Changli 49 K 3
Changling 50 D 4
Changsha 49 J 5
Changshu 49 L 4
Changting 49 K 5
Changwu 49 H 3
Changzhi 49 J 3
Changzhou 49 K 4
Chania 34 E 3
Channapatna 46 D 6
Channel Islands 32 B 2
Channel Islands (U.S.) 18 C 5
Channel Tunnel 28 E 4
Chanthaburi 47 J 6
Chany, Ozero 45 N 1
Chao Hu 49 K 4
Chao'an 49 K 6
Chaoyang 50 D 4
Chapaev 44 H 2
Chapala 20 D 3
Chapala, Laguna de 20 D 3
Chapayevsk 44 G 2
Chapleau 8 U 9
Chaplygin 44 E 2
Chara 42 G 4
Charcas 20 D 3
Chari 56 E 3
Charles City 16 E 3
Charles Island 8 W 6
Charles Louis, Pegunungan 59 C 4
Charles Point 60 E 2
Charlesbourg 8 W 9

Charleston (South Carolina, U.S.) 14 D 4
Charleston (West Virginia, U.S.) 14 C 3
Charleville 60 H 5
Charlotte 14 C 3
Charlotte Harbor 14 C 5
Charlottesville 14 D 3
Charlottetown 8 Y 9
Charlton Island 8 U 8
Charsadda 45 M 6
Charters Towers 60 H 4
Chartres 32 C 2
Chasma Barrage 46 C 2
Chasŏng 54 A 2
Châteauroux 32 C 2
Châtellerault 32 C 2
Chatham (Ontario, Canada) 14 C 2
Chatham (U.K.) 28 E 4
Chatham Islands 59 E 5
Chattahoochee 14 C 4
Chattahoochee River 14 C 4
Chattanooga 14 B 3
Chau Phu 47 K 6
Chauk 47 G 4
Chaumont 36 B 3
Chaves 33 A 1
Chaykovskiy 40 M 6
Chazhegovo 40 M 5
Cheb 36 C 2
Cheboksary 40 L 6
Chech'on 50 E 5
Cheduba Island 47 G 5
Chegdomyn 42 K 6
Cheju 50 E 6
Cheju-do 50 E 6
Cheju-haehyŏb 50 E 6
Chekanovskiy 41 W 6
Chekhov 54 D 1
Chełm 36 E 2
Chelmsford 28 E 4
Cheltenham 28 C 4
Chelyabinsk 40 O 6
Chelyuskin, Mys 63 E 1
Chemnitz 36 C 2
Chemult 18 B 3
Chencoyi 20 F 4
Cheng'an 49 J 3
Chengde 50 C 4
Chengdu 49 G 4

Chengmai 47 L 5
Chennai 46 E 6
Chenxi 49 J 5
Chenzhou 49 J 5
Ch'ŏnan 50 E 5
Cherbaniani Reef 46 C 6
Cherbourg 32 B 2
Cheremkhovo 41 W 7
Cherepanovo 41 S 7
Cherepovets 40 J 6
Cherkasy 44 D 3
Cherkessk 35 K 2
Chermoz 40 N 6
Chernigovka 54 B 2
Chernihiv 36 G 2
Chernivtsi 36 F 3
Chernogorsk 41 U 7
Chernyakhiv 36 F 2
Chernyakhovsk 36 E 2
Chernyy Yar 44 G 3
Chernyye Zemli 44 F 3
Cherokee 16 D 3
Cherokees, Lake o' the 16 E 4
Cherskiy 43 Q 3
Cherskogo, Khrebet 42 F 6
Chervonohrad 36 E 2
Chervyanka 41 V 6
Chervyen' 36 F 2
Chesapeake Bay 14 D 3
Chesapeake Bay Bridge-Tunnel 14 D 3
Cheshkaya Guba 40 L 4
Chester 28 C 3
Chesterfield 28 D 3
Chesterfield Inlet 8 S 6
Chesuncook Lake 14 E 1
Chetlat 46 C 6
Chetumal 20 G 4
Chetumal, Bahía de 20 G 4
Cheviot (New Zealand) 62 B 3
Cheviot Hills 28 C 2
Cheyenne 16 C 3
Cheyenne River 16 C 3
Cheyenne Wells 16 C 4
Cheyne Bay 60 B 6
Chhatarpur 46 D 4
Chhattīsgarh 46 E 4
Chhindwara 46 D 4
Chiai 49 L 6

Chiang Mai 47 H 5
Chiapas 20 F 4
Chiavari 34 B 2
Chiba 54 D 3
Chibougamau 8 W 9
Chicago 14 B 2
Chichagof Island 10
  P 7
Chichén Itzá 20 G 3
Chichester Range
  National Park 60
  B 4
Chickasha 16 D 4
Chiclayo 24 C 3
Chico 18 B 4
Chicoutimi 8 W 9
Chidambaram 46 D 6
Chieti 34 C 2
Chifeng 50 C 4
Chihli, Gulf of 49 K 3
Ch'ihshang 49 L 6
Chihuahua (Mexico)
  20 C 2
Chihuahua (State,
  Mexico) 20 C 2
Chikhacheva 42 N 2
Chilapa de Alvarez
  20 E 4
Chilaw 46 D 7
Childress 16 C 5
Chile 24 D 6
Chilecito 24 E 5
Chilik 44 H 2
Chlilabombwe 58
  B 3
Chilka Lake 46 F 5
Chillán 24 D 6
Chillicothe (Iowa,
  U.S.) 16 E 4
Chillicothe (Ohio,
  U.S.) 14 C 3
Chiloquin 18 B 3
Chilpancingo 20 E 4
Chilung 49 L 5
Chimaltenango 20
  F 5
Chimbote 24 C 3
Chimoio 58 C 3
Chin Hills 47 G 4
China 49 E 4
Chinandega 22 E 5
Chinchilla 60 J 5
Chinchorro, Banco
  20 G 4
Chin-do 50 E 6
Chindwin 47 G 4
Chingola 58 B 3
Chinju 50 E 5
Chioggia 36 C 3
Chios 34 F 3
Chios (Greece) 35
  B 5
Chios (Island) 34 F 3
Chippewa Falls 16
  E 3

Chippewa, Lake 16
  E 2
Chirala 46 E 5
Chirchiq 45 L 4
Chirikof Island 43
  Y 5
Chirinda 41 W 4
Chiriqui, Golfo de 22
  F 6
Chirpan 35 A 3
Chisasibi 8 V 8
Chişinău 36 F 3
Chistoozernoye 41
  R 7
Chistopol' 40 M 6
Chita 42 F 6
Chitose 54 D 2
Chitradurga 46 D 6
Chittagong 47 G 4
Chittaurgarh 46 C 4
Chittoor 46 D 6
Choiseul Island 59
  E 4
Choix 20 C 2
Chojnice 36 D 2
Cholet 32 B 2
Choluteca 20 G 5
Chomutov 36 C 2
Chon Buri 47 J 6
Chŏnan 54 A 3
Chong'an 49 K 5
Chŏngjin 54 A 2
Chŏngju 54 A 3
Chongqing 49 H 5
Chŏnju 54 A 3
Chornobyl' 36 G 2
Chorog 45 M 5
Chŏrwŏn 54 A 3
Chotanagpur Plateau
  46 E 4
Chott ech Chergui 56
  D 1
Chott Melrhir 34 B 4
Choybalsan 50 B 3
Christchurch 62 B 3
Christian IV
  Gletscher 8 Ff 5
Christianshåb 8 Aa 5
Christmas Island
  (Australia) 52 D 8
Christmas Island
  (Kiribati) 59 K 3
Chudskoye Ozero 38
  L 4
Chuginadak Island
  43 V 6
Chuhuichupa 20 C 2
Chukai 52 C 5
Chukchi Sea 43 U 3
Chukotskiy Polu-
  ostrov 43 U 3
Chula Vista 18 C 5
Chulym 41 S 6
Chum 40 O 4
Chumikan 42 L 6

Chumphon 47 H 6
Chuna 41 V 6
Ch'unch'ŏn 50 E 5
Ch'ungju 54 A 3
Chunya (Russia) 41
  V 5
Chuor Phnum Dan-
  grek 47 J 6
Chur 36 B 3
Churapcha 42 K 4
Churchill 8 S 7
Churchill Falls 8 Y 8
Churchill Lake 10
  V 7
Chureg 45 Q 2
Chureg-Tag, Gora 41
  U 7
Churu 46 C 3
Chusovoy 40 N 6
Chust 45 M 4
Chutes Boyoma
  (Stanley Falls) 58
  B 1
Chutes De La Lufira
  (Lufira Falls) 58
  B 2
Chutes Tembo
  (Tembo Falls) 58
  A 2
Chuuk Islands 59
  E 3
Chuxian 49 K 4
Chuxiong 49 G 5
Chybalsan 50 B 3
Cianjur 52 D 7
Cibuta, Cerro 18 D 5
Ciénaga 22 H 5
Cienfuegos 22 F 3
Cieza 33 B 2
Cihanbeyli 35 E 5
Cihanbeyli Platosu
  35 E 5
Cikobia 59 H 5
Cilacap 52 D 7
Cimaltepec, Sierra 20
  E 4
Cincinnati 14 C 3
Cintalapa de
  Figueroa 20 F 4
Circle (Alaska, U.S.)
  10 O 5
Circle (Montana,
  U.S.) 18 E 2
Cirebon 52 D 7
Cisco 16 D 5
Ciudad Acuña 20
  D 2
Ciudad Altamirano 20
  D 4
Ciudad Bol'var 22
  K 6
Ciudad Camargo 20
  C 2
Ciudad Cuauhtémoc
  20 F 4

Ciudad de Río
  Grande 20 D 3
Ciudad del Carmen
  20 F 4
Ciudad del Maíz 20
  E 3
Ciudad Guayana 22
  K 6
Ciudad Guzman 20
  D 4
Ciudad Hidalgo 20
  F 5
Ciudad Juárez 18
  E 5
Ciudad Lerdo 20 D 2
Ciudad Madero 20
  E 3
Ciudad Mante 20
  E 3
Ciudad Mendoza 20
  E 4
Ciudad Obregón 20
  C 2
Ciudad Ojeda 22
  H 5
Ciudad Real 33 B 2
Ciudad Rodrigo 33
  A 1
Ciudad Valles 20 E 3
Ciudad Victoria 20
  E 3
Civa Burnu 35 G 4
Civitanova Marche
  34 C 2
Civitavecchia 34 C 2
Çivril 35 C 5
Cizre 35 K 6
Clacton-on-Sea 28
  E 4
Claire Eagle Lake 18
  B 3
Claire, Lake 10 U 7
Claremorris 31 B 2
Clarendon 16 C 5
Claresholm 18 D 1
Clarinda 16 D 3
Clark Fork 18 C 2
Clark Hill Lake 14
  C 4
Clarke Island 60 H 8
Clarke Range 60 H 4
Clarksburg 14 C 3
Clarksdale 16 E 5
Clarkston 18 C 2
Clarksville 14 B 3
Claveria 52 G 2
Clavering Ø 8 Gg 4
Clear Island 31 B 3
Clear Lake 18 B 4
Clear Lake Reservoir
  18 B 3
Clearfield 18 D 3
Clearwater 14 C 5
Clearwater Moun-
  tains 18 C 2

Clermont 60 H 4
Clermont-Ferrand 32
  C 2
Cleveland (Missis-
  sippi, U.S.) 16 E 5
Cleveland (Ohio,
  U.S.) 14 C 2
Cleveland (Ten-
  nessee U.S.) 14
  C 3
Clew Bay 31 B 2
Clifden 31 A 2
Clifton 14 C 3
Clinton (Iowa, U.S.)
  16 E 3
Clinton (Oklahoma,
  U.S.) 16 D 4
Cloncurry 60 G 4
Clonmel 31 C 2
Cloquet 16 E 2
Clovis 16 C 5
Cluj-Napoca 36 E 3
Clutha 62 A 4
Clyde Inlet 8 X 4
Clyde River 8 X 4
Clyde, Firth of 28
  B 2
Coahuila 20 D 2
Coalcoman, Sierra
  de 20 D 4
Coalinga 18 B 4
Coast Mountains 10
  Q 7
Coast Range 60 J 5
Coast Range (U.S.)
  18 B 3
Coatepec 20 E 4
Coats Island 8 U 6
Coatzacoalcos 20
  F 4
Coatzacoalcos,
  Bahía 20 F 4
Coba 20 G 3
Cobán 20 F 4
Cobar 60 H 6
Cobourg Peninsula
  60 E 2
Coburg 36 C 2
Coburg Island 8 V 3
Cochabamba 24 E 4
Cochin 46 D 6
Cochrane 8 U 9
Coco Islands 47 G 6
Coco, Isla del 22 E 6
Coco, Río 20 G 5
Cocoa 14 C 5
Cocula 20 D 3
Cod, Cape 14 F 2
Cody 18 E 3
Coesfeld 36 B 2
Coëtivy 58 E 2
Coeur d'Alene 18
  C 2
Coffeyville 16 D 4
Coffs Harbour 60 J 6

Cogt-Ovoo 49 H 2
Coiba, Isla de 22 F 6
Coihaique 24 D 7
Coimbatore 46 D 6
Coimbra 33 A 1
Cojutepeque 20 G 5
Colchester 28 E 4
Coleman 16 D 5
Coleraine 31 C 1
Colfax 18 C 2
Colima (Mexico) 20
  D 4
Colima (State, Mex-
  ico) 20 D 4
Colima, Nevado de
  20 D 4
Coll 30 A 3
College Station 16
  D 5
Collier Ranges Na-
  tionalPark 60 B 4
Collingwood (New
  Zealand) 62 B 3
Collingwood (U.S.)
  14 C 2
Collooney 31 B 1
Colmar 36 B 3
Colombia 22 H 7
Colombo (Sri Lanka)
  46 D 7
Colón (Cuba) 22 F 3
Colón (Panama) 22
  G 6
Colonet 18 C 5
Colonia Morelos 18
  E 5
Colonna, Capo 34
  D 3
Colonsay 30 A 3
Colorado 18 E 4
Colorado Plateau 18
  D 4
Colorado River
  (Texas, U.S.) 16
  D 5
Colorado River
  (Utah, U.S.) 18
  D 4
Colorado Springs 16
  C 4
Colorado, Cerro
  (Mexico) 18 C 5
Colotlán 20 D 3
Columbia (Missouri,
  U.S.) 16 E 4
Columbia (South
  Carolina, U.S.) 14
  C 4
Columbia (Ten-
  nessee, U.S.) 14
  B 3
Columbia Falls 18
  D 2
Columbia Plateau 18
  C 3

Columbia River 10
  T 8
Columbus (Georgia,
  U.S.) 14 C 4
Columbus (Indiana,
  U.S.) 14 B 3
Columbus (Missis-
  sippi, U.S.) 14 B 4
Columbus (Nebraska,
  U.S.) 16 D 3
Columbus (Ohio,
  U.S.) 14 C 2
Colville Channel 62
  C 2
Colville Lake 10 R 5
Colville Lake (Lake)
  10 R 5
Colwyn Bay 28 C 3
Comalcalco 20 F 4
Comayagua 20 G 5
Comelio 20 B 2
Comino, Capo 34
  B 2
Comitán 20 F 4
Como 36 B 3
Comodoro Rivadavia
  24 E 7
Comondú 20 B 2
Comorin, Cape 46
  D 7
Compiégne 32 C 2
Comrat 36 F 3
Con Son 47 K 7
Conakry 56 B 4
Concepción 24 D 6
Concepcíon del Oro
  20 D 3
Conception Bay 58
  A 4
Conception, Point 18
  B 5
Conchos, Río 20 C 2
Concord 14 E 2
Concordia (Mexico)
  20 C 3
Condobolin 60 H 6
Condon 18 B 2
Conecuh River 14
  B 4
Conghua 49 J 6
Congo (Country) 58
  A 1
Congo (River) 58 A 2
Conn, Lough 31 B 1
Connaught 31 B 2
Connecticut 14 E 2
Connellsville 14 D 2
Conrad 18 D 2
Conroe 16 D 4
Constanta 35 C 2
Constantine 56 D 1
Constantine, Cape 43
  Y 5
Contwoyto Lake 10
  U 5

Conway (Arkansas,
  U.S.) 16 E 4
Conway (South Car-
  olina, U.S.) 14 D 4
Coober Pedy 60 E 5
Cooch Behär 47 F 3
Cook Inlet 10 M 6
Cook Islands 59 J 5
Cook Strait 62 B 3
Cookes Peak 18 E 5
Cookstown 31 C 1
Cooktown 60 H 3
Coolgardie 60 C 6
Coolidge 18 D 5
Cooma 60 H 7
Coonoor 46 D 6
Cooper Creek 61 F 5
Cooray 60 J 5
Coos Bay 18 B 3
Cootamundra 60 H 6
Copán 20 G 5
Copenhagen 38 H 4
Copiapó 24 D 5
Copper Cliff 8 U 9
Copper Harbor 8 T 9
Coral Harbour 8 U 6
Coral Sea 60 J 2
Coral Sea Islands
  Territory 60 J 3
Corato 34 D 2
Corbeil-Essonnes 32
  C 2
Corbett National Park
  46 D 3
Corcaigh 31 B 3
Cordele 14 C 4
Córdoba 24 E 6
Córdoba (Mexico) 20
  E 4
Córdoba (Spain) 33
  B 2
Cordova 10 N 6
Corigliano Calabro 34
  D 3
Corinth 14 B 4
Cork 31 B 3
Çorlu 35 B 4
Corner Brook 8 Z 9
Cornwall Island 8
  R 3
Cornwallis Island 8
  R 3
Coro 22 J 5
Coromandel Coast
  46 E 6
Coronation Gulf 10
  U 5
Corozal (Belize) 20
  G 4
Corpus Christi 20
  E 2
Corquin 20 G 5
Corrib, Lough 31 B 2
Corrientes 24 F 5
Corrientes, Cabo 22

G 6
Corrigin 60 B 6
Corse 34 B 2
Corse, Cap 34 B 2
Corsica 34 B 2
Corsicana 16 D 5
Cortegana 33 A 2
Cortez 18 E 4
Çorum 35 F 4
Corumbá 24 F 4
Corvallis 18 B 3
Cosamaloapan 20
  E 4
Cosenza 34 D 3
Coshocton 14 C 2
Costa Blanca 33 B 2
Costa Brava 32 C 3
Costa de Mosquites
  22 F 5
Costa de Mosquitos
  20 H 5
Costa del Azahar 33
  C 2
Costa del Sol 33 B 2
Costa Rica 22 E 5
Costa, Cordillera de
  la 22 J 6
Cotabato 52 G 4
Côte d'Argent 32 B 3
Côte d'Azur 34 B 2
Côte d'Ivoire 56 B 4
Cotswold Hills 28
  C 4
Cottbus 36 C 2
Cotulla 20 E 2
Coubre, Pointe de la
  32 B 2
Council Bluffs 16 D 3
Courtenay 18 A 2
Coventry 28 D 3
Covington (Georgia,
  U.S.) 14 C 4
Covington (Kentucky,
  U.S.) 14 C 3
Covington (Ten-
  nessee, U.S.) 14
  B 3
Covington (Virginia,
  U.S.) 14 D 3
Cowan, Lake 60 C 6
Cowell 60 F 6
Cox's Bazar 47 G 4
Coyame 20 C 2
Coyotitán 20 C 3
Cozumel, Isla de 20
  G 3
Cradock 58 B 5
Craig (Colorado,
  U.S.) 18 E 3
Craiova 34 E 2
Cranbrook (Canada)
  18 C 2
Crater Lake 18 B 3
Crawfordsville 14
  B 2

Crawley 28 D 4
Crazy Peak 18 D 2
Cree Lake 10 V 7
Creel 20 C 2
Creil 32 C 2
Cremona 36 C 3
Crescent City 18 B 3
Creston 16 E 3
Crestview 14 B 4
Crete 34 E 3
Creus, Cap de 32
  C 3
Crewe 28 C 3
Croatia 36 D 3
Crockett 16 D 5
Croker Island 60 E 2
Croker, Cape 60 E 2
Cromer (England,
  U.K.) 28 E 3
Cromer (Scotland,
  U.K.) 30 A 2
Crooked Creek 43
  Y 4
Crooked Island 22
  H 3
Crooked Island Pas-
  sage 22 G 3
Crookston 16 D 2
Crosby 16 C 2
Cross City 14 C 5
Crossett 16 E 5
Crotone 34 D 3
Crow Agency 18 E 2
Crow Lake 16 E 2
Crowley 16 E 5
Crown Prince Fred-
  erikIsland 8 T 5
Crowsnest Pass 18
  D 2
Croydon 60 G 3
Cruz Grande 20 E 4
Cruz, Cabo 22 G 3
Cruzeiro do Sul 24
  D 3
Cu Lao Cham 47 K 5
Cu Lao Re 52 D 2
Cuahtémoc 20 C 2
Cuando Cubango 58
  A 3
Cuango 58 A 2
Cuanza 58 A 2
Cuba 20 H 3
Cubango 58 A 3
Cucurpe 18 D 5
Cúcuta 22 H 6
Cuddalore 46 D 6
Cuddapah 46 D 6
Cue 60 B 5
Cuéllar 33 B 1
Cuenca 24 D 3
Cuenca (Spain) 32
  B 3
Cuencamé de
  Ceniceros 20 D 3
Cuernavaca 20 E 4

Cuero 20 E 2
Cuiabá 24 F 4
Cuilapa 20 F 5
Culiacán 20 C 3
Cullman 14 B 4
Cumaná 22 K 5
Cumberland 14 D 3
Cumberland Lake 10
  W 8
Cumberland Plateau
  14 B 3
Cumberland Sound 8
  X 5
Cumberland, Lake 14
  C 3
Çumra 35 E 6
Cunene 58 A 3
Cuneo 34 B 2
Cunnamulla 60 H 5
Curaçao 22 J 5
Curitaba 24 F 5
Curtis Island 60 J 4
Curupira, Sierra de
  22 K 7
Cusco 24 D 4
Cushing 16 D 4
Cuttack 46 F 4
Cuxhaven 36 B 2
Cyclades 34 E 3
Cypress Hills 18 D 2
Cyprus 35 E 7
Czech Republic 36
  C 3
Częstochowa 36 D 2
Człuchów 36 D 2
Da Lat 47 K 6
Da Nang 47 K 5
Da Yunhe 49 K 3
Daba Shan 49 H 4
Dabhoi 46 C 4
Dacca 47 G 4
Dadiangas 52 H 4
Dadu 46 B 3
Daet 52 G 3
Dafang 49 H 5
Dafeng 49 L 4
Dafni 34 E 3
Dagu 49 K 3
Dagupan 52 G 2
Daheiding Shan 54
  A 1
Dahlonega 14 C 4
Dahongliutan 48 B 3
Dahük 35 K 6
Daintree River Na-
  tional Park 60 H 3
Dajarra 60 F 4
Dakar 56 B 3
Dákura 20 H 5
Dal' 49 H 4
Dalälven 38 J 3
Dalandzadgad 49
  G 2
Dalanjagalan 50 A 3
Dalarna 38 H 3

Dalbandin 46 A 3
Dalby 60 J 5
Dale Hollow Lake 14
  B 3
Daley 60 E 2
Dalhart 16 C 4
Dali 48 G 5
Dalian 49 L 3
Dall 10 Q 8
Dallas 16 D 5
Dalles, The 18 B 2
Dal'negorsk 54 C 2
Dal'nerechensk 50
  F 3
Dal'nyaya 50 H 3
Dalou Shan 49 H 5
Dalton 14 C 4
Dältonganj 46 E 4
Dalupiri 52 G 2
Daly Waters 60 E 3
Damän 46 C 4
Damän and Diu 46
  C 4
Damar (Indonesia) 52
  H 6
Damaraland 58 A 4
Damascus 44 E 6
Damavand, Qolleh-ye
  44 H 5
Dämghän 45 H 5
Damoh 46 D 4
Dampier 60 B 4
Dampier Land 60
  C 3
Danau Toba 52 B 5
Danba 49 G 4
Dandeli 46 C 5
Danforth 14 F 1
Dangara 45 L 5
Danghe Nanshan 48
  F 3
Dangriga 20 G 4
Dangshan 49 K 4
Danilov 40 K 6
Danilovka 44 F 2
Danli 20 G 5
Danmarkshavn 8
  Hh 3
Dannevirke 62 C 3
Danube 35 B 2
Danube 36 D 3
Danville (Illinois,
  U.S.) 14 B 2
Danville (Kentucky,
  U.S.) 14 C 3
Danville (Virginia,
  U.S.) 14 D 3
Danxian 47 K 5
Danzig, Gulf of 36
  D 2
Dao Phu Quoc 47
  J 6
Daocheng 48 G 5
Daotiandi 54 B 1
Daoxian 49 J 5

Daqing 50 D 3
Dar Es Salaam 58
    C 2
Dar'a 44 E 6
Darbhanga 46 F 3
Darbod 50 D 3
Dardanelle Lake 16
    E 4
Dardanelles 34 F 3
Darganata 45 K 4
Dargaville 62 B 2
Darhan 41 X 8
Darien, Serranía del
    22 G 6
Darïya 45 M 3
Darjeeling 46 F 3
Darlag 48 F 4
Darling 60 G 6
Darling Downs 60
    J 5
Darling Range 60
    B 6
Darlington 28 D 2
Darlot, Lake 60 C 5
Darmstadt 36 B 3
Darnah 56 F 1
Darreh Gaz 45 J 5
Dartmoor 28 C 4
Dartmouth 8 Y 10
Darwin 60 E 2
Daryācheh-ye
    Orūmīyeh 44 F 5
Daryā-ye Māzan-
    darān 44 H 5
Daşhowuz 45 J 4
Dasht-e Kavīr 45
    H 5
Date 54 D 2
Datia 46 D 3
Datong 49 J 2
Datong (Qinghai,
    China) 49 G 3
Datong Shan 48 F 3
Datta 54 D 1
Daugaard-Jensen
    Land 8 Y 2
Daugava 38 L 4
Daugavpils 38 L 4
Daung Kyun 47 H 6
Dauphin 16 C 1
Dāvangere 46 D 6
Davao 52 H 4
Davenport 16 E 3
David 22 F 6
Davis Inlet 8 Y 7
Davis Strait 8 Z 5
Dawei 47 H 6
Dawson 10 P 6
Dawson Creek 10
    S 7
Dax 32 B 3
Daxian 49 H 4
Daxing 49 K 3
Dayangshu 50 D 3
Dayao 49 G 5

Dayong 49 J 5
Dayr az Zawr 44 F 5
Dayton 14 C 3
Daytona Beach 14
    C 5
Dayu 49 J 5
Dazhu 49 H 4
De Aar 58 B 5
De Kastri 42 M 6
De Land 14 C 5
De Pere 14 B 2
De Ridder 16 E 5
Deadhorse 10 N 4
Dease Lake 10 Q 7
Death Valley 18 C 4
Death Valley National
    Monument 18 C 4
Dęblin 36 E 2
Deborah East, Lake
    60 B 6
Deborah West, Lake
    60 B 6
Debre Mark'os 56
    G 3
Debrecen 36 E 3
Decatur (Alabama,
    U.S.) 14 B 4
Decatur (Illinois,
    U.S.) 14 B 3
Deccan 46 D 6
Decelles, Réservoir
    14 D 1
Decheng 49 G 5
Děčín 36 C 2
Deda 36 E 3
Dee 30 C 3
Deer Lodge 18 D 2
Dêgê 48 F 4
Dehiwala-Mount
    Lavinia 46 D 7
Dehra Dun 46 D 2
Dehui 50 E 4
Dej 36 E 3
Del City 16 D 4
Del Norte 18 E 4
Del Rio 20 D 2
Del Verme Falls 56
    H 4
Delaram 45 K 6
Delaware 14 D 3
Delaware Bay 14
    D 3
Delfoi 34 E 3
Delhi 46 D 3
Delicias 20 C 2
Déline 10 S 5
Delmenhorst 36 B 2
Delta (Colorado,
    U.S.) 18 E 4
Delta (Utah, U.S.) 18
    D 4
Delta Junction 10
    N 6
Deming 18 E 5
Demirci 35 C 5

Democratic Republic
    of the Congo 58
    B 2
Demopolis 14 B 4
Dem'yanka 40 Q 6
Dem'yanskoye 40 P 6
Denakil 56 G 3
Denali 10 N 6
Denali National Park
    10 M 6
Dengkou 49 H 2
Dengxian 49 J 4
Denia 33 C 2
Deniliquin 60 G 7
Denison (Iowa, U.S.)
    16 D 3
Denison (Texas,
    U.S.) 16 D 5
Denizli 35 C 6
Denmark 38 G 4
Denmark (Australia)
    60 B 6
Denov 45 L 5
Denpasar 52 F 7
Denton 16 D 5
D'Entrecasteaux Is-
    lands 59 E 4
Denver 18 E 4
Deoghar 46 F 4
Deolāli 46 C 5
Depoe Bay 18 B 3
Dépression du
    Mourdi 56 F 3
Dêqên 48 F 5
Deqing 49 J 6
Dequeen 16 E 5
Dera Ghāzi Khān 46
    C 2
Dera Ismāīl Khān 46
    C 2
Derbent 44 G 4
Derby (Australia) 60
    C 3
Derby (U.K.) 28 D 3
Derdap 34 E 2
Derg, Lough 31 B 2
Dergachi 44 G 2
Derweza 45 J 4
Derzhavinsk 45 L 2
Des Moines 16 E 3
Des Moines River 16
    E 3
Désappointement,
    Îles du 59 L 5
Deschambault Lake
    10 W 8
Desē 56 G 3
Desierto de Sechura
    24 C 3
Desierto do Atacama
    (Atacama Desert)
    24 E 5
Dessau 36 C 2
Destruction Bay 10
    P 6

Detmold 36 B 2
Detroit 14 C 2
Detroit Lakes 16 D 2
Deva 36 E 3
Devils Lake 16 D 2
Devon Island 8 S 3
Devonport 60 H 8
Deyang 49 G 4
Dey-Dey, Lake 60
    E 5
Dezfūl 44 G 6
Dezhou 49 K 3
Dhaka 47 G 4
Dhamtari 46 E 4
Dhanbad 46 F 4
Dharān 46 F 3
Dharmapuri 46 D 6
Dharwar 46 D 5
Dhawalāgiri 46 E 3
Dhenkanal 46 F 4
Dholpur 46 D 3
Dhorāji 46 C 4
Dhule 46 C 4
Diablo Range 18 B 4
Diamante, Punta del
    20 D 4
Diamond Peak 18
    C 4
Dianbai 49 J 6
Diane Bank 60 J 3
Dianjiang 49 H 4
Dibrugrh 47 G 3
Dickinson 16 C 2
Dicle Nehri 35 J 6
Didao 50 F 3
Dieppe 32 C 2
Digboi 47 H 3
Digby 14 F 2
Digne-les-Bains 34
    B 2
Digos 52 H 4
Dijon 36 B 3
Dikson 41 S 3
Dili 52 H 7
Dillingham 43 Y 5
Dillon 18 D 2
Dīmāpur 47 G 3
Dimashq 44 E 6
Dimbokro 56 C 4
Dimitrovgrad (Bul-
    garia) 34 F 2
Dimitrovgrad (Rus-
    sia) 44 G 2
Dinagat 52 H 3
Dinājpur 46 F 3
Dınar 35 D 5
Dindigul 46 D 6
Dinghai 49 L 4
Dingle Bay 31 A 3
Dingwall 30 B 3
Dingxi 49 G 3
Dingxing 49 K 3
Diomede Islands 10
    H 5
Dipolog 52 G 4

Dirē Dawa 56 H 3
Dirranbandi 60 H 5
Disappointment,
    Lake 60 C 4
Disko 8 Aa 5
Dispur 47 G 3
Diu 46 C 4
Divinópolis 24 G 5
Divnoye 44 F 3
Divriği 35 H 5
Dixon 14 B 2
Diyarbakır 35 J 6
Djabung, Tanjung 52
    C 6
Djelfa 56 D 1
Djember 52 E 7
Djibouti 56 H 3
Dlinnyy, Ostrov 41
    U 2
Dnipropetrovs'k 44
    E 3
Dnyapro 36 G 2
Do Gonbadān 44
    H 6
Doba 56 E 4
Doboj 34 D 2
Dobrich 35 B 3
Doctor Arroyo 20
    D 3
Dodge City 16 C 4
Dodoma 58 C 2
Doero, Rio 32 B 3
Dogai Coring 48 D 4
Dōgo 54 B 3
Doğu Karadeniz
    Dağları 35 H 4
Doi Inthanon 47 H 5
Doilungdêqên 48
    E 5
Dolak, Pulau 59 C 4
Dole 36 B 3
Dolgiy, Ostrov 40
    N 4
Dolinsk 50 H 3
Dolores Hidalgo 20
    D 3
Dolyns'ka 44 D 3
Doma Peaks 59 D 4
Dombarovskiy 40
    N 7
Dombas 38 G 3
Dominica 22 K 4
Dominican Republic
    22 J 3
Don 44 F 3
Don Benito 33 A 2
Donau 36 C 3
Donegal 31 B 1
Donegal Bay 31 B 1
Donets'k 44 E 3
Dong Hai 49 L 5
Dong Hoi 47 K 5
Dong Taijnar Hu 48
    E 3
Dongan 50 F 3

Dong'an (Hei-
    longjiang, China)
    54 B 1
Dongara 60 A 5
Dongchuan 49 G 5
Dongfang 47 K 5
Dongfeng 50 E 4
Donggou 49 L 3
Dongning 54 B 2
Dongping 49 K 3
Dongshan Dao 49
    K 6
Dongsheng 49 H 3
Dongtai 49 L 4
Dongting Hu 49 J 5
Dongxiang 49 K 5
Dønna 38 H 2
Donostia-San Sebas-
    tian 32 B 3
Door Peninsula 14
    B 2
Dooxo Nugaaleed 56
    H 4
Dorchester 28 C 4
Dorda Head 46 E 7
Dordogne 32 C 3
Dornoch 30 C 3
Dornod 50 B 3
Doro 56 C 3
Doro (Indonesia) 52
    H 5
Dorohoi 36 F 3
Döröö Nuur 48 E 1
Dorotea 38 J 3
Dortmund 36 B 2
Dos Hermanas 33
    A 2
Doshi 45 L 5
Dostyq 45 O 3
Dothan 14 B 4
Douala 56 D 4
Double Island Point
    60 J 5
Doubtful Sound 62
    A 4
Douglas (Arizona,
    U.S.) 18 E 5
Douglas (U.K.) 28
    B 2
Douglas (Wyoming,
    U.S.) 18 E 3
Douro, Rio 33 A 1
Dover (U.K.) 28 E 4
Dover (U.S.) 14 D 3
Dover, Strait of 28
    E 4
Dovois, Réservoir 14
    D 1
Dow Rūd 44 G 6
Downpatrick 28 B 2
Downpatrick Head 31
    B 1
Dozois, Réservoir 14
    D 1
Drain 18 B 3

Drama 34 E 2
Drammen 38 H 4
Drava 36 D 3
Dresden 36 C 2
Dreux 32 C 2
Drobeta-Turnu Sev-
    erin 34 E 2
Drogheda 31 C 2
Drohobych 36 E 3
Droichead Átha 31
    C 2
Dronning Louise
    Land 8 Ff 3
Dronning Maud Land
    63 P 4
Drummond 18 D 2
Drummond Range 60
    H 4
Drummondville 8
    W 9
Dry Tortugas 22 F 3
Dryden 16 E 2
Drysdale River Na-
    tional Park 60 D 3
Du Bois 14 D 2
Duarte 22 H 4
Dubăsari 36 F 3
Dubawnt Lake 10
    W 6
Dubbo 60 H 6
Dublin (Ireland) 31
    C 2
Dublin (U.S.) 14 C 4
Dubna 40 J 6
Dubno 36 F 2
Dubovka 44 F 3
Dubovskoye 44 F 3
Dubrovnik 34 D 2
Dubrovytsya 36 F 2
Dubuque 16 E 3
Duc de Gloucester,
    Îles du 59 L 5
Duchesne 18 D 3
Ducie Island 59 N 6
Dudinka 41 T 4
Dudley 28 C 3
Dudwa National Park
    46 E 3
Dudypta 41 U 3
Duero, Rio 32 B 3
Duga-Zapadnaya,
    Mys 42 M 5
Duisburg 36 B 2
Duitama 22 H 6
Duki 42 L 6
Dukou 49 G 5
Dulan 48 F 3
Dulce, Bahía 20 E 4
Dulgalakh 42 K 3
Duluth 16 E 2
Dūmā 44 E 6
Dumaguete 52 G 4
Dumai 52 C 5
Dumaran Island 52
    F 3

Dumaring 52 F 5
Dumbarton 28 B 2
Dumfries 28 C 2
Dumont d'Urville Sea
    63 T 5
Dún Dealgan 31 C 1
Dún Laoghaire 31
    C 2
Duna 36 D 3
Dunărea 36 F 3
Dunării, Delta 35 C 2
Dunaújváros 36 D 3
Dunav 34 F 2
Dunay, Ostrova 42
    H 2
Dunayivtsi 36 F 3
Dunbar 60 G 3
Duncan 16 D 5
Duncansby Head 30
    C 2
Dundalk 31 C 1
Dundalk Bay 31 C 2
Dundas Strait 60 E 2
Dundas, Lake 60
    C 6
Dundee (U.K.) 30
    C 3
Dundgovĭ 49 H 1
Dunedin 62 B 4
Dunfermline 30 C 3
Dungarvan 31 C 2
Dunhua 50 E 4
Dunkirk 14 D 2
Dunrankin 14 C 1
Dunsmuir 18 B 3
Duolun 50 C 4
Durack Ranges 60
    D 3
Durand, Récifs 59
    F 6
Durango (Mexico) 20
    D 3
Durango (Spain) 32
    B 3
Durango (State, Mex-
    ico) 20 C 3
Durango (U.S.) 18
    E 4
Durant 16 D 5
Durban 58 C 4
Durg 46 E 4
Durgāpur 46 F 4
Durham (U.K.) 28
    D 2
Durham (U.S.) 14
    D 3
Durness 30 B 2
Durrow 31 C 2
Durr's 34 D 2
Dursey Island 31 A 3
Durusu Gölü 35 C 4
D'Urville Island 62
    B 3
Dushan 49 H 5
Dushanbe 45 L 5

Düsseldorf 36 B 2
Dutch Harbor 43
    W 6
Duyun 49 H 5
Düzce 35 D 4
Dyat'kovo 36 G 2
Dyer, Cape 8 Y 5
Dyersburg 14 B 3
Dzerzhinsk 40 K 6
Dzhagdy, Khrebet 42
    J 6
Dzhalinda 50 D 2
Dzhaltyr 45 L 2
Dzhankoy 35 F 2
Dzhugdzhur, Khrebet
    42 L 5
Dzhungarian Gate 48
    C 1
Dzibalchén 20 G 4
Dzyarzhynsk 36 F 2
Eagle 10 O 6
Eagle Lake (Canada)
    16 E 2
Eagle Lake (U.S.) 18
    B 3
Eagle Pass 20 D 2
Ear Falls 10 Y 8
East Cape 62 C 2
East China Sea 49
    L 5
East Coast Bays 62
    B 2
East Kilbride 28 B 2
East London 58 B 5
East Point 14 C 4
East Siberian Sea 43
    Q 2
East Timor 52 H 7
Eastbourne 28 E 4
Eastend 18 E 2
Easter Ross 30 B 3
Eastern Ghāts 46
    E 6
Eastleigh 28 D 4
Eastmain 8 V 8
Eastman 14 C 4
Easton 14 D 2
Eastport 14 F 2
Eatonville 18 B 2
Eau Claire 16 E 3
Eauripik 59 D 3
Ebano 20 E 3
Ebe 42 M 4
Eberswalde 36 C 2
Ebingen 36 B 3
Eboli 34 D 2
Ebro, Rio 32 B 3
Ecatepec 20 E 4
Echeng 49 J 4
Echmiadzin 44 F 4
Echo Bay 10 T 5
Echuca 60 G 7
Écija 33 A 2
Eckerö 38 J 3
Ecuador 24 C 3

Ede 56 D 4
Edenton 14 D 3
Edgar Range 60 C 3
Edgell Island 8 Y 6
Edgemont 16 C 3
Edina 16 E 3
Edinburgh 28 C 2
Edineţ 36 F 3
Edirne 35 B 4
Edmonds 18 B 2
Edmonton 10 U 8
Edmundston 8 X 9
Edremit 35 B 5
Edwards Plateau 16
    C 5
Eek 43 X 4
Éfaté 59 F 5
Effingham 14 B 3
Egedesminde 8 Aa 5
Egegik 43 Y 5
Eglinton Island 10
    T 3
Egmont, Cape 62
    B 2
Egypt 56 F 2
Eiao 59 L 4
Eifel 36 B 2
Eigg 30 A 3
Eight Degree Chan-
    nel 46 C 7
Eighty Mile Beach 60
    B 3
Eiler Rasmussen,
    Kap 8 Gg 2
Eindhoven 36 B 2
Eire 31 B 2
Eisenach 36 C 2
Eisenhüttenstadt 36
    C 2
Eisleben 36 C 2
Eivissa 33 C 2
Ekarma, Ostrov 50
    K 3
Ekibastuz 45 N 2
Ekimchan 42 K 6
Ekonda 41 X 4
El Aaiún 56 B 2
El Alamo 18 C 5
El Cajon 18 C 5
El Canelo 20 D 3
El Casco 20 D 2
El Centro 18 C 5
El Descanso 18 C 5
El Dorado (Arkansas,
    U.S.) 16 E 5
El Dorado (Kansas,
    U.S.) 16 D 4
El Dorado (Mexico)
    20 C 3
El Espinal 22 H 7
El Eulma 34 B 3
El Ferrol 33 A 1

El Goléa 56 D 1
El Kef 56 D 1
El Mirador 20 F 4
El Paso 18 E 5
El Pital, Cerro 20
    G 5
El Potosi 20 D 3
El Progreso 20 G 4
El Reno 16 D 4
El Salto 20 C 3
El Salvador 22 D 5
El Sáuz 20 C 2
El Sueco 18 E 5
El Tajin 20 E 3
El Tigre 22 K 6
El Triumfo 20 B 3
El Tuito 20 C 3
Elâziğ 35 H 5
Elba 34 C 2
Elbasan 34 E 2
Elbe 36 C 2
Elbistan 35 G 5
Elbląg 36 D 2
Elbow 18 E 1
El'brus, gora 44 F 4
Elche 33 B 2
Elcho Island 60 F 2
Elda 33 B 2
El'dikan 42 L 4
Eldoret 58 C 1
Elektrostal' 40 J 6
Elephant Butte
    Reservoir 18 E 5
Eleuthera Island 14
    D 5
Elgin 30 C 3
El'ginskoye Plosko-
    gor'ye 42 L 3
Elim 43 X 4
Elista 35 L 1
Elizabeth 60 F 6
Elizabeth City 14 D 3
Elizabeth Falls 10
    V 7
Elizabethtown 14
    B 3
Elizavety, Mys 42
    M 6
Ełk 36 E 2
Elk City 16 D 4
Elkhart 14 B 2
Elkhovo 34 F 2
Elkins 14 D 3
Elko 18 C 3
Ellef Ringnes Island
    10 W 3
Ellendale 16 D 2
Ellensburg 18 B 2
Ellesmere Island 8
    U 3
Ellesmere Port 28
    C 3
Ellice Islands 59 G 4
Ellisburg 14 D 2
Elliston 60 E 6

Elmadağ 35 E 5
Elmalı 35 C 6
Elmira 14 D 2
Elmshorn 36 B 2
Eloy 18 D 5
Eltham 62 B 2
Elūru 46 E 5
Elvas 33 A 2
Ely (U.K.) 28 E 3
Ely (U.S.) 18 D 4
Embalse Ezequiel
    Ramos Mexia 24
    E 6
Embi 45 J 3
Emden 36 B 2
Emei 49 G 5
Emerald 60 H 4
Emerald Isle 10 U 3
Emiliano Zapata 20
    F 4
Eminska Planina 35
    B 3
Emirdağ 35 D 5
Emmen 36 B 2
Emmett 18 C 3
Empalme 20 B 2
Emporia (Kansas,
    U.S.) 16 D 4
Emporia (Virginia,
    U.S.) 14 D 3
Enarotali 59 C 4
Encinal 20 E 2
Endeh 52 G 7
Enderbury Island 59
    H 4
Endwell 14 D 2
Engel's 44 G 2
Enggano 52 C 7
England 28 D 3
Englee 8 Z 8
English Channel 32
    B 2
Enid 16 D 4
Eniwa 54 D 2
Eniwetok 59 F 2
Enköping 38 J 4
Enna 34 C 3
Ennadai 10 W 6
Ennadai Lake 10
    W 6
Ennis 31 B 2
Enniscorthy 31 C 2
Enniskillen 31 C 1
Ennistimon 31 B 2
Enschede 36 B 2
Ensenada 18 C 5
Enshi 49 H 4
Enterprise (Canada)
    10 T 6
Enterprise (U.S.) 18
    C 2
Entroncamento 33
    A 2
Enugu 56 D 4
Enugu Gboko 56 D 4

Envigado 22 G 6
Épernay 32 C 2
Épi 59 F 5
Épinal 36 B 3
Eqlīd 44 H 6
Équateur 58 A 1
Equatorial Guinea 56 D 4
Érd 36 D 3
Erdemlı 35 F 6
Erdenet 49 J 2
Ereğli (Turkey) 35 D 4
Ereğli (Turkey) 35 F 6
Erenhot 49 J 2
Ereymentaū 45 M 2
Erfoud 56 C 1
Erfurt 36 C 2
Ergani 35 H 5
Ergun Zuoqi 50 D 2
Erichsen Lake 8 U 4
Erie 14 C 2
Erie Canal 14 D 2
Erie, Lake 14 C 2
Erikub 59 F 3
Erimo-misaki 54 D 2
Eritrea 56 G 3
Erlangen 36 C 3
Ermenek 35 E 6
Ernest Legouve Reef 59 K 7
Erode 46 D 6
Erris Head 31 A 1
Erromango 59 F 5
Ertil' 44 F 2
Ertis 45 N 2
Ertis (River) 45 N 2
Erzgebirge 36 C 2
Erzincan 35 H 5
Erzurum 35 J 5
Esbjerg 38 G 4
Esbo 38 K 3
Escalante 18 D 4
Escalón 20 D 2
Escanaba 8 T 9
Esch-sur-Alzette 36 B 3
Escondido 18 C 5
Escuinapa de Hidalgo 20 C 3
Escuintla 20 F 5
Eşfahān 44 H 6
Esik 45 N 4
Esil 45 L 2
Esil (River) 45 L 2
Esil Zhazyghy 40 P 7
Eskilstuna 38 J 4
Eskişehir 35 D 5
Eslāmābād-e Gharb 44 G 6
Eşme 35 C 5
Esmeraldas 22 G 7
Espanola 18 E 4

Esperance 60 C 6
Esperanza (Mexico) 20 C 2
Espoo 38 K 3
Esp'ritu Santo 59 F 5
Esquel 24 D 7
Essaouira 56 C 1
Essen 36 B 2
Esso 43 P 5
Est, Pointe de l' 8 Y 9
Estaca de Bares, Punta da 33 A 1
Estacado, Llano 16 C 5
Estats, Pic d' 32 C 3
Estel' 22 E 5
Estelí 20 G 5
Estevan 16 C 2
Estherville 16 E 3
Estonia 38 K 4
Esztergom 36 D 3
Etah 8 W 3
Étampes 32 C 2
Etawah 46 D 3
Ethiopia 56 G 4
Etolin Island 10 Q 7
Etzná Tixmucuy 20 F 4
'Eua 59 H 6
Eucla Motel 60 D 6
Eufaula 14 B 4
Eufaula Lake 16 D 4
Eugene 18 B 3
Eugenia, Punta 18 C 6
Eugmo 38 K 3
Euphrates 44 F 6
Euphrates, River 35 M 7
Eureka (California, U.S.) 18 B 3
Eureka (Canada) 8 T 2
Eureka (Nevada, U.S.) 18 C 4
Evanston (Illinois, U.S.) 14 B 2
Evanston (Wyoming, U.S.) 18 D 3
Evansville 14 B 3
Everard Range 60 5
Everard, Lake 60 E 6
Everett 18 B 2
Everglades City 14 C 5
Everglades National Park 14 C 5
Everglades, The 14 C 5
Evergreen 14 B 4
Evje 38 G 4
Évora 33 A 2
Évreux 32 C 2

Evvoia 34 E 3
Excelsior Springs 16 E 4
Exeter 28 C 4
Exmoor 28 C 4
Expedition Range 60 H 4
Extremadura 33 A 2
Exuma Cays 22 G 3
Eyre Peninsula 60 F 6
Eyre, Lake (North) 60 F 5
Eyre, Lake (South) 60 F 5
Eysturoy 38 D 3
Ezine 35 B 5
Fabens 18 E 5
Faber Lake 10 T 6
Faddeyevskiy, Ostrov 42 M 1
Faenza 34 C 2
Fǎgǎras 35 A 2
Fagataufa 59 M 6
Fagatogo 59 J 5
Fair Bluff 14 D 4
Fair Isle 30 D 2
Fairbanks 10 N 6
Fairborn 14 C 3
Fairfield 18 B 4
Fairmont 16 E 3
Faisalabad 46 C 2
Faith 16 C 2
Faizabad (Afghanistan) 45 M 5
Faizabad India) 46 E 3
Fakaofo 59 H 4
Fakarava 59 L 5
Faku 50 D 4
Falam 47 G 4
Falcon Lake 20 E 2
Falfurrias 20 E 2
Falkenberg 38 H 4
Falkland Islands (Islas Malvinas, U.K.) 24 E 8
Fall River 14 E 2
Fallon 18 C 4
Falls City 16 D 3
Falmouth 28 B 4
False Pass 43 X 6
Falster 36 C 2
Fǎlticeni 36 F 3
Falun 38 J 3
Famagusta 35 E 7
Fan si Pan 47 J 4
Fanchang 49 K 4
Fang Xian 49 J 4
Fangatau 59 M 5
Fangcheng 49 H 6
Fangzheng 54 A 1
Fano 34 C 2
Fanø 38 G 4

Farafangana 58 D 4
Farāh 45 K 6
Farallon de Medinilla 59 D 2
Farallon de Pajaros 59 D 1
Farewell, Cape 62 B 3
Fargo 16 D 2
Fargūona 45 M 4
Faridpur 47 F 4
Farmington 18 E 4
Fåro 38 J 4
Faro (Canada) 10 Q 6
Faro (Portugal) 33 A 2
Faroe Islands 38 D 3
Fårösund 38 J 4
Farquhar Islands 58 E 2
Farvel, Kap 8 Cc 7
Fasano 34 D 2
Fastiv 36 F 2
Fatehabad 46 D 3
Fatsa 35 G 4
Fatu Hiva 59 M 5
Fǎurei 36 F 3
Faxaflói 38 A 3
Fayetteville (Arkansas, U.S.) 16 E 4
Fayetteville (North Carolina, U.S.) 14 D 3
Fayu 59 D 3
Fear, Cape 14 D 4
Fécamp 32 C 2
Feira de Santana 24 H 4
Feklistova, Ostrova 42 L 5
Felipe Carrillo Puerto 20 G 4
Felixstowe 28 E 4
Fener Burnu 35 H 4
Fengcheng 50 D 4
Fengdu 49 H 5
Fenghuang 49 H 5
Fengqing 48 F 6
Fengzhen 49 J 2
Feni 47 G 4
Fenyang 49 J 3
Feodosiya 35 F 2
Fergus Falls 16 D 2
Ferguson Lake 10 V 5
Ferlo 56 B 3
Ferrara 34 C 2
Ferriday 16 E 5
Fès 56 C 1
Festus 16 E 4
Feteşti 34 F 2
Fethiye 35 C 6
Fetlar 30 D 1

Fezzan 56 E 2
Fianarantsoa 58 D 4
Fichē 56 G 3
Fier 34 D 2
Fife Ness 30 C 3
Figueres 32 C 3
Figuig 56 C 1
Fiji Islands 59 G 5
Filchner Ice Shelf 63 N 4
Filiaşi 34 E 2
Findlay 14 C 2
Finke 60 E 5
Finke Gorge National-alPark 60 E 4
Finland 38 L 3
Finland, Gulf of 38 K 4
Finlay Forks 10 S 7
Finlay River 10 R 7
Finnmark 38 K 1
Finnmarksvidda 38 K 2
Fiordland National Park 62 A 4
Firenze 34 C 2
Firozabad 46 D 3
Firūzābād 44 H 7
Fishguard 28 B 3
Fisterra, Cabo 33 A 1
Fitzgerald River National Park 60 B 6
Fitzroy (River) 60 C 3
Fitzroy (River) 60 J 4
Fitzroy Crossing 60 D 3
Flade Isblink 8 Hh 2
Flagler Beach 14 C 5
Flagstaff 18 D 4
Flåm 38 G 3
Flaming Gorge Reservoir 18 E 3
Flannan Isles 30 A 2
Flasher 16 C 2
Flat Island 52 F 3
Flathead Lake 18 C 2
Flattery, Cape (Australia) 60 H 2
Flattery, Cape (U.S.) 18 A 2
Fleetwood 28 C 3
Flekkefjord 38 G 4
Flensburg 36 B 2
Flers 32 B 2
Flin Flon 10 W 7
Flinders 60 G 3
Flinders Chase National Park 60 F 7
Flinders Island 60 H 7

Flinders Range 60 F 6
Flinders Ranges National Park 60 F 6
Flinders Reefs 60 H 3
Flint (Kiribati) 59 K 5
Flint (U.S.) 14 C 2
Flint Hills 16 D 4
Flint River 14 C 4
Flisa 38 H 3
Florence 34 C 2
Florence (Alabama, U.S.) 14 B 4
Florence (Oregon, U.S.) 18 B 3
Florence (South Carolina, U.S.) 14 D 4
Florencia 22 G 7
Flores (Guatemala) 20 G 4
Flores (Indonesia) 52 G 7
Flores Sea 52 F 7
Flores, Laut 52 F 7
Florianópolis 24 G 5
Florida (Cuba) 22 G 3
Florida (U.S.) 14 C 5
Florida Keys 14 C 6
Florida, Straits of 22 F 3
Floridablanca 22 H 6
Florina 34 E 2
Florø 38 F 3
Flowers Cove 8 Z 8
Fluk 52 H 6
Focşani 36 F 3
Foggia 34 D 2
Fogo 56 A 3
Fogo Island 8 Aa 9
Foley Island 8 V 5
Foleyer 8 U 9
Folkestone 28 E 4
Folkston 14 C 4
Fond du Lac 10 V 7
Fond du Lac (U.S.) 14 B 2
Fonseca, Golfo de 20 G 5
Fontas 10 S 7
Fontur 38 C 2
Fonualei 59 H 6
Forest 14 B 4
Forfar 30 C 3
Forlì 34 C 2
Formentera 33 C 2
Formentor, Cap de 32 C 3
Formia 34 C 2
Formosa 24 F 5
Formosa 49 L 6
Formosa Strait 49 L 6

Forrest 60 D 6
Forrest City 16 E 4
Forsayth 60 G 3
Forst 36 C 2
Fort Albany 8 U 8
Fort Augustus 30
 B 3
Fort Beaufort 58 B 5
Fort Benton 18 D 2
Fort Black 10 V 7
Fort Bragg 18 B 4
Fort Bridger 18 D 3
Fort Chimo 8 X 7
Fort Chipewyan 10
 U 7
Fort Collins 18 E 3
Fort Collinson 10 T 4
Fort Dodge 16 E 3
Fort Edward 14 E 2
Fort Frances 16 E 2
Fort Good Hope 10
 R 5
Fort Kent 14 F 1
Fort Knox 14 B 3
Fort Lauderdale 14
 C 5
Fort Liard 10 S 6
Fort Mackay 10 U 7
Fort Macleod 18 D 2
Fort Madison 16 E 3
Fort McMurray 10
 U 7
Fort McPherson 10
 Q 5
Fort Morgan 16 C 3
Fort Myers 14 C 5
Fort Nelson 10 S 7
Fort Peck 18 E 2
Fort Peck Dam 18
 E 2
Fort Peck Lake 18
 E 2
Fort Pierce 14 C 5
Fort Providence 10
 T 6
Fort Qu'Appelle 16
 C 1
Fort Saint James 10
 S 8
Fort Saint John 10
 S 7
Fort Saskatchewan
 10 U 8
Fort Scott 16 E 4
Fort Severn 8 T 7
Fort Simpson 10 S 6
Fort Smith (Canada)
 10 U 6
Fort Smith (U.S.) 16
 E 4
Fort Stockton 16 C 5
Fort Summer 16 C 5
Fort Vermillion 10 T 7
Fort Walton Beach 14
 B 4

Fort Wayne 14 B 2
Fort William 30 B 3
Fort Worth 16 D 5
Fort Yukon 10 O 5
Fortaleza 24 H 3
Fort-de-France 22 5
Forth, Firth of 30 C 3
Foshan 49 J 6
Fosna 38 H 3
Fou-ling 49 H 5
Foumban 56 E 4
Foveaux Strait 62
 A 4
Fox Islands 43 W 6
Foxe Basin 8 V 5
Foxe Channel 8 U 5
Foxford 31 B 2
Foyle, Lough 31 C 1
Franca 24 G 5
France 32 B 2
France, Île de 8 Hh 3
Francia, Cabo 20
 H 3
Francis Case, Lake
 16 D 3
Francisco Escárcega
 20 F 4
Francistown 58 B 4
Francs Peak 18 E 3
Frankfort 14 C 3
Frankfurt am Main 36
 B 2
Frankfurt an der Oder
 36 C 2
Franklin Lake 8 R 5
Franz Josef Land 40
 L 2
Franzz 8 U 9
Fraser Island 60 J 5
Fraser Plateau 10
 S 8
Fraser River 10 S 8
Fraserburgh 30 C 3
Frederick Hills 60
 E 2
Frederick Reefs 61
 K 4
Fredericksburg 14
 D 3
Fredericton 8 X 9
Frederikshåb 8 Bb 6
Frederikshåb Isblink
 8 Aa 6
Frederikshavn 38
 H 44
Fredrikstad 38 H 4
Freeport (Bahamas)
 14 D 5
Freeport (Illinois,
 U.S.) 14 B 2
Freeport (Texas,
 U.S.) 20 E 2
Freetown 56 B 4
Freiberg 36 C 2
Freiburg 36 B 3

Freising 36 C 3
Fréjus 34 B 2
Fremantle 60 B 6
French Guiana
 (France) 24 F 2
French Polynesia 59
 L 6
Frenchman River 18
 E 2
Fresnillo 20 D 3
Fresno 18 C 4
Freuchen Land 8
 Cc 2
Freycinet Peninsula
 60 H 8
Frisian Islands 36
 B 2
Friza, Proliv 54 E 1
Frolovo 44 F 3
Front Range 18 E 3
Frontera 20 F 4
Fronteras 18 E 5
Frosione 34 C 2
Frøya 38 G 3
Frýdek-M'stek 36
 D 3
Fu'an 49 K 5
Fuding 49 L 5
Fuga 52 G 2
Fugloy 38 D 3
Fuji 54 C 3
Fujian 49 K 5
Fujin 50 F 3
Fuji-san 54 C 3
Fukue 54 A 4
Fukue-Jima 54 A 4
Fukui 54 C 3
Fukuoka 54 B 4
Fukushima
 (Hokkaidō, Japan)
 54 D 2
Fukushima (Honshū,
 Japan) 54 D 3
Fukuyama 54 B 4
Fulaga 59 H 5
Fulda 36 B 2
Funabashi 54 C 3
Funchal 56 B 1
Fundy, Bay of 14 F 2
Funing 49 K 4
Fuqing 49 K 5
Furano 54 D 2
Furmanov 40 K 6
Furneaux Group 60
 H 8
Fürstenwalde 36 C 2
Fürth 36 C 3
Furukawa 54 D 3
Fushun 50 D 4
Fusong 50 E 4
Futuna, Île 59 H 5
Fuxian 49 L 3
Fuxin 50 D 4
Fuyang 49 K 4
Fuyu 50 D 3

Fuyuan 49 G 5
Fuyuan (Hei-
 longjiang, China)
 54 B 1
Fuyun 48 D 1
Fuzhou (Fujian,
 China) 49 K 5
Fuzhou (Jiangxi,
 China) 49 K 5
Fyn 38 H 4
Fyne, Loch 30 B 3
Gabbs 18 C 4
Gabon 56 D 5
Gaborone 58 B 4
Gäddede 38 H 3
Gadsden 14 B 4
Gadwāl 46 D 5
Gaffney 14 C 3
Gag 52 H 6
Gagarin 40 H 6
Gagnon 8 X 8
Gagra 35 J 3
Gaillimh 31 B 2
Gainesville (Florida,
 U.S.) 14 C 5
Gainesville (Texas,
 U.S.) 16 D 5
Gainsville 14 C 4
Gairdner, Lake 60
 F 6
Gaixian 50 D 4
Gakona 10 N 6
Galapagos Islands
 (Ecuador) 24 B 2
Galashiels 28 C 2
Galaţi 35 C 2
Galatina 34 D 2
Galeana 18 E 5
Galela 52 H 5
Galena 43 Y 4
Galesburg 16 E 3
Gali 35 J 3
Galich 40 K 6
Galicia 33 A 1
Galicia 36 E 3
Galle 46 E 7
Gallinas, Punta 22
 H 5
Gällivare 38 K 2
Gailo Mountains 18
 E 5
Gallup 18 E 4
Galnesvelle 14 C 4
Galveston 20 F 2
Galveston Bay 20 F 2
Galway 31 B 2
Galway Bay 31 B 2
Gambia 56 B 3
Gambier, Îles 59 M 6
Ganāveh 44 H 7
Gǎncǎ 44 G 4
Gand'a 33 B 2
Gandajika 58 B 2
Gāndhi Sāgar 46
 D 4

Gándhinagar 46 C 4
Ganga 46 F 3
Gangānagar 46 C 3
Gangapur 46 C 3
Gangaw 47 G 4
Gangawati 46 D 5
Gangdisê Shan 48
 C 4
Ganges 46 F 3
Ganges, Mouths of
 the 47 F 4
Gangtok 46 F 3
Gangu 49 H 4
Gannan 50 D 3
Gannett Peak 18 E 3
Ganquan 49 H 3
Gansu 49 G 3
Ganzhou 49 J 5
Gao 56 D 3
Gao'an 49 K 5
Gaoyou 49 K 4
Gaozhou 49 J 6
Gap 34 B 2
Gapan 52 G 2
Garabogazköl Aylagy
 44 H 4
Garagum Kanaly 45
 K 5
Garanhuns 24 H 3
Garberville 18 B 3
Gardaneh-ye Āvej 44
 G 5
Garden City 16 C 4
Garden Reach 46
 F 4
Gardez 45 L 6
Gardiner 18 D 2
Gariep Dam 58 B 5
Garmisch-
 Partenkirchen 36
 C 3
Garnett 16 D 4
Garonne 32 B 3
Garoua 56 E 4
Garrison Dam 16
 C 2
Garry Lake 10 W 5
Garut 52 D 7
Gary 14 B 2
Garyarsa 48 C 4
Garzê 48 F 4
Gascogne 32 B 3
Gascoyne Junction
 60 B 5
Gashua 56 E 3
Gaspé 8 Y 9
Gaspé, Cap de 8 Y 9
Gastonia 14 C 3
Gāstrikland 38 J 3
Gata, Cabo de 33
 B 2
Gatchina 40 H 6

Gatehouse of Fleet
 28 B 2
Gates of the Arctic
 National Park 10
 M 5
Gateshead Island 8
 R 4
Gatineau, Parc de la
 8 V 9
Gaua 59 F 5
Gauhati 47 G 3
Gāuwän 46 E 4
Gävle 38 J 3
Gawler Ranges 60
 F 6
Gaya (India) 46 E 4
Gaylord 14 C 1
Gayndah 60 J 5
Gaza 44 D 6
Gaziantep 35 G 6
Gdańsk 36 D 2
Gdynia 36 D 2
Gearhart Mountain
 18 B 3
Gebe 52 H 6
Gebze 35 C 4
Gediz (Turkey) 35
 C 5
Gedser 36 C 2
Geelong 60 G 7
Geelvink Channel 60
 A 5
Geesthacht 36 C 2
Gejiu 49 G 6
Gela 34 C 3
Gelendzhik 44 E 4
Gelibolu 35 B 4
Gemena 58 A 1
General Bravo 20
 E 2
General Santos 52
 H 4
General Treviño 20
 E 2
General Trías 20 C 2
Geneva 14 D 2
Geneva, Lake 36
 B 3
Genève 36 B 3
Gengma 48 F 6
Genova 34 B 2
Geographical Society
 Ø 8 Gg 4
George Town (Cay-
 man Islands) 22 F 4
George Town
 (Malaysia) 52 C 4
George V Land 63 ·
 U 5
George, Lake 60 C 4
George, Lake
 (Florida, U.S.) 14
 C 5
George, Lake (New
 York, U.S.) 14 E 2

Georgetown 14 D 6
Georgetown 24 F 2
Georgetown (South Carolina, U.S.) 14 D 4
Georgetown (Texas, U.S.) 16 D 5
Georgia 44 E 4
Georgia (U.S.) 14 C 4
Georgian Bay 8 U 9
Georgīevka 45 O 3
Georgiyevsk 35 K 2
Gera 36 C 2
Geraldton 60 A 5
Geraldton (Canada) 14 B 1
Gerba 43 O 4
Gerede 35 E 4
Gereshk 45 K 6
Gering 16 C 3
Germania Land 8 Gg 3
Germany 36 B 2
Getafe 32 B 3
Gettysburg 16 D 2
Geysir 38 A 3
Geyve 35 D 4
Ghana 56 C 4
Gharb Dārfūr 56 F 3
Ghardaïa 56 D 1
Ghazni 45 L 6
Gheorghieni 36 F 3
Ghurian 45 K 6
Giannitsa 34 E 2
Gibraltar 33 A 2
Gibraltar, Estrecho de 33 A 2
Gibraltar, Strait of 33 A 2
Gibson Desert 60 C 4
Gichgeniyn Nuruu 48 E 1
Gideälven 38 J 3
Gidgi, Lake 60 D 5
Gifu 54 C 3
Gijón 33 A 1
Gila Bend 18 D 5
Gila River 18 D 5
Gilbert Islands 59 G 3
Gilgit 45 M 5
Gillen, Lake 60 D 5
Gillette 18 E 3
Gilroy 18 B 4
Gimli 16 D 1
Gingoog 52 H 4
Gir National Park 46 C 4
Gīr Range 46 C 4
Girardot 22 H 7
Giresun 35 H 4
Giridih 46 F 4
Girona 32 C 3

Girvan 28 B 2
Gisborne 62 C 2
Giurgiu 34 F 2
Gizjiga 43 Q 4
Giżycko 36 E 2
Gjirokastër 34 E 2
Gjoa Haven 8 R 5
Gjøvik 38 H 3
Glacier Bay National Park and Reserve 10 P 7
Glacier National Park 18 D 2
Gladstone 60 J 4
Glasgow (Kentucky, U.S.) 14 B 3
Glasgow (Montana, U.S.) 18 E 2
Glasgow (U.K.) 28 B 2
Glazov 40 M 6
Glen Canyon National Recreation Area 18 D 4
Glen Innes 60 J 5
Glen Mòr 30 B 3
Glendale 18 D 5
Glendive 16 C 2
Glennallen 10 N 6
Glenrock 18 E 3
Glenrothes 30 C 3
Glens Falls 14 E 2
Glenwood Springs 18 E 4
Gliwice 36 D 2
Globe 18 D 5
Głogów 36 D 2
Glomfjord 38 H 2
Glomma 38 H 4
Glommersträsk 38 J 2
Gloucester (U.K.) 28 C 4
Gloucester (U.S.) 14 E 2
Glūbokoe 45 O 2
Gniezno 36 D 2
Goa 46 C 5
Gobi Desert 49 G 2
Godavari 46 E 5
Godavari, Mouths of the 46 E 5
Godby 38 J 3
Godhavn 8 Aa 5
Godhra 46 C 4
Gödöllő 36 D 3
Gods Lake 10 Y 8
Godthåb 8 Aa 6
Gogebic Range 16 E 2
Gogland, Ostrov 38 L 4
Goiânia 24 F 4
Gojra 46 C 2
Gökçeada 34 F 2

Gökırmak 35 F 4
Göksun 35 G 5
Gol 38 G 3
Gol'chikha 41 S 3
Golconda 18 C 3
Gold Rock 16 E 2
Golden 10 T 8
Golden Hinde 18 A 2
Goldfield 18 C 4
Goldsboro 14 D 3
Golfo de Cintra 56 B 2
Golfo de San Jorge 24 E 7
Golfo San Matías 24 E 7
Gölköy 35 G 4
Golmud 48 E 3
Golpāyegān 44 H 6
Gombe 56 E 3
Gomera 56 B 2
Gómez Palacio 20 D 2
Gomo Co 48 D 4
Gonaïves 22 H 4
Gonáve, Île de la 22 H 4
Gonbad-e Qābūs 45 J 5
Gondal 46 C 4
Gonder 56 G 3
Gondia 46 E 4
Gönen 35 B 4
Gongan 49 J 4
Gongcheng 49 J 6
Gongga Shan 49 G 5
Gonghe 48 G 3
Gongliu 48 C 2
Gonzalés 20 E 3
Gooding 18 D 3
Goodland 16 C 4
Goodnews Bay 43 X 5
Goondiwindi 60 J 5
Goose Lake 18 B 3
Gorakhpur 46 E 3
Goražde 34 D 2
Gore 62 A 4
Görele 35 H 4
Gorey 31 C 2
Gorgan 45 H 5
Gorgona, Isla 22 G 7
Gori 35 L 4
Gorizia 36 C 3
Gorkiy 40 K 6
Gorna Oryakhovitsa 34 F 2
Gorno-Altaysk 41 T 7
Gornozavodsk 50 H 3
Gornozavodsk (Russia) 54 D 1
Gornyak 45 O 2

Gorodets 40 K 6
Goroka 59 D 4
Gorong 52 J 6
Gorontalo 52 G 5
Gorzów Wielkopolski 36 D 2
Goshogahara 54 D 2
Gosnells 60 B 6
Götaland 38 H 4
Göteborg 38 H 4
Gotha 36 C 2
Gothenburg (U.S.) 16 C 3
Gotland 38 J 4
Gotō-rettō 54 A 4
Gotse Delchev 34 E 2
Gotska Sandön 38 J 4
Gōtsu 54 B 4
Göttingen 36 B 2
Goulburn 60 H 6
Goulburn Island 60 E 2
Governador Valadares 24 G 4
Governor's Harbour 14 D 5
Govind Ballabah Pant Sagar 46 E 4
Gozho Co 48 C 3
Graaff Reinet 58 B 5
Grace, Lake 60 B 6
Gracias a Dios, Cabo de 22 E 5
Grafton 60 J 5
Grafton (U.S.) 16 D 2
Graham 16 E 2
Graham Island (British Columbia, Canada) 10 Q 8
Graham Island (Nunavut, Canada) 8 S 3
Grahamstown 58 B 5
Grain Coast 56 B 4
Grajewo 36 E 2
Grampian Mountains 30 B 3
Gran Altiplanicie Central 24 D 7
Gran Canaria 56 B 2
Gran Chaco 24 E 5
Granada (Nicaragua) 22 E 5
Granada (Spain) 33 B 2
Granby 8 W 9
Grand Bahama Island 14 D 5
Grand Canal 31 C 2
Grand Canal 49 K 3

Grand Canyon 18 D 4
Grand Canyon National Park 18 D 4
Grand Cayman 22 F 4
Grand Coulee 18 C 2
Grand Coulee Dam 18 C 2
Grand Forks 16 D 2
Grand Island 16 D 3
Grand Junction 18 E 4
Grand Manan Island 8 X 10
Grand Marais (Michigan, U.S.) 14 B 1
Grand Marais (Minnesota, U.S.) 16 E 2
Grand Portage 14 B 1
Grand Rapids (Michigan, U.S.) 14 B 2
Grand Rapids (Minnesota, U.S.) 16 E 2
Grand River 14 B 2
Grand Teton 18 D 3
Grand Traverse Bay 14 B 1
Grand-Bassam 56 C 4
Grande de Matagalpa, Rio 20 G 5
Grande de Santiago, Río 20 D 3
Grande Prairie 10 T 7
Grande Ronde River 18 C 2
Grande, Cerro 20 D 3
Grandin, Lac 10 T 6
Grane 38 H 2
Grangeville 18 C 2
Granite City 16 E 4
Granite Dam 8 Z 9
Granollers 32 C 3
Grantham 28 D 3
Grants 18 E 4
Grants Pass 18 B 3
Granville 32 B 2
Gras, Lac de 10 U 6
Gravelbourg 18 E 2
Grayling 14 C 2
Grays Harbor 18 A 2
Graz 36 D 3
Great Abaco Island 14 D 5
Great Artesian Basin 60 G 4
Great Australian Bight 60 D 6

Great Barrier Island 62 C 2
Great Barrier Reef 60 G 2
Great Basin 18 C 3
Great Bear Lake 10 S 5
Great Bear River 10 R 5
Great Bend 16 D 4
Great Dividing Range 60 G 3
Great Exuma Island 22 G 3
Great Falls 18 D 2
Great Himalaya Range 46 D 2
Great Inagua Island 22 H 3
Great Indian Desert 46 B 3
Great Malvern 28 C 3
Great Namaqualand 58 A 4
Great Nicobar Island 47 G 7
Great Ouse 28 E 3
Great Pee Dee River 14 D 4
Great Plain of the Koukdjuak 8 W 5
Great Plains 16 C 3
Great Plains (Canada) 10 T 7
Great Salt Lake 18 D 3
Great Salt Lake Desert 18 D 4
Great Sandy Desert 60 C 4
Great Sitkin Island 43 U 6
Great Slave Lake 10 T 6
Great Victoria Desert 60 D 5
Great Victoria Desert Nature Reserve 60 D 5
Great Yarmouth 28 E 3
Greater Antilles 22 H 4
Gredos, Sierra de 33 A 2
Greece 34 E 3
Greeley (Colorado, U.S.) 16 C 3
Greeley (Nebraska, U.S.) 16 D 3
Greemville 16 D 5
Green Bay (Michigan, U.S.) 14 B 1
Green Bay (-

Wisconsin, U.S.) 14 B 2
Green Islands 59 E 4
Green River (Kentucky, U.S.) 14 B 3
Green River (River, Utah, U.S.) 18 D 4
Green River (Utah, U.S.) 18 D 4
Green River (Wyoming, U.S.) 18 E 3
Greenland 8 Aa 3
Greenland Sea 38 B 2
Greenock 28 B 2
Greensboro (Georgia, U.S.) 14 C 4
Greensboro (North Carolina, U.S.) 14 D 3
Greenville (Alabama, U.S.) 14 B 4
Greenville (Maine, U.S.) 14 F 1
Greenville (Mississippi, U.S.) 16 E 5
Greenville (North Carolina, U.S.) 14 D 3
Greenville (South Carolina, U.S.) 14 C 4
Greenwood 14 C 4
Gregory Range 60 G 3
Gregory, Lake (South Australia) 60 F 5
Gregory, Lake (Western Australia) 60 B 5
Gregory, Lake (Western Australia) 60 D 4
Greifswald 36 C 2
Grenå 38 H 4
Grenada 22 K 5
Grenada (U.S.) 14 B 4
Grenadine Islands 22 K 5
Grenoble 36 B 3
Grenville, Cape 60 G 2
Gresik 52 E 7
Gretna (Louisiana, U.S.) 20 G 2
Grey Islands 8 Z 8
Grey Range 60 G 5
Greymouth 62 B 3
Griffin 14 C 4
Griffith 60 H 6
Grimsby 28 D 3
Grimshaw 10 T 7
Grinnell 16 E 3

Grise Fjord 8 U 3
Gris-Nez, Cap 28 E 4
Grodekovo 54 B 2
Groix, Île de 32 B 2
Grong 38 H 3
Groningen 36 B 2
Groote Eylandt 60 F 2
Grosseto 34 C 2
Grotte de Lascaux 32 C 2
Groundhog River 14 C 1
Groznyy 35 L 3
Grudziądz 36 D 2
Grundy 14 C 3
Gryada Chernysheva 40 N 4
Gryazi 44 E 2
Gryfice 36 D 2
Guadalajara (Spain) 32 B 3
Guadalajara Tepatitlán 20 D 3
Guadaloupe Mountains 16 C 5
Guadalquivir, Río 33 A 2
Guadalupe (Island, Mexico) 20 B 3
Guadalupe (Mexico) 20 D 2
Guadeloupe 22 K 4
Guadiana, Río 33 A 2
Guadix 33 B 2
Guaini, Rio 22 H 7
Guam 59 D 2
Guamúchil 20 C 2
Guan Xian 49 G 4
Guanajuato (Mexico) 20 D 3
Guanajuato (State, Mexico) 20 D 3
Guanare 22 J 6
Guane 20 H 3
Guangdong 49 J 6
Guanghua 49 J 4
Guangji 49 K 5
Guangxi Zhuangzu Zizhiqu 49 H 6
Guangyaun 49 H 4
Guangzhou 49 J 6
Guantanamo 22 G 3
Guanyun 49 K 4
Guarda 33 A 1
Guárico, Embalse del 22 J 5
Guasave 20 C 2
Guatemala 22 D 5
Guatemala (Country) 20 F 4
Guatemala (Guatemala) 20 F 5

Guayaquil 24 C 3
Guaymas 20 B 2
Gubakha 40 N 6
Guben 36 C 2
Gubkin 44 E 2
Gudbrandsdalen 38 G 3
Gudermes 35 M 3
Gudivāda 46 E 5
Gudur 46 D 6
Guelma 34 B 3
Guelph 14 C 2
Guéra Baguirmi 56 E 3
Guernsey 32 B 2
Guerrero (Mexico) 20 E 2
Guerrero (State, Mexico) 20 D 4
Guguan (Mariana Islands, U.S.A.) 59 D 2
Guguan (Micronesia) 59 F 3
Guiana Highlands 22 K 7
Guichi 49 K 4
Guiding 49 H 5
Guildford 28 D 4
Guilin 49 J 5
Guimaras Island 52 G 3
Guinea 56 B 3
Guinea-Bissau 56 B 3
Güines 22 F 3
Guisikha 41 X 3
Guixi 49 K 5
Guixian 49 H 6
Guiyang 49 H 5
Guizhou 49 H 5
Gujar Khan 45 M 6
Gujarat 46 B 4
Gujrānwāla 46 C 2
Gujrat 46 C 2
Gulbarga 46 D 5
Gulf of Aden 56 H 3
Gulf of Guinea 56 D 4
Gulfport 14 B 4
Gulian 50 D 2
Gull Lake 10 V 8
Gullfoss 38 B 3
Gulu 58 C 1
Gumdag 45 H 5
Guna 46 D 4
Güneydoğu Toroslar 35 H 5
Gunnarn 38 J 3
Gunnbjørn Fjeld 8 Ff 5
Gunnison 18 E 4
Guntakal 46 D 5
Guntersville Lake 14 B 4

Guntūr 46 E 5
Gunungsitoli 52 B 5
Guoyang 49 K 4
Gurbantünggüt Shamo 48 D 1
Guri, Embalse de 22 K 6
Gurskøy 38 F 3
Gurskoye 42 L 6
Gürun 35 G 5
Gurvan Sayhan Uul 49 G 2
Guryevsk 41 T 7
Gusau 56 D 3
Guşgy 45 K 5
Gushi 49 K 4
Gusicha 41 X 3
Gusinoozersk 41 X 7
Gus'-Khrustal'nyy 40 K 6
Gusmp, Ostrov 43 Q 3
Gustav Holm, Kap 8 Ee 5
Gustavus 10 P 7
Guthrie (Oklahoma, U.S.) 16 D 4
Guthrie (Texas, U.S.) 16 C 5
Guyana 24 E 2
Gwalior 46 D 3
Gweru 58 C 3
Gya La 48 C 5
Gydanskiy, Poluostrov 41 R 3
Gympie 60 J 5
Gyöngyös 36 D 3
Győr 36 D 3
Gyula 36 E 3
Gyumri 35 K 4
Gyzylarbat 45 J 5
Ha Dong 47 K 4
Ha Giang 47 J 4
Ha Nôi 47 K 4
Ha Tinh 47 K 5
Ha'apai Group 59 H 6
Haapsalu 38 K 4
Haast 62 A 3
Habay 10 T 7
Hachijō-jima 54 C 4
Hachinohe 54 D 2
Hadejia 56 D 3
Hadim 35 E 6
Hadrian's Wall 28 C 2
Haeju 50 E 5
Hafnarfjörður 38 A 3
Hagemeister Island 43 X 5
Hagerstown 14 D 3
Hagfors 38 H 4
Häggenäs 38 H 3
Hagi 54 B 4
Hags Head 31 B 2

Hague, Cap de la 32 B 2
Hami 48 E 2
Hai'an 49 L 4
Haikang 49 J 6
Haikou 47 L 5
Hailar 50 C 3
Hailin 50 E 4
Hailong 54 A 2
Hailun 50 E 3
Hailuoto 38 K 2
Haimen (Guangdong, China) 49 K 6
Haimen (Zhejiang, China) 49 L 5
Hainan 47 K 5
Hainan Dao 52 E 2
Haines 10 P 7
Haines Junction 10 P 6
Haining 49 L 4
Haiphong 47 K 4
Haiti 22 H 4
Haizhou Wan 49 K 4
Hakkâri 35 K 6
Hakodate 54 D 2
Haku-san 54 C 3
Halab 35 G 6
Halbei 50 E 3
Halberstadt 36 C 2
Halden 38 H 4
Halifax (Canada) 8 Y 10
Halifax (U.K.) 28 C 3
Halkett, Cape 10 M 4
Hall Beach 8 U 5
Hall Islands 59 E 3
Hall Land 8 Y 2
Halland 38 H 4
Halla-san 54 A 4
Halle 36 C 2
Halle-san 50 E 6
Hällnäs 38 J 3
Halls Creek 60 D 3
Halmahera 52 H 5
Halmstad 38 H 4
Hälsingland 38 J 3
Hamada 54 B 4
Hamadān 44 G 6
Hamāh 44 E 5
Hamamatsu 54 C 4
Hamanaka 54 E 2
Hamar 38 H 3
Hambantota 46 E 7
Hamburg 36 B 2
Häme 38 K 3
Hämeenlinna 38 K 3
Hameln 36 B 2
Hamersley Range 60 B 4
Hamersley Range National Park 60 B 4
Hamgyŏng-sanmaek 54 A 2

Hamhŭng 50 E 5
Hami 48 E 2
Hamilton (Australia) 60 G 7
Hamilton (Canada) 14 D 2
Hamilton (New Zealand) 62 C 2
Hamilton (U.S.) 18 D 2
Hammamet, Golfe de 34 C 3
Hammerdal 38 J 3
Hammerfest 38 K 1
Hammond 16 E 5
Hampden 62 B 4
Hampton Tableland 60 D 6
Hāmūn-i-Lora 45 K 7
Hanahan 14 C 4
Hanamaki 54 D 3
Hânceşti 36 F 3
Hanceville 10 S 8
Hancheng 49 J 3
Hanchuan 49 J 4
Handan 49 J 3
Hangayn Nuruu 41 V 8
Hanggin Houqi 49 H 2
Hangö 38 K 4
Hangu 49 K 3
Hangzhou 49 L 4
Hanko 38 K 4
Hanksville 18 D 4
Hanna 10 U 8
Hannibal 16 E 4
Hannover 36 B 2
Hanöbukten 38 H 4
Hanstholm 38 G 4
Hanumangarh 46 C 3
Hanzhong 49 H 4
Hao 59 L 5
Haora 46 F 4
Haparanda 38 K 2
Hapo 52 H 5
Happy Valley-Goose Bay 8 Y 8
Har Us Nuur 41 U 8
Haraiki 59 L 5
Harare 58 C 3
Har-Ayrag 50 A 3
Harbin 50 E 3
Harbor Beach 14 C 2
Harda Khas 46 D 4
Hardin 18 E 2
Härer 56 H 4
Hargeysa 56 H 4
Haridwär 46 D 3
Harihari 62 B 3
Harlingen 20 E 2
Harlow 28 E 4
Harney Basin 18 B 3

Harney Peak 16 C 3
Härnön 38 J 3
Härnösand 38 J 3
Harrington Harbour 8
Z 8
Harris, Sound of 30
A 3
Harrisburg 14 D 2
Harrison 16 E 4
Harrisonburg 14 D 3
Harrogate 28 D 3
Harry S. Truman
Reservoir 16 E 4
Hartford 14 E 2
Hartland Point 28
B 4
Hartlepool 28 D 2
Hartwell Lake 14 C 4
Hartz Mountains Na-
tional Park 60 H 8
Harve-Saint-Pierre 8
Y 8
Harvey (U.S.) 16 D 2
Harwich 28 E 4
Haryāna 46 D 3
Hastings (Minnesota,
U.S.) 16 E 3
Hastings (Nebraska,
U.S.) 16 D 3
Hastings (New
Zealand) 62 C 2
Hastings (U.K.) 28
E 4
Hat Yai 47 J 7
Hattiesburg 14 B 4
Hatutu 59 L 4
Haukeligrend 38 G 4
Hauraki Gulf 62 B 2
Haut Atlas 56 C 1
Havana 20 H 3
Havelock Island 47
G 6
Haverhill 14 E 2
Havlíčkuv Brod 36
D 3
Havre 18 E 2
Havsa 34 F 2
Havza 35 F 4
Hawaii 12 D 8
Hawaiian Islands 12
E 7
Hawera 62 B 2
Hawick 28 C 2
Hawke Bay 62 C 2
Hawthorne 18 C 4
Hay 60 G 6
Hay River 10 T 6
Hayes, Mount 10
N 6
Hays 16 D 4
Haysyn 36 F 3
Hayward 18 B 4
Hazaradjat 45 K 6
Hazard 14 C 3
Hazaribagh 46 F 4

Hazelton 10 R 7
Hazen Strait 10 U 3
Hazen, Lake 8 W 2
Hazlehurst 14 C 4
Hazleton 14 D 2
Hazlett, Lake 60 D 4
Hearne 16 D 5
Hearst 8 U 9
Hebei 49 J 3
Hebi 49 J 3
Hebrides, Sea of the
30 A 3
Hebron 8 Y 7
Hechi 49 H 6
Hechuan 49 H 4
Hecla, Cape 8 Y 2
Hede 38 H 3
Hedmark 38 H 3
Hefei 49 K 4
Hegang 50 F 3
Heidelberg 36 B 3
Heidenheim 36 C 3
Heilbronn 36 B 3
Heilongjiang 50 E 3
Heilprin Land 8 2
Heilprin Ø 8 Y 3
Heimaey 38 A 3
Heishan 50 D 4
Hejiang 49 H 5
Hejlong-Jiang 50
D 2
Hekimhan 35 G 5
Helena (Arkansas,
U.S.) 16 E 5
Helena (Montana,
U.S.) 18 D 2
Helensville 62 B 2
Helgoländer Bucht 36
B 2
Helgøy 38 J 1
Heli 50 F 3
Hell'n 33 B 2
Holmsdale 30 C 2
Helodrano Antongila
58 D 3
Helong 54 A 2
Helsingborg 38 H 4
Helsingfors 38 K 3
Helsinki 38 K 3
Helston 28 B 4
Hemsön 38 J 3
Henan 49 J 4
Henderson (Nevada,
U.S.) 18 D 4
Henderson (North
Carolina, U.S.) 14
D 3
Henderson (Texas,
U.S.) 16 E 5
Henderson Island 59
N 6
Hendersonville
(North Carolina,
U.S.) 14 C 3
Hendersonville

(Tennessee, U.S.)
14 B 3
Hengdnan Shan 48
F 5
Hengshan 49 J 5
Hengshui 49 K 3
Hengxian 49 H 6
Hengyang 49 J 5
Heniches'k 35 F 1
Henrietta Maria,
Cape 8 U 7
Henryetta 16 D 4
Henzada 47 H 5
Hepu 49 H 6
Herat 45 K 6
Herbert 18 E 1
Hereford (U.K.) 28
C 3
Hereford (U.S.) 16 C
5
Herlen Gol 50 B 3
Hermanas 20 D 2
Hermiston 18 C 2
Hermit Islands 59 D
4
Hermosillo 20 B 2
Herning 38 G 4
Heroica Zitácuaro 20
D 4
Herrero, Punta 20
G 4
Herschel Island 10
P 5
Hertungen af Orléans
Land 8 Gg 3
Hexian 49 J 6
Heyuan 49 J 6
Heze 49 K 3
Hialeah 14 C 5
Hibbing 16 E 2
Hibernia Reef 60
C 2
Hidaka-Sammyaku
54 D 2
Hidalgo 20 E 3
Hidalgo del Parral 20
C 2
High Level 10 T 7
High Point 14 D 3
High Prairie 10 T 7
High River 18 D 1
High Wycombe 28
D 4
Highrock Lake 10
W 7
Hiiumaa 38 K 4
Hikueru 59 L 5
Hildesheim 36 B 2
Hill Bank 20 G 4
Hillsboro 16 D 5
Hilo 59 K 2
Hilo Bay 20 G 4
Hilton Head Island 14
C 4
Himachal 46 D 2

Himalayas 46 D 2
Himi 54 C 3
Hims 44 E 6
Hinchinbrook Island
(Australia) 60 H 3
Hinchinbrook Island
(U.S.) 10 N 6
Hindukush 45 L 6
Hindupur 46 D 6
Hinganghat 46 D 4
Hinnøya 38 J 2
Hinton 10 T 8
Hirado 54 A 4
Hiriyūr 46 D 6
Hirosaki 54 D 2
Hiroshima 54 B 4
Hirtshals 38 G 4
Hisär 46 D 3
Hispaniola 22 H 4
Hita 54 B 4
Hitachi 54 D 3
Hiti 59 L 5
Hitra 38 G 3
Hlukhiv 36 G 2
Ho Chi Minh 47 K 6
Hoa Binh 47 K 4
Hobart 60 H 8
Hobart (U.S.) 16 D 4
Hobbs 16 C 5
Hoburgen 38 J 4
Hochstetter Forland 8
Gg 3
Hodh 56 C 3
Hódmezővásárhely
36 E 3
Hodonin 36 D 3
Hofsjökull 38 B 3
Höfu 54 B 4
Hogback Mountain
18 D 3
Hoggar 56 D 2
Hoh Sai Hu 48 E 3
Hoh XII Hu 48 E 3
Hoh Xil Shan 48 D 3
Hoi An 47 K 5
Hokitika 62 B 3
Hokkaidō 54 D 2
Hoktemberyan 35
L 4
Hol 38 G 3
Hola Prystan 44 D 3
Holbox, Isla 20 G 3
Holbrook 18 D 5
Holdenville 16 D 4
Holdrege 16 D 3
Holguín 22 G 3
Holland 14 B 2
Holly Springs 14 B 4
Hollywood 14 C 5
Holm Land 8 Hh 2
Holman 10 T 4
Holmes Reefs 59
E 5
Holmön 38 K 3

Holovanivs'k 44 D 3
Holstebro 38 G 4
Holsteinsborg 8 Aa 5
Holycross 43 Y 4
Holyhead 28 B 3
Homer 43 Z 5
Homestead (U.S.) 14
C 5
Homewood 14 B 4
Homs 44 E 6
Homyel' 36 G 2
Hon Gai 47 K 4
Hon Khoci 47 J 7
Hon Tho Chau 47
J 7
Honāvar 46 C 6
Honda 22 H 6
Honduras 22 E 5
Honduras, Golfo de
20 G 4
Hönefoss 38 H 3
Hong Kong 49 J 6
Hongjiang 49 H 5
Hongor 50 B 3
Hongshui He 49 H 6
Hongwon 50 E 4
Hongyuan 49 G 4
Hongze 49 K 4
Hongze Hu 49 K 4
Honiara 59 E 4
Honningsvåg 38 L 1
Honolulu 12 E 7
Honshū 54 D 3
Hood Point 60 B 6
Hood River 18 B 2
Hoogeveen 36 B 2
Hoorn 36 B 2
Hoover Dam 18 D 4
Hope 16 E 5
Hopedale 8 Y 7
Hopes Advance, Cap
8 X 6
Hopewell, Isles 8
V 7
Hopkinsville 14 B 3
Hoquiam 18 B 2
Hordaland 38 G 3
Horlivka 44 E 3
Horn 38 A 2
Horn Plateau 10 S 6
Hornavan 38 J 2
Hornell 14 D 2
Horodenka 36 F 3
Horqin Youyi Qiahqi
50 D 3
Horqin Zuoyi Zhongqi
50 D 4
Horsens 38 G 4
Horsham 60 G 7
Horten 38 H 4
Hose Mountains 52
E 5
Hot Springs
(Arkansas, U.S.) 16
E 5

Hot Springs (New
Mexico, U.S.) 18
E 5
Hot Springs (South
Dakota, U.S.) 16
C 3
Hotan 48 B 3
Hoting 38 J 3
Hottah Lake 10 T 5
Houghton 14 B 1
Houghton Lake 14 2
Houlton 14 F 1
Houma (China) 49
J 3
Houma (U.S.) 20 F 2
Houston 20 E 2
Houterive 8 X 9
Houtman Abrolhos
60 A 5
Hovd 48 E 1
Hovgaard Ø 8 Hh 2
Hövsgöi 49 H 2
Hövsgöl Nuur 41 V 7
Howe, Cape 60 H 7
Howland 14 F 1
Howrah 46 F 4
Hoy 30 C 2
Hradec Králové 36
D 2
Hrebinka 36 G 2
Hrodna 36 E 2
Hsilo 49 L 6
Hsinchu 49 L 6
Hu Men 49 J 6
Hua Hin 47 H 6
Huadian 50 E 4
Huahine 59 K 5
Huai'an 49 J 2
Huaide 50 D 4
Huaiji 49 J 6
Huailai 50 C 4
Huainan 49 K 4
Huairen 49 J 3
Huajuapan de Léon
20 E 4
Hua-lien 49 L 6
Huambo 58 A 3
Huanan 50 F 3
Huancayo 24 D 4
Huang Hai 49 L 3
Huang He 49 J 3
Huangchuan 49 K 4
Huangliu 47 K 5
Huangshi 49 K 4
Huangxian 49 L 3
Huangyan 49 L 5
Huangzhong 49 G 3
Huanren 54 A 4
Huarmey 24 D 4
Huatabampo 20 C 2
Huauchinanco 20 E 3
Huautla 20 E 3
Huazhou 49 J 6
Hubei 49 J 4
Huddersfield 28 D 3

Huder 50 D 2
Hudiksvall 38 J 3
Hudson Bay 8 T 7
Hudson Land 8 Gg 4
Hudson Strait 8 V 6
Hue 47 K 5
Huehuetenango 20
　F 4
Huelva 33 A 2
Huesca 32 B 3
Hugh Town 28 A 5
Hughenden 60 G 4
Hugli 46 F 4
Hugo 16 D 5
Huhhot 49 J 2
Hui'an 49 K 5
Huiarau Range 62
　C 2
Hŭich'ŏn 50 E 4
Huilai 49 K 6
Huili 49 G 5
Huinin 49 K 3
Huinan 54 A 2
Huiten Nur 48 E 3
Huixtla 20 F 4
Huize 49 G 5
Hŭksan-chedo 50
　E 6
Hulan 54 A 1
Hulan Ergi 50 D 3
Hulin 50 F 3
Hull 8 V 9
Hulun Buir Meng 50
　C 3
Hulun Nur 50 C 3
Humaitá 24 E 3
Humber 28 E 3
Humboldt (U.S.) 14
　B 3
Humboldt Gletscher 8
　Y 3
Humboldt River 18
　C 4
Hunan 49 J 5
Hunchun 50 F 4
Hunedoara 36 E 3
Hungary 36 D 3
Hŭngnam 50 E 5
Hunjiang 50 E 4
Hunter Island 60 G 8
Hunterville 62 C 2
Huntington 14 C 3
Huntsville (Alabama,
　U.S.) 14 B 4
Huntsville (Canada)
　14 D 1
Huntsville (Texas,
　U.S.) 16 D 5
Hunyuan 49 J 3
Huon Peninsula 59
　D 4
Huoshan 49 K 4
Huoxian 49 J 3
Huron 16 D 3
Huron Mountains 14

B 1
Huron, Lake 14 C 2
Hurricane 18 D 4
Hurst 16 D 5
Hūsavik 38 B 2
Huskvarna 38 H 4
Huslia 10 L 5
Hutchinson (Kansas,
　U.S.) 16 D 4
Hutchinson (Min-
　nesota, U.S.) 16
　E 3
Hutou 54 B 1
Huzhou 49 L 4
Hvar 34 D 2
Hwange 58 B 3
Hyannis 14 E 2
Hyargas Nuur 41 I
Hyderabad (India) 46
　D 5
Hyderabad (Pakistan)
　46 B 3
Hyères 34 B 2
Hyesan 50 E 4
Hysham 18 E 2
Hyūga 54 B 4
Hyvinge 38 K 3
Hyvinkää 38 K 3
Iaşi 36 F 3
Ibadan 56 D 4
Ibagué 22 G 7
Ibérico, Sistema 32
　B 3
Ibonma 53 J 6
Ica 24 D 4
İçel (Turkey) 35 F 6
Iceland 38 A 3
Ichalkaranji 46 C 5
Ichchapuram 46 E 5
Ichinskaya Sopka 43
　P 5
Ichnya 36 G 2
Ichuan 49 G 4
Idabel 16 E 5
Idah 56 D 4
Idaho 18 C 3
Idaho Falls 18 D 3
idhān Awbārī 56 E 2
Idlib 44 E 5
Idre 38 H 3
Ife 56 D 4
Igarka 41 T 4
Igatpuri 46 C 5
Iğdır 35 L 5
Iglesias 34 B 3
Igloolik 8 U 5
Ignace 16 E 2
Iğneada 35 B 4
Igoumenitsa 34 E 3
Iguala 20 E 4
Igualada 32 C 3
Iguatu 24 H 3
Iguigik 43 Y 5
Ihosy 58 D 4
Iida 54 C 3

Ilhéus 24 H 4
Iisalmi 38 L 3
IJsselmeer 36 B 2
Ikaria 44 C 5
Ikatskiy Khrebet 41
　X 7
Ikeda 54 D 2
Ila 56 D 4
Ilagan 53 G 2
Ilan 49 L 6
Iława 36 D 2
Île Des Noefs 58 E 2
Ilebo 58 B 2
Îlede 32 C 2
Îles de Los 56 B 4
Ilford 10 Y 8
Ilgın 35 D 5
Ilha de Marajó 24
　F 3
Ilha do Bananal 24
　F 4
Ilhas Selvagens (Por-
　tugal) 56 B 1
Iliamna Lake 43 Y 5
Iligan 53 G 4
Ilimananngip Nunaa
　8 Ff 4
Ilimsk 41 W 6
Ilinskiy 50 H 3
Il'inskiy (Russia) 54
　D 1
Illichivs'k 35 D 1
Illinois 14 B 2
Illinois River 16 E 4
illoqqortoormiut 8　4
Iloilo 53 G 3
Ilorin 56 D 4
Il'pi 43 S 4
Ilulissat 8 Aa 5
Ilych 40 N 5
Imabari 54 B 4
Imandra, Ozero 40
　H 4
Imatra 38 L 3
Imeni Ismail Samani,
　Pik 41 N 4
Imeni Mariny 42 N 4
Imperatriz 24 G 3
Imperia 34 B 2
Imphal 47 G 4
Inanwatan 53 J 6
Inari 38 L 2
Inarigda 41 X 5
Inarijärvi 38 L 2
İnce Burnu 35 F 3
İncekum Burnu 44
　D 5
Inch'ŏn 50 E 5
Independence
　(Kansas, U.S.) 16
　D 4
Independence (Mis-
　souri, U.S.) 16 E 4
India 46 D 5

Indian Harbour 8 Z 8
Indian Ocean 46 E 6
Indian Springs 18　4
Indiana 14 B 2
Indianapolis 14 B 3
Indias Occidentales
　22 J 3
Indiga 40 L 4
Indigirka 42 M 4
Indonesia 52 D 6
Indore 46 D 4
Indramayu 52 D 7
Indus 46 B 4
Inebolu 44 D 4
İnecik 35 B 4
İnegöl 35 C 4
Ingham 60 H 3
Inglefield Land 8
　W 3
Ing-lfshöfði 38 B 3
Ingolstadt 36 C 3
Inhulets' 44 D 3
Innamincka 60 G 5
Inner Hebrides 30
　A 4
Inner Islands 58 E 2
Innisfail 60 H 3
Innokent'yevka 54
　C 1
Innsbruck 36 C 3
Inobonto 53 G 5
Inowrocław 36 D 2
Insan-ni 54 A 2
Inta 40 O 4
Interview Island 47
　G 6
Inukjuak 8 V 7
Inuvik 10 Q 5
Inveraray 30 B 3
Invercargill 62 A 4
Inverness 30 B 3
Inya 42 M 4
Inza 44 G 2
Ioannina 34 E 3
Iokanga 40 J 4
Iona (U.K.) 30 A 3
Ionian Sea 34 D 3
Ionioi Nisoi 34 D 3
Iony, Ostrov 42 M 5
Ios 34 F 3
Iossar 40 M 5
Iowa 16 D 3
Iowa City 16 E 3
Ipatinga 24 G 4
Ipatovo 44 F 3
Ipeiros 34 E 3
Ipiales 22 G 7
Ipoh 52 C 5
İpsala 35 B 4
Ipswich (Australia) 60
　J 5
Ipswich (U.K.) 28
　E 3
Iqaluit 8 X 6
Iquique 24 D 5

Iquitos 24 D 3
Irakleio 34 F 3
Iran 44 H 6
Iran Gate 34 E 2
Iran, Pegunungan 52
　E 5
Irapuato 20 D 3
Irbit 40 O 6
Ireland 31 B 2
Iringa 58 C 2
Iriomote-jima 49 L 6
Iriona 20 G 4
Irish Sea 28 B 3
Irkutsk 41 W 7
Iron Mountain 14 B 1
Ironwood 8 T 9
Irrawaddy 47 H 4
Irrawaddy, Mouths of
　the 47 G 5
Irtysh 40 Q 6
Irún 32 B 3
Irving 16 D 5
Isabel 16 C 2
Isabella, Cordillera 20
　G 5
Isachenka, Ostrov 41
　T 2
Isachsen 10 W 3
Isachsen, Cape 10
　V 3
Ísafjörður 38 A 2
Isa-haya 54 B 4
Isaly 30 A 4
Ise 54 C 4
Isernia 34 C 2
Ise-wan 54 C 4
Isfara 45 M 4
Ishikari-wan 54 C 2
Ishikawa 50 E 7
Ishim 40 P 6
Ishim (River) 40 Q 6
Ishimbay 40 N 7
Ishinomaki 54 D 3
Isil'kul' 40 Q 7
Isiro 58 B 1
Isjichly 44 G 5
İskenderun 35 G 6
İskenderun Körfezi
　35 F 6
Iskitim 41 S 7
Isla de Chiloé 24 D 7
Isla Española 24 C 3
Isla Fernandina 24
　B 2
Isla Grande de
　Tierra del Fuego 24
　E 8
Isla Isabela 24 B 3
Isla Marchena 24
　B 2
Isla Pinta 24 B 2
Isla San Cristóbal 24
　C 3
Isla San Salvador 24
　B 3

Isla Santa Cruz 24
　B 3
Isla Santa María 24
　B 3
Islamabad 45 M 6
Island Lake 10 X 8
Islas Galápagos
　(Ecuador) 24 B 2
Islas Revillagigedo
　(Mexico) 20 B 4
Îsles Tristao 56 B 3
İsparta 44 D 5
Israel 44 D 6
İstanbul 35 C 4
İstanbul Boğazı 35
　C 4
Istra 36 C 3
Isua 8 Bb 6
Itaberaba 24 G 4
Itabuna 24 H 4
Itaguí 22 G 6
Itajaí 24 G 5
Italy 34 C 2
Itanagar 47 G 3
Itaquari 24 H 5
Itarsi 46 D 4
Ithaca 14 D 2
Ithaki 34 E 3
Itoigawa 54 C 3
Ittoqqortoormiit 8
　Gg 4
Iturup, Ostrov 54 E 2
Itzehoe 36 B 2
Iul'tin 43 U 3
Ivakoany 58 D 4
Ivalo 38 L 2
Ivanava 36 F 2
Ivanhoe 60 G 6
Ivano-Frankivs'k 36
　E 3
Ivanovka 44 H 2
Ivanovo 40 K 6
Ivao, Gora 54 E 1
Ivdel' 40 O 5
Ivittuut 8 Bb 6
Ivory Coast 56 C 4
Ivrea 36 B 3
Ivujivik 8 V 6
Iwaki 54 D 3
Iwakuni 54 B 4
Iwamisawa 54 D 2
Iwanai 54 D 2
Iwŏn 54 A 2
Izamal 20 G 3
Izhevsk 40 M 6
Izmayil 35 C 2
İzmir 35 B 5
İzmit 35 C 4
Izuhara 54 A 4
Izu-Shotō 54 C 4
Izvestiy Tsik, Ostrov
　41 S 2
Izyum 44 E 3
Jabalpur 46 D 4
Jackpot 18 D 3

Jacksboro 16 D 5
Jackson (Michigan, U.S.) 14 C 2
Jackson (Mississippi, U.S.) 16 E 5
Jackson (Tennessee, U.S.) 14 B 3
Jackson Head 62 A 3
Jackson Lake 18 D 3
Jacksonville (Florida, U.S.) 14 C 4
Jacksonville (Illinois, U.S.) 16 E 4
Jacksonville (North Carolina, U.S.) 14 D 4
Jacksonville (Texas, U.S.) 16 D 5
Jacksonville Beach 14 C 4
Jäckvik 38 J 2
Jacobabad 46 B 3
Jacona 20 D 4
Jaén (Spain) 33 B 2
Jaffa, Cape 60 F 7
Jaffna 46 E 7
Jagdalpur 46 E 5
Jagdaqi 50 D 2
Jagodina 34 E 2
Jagtiāl 46 D 5
Jaipur 46 D 3
Jaisalmer 46 C 3
Jakarta 52 D 7
Jakobshavn 8 Aa 5
Jalalabad 45 M 6
Jalapa Enríquez 20 E 4
Jalgaon 46 D 4
Jalisco 20 C 3
Jalna 46 D 5
Jālor 46 C 3
Jalostotitlán 20 D 3
Jalpa 20 D 3
Jalpāiguri 47 F 3
Jamaica 22 G 4
Jamaica Channel 22 G 4
Jambi 52 C 6
Jambusar 46 C 4
James Bay 8 U 8
James River (North Dakota, U.S.) 16 D 2
James River (Virginia, U.S.) 14 D 3
Jameson Land 8 Gg 4
Jamestown (New York, U.S.) 14 D 2
Jamestown (North Dakota, U.S.) 16 D 2
Jamiltepec 20 E 4

Jammu 46 C 2
Jammu and Kashmir 45 N 6
Jamnagar 46 C 4
Jampur 46 C 3
Jamshedpur 46 F 4
Jämtland 38 H 3
Jamuna 47 F 3
Janchuan 48 F 5
Janesville 14 B 2
Janos 18 E 5
Jaora 46 D 4
Japan 54 C 4
Japan, Sea of 54 B 2
Jardines de la Reina, Archipiélago de los 22 F 3
Jarkant 48 B 3
Jarosław 36 E 2
Järpen 38 H 3
Jarud Qi 50 D 4
Järvenpää 38 L 3
Jarvis 59 J 4
Jasło 36 E 3
Jasper 10 T 8
Jasper (Alabama, U.S.) 14 B 4
Jasper (Texas, U.S.) 16 E 5
Jasper National Park 10 T 8
Jászberény 36 D 3
Jatni 46 F 4
Jaumave 20 E 3
Jaunpur 46 E 3
Java 52 D 7
Java Sea 52 D 7
Jawa 52 D 7
Jawa, Laut 52 D 7
Jayapura 59 D 4
Jaypur 46 E 5
Jedburgh 28 C 2
Jędrzejów 36 E 2
Jefferson City 16 E 4
Jefferson River 18 D 2
Jefferson, Mount (Nevada, U.S.) 18 C 4
Jega 56 D 3
Jēkabpils 38 L 4
Jelenia Góra 36 D 2
Jelgava 38 K 4
Jemaja 52 D 5
Jena 36 C 2
Jeneponto 53 F 7
Jengish Chokusu 45 O 4
Jenny Lind Island 10 W 5
Jens Munk Island 8 U 5
Jens Munk Ø 8 Cc 6
Jequié 24 H 4

Jerada 56 C 1
Jerez dé García Salinas 20 D 3
Jeréz de la Frontera 33 A 2
Jerome 18 D 3
Jersey 32 B 2
Jessore 47 F 4
Jesup 14 C 4
Jesus Carranza 20 E 4
Jhālāwār 46 D 4
Jhang Sadar 46 C 2
Jhansi 46 D 3
Jharkhand 46 E 4
Jhelum 46 C 2
Jiahe 49 J 5
Jiaji 52 E 2
Jiamusi 50 F 3
Ji'an 49 J 5
Jian 50 E 4
Ji'an (Jilin, China) 54 A 2
Jianchuan 48 F 5
Jianghua 49 J 5
Jiangjin 49 H 5
Jiangle 49 K 5
Jiangling 49 J 4
Jiangmen 49 J 6
Jiangsu 49 K 4
Jiangxi 49 J 5
Jiangyou 49 G 4
Jianli 49 J 5
Jian'ou 49 K 5
Jianping 50 C 4
Jianshui 49 G 6
Jianyang 49 G 4
Jiaohe 50 E 4
Jiaozuo 49 J 3
Jiashan 49 K 4
Jiaxing 49 L 4
Jiayu 49 J 5
Jiayuguan 48 F 3
Jiexiu 49 J 3
Jieyang 49 K 6
Jihlava 36 D 3
Jilin 50 E 4
Jilin (China) 54 A 2
Jilin (State, China) 54 A 2
Jīma 56 G 4
Jiménez 20 D 2
Jimo 49 L 3
Jimsar 48 D 2
Jinan 49 K 3
Jingbian 49 H 3
Jingdezhen 49 K 5
Jinghai 49 K 3
Jinghe 48 C 2
Jingpo Hu 54 A 2
Jingxian 49 H 5
Jingyu 50 E 4
Jingyuan 49 G 5
Jinhua 49 K 5
Jining 49 J 2

Jining (Shandong, China) 49 K 3
Jinja 56 C 1
Jinotepe 20 G 5
Jinsha 49 H 5
Jinsha Jiang 49 G 5
Jinxi 50 D 4
Jinxian 49 L 3
Jinxiang 49 K 3
Jinzhai 49 K 4
Jinzhou 50 D 4
Jishou 49 H 5
Jisr ash-Shughūr 35 G 7
Jiujiang 49 K 5
Jiuquan 48 F 3
Jiutai 50 E 4
Jiwen 50 D 2
Jixi 54 B 1
Jizzax 45 L 4
João Pessoa 24 H 3
Jodhpur 46 C 3
Joensuu 38 L 3
Jōetsu 54 C 3
Johannesburg 58 B 4
John Day 18 C 3
John Day River 18 B 2
John o' Groats 30 C 2
Johnson 16 C 4
Johnson City (Tennessee, U.S.) 14 C 3
Johnson City (Texas, U.S.) 16 D 5
Johnsonburg 14 D 2
Johnsons Crossing 10 Q 6
Johnston Lakes, The 60 B 6
Johnstown 14 D 2
Johor Bharu 52 C 5
Joinville 24 G 5
Jokkmokk 38 J 2
Joliette 8 W 9
Jolo 52 G 4
Jolo (Island) 52 G 4
Jonava 38 K 4
Jonesboro 16 E 4
Jönköping 38 H 4
Jonquière 8 W 9
Jonuta 20 F 4
Joplin 16 E 4
Jordan (U.S.) 18 E 2
Jordan Valley 18 C 3
Jorhāt 47 G 3
Jörn 38 K 2
Jos 56 D 3
Joseph Boanparte Gulf 60 D 2
Joshua Tree National Monument 18 C 5
Jostedalsbreen 38 G 3

Jotunheimen 38 G 3
Juan Aldama 20 D 3
Juan de Fuca, Strait of 18 A 2
Juan de Nova (France) 58 D 3
Juárez, Sierra de 18 C 5
Juàzeiro 24 G 3
Juàzeiro do Norte 24 G 3
Juba 56 G 4
Jubba 58 D 1
Jubbada 58 D 1
Júcar, Rio 33 B 2
Juchitlán de Zaragoza 20 E 4
Jucuapa 20 G 5
Juigalpa 20 G 5
Juiz de Fora 24 G 5
Julianehåb 8 Bb 6
Julimes 20 C 2
Jullundur 46 D 2
Junction 16 D 5
Junction City 16 D 4
Juneau 10 Q 7
Junín 24 E 6
Junlian 49 G 5
Junsele 38 J 3
Jura (France) 36 B 3
Jura (U.K.) 30 B 3
Jura, Sound of 30 A 4
Jurhen Ul Shan 48 E 4
Jūrmala 38 K 4
Jutai 20 G 5
Juticalpa 20 G 5
Juxian 49 K 3
Juzur Qarqannah 34 C 4
Jylland 38 G 4
Jyväskylä 38 L 3
K.J.V. Steenstrup Nordre Bræ 8 Dd 5
Ka Lae 12 E 8
Kabaena 53 G 7
Kabara 59 H 5
Kabinakagami Lake 14 B 1
Kabinda 58 B 2
Kābul 45 L 6
Kabwe 58 B 3
Kachikattsy 42 J 4
Kachug 41 X 7
Kadan Kyun 47 H 6
Kadıköy 35 B 4
Kadınhanı 35 E 5
Kadirli 44 E 5
Kadoka 16 C 3
Kadoma 58 B 3
Kādugli 56 F 3
Kaduna 56 D 3

Kaechnay Darweyhān 45 K 6
Kaédi 56 B 3
Kaes ng 50 E 5
Kaesŏng 54 A 3
Kafiau 53 H 6
Kafue 58 B 3
Kagalaska Island 43 U 6
Kagayan de Sulu Island 52 F 4
Kagoshima 54 B 4
Kahoolawe 12 E 7
Kahramanmaraş 35 G 6
Kahuku Point 12 E 7
Kai Besar 53 J 7
Kai Xian 49 H 4
Kai, Kepulauan 52 J 7
Kaifeng 49 J 4
Kaikoura 62 B 3
Kaili 49 H 5
Kailu 50 D 4
Kainji Reservoir 56 D 3
Kaipara Harbour 62 B 2
Kairouan 56 E 1
Kaiserslautern 36 B 3
Kaitaia 62 B 2
Kaiyuan (Liaoning, China) 50 D 4
Kaiyuan (Yunnan, China) 49 G 6
Kajaani 38 L 3
Kajabbi 60 G 4
Kajakī Dam 45 L 6
Kakana 47 G 7
Kākināda 46 E 5
Kaktovik 10 O 4
Kalaallit Nunaat 8 Aa 4
Kalabahi 52 G 7
Kalabarri National Park 60 A 5
Kalach 44 F 2
Kalachinsk 40 Q 6
Kalach-na-Donu 44 F 3
Kalahari Desert 58 B 4
Kalaheo 12 E 7
Kalakan 42 G 5
Kalamata 34 E 3
Kalamazoo 14 B 2
Kalana 38 K 4
Kalao 53 G 7
Kalaotoa 52 G 7
Kalasin 46 B 3
Kalat 46 B 3
Kalegauk 47 H 5
Kalémié 58 B 2
Kalevala 40 H 4
Kalgoorlie 60 C 6

Kalibo 52 G 3
Kalima 58 B 2
Kalimantan 52 E 6
Kalinin 40 J 6
Kaliningrad 36 E 2
Kalinino 54 A 1
Kalinkavichy 36 F 2
Kalispell 18 D 2
Kalisz 36 D 2
Kalix 38 K 2
Kalixälven 38 K 2
Kalmar 38 J 4
Kalsong 53 G 4
Kaltag 43 Y 4
Kaltan 41 T 7
Kaluga 44 E 2
Kalukalukuang 52
F 7
Kalush 36 E 3
Kalutara 46 E 7
Kalyazin 40 J 6
Kalymnos 34 F 3
Kalymnos (Greece)
35 B 6
Kalymnos (Island,
Greece) 35 B 6
Kama 40 M 6
Kamaishi 54 D 3
Kaman 35 E 5
Kamas 18 D 3
Kambarka 40 M 6
Kamchatka, Polu-
ostrov 43 P 5
Kamchatskiy Polu-
ostrov 43 Q 5
Kamenjak, Rt 34 C 2
Kamenka 44 F 2
Kamen'-na-Obi 41
S 7
Kamensk 41 X 7
Kamenskoye 43 R 4
Kamensk-Shakhtin-
skiy 44 F 3
Kamensk-Ural'skiy 40
O 6
Kamina 58 B 2
Kaminak Lake 8 R 6
Kaminuriak Lake 8
RS 6
Kamkaly 45 M 4
Kamloops 10 S 8
Kamo 35 L 4
Kampala 58 C 1
Kampar 52 C 5
Kampen 36 B 2
Kamphaeng Phet 52
B 2
Kâmpóng Cham 52
D 3
Kâmpóng Chhnăng
52 C 3
Kampuchea 52 C 3
Kämthï 46 D 4
Kam"yanets'-
Podil's'kyy 36 F 3

Kamyshin 44 G 2
Kamyshlov 40 O 6
Kanab 18 D 4
Kanaga Island 43
U 6
Kananga 58 B 2
Kanangra Boyd Na-
tional Park 60 J 6
Kanazawa 54 C 3
Kanchana-buri 52
B 3
Kanchenjunga 48
D 5
Kānchipuram 46 D 6
Kandahār 46 B 2
Kandalaksha 40 H 4
Kandavu Island 59
G 5
Kandhkot 46 B 3
Kandi, Tanjung 52
G 5
Kandukür 46 D 5
Kandy 46 E 7
Kane Basin 8 X 3
Kanem 56 E 3
Kanevskaya 35 H 1
Kangaarsussuaq 8
W 3
Kangar 52 C 4
Kangaroo Island 60
F 7
Kangävar 44 G 6
Kangbao 49 J 2
Kangding 49 G 4
Kangean 52 F 7
Kangerlussuaq 8
Aa 5
Kangersuatsiaq 8
Z 4
Kanggye 50 E 4
Kangikajik 8 Gg 4
Kangiqsualujjuaq 8
X 7
Kangirsuk 8 W 6
Kangnŭng 50 E 5
Kangping 50 D 4
Kangshan 49 L 6
Kangto 47 G 3
Kaniet Islands 59
D 4
Kanin Nos 40 K 4
Kanin Nos, Mys 40
K 4
Kankakee 14 B 2
Kankan 56 C 3
Känker 46 E 4
Kankesanturai 46
E 7
Kanmaw Kyun 47
H 6
Kannapolis 14 C 3
Kano 56 D 3
Kanowit 52 E 5
Kanoya 54 B 4
Kanpur 46 E 3

Kansas 16 C 4
Kansas City 16 E 4
Kansk 41 V 6
Kansŏng 54 A 3
Kantang 52 B 4
Kanton 49 J 6
Kanye 58 B 4
Kaohsiung 49 L 6
Kaolack 56 B 3
Kapfenberg 36 D 3
Kaposvár 36 D 3
Kapuskasing 8 U 9
Kara Sea 40 Q 3
Karabalta 45 M 4
Karabash 40 O 6
Karabük 35 E 4
Karabula 41 V 6
Karacabey 34 F 2
Karachev 36 G 2
Karachi 46 B 4
Karad 46 C 5
Karaginskiy, Ostrov
43 Q 5
Karaikkudi 46 D 6
Karakelong 53 H 5
Karakol 45 N 4
Karakoram Range 45
N 5
Karaman 35 E 6
Karamea Bight 62
B 3
Karapınar 35 E 6
Karaqoyyn Köli 45
L 3
Karasjok 38 L 2
Karasu 44 F 5
Karasu (Turkey) 35
D 4
Karasu-Aras Dağları
35 J 5
Karasuk 41 R 7
Karaul 41 S 3
Karawang 52 D 7
Karbalā' 44 F 6
Karditsa 34 E 3
Karen 47 G 6
Karesuando 38 K 2
Kargasok 41 S 6
Kargopol' 40 J 5
Karigasniemi 38 L 2
Karik Shan 48 E 2
Karimata 52 D 6
Karimata, Selat 52
D 6
Kárimganj 47 G 4
Karkar Island 59 D 4
Karkinits'ka Zatoka
35 E 2
Karlovac 36 D 3
Karlovy Vary 36 C 2
Karlshamn 38 J 4
Karlskoga 38 H 4
Karlskrona 38 J 4
Karlsruhe 36 B 3

Karlstad 38 H 4
Karluk 43 Z 5
Karmøy 38 F 4
Karnätaka 46 D 6
Karnobat 34 F 2
Karossa, Tanjung 52
F 7
Karpathos 34 F 3
Karpinsk 40 N 6
Kars 35 K 4
Kārsava 38 L 4
Karskiye Vorota, Pro-
liv 40 N 3
Karskoye More 40
P 2
Kartaly 45 K 2
Karūr 46 D 6
Karviná 36 D 3
Kārwār 46 C 6
Karymskoye 42 F 6
Kasaï-Occidental 58
B 2
Kasaï-Oriental 58
B 2
Kasaragod 46 D 6
Kasba Lake 10 W 6
Kāshān 44 H 6
Kashi 48 B 3
Kashin 40 J 6
Kashiwazaki 54 C 3
Kashmor 46 B 3
Kasimov 44 F 2
Kasiruta 53 H 6
Kaskinen 38 K 3
Kaskö 38 K 3
Kasongo 58 B 2
Kasos 34 F 3
Kaspiskoye More 44
G 4
Kaspïy Mangy Oy-
paty 44 G 3
Kaspiyskoye More 44
G 3
Kassalä 56 G 3
Kassel 36 B 2
Kastamonu 35 E 4
Kastoria 34 E 2
Kasungan 52 E 6
Katanga (Dem. Rep.
of the Congo) 58
B 2
Katanga (River, Rus-
sia) 41 V 5
Katangli 42 M 6
Katanning 60 B 6
Katav-Ivanovsk 40
N 7
Katchall Island 47
G 7
Katerini 34 E 2
Katherine 60 E 2
Kathmandu 46 F 3
Katihar 46 F 3
Katiu 59 L 5
Katowice 36 D 2

Katsina 56 D 3
Kattaqo'rg'on 45 L 5
Kattegat 38 H 4
Kauai 12 E 7
Kauai Channel 12
E 7
Kaufbeuren 36 C 3
Kaukura 59 L 5
Kaunas 36 E 2
Kaura-Namoda 56
D 3
Kautokeino 38 K 2
Kavaj' 34 D 2
Kavala 34 E 2
Kavali 46 D 6
Kavaratti 46 C 6
Kavïr-e Namak 45
J 6
Kawakawa 62 B 2
Kawalusu 53 H 5
Kawerau 62 C 2
Kawich Peak 18 C 4
Kawio, Kepulauan 53
H 5
Kawm Umbū 56 G 2
Kayak Island 10 O 7
Kayan 47 H 5
Kayangel Islands 53
J 4
Kayenta 18 D 4
Kayes 56 B 3
Kayseri 35 F 5
Kayuagung 52 C 6
Kazachinskoye 41
X 6
Kazach'ye 42 L 2
Kazakhstan 45 J 3
Kazan' 40 L 6
Kazanka 44 D 3
Kazanlük 34 F 2
Kazantip, Mys 44
E 3
Kazbek 44 F 4
Kāzerūn 44 H 7
Kazincbarcika 36
E 3
Kazyatyn 36 F 3
Kazym 40 P 5
Kealakekua Bay 12
E 8
Keams Canyon 18
D 4
Kearney 16 D 3
Kebumen 52 D 7
Kecskemét 36 D 3
Kediri 52 E 7
Keewatin 16 E 2
Kefallonia 34 D 3
Kefamenanu 52 G 7
Keffi 56 D 4
Keflav'k 38 A 3
Kegul'ta 44 F 3
Keitele 38 L 3
Keith (Scotland) 30
C 3

Kekaha 12 E 7
Kelaa Kebira 34 C 3
Kelang 52 C 5
Kelkit Cayı 35 G 4
Kellett, Cape 10 R 4
Kellogg 18 C 2
Kelloselkä 38 L 2
Kélo 56 E 4
Kelowna 18 C 2
Kelsey Bay 10 R 8
Kelso 18 B 2
Keluang 52 C 5
Kem' 40 H 5
Kemerovo 41 T 6
Kemi 38 K 2
Kemijärvi 38 L 2
Kemijoki 38 L 2
Kempendyayi 42 G 4
Kempt, Lac 14 E 1
Kempten 36 C 3
Kenai Fjords
National Park 43
Aa 5
Kenal 10 M 6
Kendal 28 C 2
Kendallville 14 B 2
Kendari 53 G 6
Kendawangan 52   6
Kenema 56 B 4
Keng Tung 47 H 4
Kenitra 56 C 1
Kenmare (Ireland) 31
B 3
Kenmare (U.S.) 16
C 2
Kennedy Channel 8
X 2
Kennedy Peak 47
G 4
Kennedy Range Na-
tional Park 60 A 4
Kennett 16 E 4
Kennewick 18 C 2
Keno Hill 10 P 6
Kenora 16 E 2
Kentaü 45 L 4
Kentucky 14 B 3
Kentucky Lake 14
B 3
Kentucky River 14
C 3
Kenya 58 C 1
Keokuk 16 E 3
Keoladao National
Park 46 D 3
Kep Kai 59 C 4
Kepi i Gjuhëzës 34
D 2
Kepulanan Aru 59
C 4
Kepulanan Tanimbar
59 C 4
Kerala 46 D 6
Kerama-rettō 50 E 7
Kerch 44 E 3

Kerempe Burnu 35 E 3
Keren 56 G 3
Kerinci, Gunung 52 C 6
Keriya Shankou 48 C 3
Kerki 45 L 5
Kerkyra 34 D 3
Kerkyra (Island) 34 D 3
Kermadec Islands 59 H 6
Kermān 45 J 6
Kermānshāh 44 G 6
Kermit 16 C 5
Kerrville 16 D 5
Kerry Head 31 A 2
Kertamulta 52 D 6
Kerteh 52 C 5
Kerulen 50 B 3
Keşan 35 B 4
Kesen'numa 54 D 3
Keshan 50 E 3
Keskin 35 E 5
Ket' 41 S 6
Ketapang 52 D 6
Ketchikan 10 Q 7
Ketchum Mountain 16 C 5
Ket-Kap, Khrebet 42 K 5
Kettle River Range 18 C 2
Kewanee 14 B 2
Keweenaw Peninsula 14 B 1
Key Largo 14 C 5
Key West 14 C 6
Keyano 8 W 8
Kezhma 41 W 6
Khabarovsk 54 C 1
Khābūr, Nahr al 35 J 7
Khadki 46 C 5
Khairpur 46 B 3
Khalīj Surt (Gulf of Sidra) 56 E 1
Khal'mer-Yu 40 O 4
Khalturin 40 L 6
Khambhaliya 46 B 4
Khambhat 46 C 4
Khambhāt, Gulf of 46 C 4
Khammam 46 E 5
Khampa 42 H 4
Khamseh 44 G 5
Khanabad 45 L 5
Khandwa 46 D 4
Khandyga 42 L 4
Khanka, Ozero 50 F 4
Khānpur 46 C 3
Khantayskoye Vodokhranilishche 41 T 4

Khantayskoye, Ozero 41 T 4
Khanty-Mansiysk 40 P 5
Khapcheranga 42 F 7
Kharagpur 46 F 4
Kharal 41 V 7
Kharaulakhskiy Khrebet 42 J 2
Kharkiv 44 E 3
Kharmanli 35 A 4
Kharovsk 40 K 6
Khasav'yurt 44 G 4
Khashuri 35 K 4
Khaskovo 34 F 2
Khatanga 41 W 3
Khatangskiy Zaliv 41 X 3
Khatyrka 43 T 4
Khenchela 34 B 3
Kherson 44 D 3
Kheta 41 V 3
Khimki 40 J 6
Khmel'nyts'kyy 36 F 3
Khok Kloi 52 B 4
Kholm 40 H 6
Kholmogory 40 K 5
Kholmsk 50 H 3
Khomeynīshahr 44 H 6
Khon Khaen 47 J 5
Khor 50 F 3
Khorugh 45 M 5
Khowst 45 L 6
Khoyinki 36 F 2
Khromtaū 45 J 2
Khrustal'nyy 54 C 2
Khujand 45 L 4
Khulna 47 F 4
Khust 36 E 3
Khuzdār 46 B 3
Khvalynsk 44 G 2
Khvoy 44 F 5
Khyber Pass 45 M 6
Kiatassuaq 8 Z 4
Kichiga 43 Q 5
Kicking Horse Pass 10 T 8
Kidnappers, Cape 62 C 2
Kiel 36 C 2
Kielce 36 E 2
Kiev 36 G 2
Kigali 58 B 2
Kigilyakh 42 L 2
Kihnu Saar 38 K 4
Kii-suidō 54 B 4
Kikaishima 50 F 7
Kikinda 36 E 3
Kikwit 58 A 2
Kilauea 12 E 7
Kilchu 50 E 4
Kildare 31 C 2

Kil'din 40 J 3
Kili 59 F 3
Kilian Island 10 V 4
Kilindini 58 C 2
Kilis 35 G 6
Kiliya 36 F 3
Kilkee 31 B 2
Kilkenny 31 C 2
Kilkis 34 E 2
Killarney 31 B 2
Killeen 16 D 5
Killiniq Island 8 Y 6
Kilmarnock 28 B 2
Kil'mez' 40 M 6
Kil'mez' (River) 40 M 6
Kilpisjärvi 38 K 2
Kilttān Island 46 C 6
Kimball 16 D 3
Kimberley 18 C 2
Kimberley 58 B 4
Kimberley Plateau 60 D 3
Kimch'aek 54 A 2
Kimch'ŏn 54 A 3
Kimito Kemiö 38 K 3
Kimmirut 8 X 6
Kimovsk 44 E 2
Kimry 40 J 6
Kinchega National Park 60 G 6
Kinder 16 E 5
Kindu 58 B 2
Kineshma 40 K 6
King Christian Island 10 W 3
King City 18 B 4
King George Islands 8 V 7
King Island 60 G 7
King Leopold and Astrid Coast 63 R 5
King Leopold Ranges 60 C 3
King William Island 8 R 5
Kingisepp 38 L 4
Kingman 18 D 4
King's Lynn 28 E 3
Kingsport 14 C 3
Kingston (Australia) 60 F 7
Kingston (Canada) 14 D 2
Kingston (Jamaica) 22 G 4
Kingston upon Hull 28 D 3
Kingstown 22 K 5
Kingsville 20 E 2
Kinnaird Head 30 D 3
Kinnegad 31 C 2
Kinsale 31 B 3

Kinshasa 58 A 2
Kinston 14 D 3
Kintyre 28 B 2
Kipawa, Lac 14 D 1
Kipnuk 43 X 5
Kipti 36 G 2
Kirandul 46 E 5
Kirensk 41 X 6
Kiribati 59 J 4
Kiritimati 59 K 3
Kiriwina Island 59 E 4
Kirkcaldy 30 C 3
Kirkenes 38 L 2
Kirkland Lake 14 C 1
Kırklareli 35 B 4
Kirksville 16 E 3
Kirkük 44 F 5
Kirkwall 30 C 2
Kirkwood (U.S.) 16 E 4
Kirov (Russia) 36 G 2
Kirov (Russia) 40 L 6
Kirova, Ostrov 41 U 2
Kirovabad 44 G 4
Kirovo-Chepetsk 40 M 6
Kirovohrad 44 D 3
Kīrovskiy 45 N 4
Kirovskiy (Russia) 42 J 6
Kirovskiy (Russia) 43 P 6
Kirs 45 M 6
Kirsanov 44 F 2
Kirşehir 35 F 5
Kirthar National Park 46 D 3
Kirthar Range 46 B 3
Kiruna 38 K 2
Kisangani 58 B 1
Kisar 53 H 7
Kisaran 52 B 5
Kishangarh Bās 46 C 3
Kishoreganj 47 F 3
Kiska Island 43 T 6
Kiskunhalas 36 D 3
Kislovodsk 44 F 4
Kismaayo 58 D 2
Kisumu 58 C 2
Kita Kyūshū 54 B 4
Kitakyūshū 50 F 6
Kitale 58 C 1
Kitami 54 D 2
Kitami-sanchi 54 D 2
Kitchener 14 C 2
Kitigan Zibi 14 D 1
Kitimat 10 R 8

Kitsissut 8 W 3
Kittanning 14 D 2
Kitwe 58 B 3
Kivalina 10 K 5
Kiviöli 38 L 4
Kizel 40 N 6
Kizema 40 K 5
Kızılcahamam 35 E 4
Kızıltepe (Turkey) 35 J 6
Kizlyar 44 G 4
Kjøpsvik 38 J 2
Kladno 36 C 2
Klagenfurt 36 C 3
Klamath Falls 18 B 3
Klamath Mountains 18 B 3
Klamath River 18 B 3
Klarälven 38 H 3
Klerksdorp 58 B 4
Klimpfjäll 38 H 2
Klin 40 J 6
Klintsy 36 G 2
Klodzko 36 D 2
Klondike Plateau 10 O 6
Kluczbork 36 D 2
Klyuchevskaya Sopka 43 Q 5
Knezha 34 E 2
Knjaževac 34 E 2
Knoxville (Iowa, U.S.) 16 E 3
Knoxville (Tennessee, U.S.) 14 C 3
Knud Rasmussen Land 8 Z 2
Ko Khrot Kra 52 B 3
Ko Kut 52 C 3
Ko Phangan 52 C 4
Ko Phuket 52 B 4
Ko Samui 52 C 4
Ko Tao 52 B 3
Koba 52 D 6
Kōbe 54 C 4
København 38 H 4
Koblenz 36 B 2
Kobroor 52 J 7
Kobryn 36 E 2
Kocaeli 35 C 4
Koch Island 8 V 5
Kochenevo 41 S 7
Kochi 54 B 4
Koçhisar Ovası 35 E 5
Kodar, Khrebet 42 G 5
Kodiak 43 Z 5
Kodiak Island 43 Z 5
Koechechum 41 V 5

Koforidua 56 C 4
Kōfu 54 C 3
Kogon 45 K 5
Kohat 45 M 6
Kohīma 47 G 3
Koh-i-Mazar 45 L 6
Kohtla-Järve 38 L 4
Kohunlich 20 G 4
Koindu 56 B 4
Kokkola 38 K 3
Kokomo 14 B 2
Kökpekti 45 O 3
Kokshetaū 45 L 2
Kola 40 H 4
Kola Peninsula 40 J 4
Kolaka 52 G 6
Kolar 46 D 6
Kolari 38 K 2
Kolding 38 G 4
Kolguyev, Ostrov 40 M 4
Kolhapur 46 C 5
Kolhoa 47 G 7
Kolka 38 K 4
Kolkata 46 F 4
Kolky 36 F 2
Kollegal 46 D 6
Köln 36 B 2
Kołobrzeg 36 D 2
Kolombangara Island 59 E 4
Kolomna 40 J 6
Kolomyya 36 F 3
Kolpashevo 41 S 6
Kolpino 40 H 6
Kol'skiy Poluostrov 40 J 4
Kolwezi 58 B 3
Kolyma 43 O 3
Kolymskaya 43 P 3
Kolymskaya Nizmennost' 43 O 3
Kolymskiy, Khrebet 43 P 4
Komandorskiye Ostrova 43 R 5
Komárno 36 D 3
Komatsu 54 C 3
Komfane 53 J 7
Komló 36 D 3
Komotini 34 F 2
Komsomolets, Ostrov 41 U 1
Komsomol'sk-na-Amure 42 L 6
Komsomol'skoy Pravdy, Ostrova 41 X 2
Komusan 54 A 2
Kon Tum 47 K 6
Konakovo 40 J 6
Konarak 46 F 5
Kondagaon 46 E 5
Kondopoga 40 H 5

Kong Christian X
    Land 8 Ee 4
Kong Frederik IX
    Land 8 Aa 5
Kong Frederik VIII's
    Land 8 Ff 3
Kong Frederik VI-
    Kyst 8 Cc 6
Kong Wilhelm Land 8
    Gg 3
Konginskiye Gory 43
    P 3
Kongsvinger 38 H 3
Kongur Shan 48 B 3
Koni, Poluostrov 43
    O 5
Konin 36 D 2
Konitsa 34 E 2
Konosha 40 K 5
Konotop 36 G 2
Konstanz 36 B 3
Konya 35 E 6
Konya Ovası 35 E 5
Koolivoo, Lake 60 F 4
Kootenay National
    Park 10 T 8
Kópavogur 38 A 3
Kopeysk 40 O 6
Köping 38 J 4
Koppang 38 H 3
Kopychyntsi 36 F 3
Korāput 46 E 5
Korba 46 E 4
Korçë 34 F 2
Korčula 34 D 2
Kordestan 44 G 5
Korea Strait 50 E 6
Korenovsk 44 E 3
Korf 43 R 4
Korhogo 56 C 4
Korinthos 34 E 3
Kōriyama 54 D 3
Korkodon 43 O 4
Korkuteli 35 D 6
Korla 48 D 2
Kornat 34 D 2
Koro 59 G 5
Koro Sea 59 G 5
Köroğlu Dağları 35
    D 4
Koronadal 53 G 4
Koror 59 C 3
Korosten' 36 F 2
Korostyshiv 36 F 2
Korsakov 50 H 3
Koryakskaya Sopka
    43 P 6
Koryakskiy Khrebet
    43 R 4
Koryazhma 40 L 5
Kos 34 F 3
Kos (Greece) 35 B 6
Kos (Island, Greece)
    35 B 6
Kos ng 50 E 5

Kosava 36 F 2
Kosciusko 14 B 4
Kosiče 36 E 3
Koslan 40 L 5
Kosŏng 54 A 3
Kosovo 34 E 2
Kosovska Mitrovica
    34 E 2
Kostinó 41 T 4
Kostopil' 36 F 2
Kostroma 40 K 6
Kostyantynivka 44
    E 3
Koszalin 36 D 2
Kot Addu 46 C 2
Kota 46 D 3
Kota Bharu 52 C 4
Kota Kinabalu 52 F 4
Kotaagung 52 C 7
Kotabumi 52 C 6
Kotchevo 40 M 6
Kotel'nich 40 L 6
Kotel'nikovo 44 F 3
Kotel'nyy, Ostrov 42
    L 1
Kotikovo 54 D 1
Kotka 38 L 3
Kotlas 40 L 5
Kotlik 43 X 4
Kotovs'k 36 F 3
Kotri 46 B 3
Kottayam 46 D 7
Kotuy 41 W 3
Kotzebue 10 K 5
Kotzebue Sound 10
    K 5
Koukdjuak River 8
    W 5
Koumbi Saleh 56
    C 3
Koutiala 56 C 3
Kouvola 38 L 3
Kovel' 36 E 2
Kovrov 40 K 6
Kowloon 49 J 6
Koyuk 43 X 4
Koyukuk 43 Y 4
Kozan 35 F 6
Kozani 34 E 2
Kozel'sk 44 E 2
Kozlu 44 D 4
Kra, Isthmus of 47
    H 6
Kragerø 38 G 4
Kragujevac 34 E 2
Kraków 36 D 2
Kraljevo 34 E 2
Kramators'k 44 E 3
Kramfors 38 J 3
Kranj 36 C 3
Kraśnik 36 E 2
Krasnoarmeysk 44
    G 2
Krasnoarmeyskiy 44
    F 3

Krasnodar 44 E 3
Krasnogorsk 50 H 3
Krasnohrad 44 E 3
Krasnokamensk 42
    G 6
Krasnoperekops'k 35
    E 2
Krasnosel'kup 41
    S 4
Krasnoslobodsk 44
    F 3
Krasnotur'insk 40
    O 6
Krasnoural'sk 40 O 6
Krasnovishersk 40
    N 5
Krasnoyarsk 41 U 6
Krasnoyarskoye
    Vodokhranilishche
    41 U 7
Krasnozatonskiy 40
    M 5
Krasnoznamenskoe
    45 L 2
Krasnystaw 36 E 2
Krasnyy Kut 44 G 2
Krasnyy Luch 44 E 3
Krasnyy Yar (Russia)
    44 F 2
Krasyliv 36 F 3
Kraulshavn 8 Z 4
Kremenchuk 44 D 3
Kremenets' 36 F 2
Kremmling 18 E 3
Kretinga 38 K 4
Krishna, Mouths of
    the 46 E 5
Kristiansand 38 G 4
Kristianstad 38 H 4
Kristiansund 38 G 3
Kriti 34 E 3
Kriti (Crete) 35 B 7
Kronotskiy Poluostrov
    43 Q 6
Kronprins Christian
    Land 8 Gg 2
Kronprinsesse
    Märtha Kyst 63
    O 5
Kronshtadt 38 L 4
Kroonstad 58 B 4
Kropotkin 44 F 3
Kropotkin (Russia) 35
    J 2
Krosno 36 E 3
Kruglikovo 54 C 1
Krui 52 C 7
Krung Thep 47 J 6
Kruševac 34 E 2
Kruzof Island 10 P 7
Krychaw 36 G 2
Krym 35 E 2
Krymsk 44 E 4
Krytiko Pelagos 34
    F 3

Krytiko Pelagos (Sea
    of Crete) 35 B 6
Kuala Dungun 52
    C 5
Kuala Kangsar 52
    C 5
Kuala Kerai 52 C 4
Kuala Lipis 52 C 5
Kuala Lumpur 52
    C 5
Kuala Selangor 52
    C 5
Kuala Terengganu 52
    C 4
Kualakapuas 52 E 6
Kualamanjual 52 E 6
Kuandian 50 D 4
Kuantan 52 C 5
Kuban' 44 F 3
Kuchaman 46 C 3
Kuching 52 E 5
Kuçov' 34 D 2
Kudat 53 F 4
Kudus 52 E 7
Kudymkar 40 M 6
Kugaaruk 8 T 5
Kugluktuk 10 T 5
Kuhn Ø 8 Gg 4
Kūhpāyeh 45 J 6
Kuiu Island 10 Q 7
Kuji 54 D 2
Kukan 54 B 1
Kukës 34 E 2
Kula, Kryazh 42 K 3
Kūlagīno 44 H 3
Kuldīga 38 K 4
Kul'dur 54 B 1
Kulgera 60 E 5
Kulob 45 L 5
Kultuk 41 W 7
Kulu (Turkey) 35 E 5
Kulunda 45 N 2
Kulundinskoye,
    Ozero 45 N 2
Kulusuk 8 Dd 5
Kumagaya 54 C 3
Kumai 52 E 6
Kumamoto 54 B 4
Kumanovo 34 E 2
Kumara 50 E 2
Kumasi 56 C 4
Kumbakonam 46
    D 6
Kume-jima 50 E 7
Kumertau 40 N 7
Kumluca 35 D 6
Kumukahi, Cape 12
    F 8
Kūmüx 48 D 2
Kundāpura 46 C 6
Kunduz 45 L 5
Kungälv 38 H 4
Kunlun Shan 48 C 3
Kunming 49 G 5
Kunsan 50 E 5

Kununurra 60 D 3
Kuopio 38 L 3
Kuoqiang 48 D 3
Kupang 53 G 8
Kupino 41 R 7
Kupreanof Island 10
    Q 7
Kup"yans'k 44 E 3
Kuqa 48 C 2
Kurashiki 54 B 4
Kŭrdzhali 34 F 2
Kure 54 B 4
Küre Dağları 35 F 4
Kuressaare 38 K 4
Kurgan 40 P 6
Kuria 59 G 3
Kuril'sk 54 E 1
Kuril'skiye Ostrova 50
    J 3
Kurkure Bazhi, Gora
    41 T 7
Kurnool 46 D 5
Kuroiso 54 D 3
Kursk 44 E 2
Kurskaya 44 F 4
Kurskiy Zaliv 38 K 4
Kurtalan 35 J 6
Kurtamysh 40 O 7
Kurume 54 B 4
Kurunegala 46 E 7
Kushiro 54 D 2
Kuskokwim Bay 43
    X 5
Kuskokwim Moun-
    tains 10 L 6
Kuskokwim River 43
    X 4
Kussharo-Ko 54 D 2
Küstī 56 G 3
Kütahya 35 C 5
K'ut'aisi 44 F 4
Kutan 44 G 4
Kutch Peninsula 46
    B 4
Kutch, Gulf of 46 B 4
Kutno 36 D 2
Kutubdia 8 X 7
Kuummiut 8 Dd 5
Kuusamo 38 L 2
Kuwait 44 G 7
Kuya 40 K 4
Kuybyshev 44 H 2
Kuybysheva, Mys 41
    U 1
Kuybyshevo 54 E 1
Kuybyshevskoye
    Vodokhranilishche
    44 G 2
Kuytun, Gora 41
    T 8
Kuznetsk 44 G 2
Kuznetsova 50 G 3
Kuznetsovo 54 C 1
Kvaløy 38 J 2
Kvikkjokk 38 J 2

Kwajalein 59 F 3
Kwangju 50 E 5
Kwanmo-Bong 50
    E 4
Kwekwe 58 B 3
Kwidzyń 36 D 2
Kwoka, Gunung 52
    J 6
Ky ngju 50 E 5
Kyaikto 47 H 5
Kyancutta 60 F 6
Kyaukse 47 H 4
Kyiv 36 G 2
Kyklades 34 E 3
Kyle of Lochalsh 30
    B 3
Kymi 34 E 3
Kyŏngju 54 A 3
Kyōto 54 C 3
Kyparissiakos
    Kolpos 34 E 3
Kyrgyzstan 45 M 4
Kyshchevskya 35
    H 1
Kyshtym 40 O 6
Kythira 34 E 3
Kythnos 34 E 3
Kyūshū 54 B 4
Kyustendil 34 E 2
Kyusyur 42 J 2
Kyzyl 41 U 7
Kyzyl-Dzhar 45 L 3
Kyzylkum 45 K 4
La Boquilla,
    Presa de 20 C 2
La Cadena 20 D 2
La Carolina 33 B 2
La Ceiba (Honduras)
    20 G 4
La Chorrera 22 G 6
La Colorada 20 B 2
La Crosse 16 E 3
La Cruz (Mexico) 20
    C 3
La Dorada 22 H 6
La Encantada, Cerro
    de 18 C 5
La Encantada,
    Sierra de 20 D 2
La Fuente de San
    Esteban 33 A 1
La Gatineau, Parc de
    14 D 1
La Giganta, Sierra de
    20 B 2
La Gran Sabana 22
    K 6
La Grande 18 C 2
La Grande Riviére 8
    W 8
La Grange 14 B 4
La Habana 20 H 3
La Huacan 20 D 4
La Junta (Mexico) 20
    C 2

La Junta (U.S.) 16 C 4
La Juventud Isla de 20 H 3
La Libertad 20 G 5
La Loche 10 V 7
La Malbaie 8 W 9
La Mancha 33 B 2
La Marque 20 E 2
La Marsa 56 E 1
La Mauricie National Park 8 W 9
La Oroya 24 D 4
La Paz 24 E 4
La Paz (Mexico) 20 B 3
La Paz, Bahía 20 B 3
La Pesca 20 E 3
La Piedad 20 D 3
La Plata 24 F 6
La Rioja (Spain) 32 B 3
La Rochelle 32 B 2
La Roche-sur-Yon 32 B 2
La Roda 33 B 2
La Romana 22 J 4
La Ronge 10 V 7
La Salina 18 D 5
La Salle 14 B 2
La Serena 24 D 5
La Serena (Spain) 33 A 2
La Spezia 34 B 2
La Tasajera, Sierra de 20 C 2
La Tuque 8 W 9
La Union (El Salvador) 20 G 5
La Unión (Mexico) 20 D 4
La Vega 22 H 4
La Venta 20 F 4
La Ventura 20 D 3
La Zarca 20 D 2
Labé 56 B 3
Labelle 14 E 1
Labengke 53 G 6
Labinsk 35 J 2
Labis 52 C 5
Labrador 8 Cc 8
Labrador City 8 X 8
Labrador Sea 8 Z 7
Labrador, Coast of 8 Y 7
Labuhan 52 D 7
Labuhanbadjo 53 G 7
Labuhanbilik 52 C 5
Labytnangi 40 P 4
Lac Mai-Ndombe 58 A 2
Lac Moero 58 B 2

Laccadive Islands 46 C 6
Lacepede Bay 60 F 7
Lackawanna 14 D 2
Lac-Mégantic 14 E 1
Ladakh Range 45 N 6
Ladnūn 46 C 3
Ladozhskoye Ozero 40 H 5
Ladysmith 58 B 4
Lae (Marshall Islands) 59 F 3
Lae (Papua New Guinea) 59 D 4
Lafayette (Indiana, U.S.) 14 B 2
Lafayette (Louisiana, U.S.) 16 E 5
Laghouat 56 D 1
Lago do Erepecu 24 F 3
Lago Titicaca 24 D 4
Lagoa dos Patos 24 F 6
Lagoa Mirim 24 F 6
Lagos 56 D 4
Lagos (Portugal) 33 A 2
Lagos de Moreno 20 D 3
Laha 50 D 3
Lahad Datu 52 F 4
Lahat 52 C 6
Lāhījān 44 G 5
Lahore 46 C 2
Lahr 36 B 3
Lahti 38 L 3
Lai 56 E 4
Lais 52 C 6
Laiyang 49 L 3
Laizhou Wan 49 K 3
Lajes 24 F 5
Lake Bangweulu 58 B 3
Lake Chad 56 E 3
Lake Charles 16 E 5
Lake City (Florida, U.S.) 14 C 4
Lake City (South Carolina, U.S.) 14 D 4
Lake Clark National Park 10 M 6
Lake District 28 C 2
Lake Edward 58 B 2
Lake Eyasi 58 C 2
Lake Harbour 8 X 6
Lake Havasu City 18 D 5
Lake Jackson 20 E 2
Lake Kariba 58 B 3
Lake Kyoga 58 C 1
Lake Malawi 58 C 3
Lake Mead National

Recreational Area 18 D 4
Lake Minchumina 10 M 6
Lake Nasser 56 G 2
Lake Placid 14 E 2
Lake River 8 U 8
Lake Rukwa 58 C 2
Lake Tanganyika 58 B 2
Lake Turkana 58 C 1
Lake Victoria 58 C 2
Lake Volta 56 C 4
Lake Worth 14 C 5
Lakeland 14 C 5
Lakeview 18 B 3
Lakewood 18 E 4
Lakselv 38 L 1
Lakshadweep 46 C 6
Lalitpur 46 D 4
Lama, Ozero 41 T 4
Lamar 16 C 4
Lambaréné 56 E 5
Lambert Land 8 Gg 3
Lambert, Cape 59 E 4
Lamesa 16 C 5
Lamezia Terme 34 D 3
Lamia 34 E 3
Lamington National Park 60 J 5
Lampang 47 H 5
Lampasas 16 D 5
Lampazos de Naranjo 20 D 2
Lamphun 47 H 5
Lanai 12 E 7
Lanbi Kyun 47 H 6
Lancang Jiang 48 G 6
Lancaster (U.K.) 28 C 2
Lancaster (U.S.) 18 C 5
Lancaster Sound 8 T 4
Lancun 49 L 3
Landegode 38 H 2
Lander 18 E 3
Landes 32 B 3
Landfall Island 47 G 6
Lands End (Canada) 10 S 3
Land's End (U.K.) 28 B 4
Landshut 36 C 3
Lang Son 49 H 6
Langdon 16 D 2
Langjökull 38 A 3
Langkawi 52 B 4
Langlade 14 D 1

Langon 32 B 3
Langøya 38 H 2
Langres 36 B 3
Langsa 52 B 5
Languedoc 32 C 3
Langzhong 49 H 4
Länkäran 44 G 5
Lansing 14 C 2
Lanxi 49 K 5
Lanzhou 49 G 3
Lao Cai 47 J 4
Laoag 53 G 2
Laoang 53 H 3
Laoye Ling 54 B 2
Lapine 18 B 3
Lappeenranta 38 L 3
Lappland 38 J 2
Lâpseki 34 F 2
Laptevykh, More 42 H 1
Lapua 38 K 3
L'Aquila 34 C 2
Lär Koh 45 K 6
Larache 56 C 1
Laramie 18 E 3
Laramie Mountains 18 E 3
Laramie River 18 E 3
Larantuka 53 G 7
Laredo (U.S.) 20 E 2
Larisa 34 E 3
Larkana 46 B 3
Larnaka 44 D 6
Larne 28 B 2
Larned 16 D 4
Lar'yak 41 S 5
Las Ballenas, Canal de 20 B 2
Las Cruces 18 E 5
Las Mesas, Cerro de 20 E 4
Las Minas, Cerro 20 G 5
Las Minas, Sierra de 20 F 5
Las Palmas 56 B 2
Las Palomas 18 E 5
Las Tres Vírgenes,Volcán 20 B 2
Las Tunas, Sierra de 18 E 5
Las Vegas (Nevada, U.S.) 18 C 4
Las Vegas (New Mexico, U.S.) 18 E 4
Lasan 52 F 5
Lāsh-e Joveyn 45 K 6
Lashkar Gāh 45 K 6
Latakia 44 E 5

Latehar 46 E 4
Latina 34 C 2
Lātūr 46 D 5
Latvia 38 L 4
Lau Group 59 H 5
Launceston 60 H 8
Laurel (Mississippi, U.S.) 14 B 4
Laurel (Montana, U.S.) 18 E 2
Laurentian Scarp 8 V 9
Laurentides, Plateau 8 W 9
Lausanne 36 B 3
Laut (Indonesia) 52 D 5
Laut (Indonesia) 53 F 6
Lautoka 59 G 5
Laval (Canada) 8 W 9
Laval (France) 32 B 2
Laverton 60 C 5
Lavka Integralsoyuza 43 R 3
Lavrentiya 43 V 3
Lawrence 16 D 4
Lawrenceburg 14 B 3
Lawton 16 D 5
Layton 18 D 3
Lazarevac 34 E 2
Lazo (Russia) 54 B 2
Le Chaux de-Fonds 36 B 3
Le Creusot 32 C 2
Le Havre 32 C 2
Le Mans 32 C 2
Le Mars 16 D 3
Le Mont-Saint-Michel 32 B 2
Le Puy-en-Velay 32 C 2
Leadville 18 E 4
Leavenworth 16 D 4
Lebanon 44 D 6
Lebanon (U.S.) 16 E 4
Lebedyan' 44 E 2
Lebedyn 36 G 2
Lębork 36 D 2
Lebrija 33 A 2
Lecce 34 D 2
Lecco 36 B 3
Leduc 10 U 8
Leeds 28 D 3
Leeuwarden 36 B 2
Leeuwin, Cape 60 B 6
Leeward Islands (Caribbean Sea) 22 K 4

Leeward Islands (Polynesia) 59 K 5
Lefkada 34 E 3
Lefroy, Lake 60 C 6
Lefkosia 44 D 5
Leganés 32 B 3
Legaspi 53 G 3
Legnica 36 D 2
Lehi 18 D 3
Leiah 46 C 2
Leicester 28 D 3
Leinster 31 C 2
Leipzig 36 C 2
Leira 38 G 3
Leiria 33 A 2
Leiyang 49 J 5
Leizhou Wan 49 J 6
Leka 38 H 2
Lemesos 44 D 6
Lemieux Islands 8 Y 6
Lemmon 16 C 2
Lemtybozh 40 N 5
Len Malaäs 53 J 6
Lena 42 J 2
Lenger 45 L 4
Lenin Atyndagy Choku 45 M 5
Leninogorsk 44 H 2
Leninogorsk 45 O 2
Leninsk-Kuznetskiy 41 T 7
Leninskoe 44 G 3
Leninskoye 54 B 1
Leno Angarskoye Plato 41 W 7
Lensk 41 Y 5
Lentini 34 C 3
Leoben 36 D 3
Leominster 28 C 3
León (Mexico) 20 D 3
León (Nicaragua) 22 E 5
León (Spain) 33 A 1
Leonora 60 C 5
Leopold M'clintock, Cape 10 T 3
Lepar 52 D 6
Leping 49 K 5
Lerwick 30 D 1
Leshan 49 G 5
Leskovac 34 E 2
Lesogorsk 50 H 3
Lesogorskiy 38 L 3
Lesosibirsk 41 U 6
Lesotho 58 B 4
Lesozavodsk 50 F 3
Lesser Antilles (Caribbean Sea) 22 K 4
Lesser Antilles (Netherlands) 22 J 5

Lesser Slave Lake 10 T 7
Lesser Sunda Islands 52 G 7
Lesvos 34 F 3
Leszno 36 D 2
Lethbridge 18 D 2
Leti, Kepulauan 53 H 7
Letnyaya Zolotitsa 40 J 5
Letsok-aw Kyun 47 H 6
Letterkenny 31 C 1
Leuser, Gunong 52 B 5
Levanger 38 H 3
Lévêque, Cape 60 C 3
Levice 36 D 3
Levin 62 C 3
Lévis 8 W 9
Levokumskoye 44 F 4
Lewis, Isle of 30 A 2
Lewiston (Maine, U.S.) 14 E 2
Lewiston (Montana, U.S.) 18 C 2
Lewistown (Montana, U.S.) 18 E 2
Lewistown (Pennsylvania, U.S.) 14 D 2
Lexington (Kentucky, U.S.) 14 C 3
Lexington (North Carolina, U.S.) 14 C 3
Leyte 53 H 3
L'gov 44 E 2
Lhasa 48 E 5
Lhaze 48 D 5
Lhokseumawe 52 B 4
l'Hospitalet de Llobregat 32 C 3
Lhünzê 48 E 5
Liancheng 49 K 5
Lianga 52 H 4
Lianhua Shan 49 J 5
Lianjiang 49 J 6
Lianxian 49 J 6
Lianyungang 49 K 4
Liaodong 49 L 3
Liaodong Wan 49 L 2
Liaoning 50 D 4
Liaoyang 50 D 4
Liaoyuan 50 E 4
Liard River 10 R 7
Liard River (River) 10 Q 6
Libby 18 C 2
Liberal 16 C 4
Liberec 36 D 2
Liberia 56 B 4

Libobo, Tanjung 52 H 6
Libreville 56 D 4
Libro Point 52 F 3
Libya 56 E 2
Libyan Desert 56 F 2
Licata 34 C 3
Lichinga 58 C 3
Lichuan (Hubei, China) 49 H 4
Lichuan (Jiangxi, China) 49 K 5
Lida 36 F 2
Lidzbark Warmiński 36 E 2
Liechtenstein 36 B 3
Liège 36 B 2
Liepāja 38 K 4
Lifou 59 F 6
Ligurian Sea 34 B 2
Lihue 50 E 4
Lijiang 48 G 5
Likasi 58 B 3
Likiep 59 F 2
Lillehammer 38 H 3
Lillestrøm 38 H 4
Lillooet 10 S 8
Lilongwe 58 C 3
Lima 24 D 4
Lima (Idaho, U.S.) 18 D 3
Lima (Ohio, U.S.) 14 C 2
Limassol 44 D 6
Limburg 36 B 2
Limerick 31 B 2
Limnos 34 E 3
Limoges 32 C 2
Limón 22 F 6
Limon 16 C 4
Limoux 32 C 3
Limpopo 58 C 4
Linares (Mexico) 20 E 3
Linares (Spain) 33 B 2
Lincoln (Illinois, U.S.) 14 B 2
Lincoln (Nebraska, U.S.) 16 D 3
Lincoln (U.K.) 28 D 3
Lincoln City 18 B 3
Lincolnshire Wolds 28 D 3
Line Islands 59 K 4
Linfen 49 J 3
Lingayen 52 G 2
Lingayen Gulf 52 G 2
Lingen 36 B 2
Lingga 52 C 6
Lingga, Kepulauan 52 D 6
Lingling 49 J 5
Lingshan 49 H 6

Lingshui 52 E 2
Linhai 49 L 5
Linhe 49 H 2
Linköping 38 J 4
Linkou 50 F 3
Lintao 49 G 3
Linton 16 C 2
Linxi 50 C 4
Linxia 49 G 3
Linyi 49 K 3
Linz 36 C 3
Lion, Golfe du 32 C 3
Lipa 52 G 3
Lipetsk 44 E 2
Lipova 36 E 3
Lipu 49 J 6
Lisboa 33 A 2
Lisbon 33 A 2
Lisburne, Cape 10 J 5
Lishu 50 D 4
Lishui 49 K 5
Liskeard 28 B 4
Liski 44 E 2
Lismore 60 J 5
Litang 49 H 6
Lithgow 60 J 6
Lithuania 38 K 4
Litoměřice 36 C 2
Litovko 50 G 3
Little Abaco Island 14 D 5
Little Andaman 47 G 6
Little Cayman 22 F 4
Little Colorado River 18 D 4
Little Desert National Park 60 G 7
Little Falls 16 E 2
Little Inagua Island 22 H 3
Little Minch 30 A 3
Little Missouri River 16 C 2
Little Nicobar 47 G 7
Little Rock 16 E 5
Little Sitkin Island 43 T 6
Littlefield 16 C 5
Littleton 18 E 4
Liuhe 54 A 2
Liuyuan 48 F 2
Liuzhou 49 H 6
Livengood 10 N 5
Liverpool (U.K.) 28 C 3
Liverpool Land 8 Gg 4
Liverpool Range 60 H 6
Livingston (U.S.) 18 D 2
Livingstone 58 B 3

Livny 44 E 2
Livorno 34 C 2
Lixian 49 J 5
Lizard Point 28 B 5
Ljubljana 36 C 3
Ljungby 38 H 4
Ljusdal 38 J 3
Llandovery 28 C 3
Llandudno 28 C 3
Llanelli 28 B 4
Llano River 16 C 5
Llanos 22 H 7
Lleida 32 C 3
Lleyn Peninsula 28 B 3
Lobito 58 A 3
Lobva 40 O 6
Lochboisdale 30 A 3
Lochinver 30 B 2
Lodeynoye Pole 40 H 5
Łódź 36 D 2
Lofoten 38 H 2
Logan 18 D 3
Logan, Mount 10 O 6
Logansport 14 B 2
Logashkino 42 O 2
Logroño 32 B 3
Loikaw 47 H 5
Loire 32 B 2
Lokan tekojärvi 38 L 2
Lokoja 56 D 4
Lokosovo 40 Q 5
Loks Land 8 Y 6
Lolland 36 C 2
Lom (Bulgaria) 34 E 2
Lom (Norway) 38 G 3
Loma Bonita 20 E 4
Lomblen 53 G 7
Lombok 53 F 7
Lomé 56 D 4
Lomond, Loch 30 B 3
Lompoc 18 B 5
Łomża 36 E 2
London (Canada) 14 C 2
London (U.K.) 28 D 4
Londonderry 31 C 1
Londonderry, Cape 60 D 2
Londrina 24 F 5
Lone Pine 18 C 4
Long Bay 14 D 4
Long Beach (California, U.S.) 18 C 5
Long Beach (Washington, U.S.) 18 B 2
Long Island (Bahamas) 22 H 3

Long Island (Canada) 8 V 8
Long Island (Papua New Guinea) 59 D 4
Long Kuyen 47 K 6
Long Lake 14 B 1
Longford (Ireland) 31 C 2
Longiram 52 F 6
Longjiang 50 D 3
Longlac 8 T 9
Longmont 18 E 3
Longnan 49 J 6
Longquan 49 K 5
Longreach 60 G 4
Longs Peak 18 E 3
Longview (Oregon, U.S.) 18 B 2
Longview (Texas, U.S.) 16 E 5
Longxi 49 G 3
Longyan 49 K 5
Longzhen 54 A 1
Longzhou 49 H 6
Lookout, Cape 14 D 4
Loop Head 31 A 2
Lop Buri 47 J 6
Lop Nor 48 E 2
Lop Nur 48 E 2
Lopatka 43 P 6
Lopatka, Mys 43 P 3
Loralai 46 B 2
Lorca 33 B 2
Lordsburg 18 E 5
Loreto (Baja California Sur, Mexico) 20 B 2
Loreto (Zacatecas, Mexico) 20 D 3
Lorient 32 B 2
Lorn, Firth of 30 A 3
Lorraine 36 B 3
Los Alamitos, Sierra de 20 D 2
Los Alamos 18 E 4
Los Angeles 18 C 5
Los Cuchumatanes, Sierra de 20 F 4
Los Huicholes, Sierra de 20 D 3
Los Mochis 20 C 2
Los Palacios 20 H 3
Los Reyes de Salgado 20 D 4
Los Teques 22 J 5
Los Testigos 22 K 5
Lošinj 34 C 2
Lost Trial Pass 18 D 2
Loubomo 58 A 2
Louga 56 B 3
Lougheed Island 10 V 3

Loughrea 31 B 2
Louisa 14 C 3
Louisiade Archipelago 60 J 2
Louisiana 16 E 5
Louisville 14 B 3
Loum 56 D 4
Louny 36 C 2
Loup River 16 C 3
Lourdes 32 B 3
Loushan 49 J 4
Louth (U.K.) 28 D 3
Lovech 34 E 2
Loveland 18 E 3
Lovell 18 E 3
Lovelock 18 C 3
Lovington 16 C 5
Lovozero 40 J 4
Low, Cape 8 T 6
Lowell 14 E 2
Lower California 20 B 2
Lower Hutt 62 B 3
Lower Lough Erne 31 C 1
Lower Red Lake 16 D 2
Lowestoft 28 E 3
Łowicz 36 D 2
Loyauté, Îles 59 F 6
Lualaba 58 B 2
Lu'an 49 K 4
Luanda 58 A 2
Luang Prabang 47 J 5
Luanshya 58 B 3
Lubang Islands 53 F 3
Lubango 58 A 3
Lubao 58 B 2
Lubbock 16 C 5
Lübeck 36 C 2
Lubin 36 D 2
Lublin 36 E 2
Lubny 36 G 2
Lubuklinggau 52 C 6
Lubumbashi 58 B 3
Lucas, Lake 60 D 4
Luce Bay 28 B 2
Lucena (Philippines) 52 G 3
Lucena (Spain) 33 B 2
Lučenec 36 D 3
Lucera 34 D 2
Lucero 18 E 5
Lucknow 46 E 3
Luçon 32 B 2
Ludhiana 46 D 2
Ludington 14 B 2
Ludwigshafen 36 B 3
Lüeyang 49 H 4
Lufeng 49 K 6
Lugano 36 B 3
Lugo 33 A 1

Lugoj 36 E 3
Luhans'k 44 E 3
Luimneach 31 B 2
Lukeville 18 D 5
Lukoyanov 40 K 6
Luleå 38 K 2
Luleälven 38 K 2
Lultin 43 U 3
Lumajangdong Co 48 C 4
Lumberton 14 D 4
Lumding 47 G 3
Lumsden 62 A 4
Lund 38 H 4
Lundu 52 D 5
Lundy 28 B 4
Lüneburg 36 C 2
Luninyets 36 F 2
Luobei 54 B 1
Luoding 49 J 6
Luohe 49 J 4
Luong Nam Tha 47 J 4
Luoxiao Shan 49 J 5
Luoyang 49 J 4
Luoyuan 49 K 5
Lupeni 36 E 3
Luqu 49 G 4
Lurgan 31 C 1
Lusaka 58 B 3
Lüshun 49 L 3
Lusk 16 C 3
Luton 28 D 4
Łutselk'e 10 U 6
Luts'k 36 F 2
Luvua 58 B 2
Luwuk 52 G 6
Luxembourg 36 B 3
Luxi (Yunnan, China) 48 F 6
Luza 40 L 5
Luzern 36 B 3
Luzhou 49 H 5
Luzon 52 G 2
Luzon Strait 49 L 7
L'viv 36 E 3
Lycksele 38 J 3
Lyell Land 8 Ff 4
Lyepyel' 36 F 2
Lyme Bay 28 C 4
Lynchburg 14 D 3
Lyngdal 38 G 4
Lynx Lake 10 V 6
Lyon 32 C 2
Lys'va 40 N 6
Lyudinovo 36 G 2
Ma'anshan 49 K 4
Maarianhamina 38 J 3
Maas 36 B 2
Maastricht 36 B 2
Mablethorpe 28 E 3
Mac. Robertson Land 63 Q 5

Macadam Plains 60 B 5
Macalpine Lake 10 W 5
Macapá 24 F 2
Macarena, Serranía de la 22 H 7
Macau 49 J 6
Macauley Island 59 H 7
Macclesfield 28 C 3
Macdonald, Lake 60 D 4
Macdonnell Ranges 60 E 4
Macedonia 34 E 2
Maceió 24 H 3
Macerata 34 C 2
Machala 24 C 3
Machong 49 K 4
Machilipatnam 46 E 5
Machiques 22 H 5
Ma-chuan Ho 48 D 5
Mackay 60 H 4
Mackay, Lake 60 D 4
Mackenzie King Island 10 U 3
Mackenzie Mountains 10 Q 6
Mackenzie River 10 Q 5
Mackinaw City 14 C 1
Macmillan Pass 10 R 6
Mâcon 32 C 2
Macon (Georgia, U.S.) 14 C 4
Macon (Mississippi, U.S.) 14 B 4
Macroom 31 B 2
Madagascar 58 D 3
Madang 59 D 4
Madau Island 59 E 4
Madawaska Highlands 8 V 9
Madeira (Portugal) 56 B 1
Madeleine, Îles de la 8 Y 9
Maden 35 H 5
Madera 18 B 4
Madhya Pradesh 46 D 4
Madison (Indiana, U.S.) 14 B 3
Madison (Wisconsin, U.S.) 14 B 2
Madison River 18 D 2
Madisonville (Kentucky, U.S.) 14 B 3
Madisonville (Texas, U.S.) 16 D 5

Madium 52 E 7
Madras (India) 46 E 6
Madras (Oregon, U.S.) 18 B 3
Madre de Chiapas, Sierra 20 F 4
Madre del Sur, Sierra 20 D 4
Madre Occidental, Sierra 20 C 2
Madre Oriental, Sierra 20 D 2
Madre, Laguna (Mexico) 20 E 3
Madre, Laguna (U.S.) 20 E 2
Madre, Sierra 53 G 2
Madrid 32 B 3
Madura 52 E 7
Madurai 46 D 7
Mae Sot 47 H 5
Maebashi 54 C 3
Maevatanana 58 D 3
Maéwo 59 F 5
Magadan 43 O 5
Magdagachi 42 J 6
Magdeburg 36 C 2
Magdelena, Isla (Mexico) 20 B 3
Magelang 52 E 7
Magerøya 38 L 1
Magnitogorsk 45 J 2
Magnolia 16 E 5
Magwe 47 H 4
Maha Sarakham 47 J 5
Mahābād 44 G 5
Mahabalipuram 46 E 6
Mahābhārat Lek 46 E 3
Mahādeo Hills 46 D 4
Mahajanga 58 D 3
Mahallāt 44 H 6
Mahanoro 58 D 3
Maharashtra 46 C 4
Mahasamund 46 E 4
Mahbunagar 46 D 5
Mahé 58 E 2
Mahesana 46 C 4
Mahetia 59 L 5
Mahia Peninsula 62 C 2
Mahilyow 36 G 2
Mahón 33 C 2
Mahuva 46 C 4
Maiana 59 G 3
Maicao 22 H 5
Maidstone 28 E 4
Maiduguri 56 E 3
Maikala Range 46 E 4

Maimana 45 K 5
Main Barrier Range 60 G 6
Main Channel 14 C 1
Madras (Oregon,
Maine 8 X 9
Maine, Gulf of 14 F 2
Mainland (Orkney, U.K.) 30 C 2
Mainland (Shetland, U.K.) 30 D 1
Maintirano 58 D 3
Mainz 36 B 2
Maio 56 A 3
Maitland 60 J 6
Maizuru 54 C 3
Majene 52 F 6
Majuro 59 G 3
Makalu 46 F 3
Makarov 50 H 3
Makar'yev 40 K 6
Makassar 52 F 7
Makassar, Selat 52 F 7
Makat 44 H 3
Makedonia 34 E 2
Makemo 59 L 5
Makeni 56 B 4
Makgadikgadi Pan 58 B 4
Makhachkala 44 G 4
Makian 52 H 5
Makin 59 G 3
Makīnsk 45 M 2
Makiyivka 44 E 3
Makkovik 8 Z 7
Makó 36 E 3
Makrana 46 C 3
Maksimovka 54 C 1
Makurazuki 54 B 4
Makurdi 56 D 4
Mala, Punta 22 G 6
Malabar Coast 46 C 6
Malabo 56 D 4
Malacca, Strait of 52 B 5
Malad City 18 D 3
Maladzyechna 36 F 2
Málaga 33 B 2
Malaita 59 F 4
Malakāl 56 G 4
Malakula 59 F 5
Malang 52 E 7
Malanje 58 A 2
Mälaren 38 J 4
Malaspina Glacier 10 O 6
Malatya 35 H 5
Malawi 58 C 3
Malay Peninsula 52 B 4
Malaya 52 C 5

Malaya Kuril'skaya Gr'ada 54 D 2
Malaya Vishera 40 H 6
Malaybalay 52 H 4
Malaysia 52 D 4
Malbork 36 D 2
Malden 59 K 4
Maldives 46 C 7
Malé 46 C 8
Malea Atoll 46 C 8
Malegaon 46 C 4
Malheur Lake 18 C 3
Mali 56 C 3
Malin Head 31 C 1
Malinovoye Ozero 45 N 2
Mallaig 30 B 3
Mallawī 56 G 2
Mallery Lake 8 R 6
Mallorca 33 C 2
Mallow 31 B 2
Malmö 38 H 4
Maloelap 59 G 3
Malolos 53 G 3
Maloshuyka 40 J 5
Måløy 38 G 3
Malpelo, Isla del 22 F 7
Malta 34 C 3
Malta (U.S.) 18 E 2
Malta, Canale di 34 C 3
Maluku 53 H 6
Maluku, Laut 52 G 6
Malung 38 H 3
Malvan 46 C 5
Malyn 36 F 2
Malyy Lyakhovskiy, Ostrov 42 M 2
Malyy Taymyr, Ostrov 41 X 2
Malyy Yenisey 41 V 7
Mama 42 F 5
Mamburao 52 G 3
Mamonta, Poluostrov 41 R 3
Mamuju 52 F 6
Man 56 C 4
Man, Isle of 28 B 2
Manado 53 G 5
Managua 22 E 5
Manakara 58 D 4
Mananjary 58 D 4
Manapouri 62 A 4
Manas 48 D 2
Manas Hu 48 D 1
Manāslu 46 E 3
Manaus 24 F 3
Manavgat 35 D 6
Manawan 14 E 1
Manawoka 52 J 6
Manchester 28 C 3
Mandalay 47 H 4

Mandan 16 C 2
Mandioli 52 H 6
Mandla 46 E 4
Mandsaur 46 D 4
Mandvi 46 B 4
Mandya 46 D 6
Manfredonia 34 D 2
Mangaia 59 K 6
Mangalia 34 F 2
Mangalore 46 C 6
Mangareya 59 M 6
Mange 48 C 4
Mangkalihat, Tanjung 52 F 5
Manglares, Cabo 22 G 7
Mangnai 48 E 3
Mangoky 58 D 4
Mangole 52 H 6
Mangshi 48 F 6
Manhattan 16 D 4
Manicouagan 8 X 8
Manicouagan, Réservoir 8 X 8
Manihi 59 L 5
Manihiki 59 J 5
Maniitsoq 8 Aa 5
Manila 52 G 3
Manipur 47 G 4
Manisa 35 B 5
Manistique 14 B 1
Manitoba 10 X 8
Manitoba, Lake 10 X 8
Manitou Springs 16 C 4
Manitoulin Island 8 U 9
Manitowoc 14 B 2
Manizales 22 G 6
Manja 58 D 4
Manjimup 60 B 6
Mankato 16 E 3
Manley Hot Springs 10 M 5
Manmad 46 C 4
Manna 52 C 6
Mannheim 36 B 3
Manning, Cape 10 S 3
Manokwari 52 J 6
Manono 58 B 2
Manp'ojin 50 E 4
Manra 59 H 4
Manresa 32 C 3
Mansel Island 8 U 6
Mansfield (U.K.) 28 D 3
Mansfield (U.S.) 14 C 2
Manta 24 C 3
Manteo 14 D 3
Mantova 36 C 3

Manua Islands 59
   J 5
Manuae 59 K 5
Manuangi 59 L 5
Manuel Benaivdes 20
   D 2
Manui 52 G 6
Manukau 62 B 2
Manus Island 59 D 4
Manzanares 33 B 2
Manzanillo (Cuba) 22
   G 3
Manzanillo (Mexico)
   20 D 4
Manzhouli 50 C 3
Mao 22 H 4
Maoke, Pegunungan
   53 K 6
Maoming 49 J 6
Mapaga 52 F 5
Mapimi, Bolsón de 20
   D 2
Maple Creek 18 E 2
Maputo 58 C 4
Maqat 44 H 3
Mar del Plata 24 F 6
Mar Ionio 34 D 3
Marabá 24 G 3
Maracaibo 22 H 5
Maracaibo, Lago de
   22 H 6
Maracay 22 J 5
Maradi 56 D 3
Marägheh 44 G 5
Maramasike Ulawa
   59 F 4
Maränd 44 G 5
Marathon (Canada)
   14 B 1
Marathon (U.S.) 16
   C 5
Marawi 52 G 4
Marbella 33 B 2
Marble Canyon 18
   D 4
Marburg 36 B 2
Marcala 20 G 5
Mardän 45 M 6
Mardin 35 J 6
Maré 59 F 6
Mareeba 60 H 3
Marfa 16 C 5
Margai Caka 48 D 4
Margarita, Isla de 22
   K 5
Margate 28 E 4
Margie 10 U 7
Margüilon 45 M 4
Maria (French
   Polynesia) 59 K 6
Maria (French Poly-
   nesia) 59 M 6
Maria Island 60 F 2
Maria Theresa Reef
   59 K 7

Maria van Diemen,
   Cape 62 B 1
Mariana Islands 59
   D 2
Marianao 20 H 3
Mariar 52 J 6
Marias River 18
   D 2
Marías, Islas 20 C 3
Mariato, Punta 22
   F 6
Maribor 36 D 3
Marie Byrd Land 63
   W 4
Marie-Galante 22
   K 4
Mariehamn 38 J 3
Marietta 14 C 4
Mariinsk 41 T 6
Marijampolė 36 E 2
Mar"ina Horka 36
   F 2
Marinduque 52 G 3
Marinette 8 T 9
Maringá 24 F 5
Marion (Illinois, U.S.)
   14 B 3
Marion (Indiana,
   U.S.) 14 B 2
Marion (Iowa, U.S.)
   16 E 3
Marion (Ohio, U.S.)
   14 C 2
Marion Reef 60 J 3
Marion, Lake 14 C 4
Mariupol' 44 E 3
Marka 56 H 4
Markam 48 F 5
Märkäpur 46 D 5
Markha 42 G 4
Markovo 41 T 5
Marlin 16 D 5
Marmara Denizi 35
   C 4
Marmara, Sea of 34
   F 2
Marmorilik 8 Aa 4
Maroantsetra 58 D 3
Marokau 59 L 5
Maros 52 F 6
Marotiri 59 L 6
Marovoay 58 D 3
Marquises, Archipel
   des 59 M 4
Marrakech 56 C 1
Marree 60 F 5
Marsala 34 C 3
Marseille 34 B 2
Marsh Harbour 14 D
   5
Marsh Island 20 F 2
Marshall (Minnesota,
   U.S.) 16 D 3
Marshall (Texas,
   U.S.) 16 E 5

Marshall Islands 59
   F 2
Marshalltown 16 E 3
Marshfield 16 E 3
Martapura (Indone-
   sia) 52 C 6
Martapura (Indone-
   sia) 52 E 6
Martigues 34 B 2
Martin 36 D 3
Martin (U.S.) 16 C 3
Martinez de la Torre
   20 E 3
Martinique 22 K 5
Martinsburg 14 D 3
Martinsville 14 D 3
Marton 62 C 3
Martre, Lac la 10 T 6
Marutea 59 L 5
Marv Dasht 44 H 7
Mary 45 K 5
Mary River 8 V 4
Maryborough 60 J 5
Maryland 14 D 3
Marysville (California,
   U.S.) 18 B 4
Marysville (Kansas,
   U.S.) 16 D 4
Maryville 16 E 3
Masaka 58 C 2
Masalembu Besar 52
   E 7
Masan 50 E 5
Masaya 22 E 5
Masbate 52 G 3
Masbate (Island) 52
   G 3
Mascarene Islands
   58 E 4
Mascota 20 D 3
Masela 52 H 7
Maseru 58 B 4
Mashhad 45 J 5
Masjed Soleymän 44
   G 6
Maslyanskiy 40 Q 6
Mason City 16 E 3
Massachusetts 14
   E 2
Massafra 34 D 2
Massawa 56 G 3
Massena 14 E 2
Massif Central 32
   C 2
Massif du Makay 58
   D 4
Massif du
   Tsaratanana 58
   D 3
Masterton 62 C 3
Mastung 46 B 3
Masvingo 58 C 4
Mata 52 G 7
Matachewan 8 U 9
Matachic 20 C 2

Matadi 58 A 2
Matador 16 C 5
Matagalpa 20 G 5
Matagami 8 V 9
Matagorda Island 20
   E 2
Mataiva 59 L 5
Matale 46 E 7
Matamoros (Mexico)
   20 D 2
Matancita 20 B 2
Matane 8 X 9
Matanzas 22 F 3
Matara 46 E 7
Mataram 52 F 7
Mataró 32 C 3
Matata 62 C 2
Mätätïla Dam 46 D 3
Matehuala 20 D 3
Matera 34 D 2
Matheson 14 C 1
Mathura 46 D 3
Mati 52 H 4
Mätla 46 F 4
Matochkin Shar 40
   N 3
Matosinhos 33 A 1
Matsudo 54 D 3
Matsue 54 B 3
Matsumoto 54 C 3
Matsuyama 50 F 6
Matsuzaki 54 C 4
Matterhorn (U.S.) 18
   C 3
Mattoon 14 B 3
Matua, Ostrov 50
   K 3
Maturín 22 K 6
Matyl'ka 41 T 5
Maug Islands 59 D 2
Mauganj 46 E 4
Maui 12 E 7
Mauke 59 K 6
Maumere 52 G 7
Mauna Kea 59 K 2
Maunoir, Lac 10 S 5
Maupihaa 59 K 5
Maupin 18 B 2
Maupiti 59 K 5
Maurice, Lake 60
   E 5
Mauritania 56 B 3
Mauritius 58 E 3
Mauritius (Island) 58
   E 4
Mawlaik 47 G 4
Maxcanú 20 G 3
May Pen 22 G 4
Maya 52 D 6
Maya Mountains 20
   G 4
Mayaguana Island 22
   H 3
Mayagüez 22 J 4
Mayämey 45 J 5

Mayapán 20 G 3
Maykop 44 E 4
Maymyo 47 H 4
Mayn 43 S 4
Mayo 10 P 6
Mayotte (France) 58
   D 3
Mayqayyng 45 N 2
Mayraira Point 52
   G 2
Maysville 14 D 4
Mayya 42 K 4
Mazatenango 20 F 5
Mazatlán 20 C 3
Mazyr 36 F 2
Mazär-e Sharïf 45
   L 5
Mbabane 58 C 4
Mbandaka 58 A 1
Mbanza-Ngungu 58
   A 2
Mbeya 58 C 2
Mbuji-Mayi 58 B 2
McAlester 16 D 5
McAllen 20 E 2
McCamey 16 C 5
McCarthy 10 O 6
McComb 16 E 5
McCook 16 C 3
McDame 10 R 7
McDermitt 18 C 3
McGill 18 D 4
McGrath 43 Y 4
McKean Island 59
   H 4
McKeesport 14 D 2
McKenzie Island 16
   E 1
McKinney 16 D 5
McLarty Hills 60 C 3
McLeod Lake 10 S 8
M'Clintock Channel
   10 W 4
McPherson 16 D 4
McPherson Range 60
   J 5
Mead, Lake 18 D 4
Meadow Lake 10
   V 8
Meander River 10
   T 7
Meath 31 C 2
Meaux 32 C 2
Medak 46 D 5
Medan 52 B 5
Medell'n 22 G 6
Medelpad 38 J 3
Medford 18 B 3
Medgidia 34 F 2
Medical Lake 18 C 2
Medicine Bow 18 E
   3
Medicine Hat 10 U 8
Medina del Campo
   33 B 1

Mediterranean Sea
   33 C 2
Mednogorsk 45 J 2
Mednyy, Ostrov 43
   R 6
Medvezhiy Yar 41
   U 3
Medvezh'ya, Gora 54
   C 1
Medvezh'yegorsk 40
   H 5
Meekatharra 60 B 5
Meeker 18 E 3
Meerut 46 D 3
Mega 52 J 6
Meghälaya 47 G 3
Megra 40 K 5
Mehanom, Mys 44
   E 4
Mehar 46 B 3
Meighen Island 8
   R 3
Meiktila 47 H 4
Meiningen 36 C 2
Meishan 49 G 4
Meißen 36 C 2
Meixian 49 K 6
Mek'elë 56 G 3
Meknès 56 C 1
Mekong (Cambodia)
   47 K 6
Mekong (China) 48
   F 4
Mekong, Mouths of
   the 47 K 7
Melaka 52 C 5
Melanesia 59 E 4
Melappälaiyam 46
   D 7
Melbourne 60 G 7
Melcho Múzquiz 20
   D 2
Melchor Ocampo 20
   D 4
Melenki 40 K 6
Meleuz 40 K 5
Melitopol' 35 F 1
Melrose (U.S.) 18
   D 2
Melun (France) 32
   C 2
Melun (Myanmar) 47
   G 4
Melville 10 W 8
Melville Island
   (Australia) 60 E 2
Melville Island
   (Canada) 10 U 3
Melville Land 8 Ee 2
Melville, Cape 60
   G 2
Melville, Lake 8 Z 8
Mêmar Co 48 C 4
Memboro 52 F 7
Memmingen 36 C 3

Memphis 16 E 4
Mena (U.S.) 16 E 5
Mendoza 24 E 6
Menemen 35 B 5
Mengcheng 49 K 4
Mengzi 49 G 6
Menkere 42 H 3
Menominee 8 T 9
Menorca 33 C 2
Menshikova 50 G 2
Mentawai, Kepulauan 52 B 6
Mentekab 52 C 5
Mentese 35 C 6
Menzelinsk 40 M 6
Menzies 60 C 5
Meoqui 20 C 2
Meppen 36 B 2
Merano 36 C 3
Merced 18 B 4
Mercedes 24 E 6
Mercy, Cape 8 Y 6
Merefa 44 E 3
Mergui 47 H 6
Mergui Archipelago 47 H 6
Mérida (Mexico) 20 G 3
Mérida (Spain) 33 A 2
Mérida (Venezuela) 22 H 6
Mérida, Cordillera de 22 H 6
Meridian 14 B 4
Mérignac 32 B 3
Merke 45 M 4
Merkenes 38 J 2
Merredin 60 B 6
Merrill 14 B 1
Mersin 35 F 6
Mersing 52 C 5
Merthyr Tydfil 28 C 4
Mértola 33 A 2
Mertuyy 44 H 3
Merville Bugt 63 L 2
Merzifon 44 E 4
Mesabi Range 16 E 2
Mescalero 18 E 5
Meschede 36 B 2
Meseta de Chiapas 20 F 4
Mesolongi 34 E 3
Mesopotamia 44 F 5
Mesquite 16 D 5
Messerian 45 H 5
Messina 34 D 3
Messoyakna 41 R 4
Mestre 36 C 3
Metairie 16 E 5
Metapan 20 G 5
Meteghen 14 F 2
Metro 52 D 7
Metz 36 B 3

Meuse 36 B 3
Mexicali 18 C 5
Mexican Hat 18 E 4
Mexican Highlands 20 D 3
Mexico (Country) 20 D 3
México (Mexico) 20 E 4
México (State, Mexico) 20 E 4
Mexico (U.S.) 16 E 4
Mexico, Gulf of 20 F 3
Meyanobab 53 J 7
Meynopil'gyno 43 T 4
Mezcalapa, Río 20 F 4
Mezen' 40 K 4
Mezenskaya Guba 40 K 4
Mezhdurechensk 41 T 7
Mezhdurechenskiy 40 P 6
Mgachi 42 M 6
Mhow 46 D 4
Miami (Florida, U.S.) 14 C 5
Miami (Oklahoma, U.S.) 16 E 4
Miami Beach 14 C 5
Miandrivazo 58 D 3
Mianduhe 50 D 3
Mīāneh 44 G 5
Mianwali 46 C 2
Mianyang 49 G 4
Mianzhu 49 G 4
Michigan 14 B 2
Michigan City 14 B 2
Michigan, Lake 14 B 2
Michipicoten Bay 14 B 1
Michipicoten Island 14 B 1
Michoacán 20 D 4
Michurinsk 44 F 2
Micronesia, Federated States of 59 D 3
Midai 52 D 5
Middle Andaman 47 G 6
Middlesboro 14 C 3
Middlesbrough 28 D 2
Middletown 14 C 3
Midland (Michigan, U.S.) 14 C 2
Midland (Texas, U.S.) 16 C 5
Midleton 31 B 3
Midsayap 52 G 4
Midwest 18 E 3

Midyat 35 J 6
Mielec 36 E 2
Mieres 33 A 1
Mikhaylovka (Russia) 44 F 2
Mikkeli 38 L 3
Mikun' 40 M 5
Mikuni-sanmyaku 54 C 3
Miladummadulu Atoll 46 C 7
Milano 36 B 3
Milas 35 B 6
Milazzo 34 D 3
Mildura 60 G 6
Mile 49 G 6
Miles City 18 E 2
Milford 18 D 4
Milford Haven 28 B 4
Milford Sound 62 A 3
Mili 59 G 3
Milk River 18 E 2
Mill Island 8 V 6
Millau 32 C 3
Mille Lacs Lake 16 E 2
Milledgeville 14 C 4
Millennium Island 59 K 4
Millerovo 44 F 3
Millington 14 B 3
Millwood Lake 16 E 5
Milne Land 8 Ff 4
Milos 34 E 3
Milton Keynes 28 D 4
Milwaukee 14 B 2
Milwaukie 18 B 2
Milyatino 36 G 2
Min Shan 49 G 4
Min Xian 49 G 4
Mīnā' 'abd Allāh 44 G 7
Minahasa Peninsula 52 F 5
Minamata 54 B 4
Minatitlán 20 F 4
Minbu 47 G 4
Mindanao 53 G 4
Mindelo 56 A 3
Minden 36 B 2
Minden (U.S.) 16 E 5
Mindon 47 G 5
Mindoro 53 G 3
Mineral Wells 16 D 5
Mineral'nyye Vody 35 K 2
Minerva Reefs North 59 H 6
Minerva Reefs South 59 H 6

Mingäcevir 44 G 4
Mingan 8 Y 8
Mingäora 45 M 6
Mingbuloq 45 K 4
Ming-Kush 45 M 4
Mingshui 50 E 3
Minigwal, Lake 60 C 5
Miniocoy 46 C 7
Minneapolis (Kansas, U.S.) 16 D 4
Minneapolis (Minnesota, U.S.) 16 E 3
Minnedosa 16 D 1
Minnesota 16 E 2
Minnesota River 16 D 3
Minot 16 C 2
Minqing 49 K 5
Minsin 47 H 3
Minsk 36 F 2
Minto 10 P 6
Minusinsk 41 U 7
Miraj 46 C 5
Miranda de Ebro 32 B 3
Miri 52 E 5
Mirnoye 41 T 5
Mirnyy 41 Y 5
Mirpur Khas 46 B 3
Mirzapur 46 E 3
Mishan 50 F 3
Misima Island 60 J 2
Miskitos, Cayos 22 F 5
Miskolc 36 E 3
Misoöl 52 H 6
Mişrātah 56 E 1
Mississippi 16 E 5
Mississippi Delta 20 G 2
Mississippi River 16 E 4
Missoula 18 D 2
Missouri 16 E 4
Missouri River 16 E 4
Mistissini 8 W 8
Mistissini, Lac 8 W 8
Mitchell (Australia) 60 H 5
Mitchell (U.S.) 16 D 3
Mitchelstown 31 B 2
Mithapur 46 B 4
Mithcell 61 G 3
Mithi 46 B 4
Mitiaro 59 K 5
Mitla 20 E 4
Mito 54 D 3
Miyake-jima 54 C 4
Miyako 54 D 3
Miyakonojö 50 F 6
Miyāni 46 B 4

Miyazaki 50 F 6
Mizen Head 31 B 3
Mizil 36 F 3
Mizoram 47 G 4
Mizusawa 54 D 3
Mjölby 38 J 4
Mjösa 38 H 3
Mladá Boleslav 36 C 2
Mljet 34 D 2
Mo i Rana 38 H 2
Moab 18 E 4
Moberly 16 E 4
Mobile 14 B 4
Mobile Bay 20 G 2
Mobridge 16 C 2
Moctezuma (Mexico) 20 C 2
Moctezuma (Mexico) 20 D 3
Modena 34 C 2
Modesto 18 B 4
Modowi 53 J 6
Moe 60 H 7
Moen-jo-dar 46 B 3
Mogdy 42 K 6
Mogocha 42 G 6
Mogoytuy 42 F 6
Moguqi 50 D 3
Mohammedia 56 C 1
Mohyliv Podil'skyy 36 F 3
Mojave 18 C 4
Mojave Desert 18 C 5
Mokokcghüng 47 G 3
Mokp'o 54 A 4
Molaly 45 N 3
Moldava 36 F 3
Molde 38 G 3
Moldova 36 F 3
Molfetta 34 D 2
Moline 16 E 3
Mollendo 24 D 4
Molokai 12 E 7
Molucca Sea 52 G 6
Moluccas 52 H 6
Mombasa 58 C 2
Mombetsu 54 D 2
Momskiy Khrebet 42 M 3
Mona, Canal de la 22 J 4
Monaco 34 B 2
Monadhliath Mountains 30 B 3
Monahans 16 C 5
Monarch Mountain 10 R 8
Monastir 34 C 3
Monchegorsk 40 H 4
Mönchen-Gladbach 36 B 2
Monclova 20 D 2

Moncton 8 Y 9
Mondego, Cabo 33 A 1
Mondy 41 W 7
Money Island 52 E 2
Monfalcone 36 C 3
Monforte de Lemos 32 B 3
Monforte de Lemps 33 A 1
Mong Cai 47 K 4
Mongers Lake 60 B 5
Monghyr 46 F 3
Mongolia 41 V 8
Monjes, Islas los 22 H 5
Monkey River 20 G 4
Mono Lake 18 C 4
Monreal del Campo 32 B 3
Monroe (Louisiana, U.S.) 16 E 5
Monroe (Michigan, U.S.) 14 C 2
Monroe (North Carolina, U.S.) 14 C 4
Monrovia 56 B 4
Montague Island 10 N 7
Montague, Isla 18 D 5
Montana (Bulgaria) 34 E 2
Montana (U.S.) 18 D 2
Montauban 32 C 3
Montceau-les-Mines 32 C 2
Mont-de-Marsan 32 B 3
Monte Albán 20 E 4
Monte Cristi 22 H 4
Montego Bay 22 G 4
Montélimar 32 C 3
Montemorelos 20 E 2
Montenegro 34 D 2
Monter'a 22 G 6
Monterey 18 B 4
Monterey Bay 18 B 4
Monterotondo 34 C 2
Monterrey 20 D 2
Montes Claros 24 G 4
Montevideo 24 F 6
Montgomery 14 B 4
Monticello 18 E 4
Montluçon 32 C 2
Montmagny 8 W 9
Monto 60 J 4
Montoro 33 B 2

Montpelier (Idaho, U.S.) 18 D 3
Montpelier (Vermont, U.S.) 14 E 2
Montpellier 32 C 3
Montréal 8 W 9
Montreal Lake 18 E 1
Montrose (U.K.) 30 C 3
Montrose (U.S.) 18 E 4
Monts Timétrine 56 C 3
Montserrat 22 K 4
Monywa 47 H 4
Monza 36 B 3
Moora 60 B 6
Moore, Lake 60 B 5
Moorea 59 K 5
Moorhead 16 D 2
Moose Jaw 10 V 8
Moosehead Lake 14 E 1
Moosomin 16 C 1
Moosonee 8 U 8
Mopti 56 C 3
Mora 38 H 3
Moradabad 46 D 3
Morales, Laguna 20 E 3
Moramanga 58 D 3
Moran 18 D 3
Morane 59 M 6
Moratuwa 46 D 7
Morava 36 D 3
Moray Firth 30 C 3
Morbi 46 C 4
Morden 16 D 2
Møre og Romsdal 38 G 3
Morecambe Bay 28 C 3
Moree 60 H 5
Morehead City 14 D 4
Morelia 20 D 4
Morelos 20 E 4
Moreni 35 A 2
Moresby 10 Q 8
Moreton Island 60 J 5
Morgan City 20 F 2
Morgantown 14 D 3
Mori (Japan) 54 D 2
Moriarty 18 E 5
Morioka 54 D 3
Morjärv 38 K 2
Morkoka 41 X 4
Morlaix 32 B 2
Mornington Island 60 F 3
Moro Gulf 52 G 4
Morocco 56 C 1
Morogoro 58 C 2

Moroleón 20 D 3
Morón 22 G 3
Morón de la Frontera 33 A 2
Morondava 58 D 4
Moroni 58 D 3
Morotai 52 H 5
Morozovsk 44 F 3
Morris 16 D 2
Morris Jesup, Kap 8 Dd 2
Mors 38 G 4
Morshansk 44 F 2
Mortlock Islands 59 E 3
Morwell 60 H 7
Moscow 18 C 2
Moses Lake 18 C 2
Mosjøen 38 H 2
Moskenesøy 38 H 2
Moskva 40 J 6
Mosquitia 20 G 5
Mosquitos, Golfo de los 22 F 6
Mossoró 24 H 3
Most 36 C 2
Mostaganem 56 D 1
Mostar 34 D 2
Mosul 44 F 5
Motala 38 J 4
Mothe 59 H 5
Motherwell 28 C 2
Motril 33 B 2
Motu Ko 59 J 5
Motu One 59 K 5
Motul 20 G 3
Motutunga 59 L 5
Mould Bay 10 T 3
Moulins 32 C 2
Moulmein 47 H 5
Moultrie 14 C 4
Moultrie, Lake 14 C 4
Moundou 56 E 4
Mount Airy 14 C 3
Mount Forest 14 C 2
Mount Gambier 60 G 7
Mount Isa 60 F 4
Mount Magnet 60 B 5
Mount Pleasant (Michigan U.S.) 14 C 2
Mount Pleasant (Utah, U.S.) 18 D 4
Mount Roskill 62 B 2
Mount Vernon (Illinois, U.S.) 14 B 3
Mount Vernon (Kentucky, U.S.) 14 C 3
Mount Vernon (Ohio, U.S.) 14 C 2

Mount Willoughby 60 E 6
Mountain Grove 16 E 4
Mountain Home 18 C 3
Moutong 53 G 5
Mouydir 56 D 2
Moyahua 20 D 3
Mo'ynoq 45 J 4
Moyo 52 F 7
Moyynty 45 M 3
Mozambique 58 C 3
Mozambique Channel 58 D 3
Mozdok 44 F 4
Mozhga 40 M 6
Mstislaw 36 G 2
Mtsensk 44 E 2
Mu Us Shamo 49 H 3
Muang Khammouan 47 J 5
Muang Khongxedon 47 K 5
Muang Loei 47 J 5
Muang Nan 47 J 5
Muang Pakxan 47 J 5
Muang Phayao 47 H 5
Muang Phrae 47 J 5
Muang Sing 47 J 4
Muang Xaignabouri 47 J 5
Muar 52 C 5
Muara 52 C 6
Muarabungo 52 C 6
Muaraenim 52 C 6
Muarajuloi 52 E 6
Muaratewe 52 E 6
Muck 30 A 3
Mudanjiang 50 E 4
Mudgee 60 H 6
Mufu Shan 49 J 5
Mufulira 58 B 3
Muğla 35 C 6
Muhu 38 K 4
Mui Bai Bung 47 J 7
Mukacheve 36 E 3
Mukden 50 D 4
Mukhen 54 C 1
Mukomuko 52 C 6
Mulaku Atoll 46 C 8
Mulaly 45 N 3
Mulan 50 E 3
Mulegé 20 B 2
Mulegé, Sierra de 20 B 2
Mulhacén 33 B 2
Mulhouse 36 B 3
Muling 54 B 2
Mull 30 B 3
Mullaittivu 46 E 7

Muller, Pegunungan 52 E 6
Mullewa 60 B 5
Multan 46 C 2
Mumbai 46 C 5
Mumra 44 G 3
Muna (Indonesia) 52 G 6
Muna (Russia) 42 H 3
München 36 C 3
Muncho Lake 10 R 7
Muncie 14 B 2
Munday 16 D 5
Munising 14 B 1
Munku-Sardyk, Gora 41 W 7
Munster 31 B 2
Münster 36 B 2
Muntok 52 D 6
Muonio 38 K 2
Muqdisho (Mogadishu) 56 H 4
Murakami 54 C 3
Murashi 40 L 6
Murchison River 60 B 5
Murcia 33 B 2
Murdo 16 C 3
Murfreesboro 14 B 3
Murmansk 40 H 4
Murom 40 K 6
Muroran 54 D 2
Muros 33 A 1
Muroto 54 B 4
Murray (Kentucky, U.S.) 14 B 3
Murray (River) 60 G 6
Murray (Utah, U.S.) 18 D 3
Murray Islands 59 D 5
Murray, Lake (U.S.) 14 C 4
Mururoa 59 M 6
Murwara 46 E 4
Muş 35 J 5
Musala (Indonesia) 52 B 5
Musan 50 E 4
Musgrave 60 G 2
Musgrave Ranges 60 E 5
Musina 58 B 4
Muskegon 14 B 2
Muskogee 16 D 4
Musoma 58 C 2
Musrakaman 52 F 6
Musselshell River 18 E 2
Muswellbrook 60 J 6
Mut 35 E 6
Mutoray 41 W 5
Mutsu 54 D 2

Mutsu-wan 54 D 2
Muzaffarnagar 46 D 3
Muzaffarpur 46 F 3
Muzhi 40 O 4
Muztaū Bīigi 45 P 3
Mwali (Mohéli) 58 D 3
Mwanza 58 C 2
Mwene Ditu 58 B 2
My Tho 47 K 6
Myadzyel 36 F 2
Myanaung 47 H 5
Myanmar 47 G 4
Myaungmya 47 G 5
Myingyan 47 H 4
Myitkyinä 47 H 3
Mykines 34 E 3
Mykolayiv 44 D 3
Mykonos 34 F 3
Mylius Erichsen Land 8 Ff 2
Mymensingh 47 G 4
Myndagayy 42 K 4
Mýrdalsjökull 38 B 3
Myrhorod 44 D 3
Myrtle Beach 14 D 4
Mys Shmidta 43 U 3
Mys Zhelaniya 40 P 2
Mysore 46 D 6
Myszków 36 D 2
Mytilini 34 F 3
Mytishchi 40 J 6

Nahanni Butte 10 S 6
Nahanni National Park 10 R 6
Nahāvand 44 G 6
Naiman Qi 50 D 4
Nairn 30 C 3
Nairobi 58 C 2
Naissaar 38 K 4
Najafābād 44 H 6
Najin 54 B 2
Nakhodka 50 F 4
Nakhodka (Russia) 54 B 2
Nakhon Nayok 47 J 6
Nakhon Phanom 47 J 5
Nakhon Ratchasima 47 J 6
Nakhon Sawan 47 J 5
Nakhon Si Thammarat 47 H 7
Nakina 16 F 1
Nakuru 58 C 2
Nalayh 50 A 3
Nal'chik 44 F 4
Nallamalla Range 46 D 5
Nam Co 48 D 4
Nam Dinh 47 K 4
Namangan 45 M 4
Nameh 53 F 5
Namhkam 47 H 4
Namib Desert 58 A 3
Namibe 58 A 3
Namibia 58 A 4
Namjagbarwa Feng 48 F 5
Namlea 53 H 6
Nampa 18 C 3
Namp'o 50 E 5
Nampula 58 C 3
Namsos 38 H 3
Namtsy 42 J 4
Namu 59 F 3
Namwŏn 54 A 3
Nan Hai 47 K 7
Nan Hulsan Hu 48 F 3
Nanaimo 18 B 2
Nanam 50 E 4
Nanao 54 C 3
Nancha 50 E 3
Nanchang 49 K 5
Nancheng 49 K 5
Nanchong 49 H 4
Nanchuan 49 H 5
Nancowry 47 G 7
Nancy 36 B 3
Nanda Devi 46 D 2
Nänded 46 D 5
Nandurbār 46 C 4
Nandyāl 46 D 5

Nanfeng 49 K 5
Nānga Parbat 45 M 5
Nangatayap 52 E 6
Nangnim 54 A 2
Nangnim-sanmaek 54 A 3
Nangong 49 K 3
Nangpinch 52 E 6
Nanhua 48 G 5
Nanjing 49 K 4
Nanning 49 H 6
Nanpan Jiang 49 G 6
Nanping 49 K 5
Nansei-shotō 50 E 7
Nansen Land 8 Cc 2
Nantes 32 B 2
Nanton 18 D 1
Nantong 49 L 4
Nantucket Island 8 X 10
Nantucket Sound 14 E 2
Nanumea 59 G 4
Nanuque 24 H 4
Nanusa, Kepulauan 52 H 5
Nanxiong 49 J 5
Nanyang 49 J 4
Nanzhang 49 J 4
Nanzhao 49 J 4
Nao, Cabo de la 33 C 2
Napas 41 S 6
Napier 62 C 2
Naples 34 C 2
Naples (U.S.) 14 C 5
Napoli 34 C 2
Napuka 59 L 5
Naqadeh 35 L 6
Nara (Japan) 54 C 4
Naranjos 20 E 3
Narasapur 46 E 5
Narathiwat 47 J 7
Narayanganj 47 G 4
Narbonne 32 C 3
Nares Land 8 Bb 2
Narimanov 44 G 3
Närke 38 H 4
Naro-Fominsk 40 J 6
Narrabri 60 H 6
Narrandera 60 H 6
Narrogin 60 B 6
Narsaq 8 Bb 6
Narsimhapur 46 D 4
Narva 38 L 4
Narvik 38 J 2
Nar'yan Mar 40 M 4
Naryn 45 N 4
Naryn Qum 44 G 3
Năsăud 36 E 3
Nashik 46 C 4
Nashta Rūd 44 H 5
Nashville 14 B 3

Näsijärvi 38 K 3
Nasīrābād (India) 46 C 3
Nasirābād (Pakistan) 46 B 3
Nassau 14 D 5
Nassau Island 59 J 5
Nässjö 38 H 4
Nastapoka, Isles 8 V 7
Næstved 38 H 4
Natal 24 H 3
Natashquan 8 Y 8
Natchez 16 E 5
Natchitoches 16 E 5
Nathorst Land 8 Ff 4
Natuna Besar 52 D 5
Natuna Besar, Kepulauan 52 D 5
Natuna Selatan, Kepulauan 52 D 5
Naturaliste, Cape 60 A 6
Nauru 59 F 4
Naūrzym 45 K 2
Naushki 41 X 7
Nava 20 D 2
Navahrudak 36 F 2
Navajo Dam 18 E 4
Naval Station 22 H 4
Navalmoral de la Mata 33 A 2
Navan 31 C 2
Navarin, Mys 43 T 4
Navarra 32 B 3
Navassa Island 22 G 4
Navoiy 45 L 4
Navojoa 20 C 2
Navolato 20 C 3
Navsari 46 C 4
Nawabshah 46 B 3
Naxçivan 44 G 5
Naxçivan (Azerbai-jan) 35 L 5
Naxçivan (Region) 44 G 5
Naxi 49 H 5
Naxos 34 F 3
Nayakhan 43 P 4
Nayarit 20 C 3
Nayoro 54 D 2
Nazarovo 41 U 6
Nazas 20 D 2
Nazca 24 D 4
Naze 50 E 7
Nazimovo 41 U 6
Ndjamena 56 E 3
Ndola 58 B 3
Neagh, Lough 31 C 1
Neale, Lake 60 D 4
Near Islands 43 S 6

Neblina, Pico de 22 J 7
Neustrelitz 36 C 2
Nebraska 16 C 3
Nebraska City 16 D 3
Nechako Plateau 10 S 8
Nechako Reservoir 10 R 8
Nedong 48 E 5
Needles 18 D 5
Needles Point 62 C 2
Neftegorsk 35 H 2
Nefteyugansk 40 Q 5
Negombo 46 D 7
Negonego 59 L 5
Negros 53 G 4
Nehe 50 D 3
Nei Mongol Zizhiqu 49 J 2
Neijiang 49 H 5
Neilton 18 B 2
Neiva 22 G 7
Nejanilini Lake 8 R 7
Nekemtē 56 G 4
Nekrasovka 54 C 2
Nelidovo 40 H 6
Nel'kan 42 L 5
Nellore 46 D 6
Nel'ma 54 C 1
Nelson (Canada) 18 C 2
Nelson (New Zealand) 62 B 3
Nelson Island 43 W 4
Nelson River 10 X 8
Nelspruit 58 C 4
Nemiscau 8 V 8
Nemunas 38 K 4
Nemuro 54 E 2
Nenagh 31 B 2
Nenana 10 N 6
Nendo 59 F 5
Nenjiang 50 E 3
Nepa 41 X 6
Nepal 46 E 3
Nepalganj 46 E 3
Nephi 18 D 4
Nerchinsk 42 G 6
Nerekhta 40 K 6
Neryungri 42 H 5
Nes' 40 K 4
Neskaupstaður 38 C 2
Ness, Loch 30 B 3
Netherlands Antilles 22 J 5
Nettilling Lake 8 W 5
Neubrandenburg 36 C 2
Neuchâtel 36 B 3
Neumünster 36 B 2

Neuquén 24 E 6
Neustrelitz 36 C 2
Nevada (Missouri, U.S.) 16 E 4
Nevada (State, U.S.) 18 C 4
Nevada, Sierra 33 B 2
Nevada, Sierra (U.S.) 18 B 3
Nevel'sk 50 H 3
Never 42 H 6
Nevers 32 C 2
Nevinnomysk 44 F 4
Nevis 22 K 4
Nevşehir 35 F 5
Nev'yansk 40 O 6
New Albany 14 B 3
New Bedford 14 E 2
New Bern 14 D 3
New Braunfels 20 E 2
New Britain 59 E 4
New Brunswick 8 X 9
New Brunswick (U.S.) 14 E 2
New Castle 14 C 2
New Dehli 46 D 3
New England 14 F 2
New England Range 60 J 6
New Georgia 59 E 4
New Glasgow 8 Y 9
New Guinea 59 D 4
New Hampshire 14 E 2
New Hanover 59 E 4
New Haven 14 E 2
New Iberia 16 E 5
New Ireland 59 E 4
New Jersey 14 E 2
New Liskeard 14 D 1
New London 14 E 2
New Meadows 18 C 3
New Mexico 18 E 5
New Orleans 20 F 2
New Plymouth 62 B 2
New Providence Island 22 G 3
New Quay 28 B 3
New River 14 C 3
New Rockford 16 D 2
New Smyrna Beach 14 C 5
New South Wales 60 G 6
New Ulm 16 E 3
New Westminister 18 B 2
New York (State, U.S.) 14 D 2

New York (U.S.) 14 E 2
New Zealand 62 B 3
Newark (New Jersey, U.S.) 14 E 2
Newark (Ohio, U.S.) 14 C 2
Newark-on-Trent 28 D 3
Newberry 8 T 9
Newburgh 14 E 2
Newcastle (Australia) 60 J 6
Newcastle (Northern Ireland) 31 D 1
Newcastle (U.S.) 16 C 3
Newcastle upon Tyne 28 D 2
Newcastle Waters 60 E 3
Newcastle West 31 B 2
Newfoundland 8 Z 9
Newfoundland and Labrador 8 X 8
Newhaven 28 E 4
Newman 60 B 4
Newport (Arkansas, U.S.) 16 E 4
Newport (England, U.K.) 28 D 4
Newport (Oregon, U.S.) 18 B 3
Newport (Vermont, U.S.) 14 E 2
Newport (Wales, U.K.) 28 C 4
Newport (Washing-ton, U.S.) 18 C 2
Newport Beach 18 C 5
Newquay 28 B 4
Newry (U.K.) 31 C 1
Newton 16 E 3
Newtown 28 C 3
Newtownabbey 28 B 2
Neyshābūr 45 J 5
Nezahualcóyotl 20 E 4
Ngamiland 58 B 3
Ngamring 48 D 5
Ngangerabeli Plain 58 C 2
Ngangla Ringco 48 C 4
Ngangzê Co 48 D 4
Ngau 59 G 4
Nggatokae Island 59 E 4
Nguru 56 E 3
Nha Trang 47 K 6
Niagara Falls 14 D 2

Niagara River 14 D 2
Niah 52 E 5
Niamey 56 D 3
Nianzishan 50 D 3
Nias 52 B 5
Niau 59 L 5
Nicaragua 22 E 5
Nicaragua, Lago de 22 E 5
Nice 34 B 2
Nicholl's Town 14 D 5
Nicobar Islands 47 G 7
Nicosia 44 D 5
Nido, Sierra del 20 C 3
Nidzica 36 E 2
Nienburg 36 B 2
Niğde 35 F 6
Niger 56 D 3
Niger (River) 56 C 3
Nigeria 56 D 4
Nihiru 59 L 5
Niigata 54 C 3
Niihama 54 B 4
Niihau 12 D 7
Niitsu 54 C 3
Nijmegen 36 B 2
Nikolayevsk 44 G 2
Nikolayevsk-na-Amure 42 M 6
Nikol'sk (Russia) 40 L 6
Nikol'sk (Russia) 44 G 2
Nikolski 43 W 6
Niksar 35 G 4
Nikšić 34 D 2
Nikumaroro 59 H 4
Nikunau 59 G 4
Nila 53 H 7
Nile 56 F 3
Niles 14 B 2
Nimach 46 C 4
Nimes 32 C 3
Nincheng 50 C 4
Nine Degree Channel 46 C 7
Ninety Mile Beach 60 H 7
Ningbo 49 L 5
Ningde 49 K 5
Ningdu 49 K 5
Ninghai 49 L 5
Ninghua 49 K 5
Ningjing Shan 48 F 4
Ningxia Huizu Zizhiqu 49 H 3
Ningxiang 49 J 5
Ninh Binh 47 K 4
Niobrara River 16 C 3

Niort 32 B 2
Nipāni 46 C 5
Nipigon 8 T 9
Nipigon, Lake 8 T 9
Nipissing, Lake 8
    V 9
Nirmal 46 D 5
Niš 34 E 2
Nishino'omote 54
    B 4
Nistru 36 F 3
Nitchequon 8 W 8
Niterói 24 G 5
Nitra 36 D 3
Niuafo'ou 59 H 5
Niuatoputapu 59 H 5
Niue Island 59 J 5
Niutao 59 G 4
Nizamabad 46 D 5
Nizhnekamsk 40 M 6
Nizhneudinsk 41 V 7
Nizhnevartovsk 41
    R 5
Nizhniy Lomov 44
    F 2
Nizhniy Novgorod 40
    K 6
Nizhniy Tagil 40 N 6
Nizhnyaya Pesha 40
    L 4
Nizhnyaya Poyma 41
    V 6
Nizhnyaya Tunguska
    41 U 5
Nizhyn 36 G 2
Njazidja (Grand Co-
    more) 58 D 3
Nkayi 58 A 2
Nkongsamba 56 E 4
Nmai Hka 47 H 3
Noākhāli 47 G 4
Noatak National Re-
    serve 10 L 5
Nobel 14 C 1
Nobeoka 54 B 4
Nogales 18 D 5
Noginsk 40 J 6
Noholoho 53 G 6
Noirmoutier, Île de 32
    B 2
Nolinsk 40 L 6
Nombre de Dios 20
    D 3
Nome 43 W 4
Nonacho Lake 10
    V 6
Nonburg 40 M 4
Nong Khai 47 J 5
Nonoava 20 C 2
Nonouti 59 G 4
Nordenshel'da, Arkhi-
    pelag 41 U 2
Norderstedt 36 B 2
Nordfriesische Inseln
    36 B 2

Nordhausen 36 C 2
Nordkapp 38 L 1
Nordkjosbotn 38 J 2
Nordostrundingen 8
    Kk 2
Nord-Trøndelag 38
    H 3
Nordvik 41 Y 3
Norfolk (Nebraska,
    U.S.) 16 D 3
Norfolk (Virginia,
    U.S.) 14 D 3
Norfolk Island 59 F 6
Norfork Lake 16 E 4
Noril'sk 41 T 4
Normal 14 B 2
Norman 16 D 4
Norman Wells 10
    R 5
Normanby Island 60
    K 3
Normandie 32 B 2
Normanton 60 G 3
Norrbotten 38 K 2
Norris Lake 14 C 3
Norrköping 38 J 4
Norrland 38 J 2
Norrtälje 38 J 4
Norseman 60 C 6
Norske Øer 8 Hh 3
North Adams 14 E 2
North Andaman 47
    G 6
North Aulatsvik Island
    8 Y 7
North Battleford 10
    V 8
North Bay 8 V 9
North Belcher Islands
    8 V 7
North Bend 18 B 3
North Canadian River
    16 D 4
North Cape (New
    Zealand) 62 B 1
North Cape (Norway)
    38 L 1
North Carolina 14
    C 3
North Cascades Na-
    tional Park 18 B 2
North Channel
    (Canada) 14 C 1
North Channel (U.K.)
    28 B 2
North Dakota 16 C 2
North Downs 28 D 4
North Fork Pass 10
    P 6
North Geomagnetic
    Pole 8 X 3
North Island 62 B 2
North Kent Island 8
    S 3
North Korea 50 F 4

North Lakhimpur 47
    G 3
North Las Vegas 18
    C 4
North Little Rock 16
    E 5
North Magnetic Pole
    10 V 3
North Minch 30 B 2
North Platte 16 C 3
North Platte River 16
    C 3
North Rona 30 B 2
North Ronaldsay 30
    C 2
North Saskatchewan
    10 U 8
North Sea 38 F 3
North Slope 10 L 5
North Taranaki Bight
    62 B 2
North Uist 30 A 3
North West Cape 60
    A 4
North West High-
    lands 30 B 3
North York Moors 28
    D 2
Northam 60 B 6
Northampton (U.K.)
    28 D 3
Northeast
    Providence
    Channel 14 D 5
Northern Cook Is-
    lands 59 J 5
Northern Ireland 31
    C 1
Northern Mariana Is-
    lands 59 D 2
Northern Territory 60
    E 3
Northfield 16 E 3
Northway 10 O 6
Northwest Territories
    10 S 6
Norton (U.S.) 14 C 3
Norton Sound 43 X 4
Norvegia, Cape 63
    O 5
Norwalk 14 C 2
Norway 38 G 3
Norway (U.S.) 14
    B 1
Norwegian Bay 8
    S 3
Norwegian Sea 38
    G 3
Norwich 28 E 3
Noshiro 54 D 2
Nosy Bé 58 D 3
Nosy Boraha 58 D 3
Nottawasaga Bay 14
    C 2
Nottingham 28 D 3

Nottingham Island 8
    V 6
Nouadhibou 56 B 2
Nouakchott 56 B 3
Nouméa 59 F 6
Nouvelle Calédonie
    59 F 6
Nova Iguaçu 24 G 5
Nova Scotia 8 Y 10
Novara 36 B 3
Novaya Lyalya 40
    O 6
Novaya Sibir', Ostrov
    42 O 1
Novaya Zemlya 40
    M 3
Nové Zámky 36 D 3
Novhorod-Sivers'kyy
    36 G 2
Novi Ligure 34 B 2
Novi Pazar 34 E 2
Novi Sad 36 D 3
Novikovo (Russia) 54
    D 1
Novo Hamburgo 24
    F 5
Novoaltaysk 41 S 7
Novoanninskiy 44
    F 2
Novobogatīnskoe 44
    H 3
Novobureyskiy 54
    A 1
Novocheboksarsk 40
    L 6
Novocherkassk 44
    F 3
Novodvinsk 40 K 5
Novohrad-Volyns'kyy
    36 F 2
Novokuybyshevsk 44
    G 2
Novokuznetsk 41
    T 7
Novomoskovsk 44
    E 2
Novorossiysk 44 E 4
Novorybnoye 41 X 3
Novosergiyevka 44
    H 2
Novoshakhtinsk 44
    E 3
Novosibirsk 41 S 6
Novosi-
    birskoyeVodokhrani
    lishche 41 S 7
Novotroitsk 45 J 2
Novoukrayinka 44
    D 3
Novouzensk 44 G 2
Novovolyns'k 36 E 2
Novozybkov 36 G 2
Novvy Buh 44 D 3
Novvy Port 40 Q 4
Novyy 41 X 3

Novyy Bor 40 M 4
Novyy Oskol 44 E 2
Nowa Ruda 36 D 2
Nowa Sól 36 D 2
Nowgong 47 G 3
Nowogard 36 D 2
Nowy Sącz 36 E 3
Noyon 49 G 2
Nsukka 56 D 4
Nueces River 20 E 2
Nueltin Lake 8 R 6
Nueva Gerona 20
    H 3
Nueva Rosita 20 D 2
Nueva San Salvador
    20 G 5
Nuevo Casas
    Grandes 18 E 5
Nuevo Laredo 20
    E 2
Nuevo Léon 20 D 2
Nuevo, Cayo 20 F 3
Nui 59 G 4
Nuiqsut 10 M 4
Nuka Hiva 59 M 4
Nuku'alofa 59 H 6
Nukufetau 59 G 4
Nukunono 59 H 4
Nukus 45 J 4
Nukutepipi 59 L 6
Nullarbor Plain 60
    D 6
Numazu 54 C 3
Numbulwar Mission
    60 F 2
Numfoor 52 J 6
Nunap Isua 8 Cc 7
Nunavut 8 R 5
Nungnak 10 L 5
Nunivak Island 43
    W 4
Nunkun 45 N 6
Nuoro 34 B 2
Nurak 45 L 5
Nurakita 59 H 4
Nurlat 44 H 2
Nurmes 38 L 3
Nürnberg 36 C 3
Nushki 46 B 3
Nutak 8 Y 7
Nuuk 8 Aa 6
Nuussuaq 8 Z 4
Nyaingentanglha
    Feng 48 E 4
Nyaingentanglha
    Shan 48 D 5
Nyala 56 F 3
Nyandoma 40 K 5
Nyaunglebin 47 H 5
Nyazepetrovsk 40
    N 6
Nyda 40 Q 4
Nyeboe Land 8 Z 2
Nyingchi 48 E 5
Nykøbing 36 C 2

Nyköping 38 J 4
Nyngan 60 H 6
Nyoman 36 E 2
Ny'regyháza 36 E 3
Nysa 36 D 2
Nyslott 38 L 3
Nystad 38 K 3
Nyurba 42 G 4
Nyuya 42 G 4
Nzérékoré 56 C 4
Nzwani (Anjouan) 58
    D 3
Oahe Dam 16 C 3
Oahe, Lake 16 C 2
Oahu 12 E 7
Oak Ridge 14 C 3
Oakland 18 B 4
Oakley 16 C 4
Oakridge 18 B 3
Oakville 14 D 2
Oamaru 62 B 4
Oaxaca (Mexico) 20
    E 4
Oaxaca (State, Mex-
    ico) 20 E 4
Ob' 40 P 4
Oba 8 U 9
Oban (New Zealand)
    62 A 4
Oban (U.K.) 30 B 3
Obanazawa 54 D 3
Obeh 45 K 6
Obi 53 H 6
Obi, Kepulauan 52
    H 6
Obihiro 54 D 2
Obluch'ye 50 F 3
Obninsk 40 J 6
Oborniki 36 D 2
Oboyan' 44 E 2
Obozerskiy 40 K 5
Obrenovac 34 E 2
Obshchiy Syrt 44
    H 2
Obskaya Guba 40
    Q 4
Ocala 14 C 5
Ocampo 20 C 2
Ocaña 22 H 6
Ocean City 14 D 3
Och'amch'ire 35 J 3
Ocher 40 M 6
Ockelbo 38 J 3
Oconee River 14 C 4
Ocotlán 20 D 3
Ocotlán de Morelos
    20 E 4
Ocumare del Tuy 22
    J 5
Odate 54 D 2
Odawara 54 C 3
Odemira 33 A 2
Ödemiş 34 F 3
Odendaalsrus 58
    B 4

Odense 38 H 4
Oder 36 C 2
Odesa 44 D 3
Odessa 16 C 5
Odintsovo 40 J 6
Odra 36 C 2
Oelwein 16 E 3
Oeno Island 59 M 6
Offenbach 36 B 2
Ofu 59 H 5
Oga 54 C 3
Oga-hanto 54 C 2
Ōgaki 54 C 3
Ogallala 16 C 3
Ogbomoso 56 D 4
Ogden 18 D 3
Ogdensburg 14 D 2
Oglanly 44 H 5
Ogoron 42 J 6
Ogurjaly 44 H 5
Ohio 14 C 2
Ohio River 14 C 3
Ohrid 34 E 2
Ōita 54 B 4
Ojinaga 20 D 2
Ōka 44 E 2
Okak Islands 8 Y 7
Okara 46 C 2
Okavango 58 A 3
Okaya 54 C 3
Okayama 54 B 4
Okazaki 54 C 4
Okeechobee, Lake
   14 C 5
Okehampton 28 B 4
Okene 56 D 4
Okha 42 M 6
Okhotskoye More 43
   N 5
Okinawa-jima 50 E 7
Oki-Shotō 54 B 3
Oklahoma 16 D 5
Oklahoma City 16
   D 4
Oktyabr'sk 45 J 3
Oktyabr'skiy 44 H 2
Oktyabr'skoy
   Revolyutsii, Ostrov
   41 V 2
Okulovka 40 H 6
Okushiri-tō 54 C 2
Ólafsv'k 38 A 3
Olanchito 20 G 4
Öland 38 J 4
Olathe 16 E 4
Olbia 34 B 2
Old Harbor 43 Z 5
Old Head of Kinsale
   31 B 3
Oldenburg 36 B 2
Oldham 28 C 3
Olekma 42 G 6
Olekminsk 42 H 4
Olekminskiy Stanovik
   42 G 6

Oleksandrivka 44
   D 3
Olenegorsk 40 H 4
Olenek 41 Y 4
Olenek (River) 42
   G 3
Oleniy, Ostrov 41
   R 3
Oléron, Île d' 32 B 2
Oleśnica 36 D 2
Olevs'k 36 F 2
Ol'ga 54 C 2
Olhão 33 A 2
Öli Qoltyq Sory 44
   H 3
Olinda 24 H 3
Olmaliq 45 L 4
Olochi 42 G 6
Olomouc 36 D 3
Olonets 40 H 5
Olosega 59 J 5
Olot 32 C 3
Olovyannaya 42 G 6
Oloyskiy Khrebet 43
   Q 3
Olsztyn 36 E 2
Oltenița 35 B 2
Olympia 34 E 3
Olympia (U.S.) 18
   B 2
Olympic National
   Park 18 B 2
Olympus, Mount
   (U.S.) 18 B 2
Olyutorskiy 43 R 4
Olyutorskiy Polu-
   ostrov 43 S 4
Om' 41 R 6
Omagh 31 C 1
Omaha 16 D 3
Omarama 62 A 3
Omatako 58 A 4
Ometepec 20 E 4
Omiya 54 C 3
Omolon 43 P 3
Omoloy 42 K 3
Omsk 40 Q 7
Omsukchan 43 P 4
Omsukchanskiy Gory
   43 O 4
Omura 54 A 4
Ōmuta 54 B 4
Ornutninsk 40 M 6
Ondor Sum 49 J 2
Öndörhaan 50 B 3
Onega 40 J 5
Onega, Lake 40 J 5
O'Neill 16 D 3
Oneonta 14 D 2
Oneşti 36 F 3
Onezhskaya Guba
   40 J 5
Onezhskoye, Ozero
   40 J 5
Ongjin 50 E 5

Ongole 46 E 5
Onitsha 56 D 4
Ono-i-lau Island 59
   H 6
Onomichi 54 B 4
Onon Gol 50 B 3
Onotoa 59 G 4
Onslow 60 B 4
Onslow Bay 14 D 4
Ontario 10 Y 8
Ontario (U.S.) 18
   C 3
Ontario, Lake 14 D 2
Ontong Java 59 E 4
Oodnadatta 60 F 5
Ooldea 60 E 6
Oologah Lake 16
   D 4
Opava 36 D 3
Opelousas 16 E 5
Opole 36 D 2
Opotiki 62 C 2
Opp 14 B 4
Oppdal 38 G 3
Oppland 38 G 3
Opportunity 18 C 2
Oputo 18 E 5
Oradea 36 E 3
Orai 46 D 3
Oral 44 H 2
Oran 56 C 1
Orange 58 A 4
Orange (Australia) 60
   H 6
Orange (U.S.) 16
   E 5
Orange Park 14 C 4
Orange Walk 20 G 4
Oranienburg 36 C 2
Ord River Dam 60
   D 3
Ordos Plateau 49
   H 3
Ordu 35 G 4
Örebro 38 J 4
Oregon 18 B 3
Oregon Inlet 14 D 3
Orekhovo-Zuyevo 40
   J 6
Orel 44 E 2
Orem 18 D 3
Orenburg 40 N 7
Orestiada 34 F 2
Organ Pipe Cactus
   National Monument
   18 D 5
Orgün 45 L 6
Orhangazi 35 C 4
Orhei 36 F 3
Orhon Gol 41 W 8
Orick 18 B 3
Oriental, Cordillera
   (Colombia) 22 G 7
Orientale 58 B 1
Orillia 14 D 2

Orinoco, Rio 22 J 6
Orissa 46 E 5
Oristano 34 B 3
Oritz 20 B 2
Orivesi 38 L 3
Orizaba 20 E 4
Orizaba, Pico de 20
   E 4
Orkanger 38 G 3
Orkney Islands 30
   C 2
Orlando 14 C 5
Orléans 32 C 2
Ormoc 53 G 3
Örnsköldsvik 38 J 3
Orofino 18 C 2
Oroluk 59 E 3
Orona 59 H 4
Oroqen Zizhiqi 50
   D 2
Oroville (California,
   U.S.) 18 B 4
Oroville (Washington,
   U.S.) 18 C 2
Orsa 38 H 3
Orsha 36 G 2
Orsk 45 J 2
Ortegal, Cabo 33
   A 1
Ortigueira 33 A 1
Ortonville 16 D 2
Orulgan, Khrebet 42
   J 3
Orümīyeh 44 G 5
Oruro 24 E 4
Ōsaka 54 C 4
Osborne 16 D 4
Osceola 16 E 3
Osen 38 H 3
Osh 45 M 4
Oshakati 58 A 3
Oshawa 14 D 2
Oshkosh 14 B 2
Osijek 36 D 3
Osinniki 41 T 7
Osinovka 45 O 3
Oskaloosa 16 E 3
Oskarshamn 38 J 4
Öskemen 45 O 2
Oslo 38 H 4
Osmānābād 46 D 5
Osmaniye 35 G 6
Osnabrück 36 B 2
Osorno 24 D 7
Ossora 43 Q 5
Ostashkov 40 H 6
Östergötland 38 H 4
Östersjön 38 J 4
Östersund 38 H 3
Ostrava 36 D 3
Ostróda 36 D 2
Ostrogozhsk 44 E 2
Ostrołęka 36 E 2
Ostrov 38 L 4
Ostrów Mazowiecka

   36 E 2
Ostrów Wielkopolski
   36 D 2
Ōsumi-kaikyō 54 B 4
Ōsumi-shotō 54 B 4
Osuna 33 A 2
Oswego 14 D 2
Ōtake 54 B 4
Otaru 54 D 2
Otautau 62 A 4
Otranto 34 D 2
Ōtsu 54 C 3
Ottawa (Canada) 8
   V 9
Ottawa (U.S.) 16 D 4
Ottawa Islands 8 U 7
Ottawa River 14 D 1
Ottenby 38 J 4
Ottumwa 16 E 3
Otway, Cape 60 G 7
Otwock 36 E 2
Ouachita Mountains
   16 D 5
Ouaddaï 56 E 3
Ouagadougou 56
   C 3
Ouahigouya 56 C 3
Ouargla 56 D 1
Ouarzazate 56 C 1
Oubangui 58 A 1
Oudtshoorn 58 B 5
Oujda 56 C 1
Oulu 38 L 3
Oulujärvi 38 L 3
Oumé 56 C 4
Ourense 33 A 1
Outer Hebrides 30
   A 2
Ouvéa 59 F 6
Ouyen 60 G 7
Ovacık (Turkey) 35
   E 6
Ovamboland 58 A 3
Oviedo 33 A 1
Ovruch 36 F 2
Owatonna 16 E 3
Owen Sound 14 C 2
Owen Stanley Range
   59 D 4
Owensboro 14 B 3
Owo 56 D 4
Owosso 14 C 2
Owyhee 18 C 3
Owyhee River 18
   C 3
Owyhee, Lake 18
   C 3
Oxford (U.K.) 28 D 4
Oxford (U.S.) 14 B 4
Oymayakonskoye
   Nagor'ye 42 M 4
Oyotung 42 N 2
Oyun Khomoto 42
   L 3
Oyyl 44 H 3

Ozamiz 53 G 4
Ozark 14 B 4
Ozark Plateau 16
   E 4
Ozarks, Lake of the
   16 E 4
Ózd 36 E 3
Ozernoy, Zaliv 43
   Q 5
Ozinki 44 G 2
Ozona 16 C 5
Ozurget'i 44 F 4
Paamiut 8 Bb 6
Paarl 58 A 5
Pabna 47 F 4
Pachuca 20 E 3
Pacific Ocean 59
   G 3
Padang 52 C 6
Padang (Island) 52
   C 5
Padangpanjang 52
   C 6
Padangsidempuan
   52 B 5
Paderborn 36 B 2
Padova 36 C 3
Padrauna 46 E 3
Padre Island 20 E 2
Paducah 14 B 3
Paektu-San 50 E 4
Paeroa 62 C 2
Pag 34 C 2
Pagadian 53 G 4
Pagai Selatan 52
   C 6
Pagai Utara 52 B 6
Pagan 59 D 2
Pagoda Point 47 G 5
Pagosa Springs 18
   E 4
Paignton 28 C 4
Päijänne 38 L 3
Painan 52 C 6
Painesville 14 C 2
Painted Desert 18
Paisley 28 B 2
Pajala 38 K 2
Pak Phanang 47 J 7
Pakistan 46 B 3
Pakokku 47 H 4
Paks 36 D 3
Pakse 47 K 5
Pakuashipi 8 Z 8
Pala 56 D 4
Palana 43 P 5
Palanan Point 53
   G 2
Palangkaraya 52 E 6
Palani 46 D 6
Palanpur 46 C 4
Palatka 43 O 4
Palau 59 C 3
Palau Islands 59 C 3

Palawan 53 F 4
Palawan Passage 53
    F 4
Palayankottai 46 D 7
Paleleh 53 G 5
Palembang 52 C 6
Palencia 33 B 1
Palenque 20 F 4
Palermo 34 C 3
Palestine 16 D 5
Paletwa 47 G 4
Pālghāt 46 D 6
Pali 46 C 3
Palikir 59 E 3
Pālitāna 46 C 4
Pallasovka 44 G 2
Palliser, Cape 62
    C 3
Palliser, Îles 59 L 5
Palm Springs 18 C 5
Palma 56 B 2
Palma de Mallorca
    33 C 2
Palma Soriano 22
    G 3
Palmas 24 G 3
Palmer 10 N 6
Palmerston 59 J 5
Palmerston (New
    Zealand) 62 B 4
Palmerston North 62
    C 3
Palmira 22 G 7
Palopo 52 G 6
Palos, Cabo de 33
    B 2
Palpetu, Tanjung 52
    H 6
Palu 52 F 6
Pamekasan 52 E 7
Pamirs 45 M 5
Pamlico Sound 14
    D 3
Pampa (U.S.) 16 C 4
Pampas 24 E 6
Pamplona 22 H 6
Pamplona-Iru-a 32
    B 3
Panaji 46 C 5
Panama 22 G 6
Panama Canal 22
    G 6
Panama City 14 B 4
Panamá, Golfo de 22
    G 6
Panay 52 G 3
Pančevo 34 E 2
Pandharpur 46 D 5
Panevežys 38 K 4
Pangkadjene 52 F 6
Pangkalpinang 52
    D 6
Pangnirtung 8 X 5
Pangutaran Group 52
    F 4

Panipat 46 D 3
Panna 46 E 4
Panshi 50 E 4
Pantar 52 G 7
Pánuco 20 E 3
Pánuco, Río 20 E 3
Panxian 49 G 5
Pápa 36 D 3
Papa Westray 30
    C 2
Papantla 20 E 3
Papar 52 F 4
Paparoa 62 B 2
Papeete 59 L 5
Papua New Guinea
    59 D 4
Parabel' 41 S 6
Paracel Islands 52
    E 2
Pāradwīp 46 F 4
Paragould 16 E 4
Paraguay 24 E 5
Parakou 56 D 4
Paramaribo 24 F 2
Paramushir, Ostrov
    43 P 6
Paraná 24 F 6
Parang 52 G 4
Parangaba 24 H 3
Paraoa 59 L 5
Paray-le-Monial 32
    C 2
Parbhani 46 D 5
Pardubice 36 D 2
Parengarenga Har-
    bour 62 B 1
Parent 14 E 1
Parepare 52 F 6
Pariaman 52 C 6
Paricutín, Volcán 20
    D 4
Parima, Sierra 22
    K 7
Paris (France) 32
    C 2
Paris (Illinois, U.S.)
    14 B 3
Paris (Tennessee,
    U.S.) 14 B 3
Paris (Texas, U.S.)
    16 D 5
Park Rapids 16 D 2
Parkano 38 K 3
Parker 18 D 5
Parkersburg 14 C 3
Parklākimidi 46 E 5
Parkland 18 B 2
Parma 34 C 2
Parnaíba 24 G 3
Pärnu 38 K 4
Paropamisus 45 K 6
Parramatta 60 J 6
Parras 20 D 2
Parras, Sierra de 20
    D 2

Parry Islands 10 U 3
Parry, Kap 8 W 3
Partille 38 H 4
Partizansk 54 B 2
Pasadena 18 C 5
Pascagoula 14 B 4
Pashkovo 50 F 3
Passero, Capo 34
    D 3
Passo Fundo 24 F 5
Pastavy 38 L 4
Pasto 22 G 7
Pasul Meste Cănis
    36 F 3
Patagonia 24 D 7
Patan (India) 46 C 4
Patan (Nepal) 46 F 3
Paterna 33 B 2
Paterson 14 E 2
Pathankot 46 D 2
Pathfinder Reservoir
    18 E 3
Patiala 46 D 2
Patmos 35 B 6
Patna 46 F 3
Patra 34 E 3
Pattani 47 J 7
Pattle Island 52
    E 2
Patuākhāli 47 G 4
Patuca, Río 20 G 5
Pau 32 B 3
Paulatuk 10 S 5
Pauls Valley 16 D 5
Paungde 47 H 5
Pavla 36 B 3
Pavlodar 45 N 2
Pavlovo 40 K 6
Pavlovsk 41 S 7
Pavlovskaya 35 H 1
Paxson 10 N 6
Payakumbuh 52 C 6
Payeti 52 G 7
Pay-Khoy, Khrebet
    40 O 4
Paynes Find 60 B 5
Paysandú 24 F 6
Payson 18 D 3
Pazarcık 35 G 6
Pazardzhik 34 E 2
Peace Point 10 U 7
Peace River 10 T 7
Peach Springs 18
    D 4
Peachland 18 C 2
Pearl River 14 B 4
Pearsall 20 E 2
Peary Land 8 Dd 2
Peawanuck 8 T 7
Peć 34 E 2
Pechenga 38 M 2
Pechora 40 N 4

Pechora (River) 40
    M 4
Pechorskoye More
    40 M 4
Pecos 16 C 5
Pecos Plains 16 C 5
Pecos River 16 C 5
Pécs 36 D 3
Pedriseña 20 D 2
Peel 28 B 2
Peera Peera
    Poolanno Lake 60
    F 5
Pegasus Bay 62 B 3
Pegasus, Port 62
    A 4
Pegu 47 H 5
Pegu Yoma 47 H 4
Peikang 49 L 6
Peipsi järv 38 L 4
Peipus, Lake 38 L 4
Peixian 49 K 4
Pejantan 52 D 5
Pekalongan 52 D 7
Pekanbaru 52 C 5
Pekin 14 B 2
Peking 49 K 3
Pelabuhanratu 52
    D 7
Peleduy 42 F 5
Peleliu 59 C 3
Peleng 52 G 6
Pello 38 K 2
Pelly Crossing 10
    P 6
Peloponnisos 34 E 3
Pelotas 24 F 6
Pemalang 52 D 7
Pematangsiantar 52
    B 5
Pemba 58 D 3
Pemba Island 58 C 2
Pembina 16 D 2
Pembroke (Canada)
    8 V 9
Pembroke (U.K.) 28
    B 4
Peña Nevada, Cerro
    20 E 3
Peñas, Cabo de 33
    A 1
Pend Oreille Lake 18
    C 2
Pend Oreille River 18
    C 2
Pendleton 18 C 2
Penglai 49 L 3
Penida 52 F 7
Penmarc'h, Pointe de
    32 B 2
Penn Hills 14 D 2
Pennines 28 C 2
Pennsylvania 14 C 2
Penny Ice Cap 8
    X 5

Penobscot Bay 14
    F 2
Peñón Blanco 20
    D 3
Penong 60 E 6
Penrhyn 59 K 4
Penrith 60 J 6
Penrith (U.K.) 28 C 2
Pensacola 14 B 4
Pentecôte 59 F 5
Pentland Firth 30
    C 2
Penza 44 F 2
Penzance 28 B 4
Penzhino 43 R 4
Penzhinskiy Khrebet
    43 R 4
Peoria 14 B 2
Perabumulih 52 C 6
Percival Lakes 60
    C 4
Pereira 22 G 7
Pereslavl-Zalesskiy
    40 J 6
Pericos 20 C 2
Périgueux 32 C 2
Perija, Sierra de 22
    H 6
Perlas, Laguna de 22
    F 5
Perm' 40 N 6
Pernik 34 E 2
Perote 20 E 4
Perpignan 32 C 3
Perry 14 C 4
Perry Bay 10 W 5
Perryton 16 C 4
Perryville 43 Y 5
Perth (Australia) 60
    B 6
Perth (U.K.) 30 C 3
Perth-Andover 8 X 9
Peru 24 D 3
Perugia 34 C 2
Pervoural'sk 40 N 6
Pesaro 34 C 2
Pescara 34 C 2
Peschanyy Müyis 44
    H 4
Peschanyy, Ostrov
    42 G 2
Peshāwar 45 M 6
Pessac 32 B 3
Pestovo 40 J 6
Petacalco Bahía de
    20 D 4
Petaluma 18 B 4
Petatlán 20 D 4
Petén Itzá, Lago 20
    F 4
Petenwell Lake 16
    E 3
Peter I Øy 63 X 5
Peterborough (Aus-
    tralia) 60 F 6

Peterborough
    (Canada) 14 D 2
Peterborough (U.K.)
    28 D 3
Peterhead 30 D 3
Petermann Ranges
    60 D 5
Petermanns
    Gletscher 8 Y 2
Petersburg (Virginia,
    U.S.) 14 D 3
Petitsikapau Lake 8
    X 8
Peto 20 G 3
Petra Velikogo, Zaliv
    50 F 4
Petrila 36 E 3
Petropavlovsk 40
    P 7
Petropavlovsk-Kam-
    chatskiy 43 P 6
Petrovsk 44 G 2
Petrovsk-
    Zabaykal'skiy 41
    X 7
Petrozavodsk 40 H 5
Petukhovo 40 P 6
Pevek 43 S 3
Pforzheim 36 B 3
Phaliodi 46 C 3
Phaltan 46 C 5
Phan Rang 47 K 6
Phan Thiet 47 K 6
Phatthalung 47 J 7
Phenix City 14 B 4
Phetchabun 47 J 5
Phetchaburi 47 H 6
Phichit 47 J 5
Philadelphia 14 D 3
Philippi, Lake 60 F 4
Philippines 52 H 3
Phillipsburg 16 D 4
Philpots Island 8 V 4
Phitsanulok 47 J 5
Phnum Aôral 47 J 6
Phnum Pénh 47 J 6
Phoenix 18 D 5
Phoenix Islands 59
    H 4
Phon 47 J 5
Phôngsali 47 J 4
Phu Vinh 47 K 7
Phuket 47 H 7
Phumĭ Chhuk 47 J 6
Piacenza 36 B 3
Piatra-Neamţ 36 F 3
Pichilingue 20 B 3
Pickering 28 D 2
Pickle Lake 10 Y 8
Pickwick Lake 14
    B 3
Picos 24 G 3
Piedras Negras 20
    D 2
Pieksämäki 38 L 3

Pielinen 38 L 3
Pierre 16 C 3
Piešťany 36 D 3
Piet Retief 58 C 4
Pietermaritzburg 58 C 4
Piła 36 D 2
Pilas Group 53 G 4
Piloncillo Mountains 18 E 5
Pinar del Rio 20 H 3
Pincher Creek 18 D 2
Pine Bluff 16 E 5
Pine Bluffs 16 C 3
Pine Creek 60 E 2
Pine Falls 10 X 8
Pine Pass 10 S 7
Pine Point 10 U 6
Pine Ridge 16 C 3
Pinerolo 34 B 2
Pingdingshan 49 J 4
Pinghu 49 L 4
Pingjiang 49 J 5
Pingle 49 J 6
Pingluo 49 H 3
Pingnan 49 J 6
Pingquan 50 C 4
Pingtan 49 K 5
Pingtung 49 L 6
Pingvellir 38 A 3
Pingxiang (Guangxi,China) 49 J 5
Pingxiang (Jiangxi, China) 47 K 4
Pingyang 49 L 5
Pingyao 49 J 3
Pingyin 49 K 3
Pini 52 B 5
Pinjang 52 G 5
Pink Mountain 10 S 7
Pinnaroo 60 G 7
Pinos, Mount 18 C 5
Pinrang 52 F 6
Pinsk 36 F 2
Pinyug 40 L 5
Piombino 34 C 2
Pioner, Ostrov 41 U 2
Piotrków Trybunalski 36 D 2
Pipestone 16 D 3
Pipmuacan, Réser-voir 8 W 9
Pir Panjal Range 45 M 6
Piracicaba 24 G 5
Pirot 34 E 2
Piru 52 H 6
Pisa 34 C 2
Pisco 24 D 4
Pishan 48 B 3
Pisté 20 G 3

Pitalito 22 G 7
Pitcairn Island 59 M 6
Piteå 38 K 2
Piteälven 38 K 2
Pitești 35 A 2
Pit-Gorodoko 41 U 6
Pitt Island 10 Q 8
Pittsburg 16 E 4
Pittsburgh 14 C 2
Pittsfield 14 E 2
Piura 24 C 3
Pivdenyy Buh 36 F 3
Plainview 16 C 5
Plampang 53 F 7
Planalto do Mato Grosso 24 F 4
Plasencia 33 A 1
Plastun 54 C 2
Plateau du Djado 56 E 2
Platte 58 E 2
Platte River 16 D 3
Platteville 16 E 3
Plattsburgh 14 E 2
Plattsmouth 16 D 3
Plauen 36 C 2
Plavnikovye, Ostrova 41 S 3
Plavsk 44 E 2
Play Cu 47 K 6
Playa Azul 20 D 4
Pleasanton 20 E 2
Plenty, Bay of 62 C 2
Plentywood 16 C 2
Plesetsk 40 K 5
Pleven 34 E 2
Pligliang 49 H 3
Pljevlja 34 D 2
Płock 36 D 2
Plöckenpass 36 C 3
Ploiești 35 B 2
Plovdiv 34 E 2
Plumridge Lakes 60 C 5
Plungė 38 K 4
Plymouth (U.K.) 28 B 4
Plzeň 36 C 3
Po (Italy) 34 C 2
Pobeda, Gora 42 N 3
Pobedino 54 D 1
Pocatello 18 D 3
Pocklington Reef 60 K 2
Pocono Mountains 14 D 2
Poços de Caldas 24 G 5
Podgorica 34 D 2
Podgornoye 41 S 6
Podgornyy 54 E 1

Podkagernoye 43 Q 4
Podkamennaya Tun-guska 41 U 5
Podol'sk 40 J 6
Podosinovets 40 L 5
Podporozh'ye 40 H 5
Podyuga 40 K 5
Pogibi 42 M 6
Pogranichnyy 50 F 4
P'ohang 54 A 3
Pohapei 59 E 3
Pohjanmaa 38 K 3
Point Baker 10 Q 7
Point Hope 10 J 5
Point Lake 10 U 5
Point Lay 10 K 5
Pointe-à-Pitre 22 K 4
Pointe-Noire 58 A 2
Poitiers 32 C 2
Poltou 32 B 2
Poivre Atoll 58 E 2
Pokaran 46 C 3
Pokhara 46 E 3
Pokhvistnevo 44 H 2
Pokrovka 54 B 2
Pokrovsk 42 J 4
Poland 36 D 2
Polatlı 35 E 5
Pol-e Khomri 45 L 5
Polesye 36 E 2
Polevskoy 40 O 6
Polewali 52 F 6
Pölgyo 54 A 4
Police 36 C 2
Poliny Osipenko 42 L 6
Pollāchi 46 D 6
Polohy 44 E 3
Polokwane 58 B 4
Polousnyy, Kryazh 42 L 3
Polson 18 D 2
Polunochnoye 40 O 5
Poluostrov Rybachiy 38 M 2
Poluy 40 P 4
Polyarnyy (Russia) 42 N 2
Polyarnyy Ural 40 O 4
Polysayevo 41 T 7
Pomona 18 C 5
Pompeyevka 54 B 1
Ponca City 16 D 4
Ponce 22 J 4
Pond Inlet 8 V 4
Pondicherry 46 D 6
Ponferrada 33 A 1
Ponoj 40 J 4
Ponta Grossa 24 G 5
Pontchartrain, Lake 16 E 5

Pontevedra 33 A 1
Pontiac 14 B 2
Pontianak 52 D 6
Poole 28 D 4
Poona 46 C 5
Popayán 22 G 7
Poplar Bluff 16 E 4
Popocatépetl, Volcán 20 E 4
Poprad 36 E 3
Poptún 20 G 4
Porbandar 46 B 4
Porcupine Plain 10 P 5
Porcupine River 10 O 5
Pordenone 36 C 3
Pori 38 K 3
Porirua 62 B 3
Porkkala 38 K 4
Porlamar 22 K 5
Porog 40 J 5
Poronaysk 50 H 3
Porreres 33 C 2
Porsgrunn 38 G 4
Port Adelaide 60 F 6
Port Alberni 18 B 2
Port Angeles 18 B 2
Port Arthur 49 L 3
Port Arthur (U.S.) 20 F 2
Port Augusta 60 F 6
Port Blair 47 G 6
Port Cartier 8 X 9
Port Chalmers 62 B 4
Port Charlotte 14 C 5
Port Elgin 14 C 2
Port Elizabeth 58 B 5
Port Ellen 30 A 4
Port Gentil 56 D 5
Port Graham 43 Z 5
Port Harcourt 56 D 4
Port Hard 10 R 8
Port Hedland 60 B 4
Port Heiden 43 Y 5
Port Hope Smith 8 Z 8
Port Huron 14 C 2
Port Jackson 62 C 2
Port Láirge 31 C 2
Port Laoise 31 C 2
Port Lavaca 20 E 2
Port Lincoln 60 F 6
Port Louis 58 E 3
Port Macquarie 60 J 6
Port Moller 43 X 5
Port Moresby 59 D 4
Port of Ness 30 A 2
Port of Spain 22 K 5
Port Ontario 14 D 2

Port Phillip Bay 60 G 7
Pontiac 14 B 2
Port Pirie 60 F 6
Port Sulphur 20 G 2
Port Talbot 28 C 4
Portadown 31 C 1
Portage la-Prairie 16 D 2
Portales 16 C 5
Port-au-Prince 22 H 4
Porterville 18 C 4
Portile de Fier 34 E 2
Portland (Aust.) 60 G 7
Portland (Maine, U.S.) 14 E 2
Portland (Washing-ton, U.S.) 18 B 2
Portland, Bill of 28 C 4
Porto 33 A 1
Porto Alegre 24 F 6
Pôrto Santo 56 B 1
Porto Velho 24 E 3
Porto-Novo 56 D 4
Portoviejo 24 C 3
Portsmouth (New Hampshire, U.S.) 14 E 2
Portsmouth (Ohio, U.S.) 14 C 3
Portsmouth (U.K.) 28 D 4
Portsmouth (Virginia, U.S.) 14 D 3
Portsoy 30 C 3
Portugal 33 A 1
Posadas 24 F 5
Poso 53 G 6
Potenza 34 D 2
Potholes Reservoir 18 B 2
P'ot'i 35 J 3
Potomac River 14 D 3
Potosi 24 E 4
Potsdam 36 C 2
Pottstown 14 D 2
Považská Bystrica 36 D 3
Powassan 14 D 1
Powder River 18 E 2
Powell River 18 B 2
Powell, Lake 18 D 4
Poyarkovo 54 A 1
Poza Rica de Hidalgo 20 E 3
Požarevac 34 E 2
Poznań 36 D 2
Pozoblanco 33 B 2
Prachuap Khiri Khan 47 H 6
Pradesh 46 D 2

Prague 36 C 2
Praha 36 C 2
Praia 56 A 3
Prairie du Chien 16 E 3
Praslin 58 E 2
Pratapgarh 46 C 4
Prato 34 C 2
Pratt 16 D 4
Praya 52 F 7
Prentice 16 E 2
Prenzlau 36 C 2
Preparis Island 47 G 6
Preparis South Channel 47 G 6
Prescott 18 D 5
Prescott Island 8 R 4
Presidente Prudente 24 F 5
Prešov 36 E 3
Presque Isle 14 F 1
Preston (U.K.) 28 C 3
Preston (U.S.) 18 D 3
Prestonburg 14 C 3
Prestwick 28 B 2
Pretoria 58 B 4
Preveza 34 E 3
Priangarskoye Plato 41 V 6
Pribilof Islands 43 W 5
Priboj 34 D 2
Přibram 36 C 3
Price 18 D 4
Prichard 14 B 4
Prieta, Sierra 18 D 5
Prievidza 36 D 3
Prilep 34 E 2
Primorskiy Kray 54 B 2
Primorsko-Akhtarsk 35 H 1
Prince Albert 10 V 8
Prince Albert Na-tional Park 10 V 8
Prince Charles Island 8 V 5
Prince Edward Island (Island) 8 Y 9
Prince Edward Island (Province) 8 Y 9
Prince George 10 S 8
Prince of Wales Island (Australia) 60 G 2
Prince of Wales Island (Canada) 8 R 4
Prince of Wales Is-land (U.S.) 10 Q 7

Prince of Wales, Cape 43 W 3
Prince Patrick Island 10 T 3
Prince Regent Inlet 8 S 4
Prince Rupert 10 Q 8
Princess Charlotte Bay 60 G 2
Princess Royal Island 10 R 8
Princeton (Canada) 18 B 2
Princeton (U.S.) 14 B 3
Príncipe 56 D 4
Prineville 18 B 3
Prinsesse Astrid Kyst 63 P 5
Prinsesse Ragnhild Kyst 63 P 5
Priozersk 40 H 5
Pripolyarnyy Ural 40 N 5
Priština 34 E 2
Privolzhskaya Vozvyshennost' 44 G 2
Priyutovo 44 H 2
Prizren 34 E 2
Proddatür 46 D 6
Progreso 20 G 3
Prokhladnyy 35 K 3
Prokop'yevsk 41 T 7
Prokuplje 34 E 2
Proletarsk 44 F 3
Prome 47 H 5
Prosser 18 C 2
Prøven 8 Z 4
Provence 34 B 2
Providence 58 E 2
Providence (U.S.) 14 E 2
Providence, Cape 62 A 4
Providencia, Isla de 22 F 5
Provideniya 43 V 4
Provincetown 14 E 2
Provo 18 D 3
Prudhoe Bay 10 N 4
Pruszków 36 E 2
Pruzhany 36 E 2
Pryluki 36 G 2
Prypyats' 36 F 2
Przemyśl 36 E 3
P'sek 36 C 3
Pskov 38 L 4
Pucallpa 24 D 3
Pucheng 49 K 5
Puch'ŏn 54 A 3
Pudasjärvi 38 L 2
Pudino 41 R 6
Pudops Dam 8 Z 9

Pudozh 40 J 5
Puebla (Mexico) 20 E 4
Puebla (State, Mexico) 20 E 4
Pueblo 16 C 4
Puente Alto 24 D 6
Puente-Genil 33 B 2
Puerto Ángel 20 E 4
Puerto Arista 20 F 4
Puerto Ayacucho 22 J 6
Puerto Baquerizo Moreno 24 C 3
Puerto Barrios 20 G 4
Puerto Cabello 22 J 5
Puerto Cabezas 20 H 5
Puerto Cortés 20 G 4
Puerto Cumarebo 22 J 5
Puerto Escondito 20 E 4
Puerto Juárez 20 G 3
Puerto la Cruz 22 K 5
Puerto Lempira 20 H 4
Puerto Libertad 20 B 2
Puerto Madero 20 F 5
Puerto Montt 24 D 7
Puerto Plata 22 H 4
Puerto Princesa 53 F 4
Puerto Rico 22 J 4
Puerto Vallarta 20 C 3
Puertollano 33 B 2
Pugachev 44 G 2
Puget Sound 18 B 2
Pukapuka (Cook Islands) 59 J 5
Pukapuka (French Polynesia) 59 M 5
Pukaruha 59 M 5
Pukch'ŏng 50 E 4
Puketeraki Range 62 B 3
Pula 34 C 2
Pulap 59 D 3
Pulau Penida 60 B 1
Puławy 36 E 2
Pullman 18 C 2
Pulupandan 52 G 3
Puluwat 59 D 3
Puncak Trikora 59 C 4
Pune 46 C 5

Punjab (India) 46 D 2
Punjab (Pakistan) 46 C 2
Puno 24 D 4
Punta Arenas 24 D 8
Punta Carreta 24 D 4
Punta Cristóbal 24 B 3
Punta Gorda (Belize) 20 G 4
Punta Prieta 20 B 2
Punto Fijo 22 H 5
Puper 52 J 6
Puqi 49 J 5
Pur 41 R 4
Purekkari neem 38 L 4
Puri 46 F 5
Purnea 46 F 3
Purtuniq 8 W 6
Purwakarta 52 D 7
Purwokerto 52 D 7
Pusan 50 E 5
Pushkin 40 H 6
Putaruru 62 C 2
Putian 49 K 5
Puting, Tanjung 52 E 6
Putla de Guerrero 20 E 4
Putorana, Plato 41 U 4
Putrajaya 52 C 5
Puttalan 46 D 7
Puttgarden 36 C 2
Puvirnituq 8 V 6
Puyang 49 J 3
Pwllheli 28 B 3
Pyandzh 45 L 5
Pyapon 47 H 5
Pyasina 41 T 3
Pyasino, Ozero 41 T 4
Pyatigorsk 44 F 4
Pyatistennoy 43 Q 3
Pyhäjärvi 38 L 3
Pyinmana 47 H 5
Pylos 34 E 3
P'yŏngyang 50 E 5
Pyramid Lake 18 C 3
Pyrénées 32 B 3
Pyrgos 34 E 3
Pyryatyn 36 G 2
Pyu 47 H 5
Qaanaaq 8 X 3
Qabanbay 45 O 3
Qābis (Gabès) 56 D 1
Qafşah 56 D 1
Qaidam Pendi 48 E 3
Qala Nau 45 K 6
Qamashi 45 L 5

Qamdo 48 F 4
Qapshaghay 45 N 4
Qapshaghay Bögeni 45 N 4
Qaqortoq 8 Bb 6
Qarabutaq 45 K 3
Qaraghandy 45 M 3
Qaraghayly 45 N 3
Qaraqum 44 H 3
Qarataū 45 M 4
Qarataū Zhotasy 45 L 4
Qaratöbe 44 H 3
Qarazhal 45 M 3
Qarsaqbay 45 L 3
Qarshi 45 L 5
Qasigiannguit 8 Aa 5
Qaskeleng 45 N 4
Qaynar 45 N 3
Qazaqtyng Usaqshoqylyghy 45 J 3
Qazvīn 44 G 5
Qeqertarsuaq 8 Aa 5
Qeqertarsuaq (Island) 8 Aa 5
Qeshqantengiz 45 M 3
Qian Gorios 50 D 3
Qianwei 49 G 5
Qianxi 49 H 5
Qiemo 48 D 3
Qijiang 49 H 5
Qijiaojing 48 E 2
Qikiqtarjuaq 8 Y 5
Qilian Shan 48 F 3
Qin'an 49 H 4
Qingdao 49 L 3
Qinggang 50 E 3
Qinghai 48 E 3
Qinghai Hu 48 F 3
Qinghe 48 E 1
Qingjiang 49 K 4
Qingyuan 49 J 6
Qinhuangdao 49 K 3
Qinling Shan 49 H 4
Qinzhou 49 H 6
Qionghai 47 L 5
Qionglai 49 G 4
Qiongshan 47 L 5
Qiqihar 50 D 3
Qitai 48 D 2
Qitaihe 54 B 1
Qiyang 49 J 5
Qom 44 H 6
Qomsheh 44 H 6
Qo'ng'irot 45 J 4
Qo'qon 45 M 4
Qoraqo'l 45 K 5
Qoryooley 58 D 1
Qosköl 45 L 3
Qosshaghyl 44 H 3
Qostanay 45 K 2
Qotanqaraghay 45 P 3

Quan Dao Nam Du 47 J 7
Quang Ngai 47 K 5
Quanjyang 49 J 5
Quanzhou (Fujian, China) 49 K 6
Quanzhou (Guangxi,China) 49 J 5
Qu'Appelle River 16 C 1
Quaqtaq 8 X 6
Quartu Sant'Elena 34 B 3
Quartzsite 18 D 5
Quatro Ciénegas 20 D 2
Qūchān 45 J 5
Québec 8 W 9
Québec (Canada) 14 E 1
Québec (State) 8 V 8
Queen Charlotte Islands 10 Q 8
Queen Elizabeth Islands 8 S 3
Queen Mary Land 63 S 5
Queen Maud Gulf 10 W 5
Queensland 60 F 4
Queenstown 58 B 5
Quelimane 58 C 3
Quemado 18 E 5
Querétaro (Mexico) 20 D 3
Querétaro (State, Mexico) 20 E 3
Quesnel 10 S 8
Quetta 46 B 2
Quezaltenango 22 D 5
Quezon City 52 G 3
Qui Nhon 47 K 6
Quibdó 22 G 6
Quilá 20 C 3
Quilon 46 D 7
Quilpie 60 G 5
Quimer 49 K 5
Quimper 32 B 2
Quincy 16 E 4
Quintana Roo 20 G 4
Quiriguá 20 G 4
Quitasueño, Banco 22 F 5
Quito 24 D 3
Qujing 49 G 5
Qulsary 44 H 3
Qumarlêb Jiuzhi 48 F 4
Qürghonteppa 45 L 5
Qūs 56 G 2

Qusmurun Köli 45 K 2
Quxian 49 K 5
Qvareli 35 L 4
Qyzylorda 45 L 4
Raas Caseyr 56 J 3
Raas Xaafuun 56 J 4
Raasay, Sound of 30 A 3
Raba 53 F 7
Rabat 56 C 1
Râbniţa 36 F 3
Rach Gia 47 K 6
Racine 14 B 2
Rădăuţi 36 F 3
Radomsko 36 D 2
Radøy 38 F 3
Radviliškis 38 K 4
Radville 16 C 2
Rae-Edzo 10 T 6
Raevavae 59 L 6
Ragged Island Range 22 G 3
Ragusa 34 C 3
Rahīmyār Khān 46 C 3
Raiatea 59 K 5
Raichur 46 D 5
Raigarh 46 E 4
Rainy Lake 16 E 2
Raipur 46 E 4
Rāj Gangpur 46 E 4
Raj Nandgaon 46 E 4
Rajabasa 52 C 7
Rājahmundry 46 E 5
Rajanpur 46 C 3
Rājapālaiyam 46 D 7
Rajasthan 46 C 3
Rajkot 46 C 4
Rājmahal Hills 46 E 4
Rajshahi 47 F 4
Rakahanga 59 J 4
Rakaia 62 B 3
Rakitnoye 54 B 1
Raleigh 14 D 3
Raleigh Bay 14 D 4
Râmnicu Sărat 36 F 3
Râmnicu Vâlcea 36 E 3
Rampur 46 D 3
Ramree Island 47 G 5
Ramsey (Canada) 14 C 1
Ramsey (U.K.) 28 B 2
Ramsgate 28 E 4
Rāna Pratāp Sāgar 46 D 4
Rancagua 24 D 6
Ranchi 46 F 4

Randers 38 H 4
Rangaunu Bay 62 B 1
Ranger 16 D 5
Rangiroa 59 L 5
Rangkasbitung 52 D 7
Rangoon 47 H 5
Rangpur 47 F 3
Rangsang 52 C 5
Ranibennur 46 D 6
Rankin Inlet 8 S 6
Ranonga 47 H 7
Ransiki 53 J 6
Rantau 52 C 5
Rantauprapat 52 B 5
Raohe 54 B 1
Raoul Island 59 H 6
Rapa 59 L 6
Raper, Cape 8 X 5
Rapid City 16 C 3
Raraka 59 L 5
Raroia 59 L 5
Rarotonga 59 K 6
Ra's Ajdir 56 E 1
Râs Koh 46 B 3
Râs Tîmirist 56 B 3
Rasht 44 G 5
Rasskazovo 44 F 2
Rat Island 43 T 6
Ratak Chain 59 F 3
Ratangarh 46 C 3
Rath 46 D 3
Rathenow 36 C 2
Rathlin Island 31 C 1
Ratlam 46 D 4
Ratnagiri 46 C 5
Raton 16 C 4
Rattray Head 30 D 3
Rättvik 38 J 3
Raub 52 C 5
Rauma 38 K 3
Raumo 38 K 3
Raurkela 46 E 4
Rausu 54 E 2
Ravahere 59 L 5
Ravenna 34 C 2
Ravensthorpe 60 C 6
Rawaki 59 H 4
Rãwalpindi 45 M 6
Rawlinna 60 D 6
Rawlins 18 E 3
Rawson 24 E 7
Rãyadrug 46 D 6
Rãyagarha 46 E 5
Raychikhinsk 50 E 3
Raymond 18 B 2
Raymondville 20 E 2
Rayón 20 E 3
Rayong 47 J 6
Razgrad 34 F 2
Ré, Île de 32 B 2
Reading 28 D 4
Reao 59 M 5

Reata 20 D 2
Rebecca, Lake 60 C 6
Rebi 53 J 7
Reboly 40 H 5
Rebun-To 50 H 3
Rebun-to 54 C 1
Recherche, Archipel-ago of the 60 C 6
Rechna Doab 46 C 2
Rechytsa 36 G 2
Recife 24 H 3
Récifs Bampton 59 E 5
Red Bank 14 B 3
Red Basin 49 H 4
Red Bluff 18 B 3
Red Cloud 16 D 3
Red Deer 10 U 8
Red Deer River 10 U 8
Red Devil 43 Y 4
Red Lake 10 Y 8
Red Lake (Lake, On-tario, Canada) 16 C 1
Red Lodge 18 E 2
Red Oak 16 D 3
Red River (Canada) 16 D 2
Red River (U.S.) 16 C 5
Red Rock River 18 D 3
Red Sea 56 G 2
Red Wing 16 E 3
Redcliffe 60 J 5
Redding 18 B 3
Redditch 28 D 3
Redfield 16 D 3
Redlands 18 C 5
Redon 32 B 2
Redoubt Volcano 10 M 6
Redruth 28 B 4
Ree, Lough 31 B 2
Reef Islands 59 F 4
Reefton 62 B 3
Regensburg 36 C 3
Reggio di Calabria 34 D 3
Reggio nell' Emilia 34 C 2
Reghin 36 E 3
Regina 10 W 8
Reims 32 C 2
Reindeer Lake 10 W 7
Reine 38 H 2
Reinosa 33 B 1
Reitoru 59 L 5
Rekinniki 43 Q 4
Reliance 10 V 6
Rembang 52 E 7

Remontnoye 44 F 3
Rendsburg 36 B 2
Renfrew 14 D 1
Rengat 52 C 6
Renland 8 Ff 4
Renmark 60 G 6
Rennell Island 59 F 5
Rennes 32 B 2
Reno 18 C 4
Renton 18 B 2
Reo 52 G 7
Replot 38 K 3
Represa Boa Esper-ança 24 G 3
Represa Trés Marias 24 G 4
Republic 18 C 2
Republican River 16 D 4
Repulse Bay 8 T 5
Reşadiye 35 G 4
Reserve 18 E 5
Reshteh-ye Kūhhā-yeAlborz 44 H 5
Resistencia 24 E 5
Reşiţa 36 E 3
Resolution Island (Canada) 8 Y 6
Resolution Island (New Zealand) 62 A 4
Retalhuleu 20 F 5
Retkucha 43 S 3
Réunion (France) 58 E 4
Reus 32 C 3
Revda 40 N 6
Revelstoke 10 T 8
Revillagigedo Island 10 Q 7
Rewa 46 E 4
Rexburg 18 D 3
Rey 44 H 5
Rey, Isla del 22 G 6
Reyhanlı 35 G 6
Reykjav'k 38 A 3
Reynosa 20 E 2
Rēzekne 38 L 4
Rezh 40 O 6
Rhein 36 B 3
Rhinelander 14 B 1
Rhode Island 14 E 2
Rhodes 34 F 3
Rhondda 28 C 4
Rhône 32 C 3
Rhum 30 A 3
Riau, Kepulauan 52 C 5
Ribadeo 33 A 1
Ribe 38 G 4
Ribeirão Prêto 24 G 5
Richards, Cape 8 V 2

Richfield 18 D 4
Richland 18 C 2
Richmond (California, U.S.) 18 B 4
Richmond (New Zealand) 62 B 3
Richmond (Virginia, U.S.) 14 D 3
Riding Mountain Na-tional Park 10 W 8
Riesa 36 C 2
Rieti 34 C 2
Rīga 38 K 4
Riga, Gulf of 38 K 4
Riggins 18 C 2
Rigolet 8 Z 8
Rijeka 36 C 3
Riksgränsen 38 J 2
Riley 18 C 3
Rimatara 59 K 6
Rimini 34 C 2
Rimouski 8 X 9
Rinbung 48 D 5
Rinca 53 F 7
Ringsvassøy 38 J 2
Rio Amazonas 24 E 3
Rio Beni 24 E 4
Rio Branco 24 E 4
Río Cuarto 24 E 6
Rio das Balsas 24 G 3
Rio de Janeiro 24 G 5
Rio de Oro 56 B 2
Río Gallegos 24 E 8
Rio Grande 24 F 6
Río Grande (Nicaragua) 20 G 5
Rio Grande (U.S.) 18 E 5
Río Lagartos 20 G 3
Rio Madeira 24 E 3
Río Madre de Dios 24 E 4
Río Negro 24 E 3
Rio Paraguai 24 F 4
Río Paraná 24 F 6
Rio Parnaíba 24 G 3
Rio Roosevelt 24 E 3
Río São 24 G 4
Ric Tapajós 24 F 3
Rio Teles Pires 24 F 4
Rio Tocantins 24 G 3
Río Ucayali 24 D 3
Ríoverde (Mexico) 20 D 3
Ripon 28 D 2
Rishiri-Tô 50 H 3
Ritzville 18 C 2
Riverside 18 C 5
Riverton (Canada) 16

D 1
Riverton (New Zealand) 62 A 4
Riverton (U.S.) 18 E 3
Rivière-du-Loup 8 X 9
Rivne 36 F 2
Rivoli 36 B 3
Rize 35 J 4
Rizhao 49 K 3
Roan Plateau 18 E 4
Roanne 32 C 2
Roanoke 14 D 3
Roanoke Rapids 14 D 3
Roanoke River 14 D 3
Roatán 20 G 4
Robeson Channel 8 Y 2
Robinson Ranges 60 B 5
Robstown 20 E 2
Roca Partida, Isla 20 B 4
Rochefort 32 B 2
Rochester (Min-nesota, U.S.) 16 E 3
Rochester (New Hampshire, U.S.) 14 E 2
Rochester (New York, U.S.) 14 D 2
Rock Hill 14 C 4
Rock Island 16 E 3
Rock River 16 E 3
Rock Springs 18 E 3
Rockford 14 B 2
Rockhampton 60 J 4
Rockingham (U.S.) 14 D 4
Rocklands Reservoir 60 G 7
Rockport 20 E 2
Rockville 14 D 3
Rocky Mount 14 D 3
Rocky Mountain Na-tional Park 18 E 3
Rocky Mountains (Canada) 10 S 7
Rocky Mountains (U.S.) 18 E 5
Rodeo (Mexico) 20 D 2
Rodeo (U.S.) 18 E 5
Rodez 32 C 3
Rodney, Cape 43 W 4
Rodos 34 F 3
Rodos (Greece) 35 C 6
Rodos (Island) 34 F 3
Rodos (Rhodes) Is-land 35 C 6

Rogaland 38 G 4
Rogers Peak 18 D 4
Rogue River 18 B 3
R'ohacha 22 H 5
Rohri 46 B 3
Rohtak 46 D 3
Roi Et 47 J 5
Roi Georges, Îles du 59 L 5
Rojo, Cabo (Mexico) 20 E 3
Røldal 38 G 4
Rolla (Missouri, U.S.) 16 E 4
Rolla (North Dakota, U.S.) 16 D 2
Rolvsøya 38 K 1
Roma (Australia) 60 H 5
Roma (Italy) 34 C 2
Roman 36 F 3
Romang 52 H 7
Romania 36 E 3
Romanovka 42 F 6
Rome (Georgia, U.S.) 14 B 4
Rome (Italy) 34 C 2
Rome (New York, U.S.) 14 D 2
Romny 36 G 2
Rømø 36 B 2
Roncador Reef 59 E 4
Roncador, Cayos de 22 F 5
Rondane 38 G 3
Rondonópolis 24 F 4
Rongan 49 H 5
Rongelap 59 F 2
Rongerik 59 F 2
Rongjiang 49 H 5
Rongxian (Guangxi,China) 49 J 6
Rongxian (Sichuan,China) 49 G 5
Rønne 38 H 4
Ronneby 38 H 4
Roquefort 32 B 3
Roraima 22 K 7
Røros 38 H 3
Rosamorada 20 C 3
Rosario (Argentina) 24 E 6
Rosario (Baja Califor-nia Sur, Mexico) 20 B 2
Rosario (Sinaloa, Mexico) 20 C 3
Rosario, Bahía 18 C 5
Roscommon 31 B 2
Roscrea 31 C 2
Rose Island 59 J 5

Roseau 22 K 4
Roseburg 18 B 3
Rosenberg 20 E 2
Rosenheim 36 C 3
Rosetown 10 V 8
Roşiorii-de-Vede 34 F 2
Roskilde 38 H 4
Roslavl' 36 G 2
Roslyn 18 B 2
Ross River 10 Q 6
Rossan Point 31 B 1
Rossel Island 60 J 2
Rosslare 31 C 2
Rossosh' 44 E 2
Røst 38 H 2
Rostock 36 C 2
Rostov 40 J 6
Rostov-na-Donu 44 E 3
Roswell 16 C 5
Rota (Northern Mariana Islands) 59 D 2
Rota (Spain) 33 A 2
Rote 53 G 8
Rotorua 62 C 2
Rouen 32 C 2
Rousay 30 C 2
Rouyn 8 V 9
Rovaniemi 38 L 2
Rovigo 36 C 3
Rovnoye 44 G 2
Rowley Island 8 V 5
Roxas 53 G 3
Roxburgh 62 A 4
Roy 16 C 4
Royal Canal 31 C 2
Royal Tunbridge Wells 28 E 4
Royale, Isle 14 B 1
Royan 32 B 2
Rtishchevo 44 F 2
Ruacana Falls 58 A 3
Ruahine Range 62 C 3
Rubtsovsk 45 O 2
Ruby 10 L 6
Ruby Mountains 18 C 4
Rüd Sar 44 H 5
Rudbar 45 K 6
Rudkøbing 36 C 2
Rudnya 36 G 2
Rüdnyy 45 K 2
Rudyard 18 D 2
Rufino 24 E 6
Rugao 49 L 4
Rugby 16 C 2
Rügen 36 C 2
Ruhnu Saar 38 K 4
Rui'an 49 L 5
Ruijin 49 K 5
Rumbek 56 F 4

Rumoi 54 D 2
Runan 49 J 4
Runaway, Cape 62 C 2
Rupat 52 C 5
Rupert 18 D 3
Rurutu 59 K 6
Ruse 34 F 2
Russell (Canada) 16 C 1
Russell (New Zealand) 62 B 2
Russell Island 8 R 4
Russell Islands 59 E 4
Russell Range 60 C 6
Russellville (Alabama, U.S.) 14 B 4
Russellville (Arkansas, U.S.) 16 E 4
Russia 41 R 5
Russkiy, Ostrov 41 U 2
Rust'avi 35 L 4
Rustenburg 58 B 4
Ruston 16 E 5
Ruteng 53 F 7
Ruthin 28 C 3
Rutland 47 G 6
Rutog 48 B 4
Ruzayevka 44 F 2
Ružomberok 36 D 3
Rwanda 58 C 2
Ryazan' 44 E 2
Ryazhsk' 44 F 2
Rybinsk 40 J 6
Rybinskoye Vodokhranilishche 40 J 6
Rybnik 36 D 2
Ryegate 18 E 2
Ryl'sk 36 G 2
Ryōtsu 54 C 3
Ryukyu Islands 50 E 7
Rzeszów 36 E 2
Rzhev 40 H 6
Sa Dec 47 K 6
Saarbrücken 36 B 3
Saaremaa 38 K 4
Saariselkä 38 L 2
Šabac 34 D 2
Sabadell 32 C 3
Sabah 52 F 5
Sabanalarga 22 G 5
Sabinas 20 D 2
Sabinas Hidalgo 20 D 2
Sabine River 16 E 5
Sable Island 8 Z 10
Sable, Cape 14 F 2
Sabzevär 45 J 5

Sacajawea Peak 18 C 2
Sach'ŏn 54 A 4
Sachs Harbour 10 R 4
Saco 18 E 2
Sacramento 18 B 4
Sacramento Mountains 18 E 5
Sacramento River 18 B 3
Sacramento Valley 18 B 3
Sado 54 C 3
Sadovoye 44 F 3
Safāgis 34 C 4
Safford 18 E 5
Safi 56 C 1
Safronovo 40 L 4
Saga 54 B 4
Sagang 47 H 4
Sagar 46 D 4
Sagay 52 G 3
Saghyz 44 H 3
Saginaw 14 C 2
Saginaw Bay 14 C 2
Saglouc 8 V 6
Sagres 33 A 2
Sagua la Grande 22 F 3
Sagunto 33 B 2
Sagwon 10 N 5
Sahagun 22 G 6
Sahagún 33 A 1
Sahara 56 C 2
Saharanpur 46 D 3
Sahiwal 46 C 2
Sahrā' al Ḥajārah 44 F 6
Sahuaripa 20 C 2
Sahuayo 20 D 3
Saibai 59 D 4
Saigon 47 K 6
Saiki 54 B 4
Saimaa 38 L 3
Sain Alto 20 D 3
Saint Albans 14 E 2
Saint Albert 10 U 8
Saint Andrews 30 C 3
Saint Anthony 8 Z 8
Saint Augustine 14 C 5
Saint Austell 28 B 4
Saint Clair River 14 C 2
Saint Cloud 16 E 2
Saint Croix 22 K 4
Saint David's Head 28 B 4
Saint Eustatius 22 K 4
Saint Francis 16 C 4
Saint François 58 E 2

Saint Francois Mountains 16 E 4
Saint George (Utah, U.S.) 18 D 4
Saint George, Cape 59 E 4
Saint George's 22 K 5
Saint George's Channel (U.K.) 31 C 3
Saint Helens 28 C 3
Saint Ignace 14 C 1
Saint Ignace Island 8 T 9
Saint John 14 F 1
Saint Johns 18 E 5
Saint John's (Antigua and Barbuda) 22 K 4
Saint John's (Canada) 8 Aa 9
Saint Johns River 14 C 4
Saint Johnsbury 14 E 2
Saint Joseph 58 E 2
Saint Joseph (U.S.) 16 E 4
Saint Joseph, Lake 10 Y 8
Saint Kitts 22 K 4
Saint Kitts-Nevis 22 K 4
Saint Lawrence 8 X 9
Saint Lawrence Island 43 V 4
Saint Lawrence, Gulf of 8 Y 9
Saint Louis 16 E 4
Saint Lucia 22 K 5
Saint Marks 14 C 4
Saint Martin 22 K 4
Saint Matthew Island 43 V 4
Saint Matthias Group 59 D 4
Saint Michael 43 X 4
Saint Paul (Minnesota, U.S.) 16 E 2
Saint Petersburg (U.S.) 14 C 5
Saint Petersburgh (Russia) 40 H 6
Saint Pierre 58 D 2
Saint Pierre et Miquelon 8 Z 9
Saint Stephen 14 F 1
Saint Thomas (Canada) 14 C 2
Saint Vincent and The Grenadines 22 K 5

Saint'Antioco, Isola di 34 B 3
Saint-Brieuc 32 B 2
Saint-Dié 36 B 3
Saint-Dizier 32 C 2
Saintes 32 B 2
Sainte-Therese 8 W 9
Saint-Étienne 32 C 2
Saint-Jean-sur-Richelieu 8 W 9
Saint-Jérôme 8 W 9
Saint-Malo 32 B 2
Saint-Malo, Golfe de 32 B 2
Saint-Nazaire 32 B 2
Saint-Quentin 32 C 2
Saipan 59 D 2
Sakai 54 C 4
Sakakawea, Lake 16 C 2
Sakarya 44 D 4
Sakata 54 C 3
Sakchu 54 A 2
Sakhalin 50 H 2
Sakht Sar 44 H 5
Säki 44 G 4
Saki 56 D 4
Sakon Nakhon 47 J 5
Sakti 46 E 4
Sal 56 A 3
Salamá 20 F 4
Salamanca 33 A 1
Salamanca (Mexico) 20 D 3
Salamat 56 F 3
Salamis 44 D 5
Salar de Uyuni 24 E 5
Salavat 40 N 7
Salayar 53 G 7
Saldus 38 K 4
Sale 60 H 7
Salekhard 40 P 4
Salem (Illinois, U.S.) 14 B 3
Salem (India) 46 D 6
Salem (Oregon, U.S.) 18 B 3
Salerno 34 C 2
Salerno, Golfo di 34 C 2
Salgótarján 36 D 3
Salgueiro 24 H 3
Salhus 38 G 3
Salida 18 E 4
Salihli 35 C 5
Salihorsk 36 F 2
Salina (Kansas, U.S.) 16 D 4
Salina (Utah, U.S.) 18 D 4
Salinas (U.S.) 18 B 4
Salinas de Hidalgo

20 D 3
Salinas Grandes 24 E 5
Salines, Cap de ses 33 C 2
Salisbury (Australia) 60 F 6
Salisbury (U.K.) 28 D 4
Salisbury Island 8 V 6
Salmon 18 D 2
Salmon River 18 C 2
Salmon River Mountains 18 C 3
Salon-de-Provence 34 B 2
Sal'sk 44 F 3
Salt Fork 16 C 5
Salt Lake City 18 D 3
Salt River 18 D 5
Salta 24 E 5
Saltillo 20 D 2
Salto das Sete Quedas 24 F 5
Salton Sea 18 C 5
Sālūr 46 E 5
Salvador 24 H 4
Salvatierra 20 D 3
Salween 47 H 4
Salzburg 36 C 3
Salzgitter 36 C 2
Salzwedel 36 C 2
Sam Rayburn Reservoir 16 D 5
Samales Group 53 G 4
Samar 52 H 3
Samar Sea 52 G 3
Samara 44 H 2
Samarinda 52 F 6
Samarqand 45 L 5
Sambalpur 46 E 4
Sambas 52 D 5
Sambir 36 E 3
Samboja 52 F 6
Samburg 41 R 4
Samch'ŏk 50 E 5
Samch'ŏnp'o 50 E 6
Samoa 59 H 5
Samoa Islands 59 H 5
Samokov 34 E 2
Samos 34 F 3
Samothraki 34 F 2
Sampit 52 E 6
Samsang 48 C 4
Samsun 35 G 4
Samtredia 35 K 3
Samut Songkhram 47 H 6
San Agustin, Cape 53 H 4
San Andres Moun-

tains 18 E 5
San Andrés Tuxtla 20 E 4
San Andrés y Providencia 22 G 5
San Angelo 16 C 5
San Antonio (U.S.) 20 E 2
San Antonio Bay 20 E 2
San Antonio, Cabo 22 F 3
San Benedetto del Tronto 34 C 2
San Benedicto, Isla 20 B 4
San Bernardino 18 C 5
San Bernardo 24 D 6
San Bernardo (Mexico) 20 B 2
San Blas 20 C 2
San Blas, Cape 14 B 6
San Borjas, Sierra de 20 B 2
San Buenaventura 20 D 2
San Carlos (Mexico) 20 E 3
San Carlos de Bariloche 24 D 7
San Clemente 18 C 5
San Clemente Island 18 C 5
San Cristobal 59 F 5
San Cristóbal (Dominican Republic) 22 H 4
San Cristóbal (Venezuela) 22 H 6
San Cristóbal de las Casas 20 F 4
San Diego 18 C 5
San Felipe (Mexico) 18 D 5
San Felipe (Mexico) 20 D 3
San Felipe (Venezuela) 22 J 5
San Fernando 22 K 5
San Fernando (Mexico) 20 E 3
San Fernando (Spain) 33 A 2
San Fernando de Apure 22 J 6
San Fernando(Philippines) 53 G 2
San Francisco (U.S.) 18 B 4

San Franciscó de Macoris 22 H 4
San Francisco del Oro 20 C 2
San Francisco del Rincón 20 D 3
San Gottardo, Passo del 36 B 3
San Hilario 20 B 3
San Ignacio (Belize) 20 G 4
San Ignacio (Mexico) 20 B 2
San Joaquin River 18 C 4
San Joaquin Valley 18 B 4
San Jorge Island 59 E 4
San Jorge, Bahía de 18 D 5
San Jose 53 G 2
San José (Costa Rica) 22 F 6
San José (Guatemala) 20 F 5
San José (U.S.) 18 B 4
San Jose de Buenavista 53 G 3
San Jose de Guanipa 22 K 6
San José del Cabo 20 C 3
San José, Isla 20 B 2
San Juan 24 E 6
San Juan de Guadalupe 20 D 3
San Juan del Norte, Bah'a de 22 F 5
San Juan del Río (Durango, Mexico) 20 D 3
San Juan del Río (Queretaro, Mexico) 20 E 3
San Juan Mountains 18 E 4
San Lázaro, Sierra de 20 B 3
San Lorenzo, Río 20 C 3
San Lucas (Mexico) 20 C 3
San Lucas, Cabo 20 B 3
San Luis 24 E 6
San Luis (Mexico) 20 B 2
San Luis de la Paz 20 D 3
San Luís Gonzaga, Bahía 18 D 5

San Luis Obispo 18 B 4
San Luis Peak 18 E 4
San Luis Potosí (Mexico) 20 D 3
San Luis Potosí (State, Mexico) 20 D 3
San Marcos (Mexico) 20 D 3
San Marcos (Mexico) 20 E 4
San Marcos (U.S.) 20 E 2
San Marino 34 C 2
San Miguel 22 E 5
San Miguel de Allende 20 D 3
San Miguel de Tucumán 24 E 5
San Miguel Islands 53 F 4
San Miguel Sola de Vega 20 E 4
San Nicolás (Mexico) 20 D 2
San Pablo (Philippines) 53 G 3
San Pédro 56 C 4
San Pedro (Mexico) 20 D 2
San Pedro Pochutla 20 E 4
San Pedro Sula 20 G 4
San Pietro, Isola di 34 B 3
San Quintín 18 C 5
San Quintín, Bahía de 18 C 5
San Rafael 24 E 6
San Rafael (Mexico) 20 D 2
San Remo 34 B 2
San Salvador 22 E 5
San Salvador (El Salvador) 20 G 5
San Salvador de Jujuy 24 E 5
San Salvador Island 22 G 3
San Severo 34 D 2
San Telmo 18 C 5
San Vicente (Mexico) 18 C 5
San Vincente 52 G 2
San Vito, Capo 34 C 3
Sanaga 56 E 4
Sanak Island 43 X 6
Sanana 53 H 6
Sanandaj 44 G 5
Sancti Spiritus 22 G 3

Sand 38 G 4
Sand Cay 46 C 6
Sand Hills 16 C 3
Sandagou 54 B 2
Sandakan 52 F 4
Sandane 38 G 3
Sandanski 34 E 2
Sanday 30 C 2
Sandbukt 38 K 2
Sandefjord 38 H 4
Sandıklı 35 D 5
Sandnes 38 G 4
Sandoway 47 G 5
Sandown 28 D 4
Sandoy 38 D 3
Sandstone (Australia) 60 B 5
Sandusky 14 C 2
Sandviken 38 J 3
Sandy Cape 60 J 4
Sandy Lake 10 Y 8
Sangamner 46 C 5
Sanger 18 C 4
Sanggau 52 E 5
Sangir 53 H 5
Sangir, Kepulauan 53 H 5
Sangiyn Dalay Nuur 41 V 8
Sangju 50 E 5
Sangli 46 C 5
Sangre de Cristo Mountains 18 E 4
Sanikiluaq 8 V 8
Sanjo 54 C 2
Sankt Gallen 36 B 3
Sankt Michel 38 L 3
Sankt Pölten 36 D 3
Sankt-Peterburg 40 H 6
Sankuru 58 B 2
Şanlıurfa 35 H 6
Sanlúcar de Barrameda 33 A 2
Sanmenxia 49 J 4
Sanming 49 K 5
Sannikova 42 L 2
Sanok 36 E 3
Santa Ana (El Salvador) 22 E 5
Santa Ana (Mexico) 18 D 5
Santa Ana (Solomon-Islands) 59 F 5
Santa Ana (U.S.) 18 C 5
Santa Barbara (Mexico) 20 C 2
Santa Barbara (U.S.) 18 C 5
Santa Barbara Channel 18 B 5
Santa Catalina Island 18 C 5
Santa Clara 22 F 3

Santa Clara (Mexico) 20 C 2
Santa Clara los Gatos 18 B 4
Santa Cruz 24 E 4
Santa Cruz (U.S.) 18 B 4
Santa Cruz de la Palma 56 B 2
Santa Cruz de Tenerife 56 B 2
Santa Cruz Island 18 C 5
Santa Cruz Islands 59 F 5
Santa Elena, Cabo 22 E 5
Santa Fe 18 E 4
Santa Fé 24 E 6
Santa Inés, Bahía 20 B 2
Santa Isbel Island 59 E 4
Santa Margarita, Isla 20 B 3
Santa Maria 24 F 5
Santa Maria (U.S.) 18 B 5
Santa María del Oro 20 C 2
Santa María del Río 20 D 3
Santa Marla dl Leuca,Capo 34 D 3
Santa María, Bahía de 20 C 2
Santa Maria, Laguna de 18 E 5
Santa Marta 22 H 5
Santa Rita (U.S.) 18 E 5
Santa Rosa 24 E 6
Santa Rosa (California, U.S.) 18 B 4
Santa Rosa (New Mexico, U.S.) 16 C 5
Santa Rosa de Copán 20 G 5
Santa Rosa Island 18 B 5
Santa Rosalía 20 B 2
Santai 49 H 4
Santander (Spain) 32 B 3
Santanghon 48 E 2
Santarém 24 F 3
Santee River 14 C 4
Santiago 24 D 6
Santiago (Dominican-Republic) 22 H 4
Santiago de Compostela 33 A 1

Santiago de Cuba 22 G 3
Santiago del Estero 24 E 5
Santiago do Cacém 33 A 2
Santiago Papasquiaro 20 C 2
Santiago, Río Grande de 20 D 3
Santo Antão 56 A 3
Santo Domingo (Dominican Republic) 22 J 4
Santo Domingo (Mexico) 20 B 2
Santos 24 G 5
Sany-Tash 45 M 5
São Carlos 24 G 5
São José do Rio Preto 24 F 5
São Luís 24 G 3
São Nicolau 56 A 3
São Paulo 24 G 5
São Tiago 56 A 3
São Tomé 56 D 4
São Tomé (Island) 56 D 5
São Tomé and Príncipe 56 D 4
Sapele 56 D 4
Sapporo 54 D 2
Sapulpa 16 D 4
Saqqaq 8 Aa 4
Saraburi 47 J 6
Sarajevo 34 D 2
Sarakhs 45 K 5
Sarangani 52 H 4
Sarangarh 46 E 4
Saransk 44 G 2
Sarapul 40 M 6
Sarapul'skoye 54 C 1
Sarasota 14 C 5
Saratov 44 G 2
Saravan 47 K 5
Sarawak 52 E 5
Sarayköy 35 C 6
Sardarshahr 46 C 3
Sardegna 34 B 3
Sardinia 34 B 3
Sargodha 46 C 2
Sarh 56 E 4
Särī 44 H 5
Sarigan 59 D 2
Sarıkamış 35 K 4
Sarikei 52 E 5
Sariwon 50 E 5
Şarkışla 35 G 5
Şarköy 35 B 4
Sarnia 14 C 2
Sarny 36 F 2
Sarowbī 45 L 6
Sarqan 45 N 3
Sarych, Mys 44 D 4

Saryeh, Mys 44 D 4
Saryesik-Atyraū Qumy 45 N 3
Saryözek 45 N 4
Saryshaghan 45 M 3
Sāsarām 46 E 4
Sasebo 50 E 6
Saskatchewan 10 V 8
Saskatchewan River 10 W 8
Saskatoon 10 V 8
Saskylakh 41 Y 3
Sasovo 44 F 2
Sassari 34 B 2
Sassnitz 36 C 2
Sasyqköl 45 O 3
Sātāra 46 C 5
Sätbaev 45 L 3
Satna 46 E 4
Satpura Range 46 C 4
Satu Mare 36 E 3
Satun 47 J 7
Sauceda Mountains 18 D 5
Saucillo 20 C 2
Saudárkrókur 38 B 2
Sauk Centre 16 E 2
Sault Sainte Marie 8 U 9
Sault Ste Marie (Canada) 14 C 1
Saumarez Reef 60 J 2
Saumur 32 B 2
Saurimo 58 B 2
Sava 36 D 3
Savaii 59 H 5
Savannah 14 C 4
Savannah River 14 C 4
Savannakhet 47 J 5
Savanne 16 E 2
Savant Lake 16 E 1
Sāveh 44 H 5
Savona 34 B 2
Savonlinna 38 L 3
Savu 53 G 8
Sawāi Mādhopur 46 D 3
Sawankhalok 47 H 5
Sawhaj 56 G 2
Sawtooth Mountains 16 E 2
Sawu 60 C 2
Sayanogorsk 41 U 7
Sayaq 45 N 3
Sayat 45 K 5
Saydā 44 E 6
Sayram 45 L 4
Scammon Bay 43 W 4
Scarborough (U.K.) 28 D 2

Schaffhausen 36 B 3
Schell Creek Range 18 D 4
Schenectady 14 E 2
Schleswig 36 B 2
Schull 31 B 3
Schultz Lake 8 R 6
Schurz 18 C 4
Schwäbisch Hall 36 B 3
Schwedt 36 C 2
Schweinfurt 36 C 2
Schwerin 36 C 2
Sciacca 34 C 3
Scilly, Isles of 28 A 4
Scioto River 14 C 3
Scoresby Land 8 Gg 4
Scoresbysund 8 Gg 4
Scotland 30 C 3
Scott City 16 C 4
Scott Reef 60 C 3
Scott, Cape 60 D 2
Scottsbluff 16 C 3
Scottsdale (U.S.) 18 D 5
Scottsville 14 B 3
Scranton 14 D 2
Scugog, Lake 14 D 2
Scunthorpe 28 D 3
Sea Islands 14 C 4
Seabrook, Lake 60 B 6
Seaside 18 B 2
Seattle 18 B 2
Sebangka 52 C 5
Sebastián Vizcaíno, Bahía 18 D 6
Sebatik 52 F 5
Sebring 14 C 5
Sebuku 52 F 6
Sedalia 16 E 4
Sedanka Island 10 J 8
Seddon 62 B 3
Sedona 18 D 5
Sefrou 56 C 1
Segamat 52 C 5
Seget 52 J 6
Segezha 40 H 5
Ségou 56 C 3
Segovia 33 B 1
Seguam Island 43 V 6
Seguin 20 E 2
Segula Island 43 T 6
Sehwan 46 B 3
Seiland 38 K 1
Seinäjoki 38 K 3
Seine 32 C 2
Sekayu 52 C 6
Sekondi-Takoradi 56 C 4
Selaru 53 J 7

Selatan, Tanjung 52 E 6
Selawik Lake 10 K 5
Selawiko 10 K 5
Selbu 38 H 3
Selby 16 C 2
Selenge 41 W 8
Selennyakh 42 M 3
Selfoss 38 A 3
Sel'gon 54 C 1
Selinunte 34 C 3
Selma (Alabama, U.S.) 14 B 4
Selma (California, U.S.) 18 C 4
Selvas 24 E 3
Selwyn Lake 10 W 6
Semarang 52 E 7
Semenovskiy, Ostrov 42 K 2
Semey 45 O 2
Semichi Islands 43 S 6
Semiluki 44 E 2
Semīozernoe 45 K 2
Semitau 52 E 5
Semīyarka 45 N 2
Semnān 44 H 5
Sendai (Japan) 54 B 4
Sendai (Japan) 54 D 3
Sendai-wan 54 D 3
Setermoen 38 J 2
Senegal 56 B 3
Senftenberg 36 C 2
Senigallia 34 C 2
Senja 38 J 2
Senneterre 8 V 9
Sens 32 C 2
Senta 36 E 3
Seoni 46 D 4
Seoul 50 E 5
Sepanjang 52 F 7
Sepasu 53 F 5
Sequoia National Park 18 C 4
Seram 53 H 6
Seramban 52 C 5
Serang 52 D 7
Serasan 52 D 5
Serb Republic 34 D 2
Serbia 34 E 2
Serbia and Montene-gro 34 D 2
Serdobsk 44 F 2
Serebryansk 45 O 3
Şereflikoçhisar 35 E 5
Sergach 40 L 6
Sergeya Kirova, Os-trova 41 T 2
Sergino 40 P 5
Sergiyev Posad 40 J 6

Seria 52 E 5
Serifos 34 E 3
Serık 35 D 6
Sermersuaq 8 Z 3
Sermiligaaq 8 Dd 5
Sernovodsk 44 H 2
Sernyy Zavod 45 J 4
Serov 40 O 6
Serowe 58 B 4
Serpentine Lakes 60 D 5
Serpukhov 44 E 2
Serra do Mar 24 G 5
Serra do Paranapia-caba 24 F 5
Serra Geral 24 F 5
Serrana, Cayo de 22 F 5
Serranilla, Cayo de 22 G 4
Serres 34 E 2
Serro Duida 22 J 7
Sertavul Geçidi 44 D 5
Serui 53 K 6
Seryshevo 42 J 6
Seskarö 38 K 2
Sestao 32 B 3
Sestroretsk 40 H 5
Setana 54 C 2
Sète 32 C 3
Sete Lagoas 24 G 4
Setesdal 38 G 4
Sétif 56 D 1
Seto-naikai 54 B 4
Settat 56 C 1
Sette-Daban, Khrebet 42 L 4
Setúbal 33 A 2
Seul, Lac 10 Y 8
Sevastopol' 44 D 4
Severn 28 C 3
Severn River 10 Y 8
Severnaya Dvina 40 K 5
Severnaya Sos'va 40 O 5
Severnaya Zemlya 41 V 1
Severnoye 44 H 2
Severo-Baykal'skoye Nagor'ye 42 F 5
Severodvinsk 40 J 5
Severo-Kuril'sk 43 P 6
Severomorsk 40 H 4
Severo-SibirskayaNizmen-nost' 41 T 3
Severo-Yeniseyskiy 41 U 5
Sevier Desert 18 D 4
Sevilla 33 A 2
Seward 10 N 6

Seward (Nebraska, U.S.) 16 D 3
Seychelles 58 E 2
Seydişehir 35 D 6
Seymchan 43 O 4
Seymour (U.S.) 14 B 3
Sfântu Gheorghe 35 A 2
Sfax 56 E 1
Shaanxi 49 H 3
Shabelē Wenz 56 H 4
Shache 48 B 3
Shachun'ya 40 L 6
Shādegān 44 G 6
Shadrinsk 40 O 6
Shāhdol 46 E 4
Shahjahanpur 46 D 3
Shahpura (Madhya Pradesh, India) 46 E 4
Shahpura (Ra-jasthan,India) 46 C 3
Shahrak 45 K 6
Shahr-e Kord 44 H 6
Shāhrūd 45 J 5
Shaim 40 O 5
Shājāpur 46 D 4
Shakhtersk 50 H 3
Shakhtīnsk 45 M 3
Shakhty 44 F 3
Shalaurova 42 M 2
Shallāl as Sablūkah 56 G 3
Shalqar 45 J 3
Shamattawa 8 S 7
Shamokin 14 D 2
Shamrock 16 C 4
Shan 49 G 5
Shandan 49 G 3
Shandong 49 K 3
Shandong Bandao 49 K 3
Shang Xian 49 H 4
Shangcai 49 J 4
Shangcheng 49 K 4
Shanghai 49 L 4
Shanghang 49 K 5
Shangqiu 49 K 4
Shangrao 49 K 5
Shangzhi 50 E 3
Shannon (Kalaallit Nunaat) 8 Hh 3
Shannon (River, Ire-land) 31 B 2
Shannon, Mouth of the 31 A 2
Shanshan 48 E 2
Shantarskiye Ostrova 42 L 5
Shantou 49 K 6
Shanxi 49 J 3

Shaoguan 49 J 6
Shaowu 49 K 5
Shaoxing 49 L 5
Shaoyang 49 J 5
Shar 45 O 3
Sharbaqty 45 N 2
Shark Bay 60 A 5
Shar'ya 40 L 6
Shashi 49 J 4
Shaunavon 18 E 2
Shawinigan 14 E 1
Shawnee 16 D 4
Shchūchīnsk 45 M 2
Shchuch'ye 40 O 6
Shebekino 44 E 2
Sheboygan 14 B 2
Shebunino 54 D 1
Sheffield (U.K.) 28 D 3
Sheffield (U.S.) 14 B 4
Shehong 49 H 4
Shekhupura 46 C 2
Shelagskiy, Mys 43 S 2
Shelburne 14 F 2
Shelby 18 D 2
Sheldon Point 43 X 4
Shelek 45 N 4
Shelikof Strait 43 Y 5
Shellharbour 60 J 6
Shemonaïkha 45 O 2
Shenandoah National Park 14 D 3
Shengxian 49 L 5
Shenkursk 40 K 5
Shenmu 49 J 3
Shenyang 50 D 4
Shepetivka 36 F 2
Shepparton 60 H 7
Sherard, Cape 8 U 4
Sherbrooke 14 E 1
Sherekhov 41 W 7
Sheridan 18 E 3
Sherlovaya Gora 42 G 6
Sherman 16 D 5
Sherman Station 14 F 1
Shetland Islands 30 D 1
Sheyenne River 16 D 2
Shibarghan 45 L 5
Shibata 54 C 3
Shidao 49 L 3
Shīeli 45 L 4
Shiguai 49 J 2
Shijiazhuang 49 J 3
Shikapur 46 B 3
Shikarpur 46 B 3
Shikoku 54 B 4
Shikotan, Ostrov 54

D 2
Shilka 42 G 6
Shilla 46 D 2
Shillong 47 G 3
Shilovo 44 F 2
Shimizu 54 C 3
Shimoga 46 D 6
Shimonoseki 54 B 4
Shin, Loch 30 B 2
Shingbwiyang 47 H 3
Shingū 54 C 4
Shinjo 54 D 3
Shiping 49 G 6
Shippagan 8 Y 9
Shipunovo 45 O 2
Shira 41 T 7
Shiranuka 54 D 2
Shirley Mountains 18 E 3
Shirokostan Polu- ostrov 42 M 2
Shīrvān 45 J 5
Shivpuri 46 D 3
Shiwan Dashan 49 H 6
Shizunai 54 D 2
Shizuoka 54 C 4
Shkod'r 34 D 2
Shmidta, Ostrov 41 U 1
Shmidta, Poluostrov 42 M 6
Shokal'skogo, Ostrov 40 Q 3
Sholapur 46 D 5
Sholaqqkorghan 45 L 4
Shoshone 18 D 3
Shoshone Peak 18 C 4
Shoshoni 18 E 3
Shostka 36 G 2
Shou Xian 49 K 4
Shouchang 49 K 5
Shouguang 49 K 3
Show Low 18 D 5
Shoyna 40 K 4
Shreveport 16 E 5
Shrewsbury 28 C 3
Shū 45 M 4
Shuangcheng 50 E 3
Shuangliao 50 D 4
Shuangyang 54 A 2
Shuangyashan 54 B 1
Shuguri Falls 58 C 2
Shuicheng 49 G 5
Shulan 50 E 4
Shule 48 B 3
Shumagin Islands 43 Y 5
Shumen 34 F 2
Shumerlya 40 L 6

Shumshu, Ostrov 43 P 6
Shuoxian 49 J 3
Shurab 45 M 4
Shūshtar 44 G 6
Shuya 40 K 6
Shuyak Island 43 Z 5
Shuyang 49 K 4
Shymkent 45 L 4
Si Racha 47 J 6
Siähän Range 46 A 3
Siälkot 46 C 2
Siargao 52 H 4
Siau 52 H 5
Šiauliai 38 K 4
Sibay 45 J 2
Šibenik 34 D 2
Siberut 52 B 6
Sibi 46 B 3
Sibirskiye Uvaly 40 P 5
Sibirskoye 41 V 4
Sibirtsevo 54 B 2
Sibiryakova, Ostrov 41 R 3
Sibiu 36 E 3
Sibolga 52 B 5
Sibsagar 47 G 3
Sibu 52 E 5
Sibutu 52 F 5
Sibuyan 52 G 3
Sibuyan Sea 52 G 3
Sichuan 49 G 4
Sicilia 34 D 3
Sicilia, Canale di 34 C 3
Sicily 34 D 3
Siddhapur 46 C 4
Siddipet 46 D 5
Siderno 34 D 3
Sidi-Bel-Abbès 56 C 1
Sidney (Canada) 18 B 2
Sidney (Montana, U.S.) 16 C 2
Sidney (Nebraska, U.S.) 16 C 3
Siedlce 36 E 2
Siegen 36 B 2
Siena 34 C 2
Sieradz 36 D 2
Sierra Blanca 18 E 5
Sierra de Segura 33 B 2
Sierra Leone 56 B 4
Sierra Mojada 20 D 2
Sifnos 34 E 3
Sigep 52 B 6
Sighetu Marmaţiei 36 E 3
Sighişoara 35 A 1

Sigli 52 B 4
Siglufjörður 38 B 2
Sigulda 38 K 4
Sihanoukville 47 J 6
Siirt 35 J 6
Sikar 46 D 3
Sikaram 45 L 6
Sikasso 56 C 3
Sikeston 14 B 3
Sikhote-Alin' 54 C 1
Sikkim 46 F 3
Siktyach 42 H 3
Silchar 47 G 4
Siletitengiz Köli 45 M 2
Silifke 35 E 6
Siliguri 46 F 3
Siling Co 48 D 4
Silistra 34 F 2
Siljan 38 H 3
Silkeborg 38 G 4
Sillem Island 8 W 4
Sillon de Talbert 32 B 2
Siloam Springs 16 F 4
Silvan 35 J 5
Silver City 18 E 5
Silverton (U.S.) 18 E 4
Simao 48 G 6
Simcoe, Lake 14 D 2
Simeulue 52 B 5
Simferopol' 44 D 4
Simla 46 D 2
Simojovel de Allende 20 F 4
Simplon Pass 36 B 3
Simpson Desert 60 F 4
Simpson Desert Na- tional Park 60 F 5
Simrichamn 38 H 4
Sinabang 52 B 5
Sinaloa 20 C 3
Sincelejo 22 G 6
Sinch'ang 50 E 4
Sinch'ang-ni 54 A 2
Sindjai 52 G 7
Sines, Cabo de 33 A 2
Singapore 52 C 5
Singaradja 52 F 7
Singkang 52 G 6
Singkawang 52 D 5
Singkep 52 C 6
Singö 38 J 3
Sînnär 56 G 3
Sinoie, Lacul 35 C 2
Sinop 35 F 3
Sinp'o 54 A 2
Sintang 52 E 5
Sinŭiju 50 D 4
Sioux City 16 D 3
Sioux Falls 16 D 3

Sioux Lookout 16 E 1
Sipalay 52 G 4
Siping 50 D 4
Sipura 52 B 6
Siquijor 52 G 4
Sir Edward Pellew Group 60 F 3
Sira 46 D 6
Sirevåg 38 G 4
Sirohi 46 C 4
Sironj 46 D 4
Sirsa 46 D 3
Sisak 36 D 3
Sisaket 47 J 5
Siskiyou Mountains 18 B 3
Sisseton 16 D 2
Sissimiut 8 Aa 5
Sitapur 46 E 3
Sitka 10 P 7
Sitkalidak Island 10 M 7
Sittwe 47 G 4
Siuna 20 H 5
Sivas 35 G 5
Siverek 35 H 6
Sivrihisar 35 D 5
Siwalik Range 46 D 2
Siwan 46 E 3
Sjælland 38 H 4
Skadovs'k 35 E 1
Skagerrak 38 G 4
Skagway 10 P 7
Skåne 38 H 4
Skardu 45 N 5
Skarodnaye 36 F 2
Skarżysko Kamienna 36 E 2
Skegness 28 E 3
Skeiðarárjökull 38 B 3
Skellefteå 38 K 3
Skellefteålven 38 J 2
Ski 38 H 4
Skibotn 38 K 2
Skien 38 G 4
Skikda 56 D 1
Skomvær 38 H 2
Skopelos 34 E 3
Skopje 34 E 2
Skövde 38 H 4
Skovorodino 42 H 6
Skowhegan 14 F 2
Skvyra 36 F 3
Skye 30 A 3
Skyros 34 E 3
Slamet, Gunung 52 D 7
Slantsy 38 L 4
Slatina 34 E 2
Slave River 10 U 6
Slavgorod 45 N 2
Slavnoye 54 E 1

Slavonski Brod 36 D 3
Slavuta 36 F 2
Slavyanka 54 B 2
Slavyansk-na Kubani 44 E 3
Sleeper Islands 8 U 7
Slettuheiði 38 B 2
Sligo 31 B 1
Sliven 34 F 2
Słolin 36 F 2
Slonim 36 F 2
Slough 28 D 4
Slovakia 36 D 3
Slovenia 36 C 3
Slov"yans'k 44 E 3
Slozhnyy, Ostrov 41 T 2
Słupsk 36 D 2
Slutsk 36 F 2
Slyne Head 31 A 2
Slyudyanka 41 W 7
Småland 38 H 4
Smallwood Reservoir 8 Y 8
Smederevo 34 E 2
Smidovich 54 B 1
Smila 44 D 3
Smirnykh 50 H 3
Smith 10 U 7
Smiths Falls 14 D 2
Smokey Dome 18 D 3
Smokey Falls 8 U 8
Smoky Hill River 16 C 4
Smoky Hills 16 D 4
Smoła 38 G 3
Smolensk 36 G 2
Smolyan 34 E 2
Smythe, Mount 10 S 7
Snag 10 O 6
Snake River 18 C 3
Snake River Plain 18 D 3
Snow Mountain 18 B 4
Snowville 18 D 3
Snyder 16 C 5
Sobral 24 G 3
Soc Trang 47 K 7
Sochi 44 E 4
Société, Archipel de la 59 K 5
Society Islands 59 K 5
Socorro (U.S.) 18 E 5
Socorro, Isla 20 B 4
Sodankylä 38 L 2
Söderhamn 38 J 3
Södermanland 38 J 4

Södertälje 38 J 4
Soe 52 G 7
Sofia 34 E 2
Sofie Christensen Reef 59 L 8
Sofiya 34 E 2
Sofiysk 42 K 6
Sofporog 40 H 4
Sofronovo 40 J 6
Sōfu-gan 54 D 5
Sogamoso 22 H 6
Sogn og Fjordane 38 G 3
Sogndal 38 G 3
Soissons 32 C 2
Sōjosŏn-man 49 L 3
Sokch'o 54 A 3
Söke 35 B 6
Sokhumi 44 F 4
Sokółka 36 E 2
Solano 52 G 2
Soldotna 43 Z 4
Solenoye 44 F 3
Solikamsk 40 N 6
Sol'-Ilotok 44 H 2
Solimón, Punta 20 G 4
Solingen 36 B 2
Sollefteå 38 J 3
Solomon Islands 60 K 2
Solomon Sea 59 E 4
Solon 50 D 3
Solonchak Arys 45 L 3
Solway Firth 28 C 2
Soma 35 B 5
Somalia 56 H 4
Sombor 36 D 3
Sombreretè 20 D 3
Somerset 14 C 3
Somerset Island 8 S 4
Somoto 20 G 5
Son La 47 J 4
Son Tay 47 K 4
Sønderborg 36 B 2
Søndre Strømfjord 8 Aa 5
Sonepur 46 E 4
Song Cau 47 K 6
Song Ma 47 J 4
Songhua Hu 50 E 4
Songhua Jiang 54 A 1
Songjiang 49 L 4
Songkhla 47 J 7
Sŏngnam 54 A 3
Songnim 50 E 5
Sonmiani Bay 46 B 3
Sonneberg 36 C 2
Sonoita 18 D 5
Sonora (Mexico) 20 B 2

Sonora (U.S.) 16 C 5
Sonora, Río 20 B 2
Sonoran Desert 18 D 5
Sonqor 44 G 6
Sonsonate 22 E 5
Sonsorol Islands 52 J 4
Sopka Shiveluch 43 Q 5
Sopot 36 D 2
Sopron 36 D 3
Sor Kajdak 44 H 4
Sorada 46 E 5
Sorang 45 M 3
Sorel 8 W 9
Soria 32 B 3
Sörmjöle 38 J 3
Soroca 36 F 3
Sorocaba 24 G 5
Sorochinsk 44 H 2
Sørøya 38 K 1
Sorsele 38 J 2
Sorsogon 52 G 3
Sortavala 40 H 5
Sortland 38 J 2
Sør-Trøndelag 38 H 3
Sôsan 54 A 3
Sosnogorsk 40 M 5
Sosnovo-Ozerskoye 42 F 6
Sosnowiec 36 D 2
Sos'va 40 O 6
Sotsial 45 N 3
Soudan 60 F 4
Souk Ahras 34 B 3
Sŏul 50 E 5
Soulac-sur-Mer 32 B 2
Souris (Manitoba, Canada) 16 C 2
Sousa 24 H 3
South Africa 58 A 5
South Andaman 47 G 6
South Aulatsivik Island 8 Y 7
South Australia 60 E 6
South Bend (Indiana, U.S.) 14 B 2
South Bend (Washington, U.S.) 18 B 2
South Carolina 14 C 4
South China Sea 47 K 7
South Dakota 16 C 3
South Downs 28 D 4
South East Cape 60 H 8
South East Point 60 H 7

South Georgia (U.K.) 24 H 8
South Island 62 A 3
South Korea 50 F 5
South Lake Tahoe 18 C 4
South Molton 28 C 4
South Platte River 16 C 3
South Ronaldsay 30 C 2
South Saskatchewan River 18 D 1
South Shields 28 D 2
South Sioux City 16 D 3
South Stradbroke Island 60 J 5
South Taranaki Bight 62 B 2
South Uist 30 A 3
Southampton 28 D 4
Southampton Island 8 T 6
Southend 10 W 7
Southend-on-Sea 28 E 4
Southern Alps 62 A 3
Southern Cook Islands 59 K 5
Southern Cross 60 B 6
Southern Indian Lake 8 R 7
Southern Uplands 28 B 2
Southport (Australia) 60 J 5
Southport (U.K.) 28 C 3
Southport (U.S.) 14 D 4
Southwest Cape 62 A 4
Sovetskaya Gavan' 50 H 3
Sovetskiy 40 L 6
Spain 33 B 2
Spanish Fork 18 D 3
Spanish Town 22 G 4
Sparks 18 C 4
Spartanburg 14 C 4
Sparti 34 E 3
Spartivento, Capo 34 B 3
Spassk-Dal'niy 54 B 2
Spearfish 16 C 3
Spencer 16 D 3
Spencer Gulf 61 F 6
Spencer, Cape 60 F 7

Spenser Mountains 62 B 3
Spey 30 C 3
Split 34 D 2
Spokane 18 C 2
Spooner 16 E 2
Springdale (U.S.) 16 E 4
Springer 16 C 4
Springfield (Colorado, U.S.) 16 C 4
Springfield (Conneticut, U.S.) 14 E 2
Springfield (Illinois, U.S.) 14 B 3
Springfield (Missouri, U.S.) 16 E 4
Springfield (Oregon, U.S.) 18 B 3
Springfield (Tennessee, U.S.) 14 B 3
Springsure 60 H 4
Spurn Head 28 E 3
Squamish 18 B 2
Squillace, Golfo di 34 D 3
Srebrenica 34 D 2
Sredinnyy Khrebet 43 P 6
Sredne Sibirskoye Ploskogor'ye 41 W 4
Srednekolymsk 43 O 3
Sremska Mitrovica 34 D 2
Sretensk 42 G 6
Sri Jayawardenepura Kotte 46 E 7
Sri Kālahasti 46 D 6
Sri Lanka 46 E 7
Srīkākulam 46 E 5
Srinagar 45 M 6
Staaten River National Park 60 G 3
Stack Skerry 30 B 2
Stade 36 B 2
Stafford 28 C 3
Stakhanov 44 E 3
Stallworthy, Cape 8 S 2
Stalowa Wola 36 E 2
Stamford 14 E 2
Standerton 58 B 4
Stanke Dimitrov 34 E 2
Stanley 24 F 8
Stanley (U.S.) 16 C 2
Stanovoy Khrebet 42 H 5
Stanovoye Nagor'ye 42 F 5
Stanthorpe 60 J 5

Stara Planina 34 E 2
Stara Zagora 34 F 2
Staraya Russa 40 H 6
Starbuck Island 59 K 4
Stargard Szczeciński 36 D 2
Staritsa 54 D 1
Starobil's'k 44 E 3
Starodub 36 G 2
Starogard Gdański 36 D 2
Start Point 28 C 4
Staryy Oskol 44 E 2
State College 14 D 2
Statesboro 14 C 4
Statesville 14 C 3
Staumnes 38 A 2
Staunton 14 D 3
Stavanger 38 G 4
Stavropol' 44 F 3
Stavropolka 45 L 2
St-Denis 58 E 4
Steenstrup Gletscher 8 Z 3
Stefansson Island 10 V 4
Steinbach 16 D 2
Steinkjer 38 H 3
Stendal 36 C 2
Stephenville (U.S.) 16 D 5
Stepnyak 45 M 2
Sterling 16 C 3
Sterlitamak 40 N 7
Ste-Thérèse 14 E 1
Steubenville 14 C 2
Stevenage 28 D 4
Stevens Point 14 B 2
Stewart Crossing 10 P 6
Stewart Island 62 A 4
Stewart River 10 P 6
Steyr 36 C 3
St-Georges (Canada) 14 E 1
Stillwater 16 D 4
Štip 34 E 2
Stirling (Australia) 60 B 6
Stirling (U.K.) 30 C 3
Stirling Range 60 B 6
Stirling Range National Park 60 B 6
St-Jean-sur-Richelieu 14 E 1
St-Léonard 14 F 1
St-Louis 56 B 3
Stockholm 38 J 4
Stockport 28 C 3
Stockton 18 B 4
Stockton Plateau 16

C 5
Stockton-on-Tees 28 D 2
Stoke-on-Trent 28 C 3
Stokksnes 38 C 3
Stolbovoy, Ostrov 42 L 2
Stonehaven 30 C 3
Stora Lulevatten 38 J 2
Stora Sjöfallet 38 J 2
Storavan 38 J 2
Stord 38 F 4
Store Bælt 38 H 4
Store Koldewey 8 Hh 3
Store Sotra 38 F 3
Storlien 38 H 3
Stornoway 30 A 2
Storstrømmen 8 Gg 3
Storuman 38 J 2
Stowbtsy 36 F 2
Strabane 31 C 1
Strait of Magellan 24 E 8
Stralsund 36 C 2
Strand 58 A 5
Stranraer 28 B 2
Strasbourg 36 B 3
Stratford (Canada) 14 C 2
Stratford (New Zealand) 62 B 2
Stratford (U.S.) 16 C 4
Stratford-upon-Avon 28 D 3
Strathclyde 30 C 3
Strathspey 30 C 3
Strathy Point 30 B 2
Straubing 36 C 3
Streaky Bay 60 E 6
Strelka (Russia) 41 U 6
Strelka (Russia) 43 O 4
Strelka-Chunya 41 W 5
Streymoy 38 D 3
Stronsay 30 C 2
Stroud 28 C 4
Strumica 34 E 2
Stryy 36 E 3
Stuart Bluff Range 60 E 4
Stuart Island 43 X 4
Sturgeon Lake 16 E 2
Sturt Desert 60 G 5
Sturt National Park 60 G 5
Stutterheim 58 B 5
Stuttgart 36 B 3

Suai 53 H 7
Subi Besar 52 D 5
Subotica 36 D 3
Suceava 36 F 3
Suchumi 44 F 4
Sucre 24 E 4
Sudak 35 F 2
Sudan 56 F 3
Sudbury 8 U 9
Sudd 56 G 4
Suđuroy 38 D 3
Suess Land 8 Ff 4
Sugoy 43 P 4
Sühbaatar (Mongolia) 50 A 2
Sühbaatar (Mongolia) 50 B 3
Suhl 36 C 2
Suibin 54 B 1
Suichang 49 K 5
Suide 49 J 3
Suihua 50 E 3
Suileng 50 E 3
Suining 49 H 4
Suir 31 C 2
Suixi 49 K 4
Suiyang 54 B 2
Suizhong 50 D 4
Suizhou 49 J 4
Sujawal 46 B 4
Sukabumi 52 D 7
Sukadana 52 D 6
Sukagawa 54 D 3
Sukaraja 52 E 6
Sukhana 42 G 3
Sukhona 40 K 6
Sukhothai 47 H 5
Sukkertoppen 8 Aa 5
Sukkur 46 B 3
Sula 38 F 3
Sula Islands 52 H 7
Sula Sgeir 30 A 2
Sula, Kepulauan 52 G 6
Sulaiman Range 46 B 3
Sulawesi 52 F 6
Sule Skerry 30 B 2
Sulincheen 49 H 2
Sulphur 16 E 5
Sulphur Springs 16 D 5
Sulu Archipelago 52 F 5
Sulu Sea 52 F 4
Sumalē 56 H 4
Sumatera 52 C 6
Sumatra 52 C 6
Sumba 53 F 8
Sumbawa 52 F 7
Sumbawa Besar 52 F 7
Sumburgh Head 30 D 2
Sumedang 52 D 7

Sumenep 52 E 7
Sumisu-jima 54 D 4
Summer Lake 18 B 3
Summit Lake 10 S 7
Šumperk 36 D 3
Sumqayit 44 G 4
Sumter 14 C 4
Sumy 36 G 2
Sun Valley 18 D 3
Sunbury 14 D 2
Sunch'ŏn 54 A 4
Sunch'on (North Korea) 50 E 5
Sunderland 28 D 2
Sundsvall 38 J 3
Sungai Kolok 47 J 7
Sungai Petani 52 C 4
Sungaidareh 52 C 6
Sungalguntung 52 C 5
Sungurlu 35 F 4
Sunndalsøra 38 G 3
Sunshine 60 G 7
Suntar 42 G 4
Suntar Khayata, Khrebet 42 L 4
Sunwu 54 A 1
Sunyani 56 C 4
Suomi 38 L 3
Suomussalmi 38 L 3
Suonenjoki 38 L 3
Suoyarvi 40 H 5
Superior (Montana, U.S.) 18 D 2
Superior (Wisconsin, U.S.) 16 E 2
Superior, Lake 16 E 2
Sŭr 44 E 6
Surabaya 52 E 7
Surakarta 52 E 7
Surakarta 52 E 7
Surat 46 C 4
Surat Thani 47 H 7
Suratgarh 46 C 3
Surgut 40 Q 5
Suriapet 46 D 5
Surigao 52 H 4
Surin 47 J 6
Suriname 24 F 2
Surovikino 44 F 3
Surskoye 44 G 2
Surtsey 38 A 3
Sürüç 35 H 6
Surulangun 52 C 6
Survey Pass 10 M 5
Susanville 18 B 3
Suşehri 35 H 4
Susitna River 10 M 6
Susquehanna 14 D 2
Susurluk 35 C 5
Sutherland 30 B 2
Sutton (West Vir-

ginia, U.S.) 14 C 3
Sutwik Island 43 Y 5
Suva 59 G 5
Suvadiva 46 C 8
Suvorov 59 J 5
Suwa 54 C 3
Suwałki 36 E 2
Suwannee River 14 C 4
Suwanose-jima 50 F 7
Suwaydah 35 H 7
Suwon 50 E 5
Suzhou 49 L 4
Suzu 54 C 3
Svappavaara 38 K 2
Svatove 44 E 3
Svay Riêng 47 K 6
Svealand 38 H 4
Sveg 38 H 3
Svendborg 38 H 4
Sverdlovsk 40 O 6
Sverdrup Islands 10 W 3
Sverdrup, Ostrov 41 R 3
Svetlaya 54 C 1
Svetlograd 44 F 3
Svetlyy (Russia) 42 G 5
Svir 40 H 5
Svirsk 41 W 7
Svistov 34 F 2
Svobodnyy 42 J 6
Svyatoy Nos, Mys (Russia) 40 J 4
Svyetlahorsk 36 F 2
Swain Reefs 60 J 4
Swains Island 59 H 5
Swan Hill 60 G 7
Swan Range 18 D 2
Swan River 10 W 8
Swansea 28 B 4
Swaziland 58 C 4
Sweden 38 H 3
Sweet Home 18 B 3
Sweetwater 16 C 5
Sweetwater River 18 E 3
Świecie 36 D 2
Swift Current 10 V 8
Swift River 10 Q 6
Swindon 28 D 4
Świnoujście 36 C 2
Switzerland 36 B 3
Syanno 36 F 2
Sydney (Australia) 60 J 6
Sydney (Canada) 8 Y 9
Syeverodonets'k 44 E 3
Syktyvkar 40 M 5
Sylacauga 14 B 4

Sylhet 47 G 4
Sylt 36 B 2
Syngyrli, Mys 44 H 4
Syracuse (Kansas, U.S.) 16 C 4
Syracuse (New York, U.S.) 14 D 2
Syria 44 E 5
Syriam 47 H 5
Syrian Desert 44 E 6
Syros 34 E 3
Syverma, Plato 41 U 4
Syzran' 44 G 2
Szczecin 36 C 2
Szczecinek 36 D 2
Szczyrno 36 E 2
Szeged 36 E 3
Székesfehérvár 36 D 3
Szekszárd 36 D 3
Szentes 36 E 3
Szolnok 36 D 3
Szombathely 36 D 3
Taasiilaq Ammassalik 8 Dd 5
Tabasará, Serranía de 22 F 6
Tabasco 20 F 4
Tabasco y Campeche, Llanosde 20 F 4
Taber 18 D 2
Tabiteuea 59 G 4
Tablas 52 G 3
Table Rock Lake 16 E 4
Tabor 42 O 2
Tabora 58 C 2
Tabory 40 O 6
Tabrīz 44 G 5
Tacámbaro 20 D 4
Tacheng 48 C 1
Tacloban 52 G 3
Tacna 24 D 4
Tacoma 18 B 2
Tacuarembó 24 F 6
Tacurong 52 G 4
Tadoule Lake 8 R 7
T'aebaek-Sanmaek 54 A 3
Taegu 50 E 5
Taej n 50 E 5
Taejŏn 54 A 3
Taenga 59 L 5
Tafahi 59 H 5
Taft 52 H 3
Taganrog 44 E 3
Tagula Island 60 J 2
Tagum 52 H 4
Tahan, Gunong 52 C 5
Tahanea 59 L 5
Tahe 50 D 2
Tahiti 59 L 5

Tahkuna nina 38 K 4
Tahoe, Lake 18 B 4
Tahoua 56 D 3
Tahulandang 52 H 5
Tahuna 52 H 5
Tai Hu 49 K 4
Taiaro 59 L 5
Taibai Shan 49 H 4
Taihape 62 C 2
Taihu 49 K 4
Taikang 49 J 4
Tailai 50 D 3
T'ainan 49 L 6
T'aipei 49 L 6
Taiping 52 C 5
Taishan 49 J 6
T'aitung 49 L 6
Taivalkoski 38 L 2
Taiwan 49 L 6
Taiwan Haixia 49 K 6
Taiyuan 49 J 3
Taizhou 49 K 4
Taj Mahal 46 D 3
Tajikistan 45 L 5
Tajito 18 D 5
Tajo, R'o 33 B 2
Tajrīsh 44 H 5
Tajumulco, Volcán 20 F 4
Tak 47 H 5
Takalar 52 F 7
Takamatsu 54 B 4
Takaoka 54 C 3
Takapuna 62 B 2
Takara-jima 50 E 7
Takasaki 54 C 3
Takengon 52 B 5
Takhli 47 J 5
Takijuk Lake 10 U 5
Takikawa 54 D 2
Takla Landing 10 R 7
Takla Makan 48 C 3
Taklimakan Shamo 48 C 3
Takume 59 L 5
Takutea 59 K 5
Tala 20 D 3
Talagbetutu 52 C 6
Talaimannar 46 D 7
Talak 56 D 3
Talamanca, Cordillera de 22 E 5
Talara 24 C 3
Talas 45 M 4
Talaud, Kepulauan 52 H 5
Talavera de la Reina 33 B 2
Talca 24 D 6
Talcahuano 24 D 6
Tâlcher 46 F 4

Taldyqorghan 45 N 3
Talence 32 B 3
Talghar 45 N 4
Taliabu 52 G 6
Taliquin 45 L 5
Taliwang 52 F 7
Talkeetna 10 M 6
Tallahassee 14 C 4
Tallinn 38 K 4
Tallulah 16 E 5
Tal'menka 45 O 2
Talnakh 41 T 4
Tal'ne 44 D 3
Talok 52 F 5
Talovka 44 G 4
Taloyoak 8 S 5
Talsi 38 K 4
Talu 52 B 5
Taluk 52 C 6
Taluma 42 H 5
Tam Ky 47 K 5
Tama Abu Range 52 F 5
Tamale 56 C 4
Tamar 28 B 4
Tamaulipas 20 E 3
Tamaulipas, Llanos de 20 E 2
Tamazunchale 20 E 3
Tambacounda 56 B 3
Tambalan 52 F 5
Tambalan, Kepu-lauan 52 D 5
Tambov 44 F 2
Tamiahua, Laguna de 20 E 3
Tamil 46 D 6
Tammerfors 38 K 3
Tampa 14 C 5
Tampa Bay 14 C 5
Tampere 38 K 3
Tampico 20 E 3
Tamsagbulag 50 C 3
Tamuín 20 E 3
Tamworth 60 J 6
Tana 58 C 2
Tana (Norway) 38 L 2
Talagbetutu 52 C 6
Tanana 41 R 3
Tanami Desert Wildlife Sanctuary 60 D 3
Tanana 10 M 5
Tanch'ŏn 54 A 2
Tandag 52 H 4

Tandil 24 F 6
Tando Adam 46 B 3
Tando Muhammad Khan 46 B 3
Tandsjöborg 38 H 3
Tanega-shima 54 B 4
Tanga 58 C 2
Tanga (Russia) 42 F 6
Tanger 56 C 1
Tangerang 52 D 7
Tanggu 49 K 3
Tanggula Shan 48 E 4
Tanggula Shankou 48 E 4
Tanghe 49 J 4
Tangmai 48 F 4
Tangra Yumco 48 D 4
Tangshan 49 K 3
Tangwanghe 50 E 3
Tangyin 49 J 3
Tangyuan 50 E 3
Tanimbar, Kepulauan 52 J 7
Tanjang Karossa 60 B 1
Tanjona Bobaomby 58 D 3
Tanjona Masoala 58 D 3
Tanjona Vilanandro 58 D 3
Tanjona Vohimena 58 D 4
Tanjungbalai 52 B 5
Tanjungpandan 52 D 6
Tanjungpinang 52 C 5
Tanjungredep 52 F 5
Tanjungselor 52 F 5
Tānk 46 C 2
Tankovo 41 T 5
Tanna 59 F 5
Tännäs 38 H 3
Tannu Ola, Khrebet 41 U 7
Tanţa 56 G 1
Tantoyuca 20 E 3
Tanzania 58 B 2
Tao'an 50 D 3
T'aoyüan 49 L 5
Tapachula 22 D 5
Tapaktuan 52 B 5
Tappahannock 14 D 3
Tapul Group 53 G 4
Taqtabrod 45 L 2
Tara 40 Q 6
Tara Vai 59 M 6
Tarābulus (Lebanon) 44 E 6

Tarābulus (Tripoli) 56 E 1
Tarahumara, Sierra 20 C 2
Tarakan 53 F 5
Taranto 34 D 2
Taranto, Golfo di 34 D 2
Tararua Range 62 C 3
Taraz 45 M 4
Tarbes 32 C 3
Tarcoola 60 E 6
Tardoki-Yani, Gora 54 C 1
Taree 60 J 6
Târgu Jiu 36 E 3
Târgu Mureş 36 E 3
Tarija 24 E 5
Tarko-Sale 41 R 5
Tarlac 53 G 2
Tärnaby 38 J 2
Tarnobrzeg 36 E 2
Tarnów 36 E 3
Taroom 60 H 5
Tarpon Springs 14 C 5
Tarragona 32 C 3
Tarrassa 32 C 3
Tarsus 35 F 6
Tart 48 E 3
Tartu 38 L 4
Tartus 44 E 6
Tarutung 52 B 5
Taseyevo 41 U 6
Tash-Kömür 45 M 4
Tashkurgan 45 L 5
Tashtagol 41 T 7
Tashtyp 41 T 7
Tasiilap Karra 8 Ee 5
Tasiilaq 8 Dd 5
Tasikmalaja 52 D 7
Taşköprü 35 F 4
Tas-Kystaby, Khrebet 42 M 4
Tasman Bay 62 B 3
Tasman Peninsula 60 H 8
Tasman Sea 60 K 7
Tasmania (Island) 60 G 8
Tasmania (State) 60 G 8
Tassili n'Ajjer 56 D 2
Tas-Tumus 42 J 4
Tata 36 D 3
Tatabánya 36 D 3
Tatarsk 41 R 6
Tatarskiy Proliv 50 H 3
Tatau 52 E 5
Tataurovo 41 X 7
Tathlina Lake 10 T 6
Tatnam, Cape 8 S 7
Tatry 36 D 3

Tatta 46 B 4
Tatvan 35 K 5
Tau 59 J 5
Tauere 59 L 5
Taunggyi 47 H 4
Taunton 28 C 4
Taupo 62 C 2
Taupo, Lake 62 C 2
Taurag 38 K 4
Tauranga 62 C 2
Taurus 35 D 6
Tavas 35 C 6
Tavastehus 38 K 3
Tavda 40 P 6
Taveuni 59 H 5
Tavoy 47 H 6
Tavşanli 35 C 5
Tawas City 14 C 2
Tawau 52 F 5
Tawitawi Group 52 F 4
Taxco de Alarcón 20 E 4
Tay 30 C 3
Tay Ninh 47 K 6
Tay, Loch 30 B 3
Tayga 41 T 6
Taygonos, Mys 43 P 4
Taygonos, Poluostrov 43 Q 4
Taylor 43 X 3
Taylorville 14 B 3
Taymyr, Ozero 41 W 3
Taymyr, Poluostrov 41 U 3
Taypaq 44 H 3
Tayshet 41 V 6
Taz 41 S 5
Taza 56 C 1
Tazovskiy 41 R 4
Tazumal 22 E 5
T'bilisi 35 L 4
Te Anau, Lake 62 A 3
Te Araroa 62 C 2
Te Awamutu 62 C 2
Te Kao 62 B 1
Te Puia 62 C 2
Teapa 20 F 4
Tébessa 56 D 1
Tebingtinggi 52 B 5
Tecate 18 C 5
Tecomán 20 D 4
Tecuala 20 C 3
Tecuci 36 F 3
Tees 28 C 2
Tegal 52 D 7
Tegucigalpa 22 E 5
Tegul'det 41 T 6
Tehrān 44 H 5
Tehuacán 20 E 4
Tehuantepec 20 E 4
Tehuantepec, Golfo

de 20 E 4
Tehuantepec, Istmo de 20 F 4
Tejen 45 K 5
Tejo 33 A 2
Tekeli 45 N 4
Tekirdağ 34 F 2
Tekokota 59 L 5
T'elavi 35 L 4
Telegraph Creek 10 Q 7
Telemark 38 G 4
Telford 28 C 3
Teller 43 W 3
Tellicherry 46 D 6
Telmen Nuur 41 V 8
Teloloapan 20 E 4
Telšiai 38 K 4
Teluk Anson 52 C 5
Telukdalem 52 B 5
Téma 56 C 4
Tematangi 59 L 6
Temax 20 G 3
Tembenchi 41 V 4
Tembilahan 52 C 6
Tembisa 58 B 4
Tembleque 33 B 2
Temirtau 41 T 7
Temirtaū 45 M 2
Temoe 59 M 6
Tempe 18 D 5
Temple 16 D 5
Temryuk 35 G 2
Temuco 24 D 6
Ten Degree Channel 47 G 7
Tenāli 46 E 5
Tenasserim 47 H 6
Tenerife 56 B 2
Tengchong 48 F 5
Tenggara, Kepulauan 52 H 7
Tengger Shamo 49 G 3
Tengiz Köli 45 L 2
Tengxian (Guangxi, China) 49 J 6
Tengxian (Shandong,China) 49 K 3
Tennant Creek 60 E 3
Tennessee 14 B 3
Tennessee River 14 B 4
Tenojoki 38 L 2
Tenosique 20 F 4
Teocaltiche 20 D 3
Teófilo Otoni 24 G 4
Teotihuacan 20 E 4
Tepa 53 H 7
Tepache 20 C 2
Tepan 52 C 6
Tepic 20 D 3
Tepoca, Bahía de 18

D 5
Tequila 20 D 3
Teramo 34 C 2
Terek 44 F 4
Terempa 52 D 5
Teresina 24 G 3
Teressa 47 G 7
Términos, Laguna de 20 F 4
Termiz 45 L 5
Ternate 52 H 5
Terney 54 C 1
Terni 34 C 2
Ternopil' 36 F 3
Terpeniya, Mys 50 H 3
Terpeniya, Zaliv 54 D 1
Terrace 10 R 8
Terrace Bay 14 B 1
Terracina 34 C 2
Terre Adélie 63 T 5
Terre Haute 14 B 3
Terrebonne Bay 20 F 2
Teruel 32 B 3
Teshekpuk Lake 10 M 4
Teskey Ala-Too 45 N 4
Teslin Lake 10 Q 6
Tete 58 C 3
Tetiaroa 59 L 5
Tétouan 56 C 1
Tetovo 34 E 2
Tevriz 40 Q 6
Tevzur 47 G 3
Texarkana 16 E 5
Texas (U.S.) 16 C 5
Texas City 20 F 2
Teykovo 40 K 6
Teywarah 45 K 6
Teziutlán 20 E 4
Tezpur 47 G 3
Thai Nguyen 47 K 4
Thailand 47 H 5
Thailand, Gulf of 47 J 6
Thal 45 M 6
Thal Desert 46 C 2
Thames (New Zealand) 62 C 2
Thames (U.K.) 28 D 4
Thāne 46 C 5
Thanh Hoa 47 K 5
Thanjāvūr 46 D 6
Thar Desert 46 C 3
Thasos 34 E 2
Thaton 47 H 5
Thayetmyo 47 H 5
The Fens 28 D 3
The Gambia 56 B 3
Thedford 16 C 3
Thermaïkos Kolpos 34 E 2

Thermopilal 34 E 3
Thermopolis 18 E 3
Thessalia 34 E 3
Thessaloniki 34 E 2
Thetford 28 E 3
Thetford Mines 8 W 9
Thief River Falls 16 D 2
Thiès 56 B 3
Thika 58 C 2
Thiladummathi Atoll 46 C 7
Thimbu 47 F 3
Thimphu 47 F 3
Thionville 36 B 3
Thira 34 F 3
Thirsk 28 D 2
Thomastown 31 C 2
Thomasville (Alabama, U.S.) 14 B 4
Thomasville (Georgia, U.S.) 14 C 4
Thompson 8 R 7
Thompson Falls 18 C 2
Thon Buri 47 J 6
Thongwe 47 H 5
Thonze 47 H 5
Thraki 34 F 2
Three Forks 18 D 2
Three Hummock Island 60 G 8
Three Kings Islands 62 B 1
Three Pagodas Pass 47 H 5
Throssell, Lake 60 C 5
Thule 8 X 3
Thunder Bay 8 T 9
Thunder Bay (Canada) 14 B 1
Thunder Bay (U.S.) 14 C 2
Thung Song 47 H 7
Thurso 30 C 2
Thy 38 G 4
Tian Shan 48 B 2
Tiandong 49 H 6
Tianjin 49 K 3
Tianjun 48 F 3
Tianmen 49 J 4
Tianshui 49 H 4
Tianyang 49 H 6
Tibesti 56 E 2
Tibet 48 C 4
Tiburón, Isla 20 B 2
Ticul 20 G 3
Tieli 50 E 3
Tieling 50 D 4
Tientsin 49 K 3
Tierra Blanca 20 E 4
Tierra Colorada 20 E

4
Tifton 14 C 4
Tigalda Island 43 X 6
Tighina 36 F 3
Tigil' 43 P 5
Tigris 44 F 6
Tigris, River 35 J 7
Tijuana 18 C 5
Tikal 20 G 4
Tikamgarh 46 D 4
Tikanlik 48 D 2
Tikhoretsk 35 J 2
Tikhvin 40 H 6
Tikopia 59 F 5
Tiksi 42 J 2
Tilburg 36 B 2
Tillamook 18 B 2
Tillanchong 47 G 7
Tilos 34 F 3
Timagami, Lake 14 C 1
Timanskiy Kryazh 40 L 4
Timaru 62 B 3
Timashevsk 35 H 2
Timiskaming 8 V 9
Timiskaming, Lac 14 D 1
Timişoara 36 E 3
Timmins 8 U 9
Timon 60 C 1
Timor 52 H 7
Timor Sea 53 H 8
Timpton 42 J 5
Tinaca Point 52 G 4
Tindivanam 46 D 6
Tinian 59 D 2
Tinos 34 F 3
Tinsukia 47 H 3
Tioman 52 C 5
Tipperary (Ireland) 31 B 2
Tipton, Mount 18 D 4
Tiquisate 20 F 5
Tiranë 34 D 2
Tiraspol 36 F 3
Tire 34 F 3
Tiree 30 A 3
Tirol 36 C 3
Tirreno, Mare 34 C 3
Tiruchchirappalli 46 D 6
Tiruneveli 46 D 7
Tirupati 46 D 6
Tirūvottiyūr 46 E 6
Tisa 36 E 3
Tisza 36 E 3
Tiszántúl 36 E 3
Titlägarh 46 E 4
Titograd 34 D 2
Titusville 14 C 5
Tivoli 34 C 2
Tizi Ouzou 56 D 1
Tizimin 20 G 3
Tkvarcheli 44 F 4

Tlalnépantla 20 E 4
Tlapa de Comonfort 20 E 4
Tlapacoyan 20 E 4
Tlaxcala 20 E 4
Tlemcen 56 C 1
Toamasina 58 D 3
Toba Kākar Range 46 B 2
Tobago 22 K 5
Tobermory (Canada) 8 U 9
Tobermory (U.K.) 30 A 3
Tobol' 40 P 6
Tobol'sk 40 P 6
Tobyl 45 K 2
Tobyl (River) 45 K 2
Tobylzhan 45 N 2
Tocopilla 24 D 5
Todos Santos 20 B 3
Tofino 18 A 2
Togian, Kepulauan 52 G 6
Togo 56 D 4
Togtoh 49 J 2
Tok 10 O 6
Tokat 44 E 4
Tokelau Islands 59 H 4
Tokmok 45 N 4
Tokoroa 62 C 2
Toksun 48 D 2
Tokuno-shima 50 E 7
Tokushima 54 B 4
Tōkyō 54 C 3
Tôlañaro 58 D 4
Toledo (Spain) 33 B 2
Toledo (U.S.) 14 C 2
Toledo Bend Reservoir 16 E 5
Toledo, Montes de 33 A 2
Toliara 58 D 4
Toliary 58 D 4
Tolstoy, Mys 43 P 5
Toluca 20 E 4
Tol'yatti 44 G 2
Tom 41 S 6
Tomah 16 E 3
Tomakomai 54 D 2
Tomar 33 A 2
Tomari 54 D 1
Tomaszów Mazowiecki 36 E 2
Tomatlán 20 C 4
Tombigbee River 14 B 4
Tombouctou 56 C 3
Tomdibuloq 45 K 4
Tomelloso 33 B 2
Tomini, Teluk 52 G 6
Tomkinson Ranges

60 D 5
Tommot 42 J 5
Tomsk 41 S 6
Tonasket 18 C 2
Tondano 52 G 5
Tonekābon 44 H 5
Tonga 59 H 5
Tonga Trench 59 H 6
Tongariro National Park 62 C 2
Tongatapu 59 H 6
Tongatapu Group 59 H 6
Tongbei 50 E 3
Tongchuan 49 H 3
Tonghai 49 G 6
Tonghe 50 E 3
Tonghua 50 E 4
Tongjan 50 F 3
Tongjiang 50 F 3
Tongjiang (Heilongjiang, China) 54 B 1
Tongjoson-man 54 A 3
Tongliao 50 D 4
Tongling 49 K 4
Tongren 49 H 5
Tongxiam 49 K 3
T'ongyŏng 54 A 4
Tongyu 50 D 4
Tongzi 49 H 5
Tonichí 20 C 2
Tonk 46 D 3
Tonkin, Gulf of 47 K 5
Tonopah 18 C 4
Tonstad 38 G 4
Tooele 18 D 3
Toowoomba 60 J 5
Topeka 16 D 4
Topki 41 T 6
Topolobampo 20 C 2
Topozero, Ozero 40 H 4
Toppenish 18 B 2
Torbalı 35 B 5
Torbat-e Ḩeydarīyeh 45 J 5
Torbat-e Jām 45 K 5
Töre 38 K 2
Torgau 36 C 2
Toribulu 52 F 6
Torino 36 B 3
Tori-shima 54 D 4
Torneå 38 K 2
Torneälven 38 K 2
Torneträsk 38 K 2
Tornio 38 K 2
Tornionjoki 38 K 2
Toronto 14 D 2
Toropets 40 H 6
Toros Dağları 35 D 6
Torquay 28 C 4
Torre del Greco 34 C

2
Torrelavega 33 B 1
Torremolinos 33 B 2
Torrens, Lake 60 F 6
Torrent 33 B 2
Torreón 20 D 2
Torres Strait 59 D 5
Torrevieja 33 C 2
Torrington 16 C 3
Torsby 38 H 3
Tórshavn 38 D 3
Tortola 22 K 4
Tortolì 34 B 3
Tortosa 32 C 3
Tortue, Île de la 22 H 3
Toruń 36 D 2
Torzhok 40 H 6
Tosa-shimizu 54 B 4
Tosa-wan 54 B 4
Toscana 34 C 2
Toshkent 45 L 4
Toson Hu 48 F 3
Tosya 35 F 4
Tot'ma 40 K 6
Totonicapan 20 F 5
Tottori 54 B 3
Touggourt 56 D 1
Touliu 49 L 6
Toulon 34 B 2
Toulouse 32 C 3
Toungoo 47 H 5
Touraine 32 C 2
Touri-án, Cabo 33 A 1
Tours 32 C 2
Tovuz 35 L 4
Towada 54 D 2
Towanda 14 D 2
Townsend 18 D 2
Townshend Island 60 J 4
Townsville 60 H 3
Towson 14 D 3
Toyama 54 C 3
Toyohashi 54 C 4
Toyota 54 C 3
Tqvarch'eli 44 F 4
Trabzon 35 H 4
Trafalgar, Cabo 33 A 2
Trail 18 C 2
Traill Ø 8 Gg 4
Tralee 31 A 2
Tralee Bay 31 A 2
Trang 47 H 7
Trangan 52 J 7
Transantarctic Mountains 63 Y 4
Transylvania 36 E 3
Trapani 34 C 3
Traralgon 60 H 7
Trarza Ouarâne 56 B 3
Traverse City 14 B 2

Třebíc 36 D 3
Tremonton 18 D 3
Trenč'n 36 D 3
Trent 28 C 3
Trento 36 C 3
Trenton (Missouri, U.S.) 16 E 3
Trenton (New Jersey, U.S.) 14 E 2
Tres Arroyos 24 E 6
Tres Picos 20 F 4
Tres Zapotes 20 E 4
Treviso 36 C 3
Trevose Head 28 B 4
Triángulos, Arrecifes 20 F 3
Trichur 46 D 6
Trier 36 B 3
Triosto 36 C 3
Trikala 34 E 3
Trincomalee 46 E 7
Trinidad 24 E 4
Trinidad (California, U.S.) 18 B 3
Trinidad (Colorado, U.S.) 16 C 4
Trinidad (Cuba) 22 F 3
Trinidad (Trinidad and Tobago) 22 K 5
Trinidad and Tobago 24 F 1
Trinity Islands 43 Z 5
Trinity River 16 D 5
Tripoli 34 E 3
Tripura 47 G 4
Trivandrum 46 D 7
Trobriand Islands 59 E 4
Trois-Rivières 8 W 9
Troitsko-Pechorsk 40 N 5
Troitskoye 45 O 2
Troitskoye (Russia) 54 C 1
Trollhättan 38 H 4
Troms 38 J 2
Tromsø 38 J 2
Trona 18 C 4
Trondheim 38 H 3
Trout Lake 10 S 6
Troy 14 B 4
Troyan 34 E 2
Troyes 32 C 2
Trubchevsk 36 G 2
Trujillo 24 D 3
Trujillo (Honduras) 20 G 4
Trujillo (Venezuela) 22 H 6
Truro (Canada) 8 Y 9
Truro (U.K.) 28 B 4

Truth or Consequences 18 E 5
Tsentral'no Tungusskoye Plato 41 W 5
Tsetserleg 41 W 8
Tshikapa 58 A 2
Tsiigehtchic 10 Q 5
Tsimlyansk 44 F 3
Tsingtao 49 L 3
Tsipanda 42 L 5
Tsipikan 42 F 6
Tsiroanomandidy 58 D 3
T'skhinvali 35 K 3
Tsu 54 C 4
Tsuchiura 54 D 3
Tsugaru-Kaikyō 54 C 2
Touruga 54 C 3
Tsuruoka 54 C 3
Tsushima 50 E 6
Tsuyama 54 B 3
Tual 52 J 7
Tuam 31 B 2
Tuamot, Îles 59 L 5
Tuanake 59 L 5
Tuangku 52 B 5
Tuapse 44 E 4
Tuba City 18 D 4
Tuban 52 E 7
Tubbataha Reefs 52 G 4
Tübingen 36 B 3
Tubruq 56 F 1
Tubuai 59 L 6
Tubuai Islands 59 K 6
Tucson 18 D 5
Tucumcari 16 C 4
Tucupita 22 K 6
Tudela 32 B 3
Tudmur 44 E 6
Tuguegarao 52 G 2
Tugur 42 L 6
Tui 33 A 1
Tukangbesi, Kepulauan 52 G 7
Tuktoyaktuk 10 Q 5
Tukums 38 K 4
Tukuringra, Khrebet 42 H 6
Tula 44 E 2
Tula (Mexico) 20 E 3
Tulancingo 20 E 3
Tulare 18 C 4
Tulcea 36 F 3
Tul'chyn 36 F 3
Tüledi Araldary 44 G 3
Tulemalu Lake 10 W 6
Tulita 10 R 6
Tullahoma 14 B 3
Tully 60 H 3

Tulsa 16 D 4
Tuluksak 43 X 4
Tulum 20 G 3
Tulun 41 W 7
Tulungagung 52 E 7
Tumaco 22 G 7
Tumany 43 P 4
Tumbes 24 C 3
Tumen 54 A 2
Tumkūr 46 D 6
Tunceli 35 H 5
Tungkang 49 L 6
Tungku 52 F 4
Tungsten 10 R 6
Tūnis 56 D 1
Tunis, Golfe de 34 C 3
Tunisia 56 D 1
Tunja 22 H 6
Tunugayualok Island 8 Y 7
Tununak 43 W 4
Tunxi 49 K 5
Tuotuo He 48 E 4
Tupelo 14 B 4
Tupik 42 G 6
Tuquan 50 D 3
Tura (India) 47 G 3
Tura (Russia) 41 W 5
Turakh 42 H 2
Turan 41 U 7
Turana, Khrebet 42 K 6
Turbaco 22 G 5
Turbo 22 G 6
Turda 36 E 3
Turek 36 D 2
Türgen Uul 41 U 8
Türgovishte 35 B 3
Turgutlu 34 F 3
Turhal 35 G 4
Turinsk 40 O 6
Turiy Rog 54 B 1
Türkistan 45 L 4
Türkmenabat 45 K 5
Türkmenbashi 44 H 4
Turkmenistan 45 J 5
Türköglu 35 G 6
Turks and Caicos Islands 22 H 3
Turks Islands 22 H 3
Turku 38 K 3
Turneffe Islands 20 G 4
Turnu-Măgurele 34 E 2
Turpan 48 D 2
Turukhan 41 S 4
Turukhansk 41 T 4
Tuscaloosa 14 B 4
Tutavev 40 J 6
Tuticorin 46 D 7
Tuttle Creek Lake 16

D 4
Tuttut Nunaat 8 Ff 4
Tutuala 52 H 7
Tutuila 59 H 5
Tuvalu 59 H 4
Tuvana-i-ra 59 H 6
Tuxpán 20 C 3
Tuxpan 20 E 3
Tuxtepec 20 E 4
Tuxtla Gutiérrez 20 F 4
Tuy Hoa 47 K 6
Tuyen Quang 47 K 4
Tuymazy 44 H 2
Tuz Gölü 35 E 5
Tūz Khurmātū 44 F 6
Tuzla 34 D 2
Tver' 40 J 6
Tweed 28 C 2
Twin Falls (U.S.) 18 D 3
Twin Islands 8 U 8
Twins, The 62 B 3
Twisp 18 B 2
Two Harbors 16 E 2
Tyatino 54 E 2
Tybee Island 14 C 4
Tygda 42 J 6
Tyler 16 D 5
Tym 41 S 5
Tynda 42 H 5
Tyne 28 D 2
Tynset 38 H 3
Tyrma 42 K 7
Tyrnavos 34 E 3
Tyrrhenian Sea 34 C 3
Tysnesøy 38 F 4
Tyssedal 38 G 3
Tyukalinsk 40 Q 6
Tyumen 40 P 6
Tyung 42 G 3
Tzucacab 20 G 4
Ua Pou 59 M 4
Uashat 8 X 8
Uaxactún 20 G 4
Ube 54 B 4
Úbeda 33 B 2
Uberaba 24 G 4
Uberlândia 24 G 4
Ubon Ratchathani 47 J 5
Uchiura-Wan 54 D 2
Udachnyy 41 Y 4
Udaipur 46 C 4
Uddevalla 38 H 4
Udgīr 46 D 5
Udine 36 C 3
Udokan 42 G 5
Udokan, Khrebet 42 G 5
Udon Thani 47 J 5
Udskaya Guba 42 L 6

Udupi 46 C 6
Udzha 42 G 2
Ueda 54 C 3
Uekuli 52 G 6
Uele 58 B 1
Uelen 50 D 3
Uel'Kal 43 U 3
Uelzen 36 C 2
Ufa 40 N 7
Uganda 58 C 1
Ugashik 43 Y 5
Uglegorsk 50 H 3
Uglich 40 J 6
Ugol'nyye Kopi 43 T 4
Uig 30 A 3
'Uiha 59 H 5
Uiju 50 D 4
Uinta Mountains 18 D 3
Uitenhage 58 B 5
Ujae 59 F 3
Ujelang 59 F 3
Ujjain 46 D 4
Ujung Pandang 52 F 7
Ukhta 40 M 5
Ukiah (California, U.S.) 18 B 4
Ukiah (Oregon, U.S.) 18 C 2
Ukraine 36 F 3
Ukrainka 41 R 6
Ulaanbaatar 50 A 3
Ulakhan-Bam, Khrebet 42 L 5
Ulakhan-Chistay, Khrebet 42 M 3
Ulan Ul Hu 48 E 4
Ulan-Burgasy, Khrebet 41 X 7
Ulan-Ude 41 X 7
Ulchin 54 A 3
Uleåborg 38 L 3
Ulgal 50 C 3
Ulhāsnagar 46 C 5
Uliastal 50 C 3
Ullapool 30 B 3
Ullared 38 H 4
Ullersuaq 8 W 3
Ulm 36 B 3
Ulsan 54 A 3
Ulster 31 C 1
Ulu 42 J 4
Ulunga 54 C 1
Ulunkhan 42 F 6
Ul'yanovsk 44 G 2
Ulytaū 45 L 3
Uman' 44 D 3
Uman 53 K 6
Umboi 59 D 4
Umeå 38 K 3
Umeälven 38 J 3
Umiat 10 M 5
Umm Durmān (Om-

durman) 56 F 3
Umnak Island 43 W 6
Ueda 54 C 3
Umtata 58 B 5
Unadilla 14 C 4
Unalakleet 43 X 4
Unalaska Island 43 W 6
Unelja 36 G 2
Unga 43 X 5
Ungava Bay 8 X 7
Ungava, Péninsule d' 8 V 6
Unimak Island 43 X 5
Union City 14 B 3
United Kingdom 28 D 2
United States of America 16 C 4
University City 16 E 4
Unst 30 D 1
Upata 22 K 6
Upernavik 8 Z 4
Upington 58 B 4
Upolu 59 H 5
Upolu Point 12 E 7
Upper Arlington 14 C 2
Upper Hutt 62 C 3
Upper Klamath Lake 18 B 3
Upper Lough Erne 31 C 1
Upper Red Lake 16 D 2
Uppland 38 J 3
Uppsala 38 J 4
Urak 42 M 5
Urakawa 54 D 2
Ural Mountains 40 N 7
Uralovka 42 J 6
Ural'sk 44 H 2
Ural'skiy Gory 45 J 2
Uranium City 10 V 7
Urbino 34 C 2
Urdzhar 45 O 3
Uren' 40 L 6
Urengoy 41 R 4
Urfa 44 E 5
Urgal 42 K 6
Urganch 45 K 4
Urla 35 B 5
Uroteppa 45 L 5
Ursuq Ash Shuyūkh 44 G 6
Uruapan 20 D 4
Uruguay 24 F 6
Ürümqi 48 D 2
Uryupinsk 44 F 2
Urzhum 40 L 6
Urziceni 35 B 2
Uşak 35 C 5

Ushakova, Ostrov 41 R 1
Üsharal 45 O 3
Ushki, Zaliv 43 N 5
Üshtöbe 45 N 3
Ush-Urekchen, Khrebet 43 Q 3
Üsküdar 34 F 2
Usman' 44 E 2
Usol'ye-Sibirskoye 41 W 7
Ussuri 54 B 2
Ussuriysk 54 B 2
Ust'-Ilimsk 41 W 6
Ust'-Ilimskoye Vodokhranilishche 41 W 6
Ust'-Ishim 40 Q 6
Ust'-Kamchatsk 43 Q 5
Ust'-Kara 40 P 4
Ust'-Katav 40 N 7
Ust'-Khayryuzovo 43 P 5
Ust'-Kulom 40 M 5
Ust'-Kut 41 X 6
Ust'-Labinsk 44 E 3
Ust'-Maya 42 K 4
Ust'-Mil' 42 K 5
Ust'-Muya 42 G 5
Ust'-Nera 42 M 4
Ust'-Omchug 43 N 4
Ust'-Paden'ga 40 K 5
Ust'-Penzhino 43 R 4
Ust'-Port 41 S 4
Ust'-Sopochnoye 43 P 5
Ust'-Tatta 42 K 4
Ust'-Tsil'ma 40 M 4
Ust'-Tsima 40 M 4
Ust'-Urgal 42 K 6
Ust'-Usa 40 N 4
Ust'-Vaga 40 K 5
Ust'-Voyampolka 43 P 5
Usu 48 C 2
Usulután 22 E 5
Usumacinta, Río 20 F 4
Utah 18 D 4
Utah Lake 18 D 3
Utica 14 D 2
Utirik 59 F 2
Utrecht 36 B 2
Utsunomiya 54 C 3
Uttar Pradesh 46 D 3
Uttaradit 47 J 5
Utupua 59 F 5
Uuldza 50 B 3
Uummannaq (Kalaallit Nunaat) 8 Aa 4

Uummannaq (Kalaallit Nunaat) 8 Cc 6
Üüreg Nuur 41 U 8
Uusikaupunki 38 K 3
Uva 40 M 6
Uvalde 20 E 2
Uvarovo 44 F 2
Uvdal 38 G 3
Uvs Nuur 41 U 7
Uwajima 54 B 4
Uxmal 20 G 3
Uyedineniya, Ostrov 41 S 2
Uzbekistan 45 K 4
Uzhhorod 36 E 3
Uzhur 41 T 6
Užice 34 D 2
Uzlovaya 44 E 2
Uzunköprü 35 B 4
Vaal 58 B 4
Vaal Dam 58 B 4
Vaasa 38 K 3
Vác 36 D 3
Vacaria 24 F 5
Vache, Île-à 22 H 4
Vadodara 46 C 4
Vaduz 36 B 3
Vágar 38 D 3
Vaghena Island 59 E 4
Vaiaku 59 G 4
Vaikh 41 S 5
Valachia 34 E 2
Valday 40 H 6
Valdayskaya Vozvyshennost' 40 H 6
Valdez 10 N 6
Valdivia 24 D 6
Val-d'Or 8 V 9
Valdosta 14 C 4
Vale of White Horse 28 D 4
Valence 32 C 3
Valencia (Spain) 33 B 2
Valencia (Venezuela) 22 J 5
Valentine 16 C 3
Valera 22 H 6
Valga 38 L 4
Valjevo 34 D 2
Valladolid (Mexico) 20 G 3
Valladolid (Spain) 33 B 1
Valle 38 G 4
Valle de la Pascua 22 J 6
Valle de Zaragoza 20 C 2
Valle Hermoso 20 E 2
Valletta 34 C 3
Valley City 16 D 2

Valley Station 14 B 3
Valleyfield 14 E 1
Valmiera 38 L 4
Valparaiso 20 D 3
Valparaíso 24 D 6
Vals, Tanjung 53 K 7
Valuyki 44 E 2
Van 35 K 5
Van Buren 16 E 4
Van Dieman, Cape 60 E 2
Van Diemen Gulf 60 E 2
Van Gölü 35 K 5
Van Horn 16 C 5
van Rees, Pegunungan 53 K 6
Van Wert 14 C 2
Vanadzor 35 L 4
Vanavara 41 W 5
Vancouver 18 B 2
Vancouver Island 10 R 8
Vandalla 14 B 3
Vanderbijlpark 58 B 4
Vanderhoof 10 S 8
Vanderlin Island 60 F 3
Vänern 38 H 4
Vänersborg 38 H 4
Vangunu Island 59 E 4
Vanikoro Islands 59 F 5
Vankarem 43 U 3
Vanna 38 J 1
Vanna Levu 59 G 5
Vannatu 61 K 3
Vannes 32 B 2
Vansittart Island 8 U 5
Vanua Lava 59 F 5
Vanuatu 59 F 5
Vārānasi 46 E 3
Varangerhalvøya 38 L 1
Varaždin 36 D 3
Varberg 38 H 4
Vardø 40 H 3
Värmland 38 H 4
Varna 34 F 2
Varna (Bulgaria) 35 B 3
Värnamo 38 H 4
Varnenski Zaliv 35 C 3
Varsinais Suomi 38 K 3
Varzuga 40 J 4
Vasa 38 K 3
Vaşac 36 F 3
Vasai 46 C 5
Vaslui 36 F 3
Vasta 44 G 3

Västerås 38 J 4
Västerbotten 38 J 3
Västergötland 38 H 4
Västervik 38 J 4
Västmanland 38 J 4
Vasyl'kiv 36 G 2
Vasyugan 41 R 6
Vatican City State 34 C 2
Vatnajökull 38 B 3
Vatoa 59 H 5
Vatomandry 58 D 3
Vatra Dornei 36 F 3
Vättern 38 H 4
Vaughn 18 E 5
Vava'u Group 59 H 5
Vavuniya 46 E 7
Vawkavysk 36 E 2
Väydaghch 40 N 3
Vega 38 H 2
Vejle 38 G 4
Veles 34 E 2
Velikaya Kema 54 C 1
Velikiy Ustyug 40 L 5
Velikiye-Luki 40 H 6
Veliko Türnovo 34 F 2
Velikonda Range 46 D 5
Vellore 46 D 6
Vel'sk 40 K 5
Vendinga 40 L 5
Vendôme 32 C 2
Venetie 10 N 5
Venezia 36 C 3
Venezuela 24 E 2
Venezuela, Golfo de 22 H 5
Venice, Gulf of 36 C 3
Ventspils 38 K 4
Ventura 18 C 5
Venustiano Carranza 20 F 4
Veracruz (Mexico) 20 E 4
Veracruz (State, Mexico) 20 E 3
Veraval 46 C 4
Verde River 18 D 4
Vereeniging 58 B 4
Vereshchagino 40 M 6
Verkhneangarskiy ·Khrebet 41 X 6
Verkhneimbatskoye 41 T 5
Verkhnevilyuysk 42 H 4
Verkhniy Ufaley 40 O 6
Verkhnyaya Amga 42

J 5
Verkhnyaya Salda 40 O 6
Verkhnyaya Toyma 40 K 5
Verkhotur'ye 40 O 6
Verkhoyansk 42 K 3
Verkhoyanskiy Khrebet 42 J 3
Vermilion Bay 16 E 2
Vermont 14 E 2
Vernal 18 E 3
Vernon (Canada) 10 T 8
Vernon (U.S.) 16 D 5
Vero Beach 14 C 5
Veroia 34 E 2
Verona 36 C 3
Versailles 32 C 2
Veshenskaya 44 F 3
Vest-Agder 38 G 4
Vesterålen 38 H 2
Vestfjorden 38 H 2
Vestmannaeyjar 38 A 3
Vestvågøy 38 H 2
Ves'yegonsk 40 J 6
Vétaoundé 59 F 5
Vetlanda 38 J 4
Vevelstad 38 H 2
Vezh'ydor 40 M 5
Viana do Castelo 33 A 1
Viangchan 47 J 5
Vibo Valentia 34 D 3
Viborg 38 G 4
Vic 32 C 3
Vicenza 36 C 3
Vichuga 40 K 6
Vichy 32 C 2
Vicksburg 16 E 5
Victoria 58 E 2
Victoria (Australia) 60 G 7
Victoria (Canada) 18 B 2
Victoria (Malaysia) 52 F 4
Victoria (U.S.) 20 E 2
Victoria de las Tunas 22 G 3
Victoria Island 10 U 4
Victoria River Downs 60 E 3
Victoria Strait 10 W 5
Victorias 52 G 3
Victoriaville 14 E 1
Victorville 18 C 5
Videle 35 A 2
Vidin 34 E 2
Vidisha 46 D 4
Vidra 34 F 2

Viedma 24 E 7
Viejo, Cerro (Mexico) 18 D 5
Vienna 36 D 3
Vienna (U.S.) 14 C 3
Vienne 32 C 2
Vientiane 47 J 5
Vieques, Isla de 22 K 4
Vierzon 32 C 2
Viesca 20 D 2
Viet Triu 47 K 4
Vietnam 47 K 5
Vigan 52 G 2
Vigo 33 A 1
Vihari 46 C 2
Vijayawāda 46 E 5
Vikhorevka 41 W 6
Vikna 38 H 3
Vila 59 F 5
Vila Real 33 A 1
Vila Real 33 B 2
Vilalba 33 A 1
Vilanova i la Geltrú 32 C 3
Vila-real 32 B 3
Vilhelmina 38 J 3
Viliga-Kushka 43 P 4
Viljandi 38 L 4
Vil'kitskogo, Ostrov 41 R 3
Vil'kitskogo, Proliv 41 W 2
Villa Ahumada 18 E 5
Villa Coronado 20 C 2
Villa de Cos 20 D 3
Villa Flores 20 F 4
Villa Frontera 20 D 2
Villa Hidalgo 20 D 2
Villa María 24 E 6
Villa Ocampo (Mexico) 20 C 2
Villa Union 20 C 3
Villach 36 C 3
Villahermosa 20 F 4
Villaldama 20 D 2
Villavicencio 22 H 7
Ville de Reyes 20 D 3
Villeurbanne 32 C 2
Villmanstrand 38 L 3
Villupuram 46 D 6
Vilnius 36 F 2
Vilye 36 F 2
Vilyuy 42 G 4
Vilyuyskoye Plato 41 X 4
Vi-lyuyskoyeVodokhranilishche 41 X 5
Viña del Mar 24 D 6
Vinaròs 32 C 3
Vincennes 14 B 3

Vindhya Range 46 C 4
Vineland 14 D 3
Vinh 47 K 5
Vinh Loi 47 K 7
Vinkovci 36 D 3
Vinnytsya 36 F 3
Virac 52 G 3
Viramgam 46 C 4
Virden 16 C 2
Virgin Islands 22 J 4
Virginia (Minnesota, U.S.) 16 E 2
Virginia (State, U.S.) 14 D 3
Virginia Beach 14 D 3
Virginia Falls 10 R 6
Virudunager 46 D 7
Visalia 18 C 4
Visayan Sea 52 G 3
Visby 38 J 4
Viscount Melville Sound 10 U 4
Viseu 33 A 1
Viseul de Sus 36 E 3
Vishakhapatnam 46 E 5
Visnagar 46 C 4
Vistula 36 D 2
Viterbo 34 C 2
Viti Levu 59 G 5
Vitim 42 G 5
Vitimskoye Ploskogor'ye 42 F 6
Vitória 24 H 5
Vitória da Conquista 24 G 4
Vitoria-Gasteiz 32 B 3
Vitsyebsk 40 H 6
Vittoria 34 C 3
Vittorio Veneto 36 C 3
Vivi 41 V 5
Vizcaíno, Desierto de 20 B 2
Vizcaíno, Sierra 20 B 2
Vize, Ostrov 41 R 2
Vizianagaram 46 E 5
V'k 38 B 3
Vladikavkaz 35 L 3
Vladimir 40 K 6
Vladivostok 54 B 2
Vlor' 34 D 2
Vojvodina 36 D 3
Volga 44 G 3
Volgo-Balt Kanal 40 J 5
Volgodonsk 44 F 3
Volgograd 44 F 3
Volkhov 40 H 6
Volnovakha 44 E 3
Volochanka 41 U 3

Volodymyr-Volyns'kyy 36 E 2
Vologda 40 J 6
Volos 34 E 3
Vol'sk 44 G 2
Volzhsk 40 L 6
Volzhskiy 44 F 3
Vongping 48 F 5
Voranava 36 F 2
Voreioi Sporades 34 E 3
Vorkuta 40 O 4
Vormsi 38 K 4
Voronezh 44 E 2
Voronina, Ostrov 41 U 2
Võru 38 L 4
Voss 38 G 3
Vostochno-Sibirskoye More 43 P 2
Vostochnyy (Russia) 54 D 1
Vostochnyy Sayan 41 U 7
Vostok Island 59 K 5
Votkinsk 40 M 6
Voyvozh 40 N 5
Vozhgora 40 L 5
Voznesens'k 44 D 3
Vozrozhdeniya 45 J 3
Vozvrashcheniye 54 D 1
Vrangelya, Ostrov 43 T 2
Vranje 34 E 2
Vratsa 34 E 2
Vryburg 58 B 4
Vset'n 36 D 3
Vsevolozhsk 40 H 6
Vukovar 36 D 3
Vung Tau 47 K 6
Vyatka 40 L 6
Vyatskiye Polyany 40 M 6
Vyaz'ma 40 H 6
Vyborg 38 L 3
Vyksa 40 K 6
Vyselki 35 H 2
Vyshniy Volochek 40 H 6
Vysokiy, Mys 42 N 1
Vysokogorsk 54 C 2
Vytegra 40 J 5
W nsan 50 E 5
Wa 56 C 4
Wa Keeney 16 D 4
Wabash River 14 B 3
Waboden 10 X 8
Wabowden 10 X 8
Waco (U.S.) 16 D 5
Waconda Lake 16 D 4
Wad Madanī 56 G 3

Wadi Drâa 56 B 2
Wādī Sawbā 56 G 4
Wadley 14 C 4
Wadsworth 18 C 4
Wagga Wagga 60 H 7
Wagin 60 B 6
Wagon Mound 16 C 4
Wagoner 16 D 4
Wäh Cantonment 45 M 6
Wahai 52 H 6
Wahiawa 12 E 7
Wahpeton 16 D 2
Waiau 62 B 3
Waibeem 52 J 6
Waigeo 52 J 5
Waija 52 H 6
Waikato 62 C 2
Waikouaiti 62 B 4
Waimate 62 B 3
Wainwright 10 K 4
Waiotira 62 B 2
Waipara 62 B 3
Wairau 62 B 3
Wairoa 62 C 2
Waitaki 62 B 3
Waitara 62 B 2
Waitemata 62 B 2
Waiwo 52 J 6
Wakasa-wan 54 C 3
Wakatipu, Lake 62 A 4
Wakayama 54 C 4
Wakema 47 H 5
Wakkanai 50 H 3
Wałbrzych 36 D 2
Wałcz 36 D 2
Waldport 18 B 3
Wales (U.K.) 28 C 3
Wales (U.S.A.) 43 W 3
Wales Island 8 T 5
Walker Lake 18 C 4
Wall 16 C 3
Walla Walla 18 C 2
Wallaceburg 14 C 2
Wallaroo 60 F 6
Wallis and Futuna 59 H 5
Wallis, Îles 59 H 5
Walsall 28 D 3
Walsenburg 16 C 4
Walt Disney World 14 C 5
Walterboro 14 C 4
Waltershausen Gletscher 8 Ff 4
Walvis Bay 58 A 4
Wanaka 62 A 3
Wanaka, Lake 62 A 3
Wandel Sea 8 Gg 2
Wanganui 62 C 2

Wangaratta 60 H 7
Wangiwangi 52 G 7
Wangkui 50 E 3
Wangqing 54 A 2
Wanneroo 60 B 6
Wanning 47 L 5
Wanxian 49 H 4
Wanyuan 49 H 4
Warangal 46 D 5
Warburton Range 60 D 5
Ward 62 B 3
Ware 10 R 7
Waren 53 K 6
Warin Chamrap 47 J 5
Warm Springs 18 C 4
Warming Land 8 Aa 2
Warner Mountains 18 B 3
Warner Peak 18 C 3
Warner Robins 14 C 4
Warren (U.S.) 14 C 2
Warri 56 D 4
Warrington 28 C 3
Warrnambool 60 G 7
Warrumbungle Range 60 H 6
Warsaw 36 E 2
Warszawa 36 E 2
Warwick 60 J 5
Wasatch Range 18 D 3
Wasco 18 C 4
Wasgomuwa National Park 46 E 7
Wash, The 28 E 3
Washburn Lake 10 V 4
Washim 46 D 4
Washington (Indiana, U.S.) 14 B 3
Washington (Maryland, U.S.) 14 D 3
Washington (North Carolina, U.S.) 14 D 3
Washington (State, U.S.) 18 B 2
Washington Court House 14 C 3
Washington Land 8 X 2
Wasior 52 J 6
Waskaganish 8 V 8
Waspán 20 H 5
Watampone 52 G 6
Waterbury 14 E 2
Waterford 31 C 2
Waterloo (U.S.) 16 E 3
Waterton Lakes Na-

tional Park 18 D 2
Watertown (New York, U.S.) 14 D 2
Watertown (South Dakota, U.S.) 16 D 3
Watertown (Wisconsin, U.S.) 14 B 2
Waterville 8 X 10
Watford City 16 C 2
Watrous (U.S.) 16 C 4
Watson Lake 10 R 6
Watts Bar Lake 14 C 3
Watubela, Kepulauan 52 J 6
Waukara, Gunung 52 F 6
Waukarlycarly, Lake 60 C 4
Waukegan 14 B 2
Waukesha 14 B 2
Wausau 14 B 2
Wave Hill 60 E 3
Waverly 16 E 3
Wāw 56 F 4
Wawa 8 U 9
Way, Lake 60 C 5
Waycross 14 C 4
Wayland 14 C 3
Wayne 14 C 3
Webster 16 D 2
Webster City 16 E 3
Weda 52 H 5
Weh 52 B 4
Wehē 56 H 4
Wei He 49 J 4
Weichang 50 C 4
Weiden in der Oberpfalz 36 C 3
Weifang 49 K 3
Weihai 49 L 3
Weinan 49 H 4
Weirton 14 C 2
Weiser 18 C 3
Weishan Hu 49 K 4
Weißwasser 36 C 2
Wejherowo 36 D 2
Welkom 58 B 4
Wellesley Islands 60 F 3
Wellington (Kansas, U.S.) 16 D 4
Wellington (Nevada, U.S.) 18 C 4
Wellington (New Zealand) 62 B 3
Wells 18 D 3
Wellsboro 14 D 2
Wellton 18 D 5
Wels 36 C 3
Wenatchee 18 B 2
Wenchang 47 L 5
Wendeng 49 L 3

Wendover 18 D 3
Wenling 49 L 5
Wenshan 49 G 6
Wentworth 60 G 6
Wenzhou 49 L 5
Weri 52 J 6
Weslaco 20 E 2
Wessel Islands 60 F 2
Wessel, Cape 60 F 2
West Allis 14 B 2
West Bend 14 B 2
West Bengal 46 F 4
West Cape Howe 60 B 7
West Memphis 16 E 4
West Palm Beach 14 C 5
West Plains 16 E 4
West Point 14 B 4
West Virginia 14 C 3
West Wyalong 60 H 6
West Yellowstone 18 D 3
Westbrook 14 E 2
Wester Ross 30 B 3
Western Australia 60 B 4
Western Ghāts 46 C 5
Western Port 60 G 7
Western Sahara (Morocco) 56 B 2
Weston 14 C 3
Weston-super-Mare 28 C 4
Westport 62 B 3
Westray 30 C 2
Westree 14 C 1
Westwood 18 B 3
Wetar 52 H 7
Wetzlar 36 B 2
Wewak 59 D 4
Wexford 31 C 2
Weyburn 16 C 2
Weymouth 28 C 4
Whakatane 62 C 2
Whale Cove 8 S 6
Whalsay 30 D 1
Whangarei 62 B 2
Whapmagoostui 8 V 7
Wharton Lake 10 W 6
Wheatland 16 C 3
Wheeler Peak (Nevada, U.S.) 18 D 4
Wheeler Peak (New Mexico, U.S.) 18 E 4
Wheeling 14 C 2
White Butte 16 C 2

White Island 8 T 5
White River 8 T 9
White River (Arkansas, U.S.) 16 E 5
White River (Indiana, U.S.) 14 B 3
White River (Ontario, Canada) 14 B 1
White River (South Dakota, U.S.) 16 C 3
White Sulphur Springs 18 D 2
White Volta 56 C 4
Whitecourt 10 T 8
Whitefish Bay 14 C 1
Whitefish Point 14 B 1
Whitehaven 28 C 2
Whitehorse 10 P 6
Whitewater Bay 14 C 5
Whitney 14 D 1
Whitsunday Island 60 H 4
Whittier 10 N 6
Whiyby 28 D 2
Wholdaia Lake 10 V 6
Whyalla 60 F 6
Wibaux 16 C 2
Wichita 16 D 4
Wichita Falls 16 D 5
Wick 30 C 2
Wickenburg 18 D 5
Wickham, Cape 60 G 7
Wicklow 31 C 2
Wicklow Head 28 B 3
Wicklow Mountains 31 C 2
Wien 36 D 3
Wiener Neustadt 36 D 3
Wiesbaden 36 B 2
Wight, Isle of 28 D 4
Wilbur 18 C 2
Wilcannia 60 G 6
Wilhelm II Land 63 R 5
Wilhelmshaven 36 B 2
Wilkes Barre 14 D 2
Willamette River 18 B 3
Willapa Bay 18 A 2
Willard 18 E 5
Willcox 18 E 5
Willemstad 22 J 5
Williams 18 D 4
Williams Lake 10 S 8
Williamsburg (Kentucky, U.S.) 14 C 3

Williamsburg (Virginia, U.S.) 14 D 3
Williamsport 14 D 2
Willis Group 60 J 3
Williston (U.S.) 16 C 2
Williston Lake 10 S 7
Willow Bunch 18 E 2
Willows 18 B 4
Wilmington (New Jersey, U.S.) 14 D 3
Wilmington (North Carolina, U.S.) 14 D 4
Wilson 14 D 3
Wilson Lake 14 B 4
Wilson, Cape 8 U 5
Wilson's Promontory National Park 60 H 7
Wiluna 60 C 5
Winchester (U.K.) 28 D 4
Winchester (U.S.) 14 C 3
Wind River 18 E 3
Wind River Range 18 E 3
Windermere 28 C 2
Windhoek 58 A 4
Windorah 60 G 5
Window Rock 18 E 4
Windsor (Ontario, Canada) 14 C 2
Windsor (U.K.) 28 D 4
Windsor Forest 14 C 4
Windsor Locks 14 E 2
Windward Islands (Caribbean) 22 K 5
Windward Islands (French Polynesia) 59 K 5
Winfield (Alabama, U.S.) 14 B 4
Winfield (Kansas, U.S.) 16 D 4
Winnebago, Lake 14 B 2
Winnemucca 18 C 3
Winnfield 16 E 5
Winnipeg 16 D 2
Winnipeg, Lake 10 X 8
Winnipegosis, Lake 10 W 8
Winnipesaukee, Lake 14 E 2
Winona 16 E 3
Winslow 18 D 4
Winslow Reef 59 H 4
Winston-Salem 14 C 3

Winter Park 14 C 5
Winton 60 G 4
Winton (New Zealand) 62 A 4
Wisconsin 16 E 2
Wiseman 10 M 5
Wisła 36 D 2
Wismar 36 C 2
Witbank 58 B 4
Witney 28 D 4
Wittenberg 36 C 2
Wittenberge 36 C 2
Włocławek 36 D 2
Wokam 52 J 7
Woking 28 D 4
Wolf Creek 18 D 2
Wolf Point 18 E 2
Wolf Rock 28 B 5
Wolfsberg 36 C 3
Wollaston Forland 8 Gg 4
Wollaston Lake 10 W 7
Wollongong 60 J 6
Wolseley 16 C 1
Wolverhampton 28 C 3
Wonju 54 A 3
Wŏnsan 54 A 3
Wood Buffalo National Park 10 U 7
Woodland 18 B 4
Woodlark Island 59 E 4
Woods, Lake 60 E 3
Woods, Lake of the 16 D 2
Woodstock (Canada) 14 F 1
Woodstock (U.S.) 14 E 2
Woodville 16 E 5
Woodward 16 D 4
Woomera 60 F 6
Worcester 58 A 5
Worcester (U.K.) 28 C 3
Worcester (U.S.) 14 E 2
Wordie Gletscher 8 Gg 4
Workington 28 C 2
Worland 18 E 3
Worthing 28 D 4
Worthington 16 D 3
Wosi 52 H 6
Wosu 52 G 6
Wotho 59 F 2
Wotje 59 G 3
Wotu 52 G 6
Wowoni 52 G 6
Woy Woy 60 J 6
Wozrojdeniye Orol 45 J 3
Wrangell 10 Q 7

Wrangell Mountains 10 O 6
Wrangell Saint Elias National Park 10 O 6
Wrangell, Cape 43 S 6
Wrath, Cape 30 B 2
Wrexham 28 C 3
Wright Patman Lake 16 D 5
Wrigley 10 S 6
Wrocław 36 D 2
Wu Shan 49 J 4
Wuchang (Hei-longjiang, China) 50 E 4
Wuchang (Hubei, China) 49 J 4
Wuchuan 49 J 6
Wuda 49 H 3
Wudu 49 G 4
Wugang 49 J 5
Wuhai 49 H 3
Wuhan 49 J 4
Wuhu 49 K 4
Wuji Shan 49 K 5
Wulff Land 8 Aa 2
Wuling Shan 49 H 5
Wumeng 49 G 5
Wunnummin Lake 8 T 8
Wuppertal 36 B 2
Wuqing 49 K 3
Würzburg 36 B 3
Wutai Shan 49 J 3
Wutunghliao 49 G 5
Wuwei (Anhui, China) 49 K 4
Wuwei (Gansu, China) 49 G 3
Wuxi 49 L 4
Wuyiling 54 A 1
Wuyuan 49 H 2
Wuzhong 49 H 3
Wuzhou 49 J 6
Wye 28 C 3
Wyndham 60 D 3
Wyoming (Michigan, U.S.) 14 B 2
Wyoming (State, U.S.) 18 E 3
Wyperfeld National Park 60 G 7
Xaidulla 48 B 3
Xam Nua 47 J 4
Xankändi 44 G 5
Xanthi 34 E 2
Xayar 48 C 2
Xenia 14 C 3
Xi Jiang 49 J 6
Xiachengzi 54 B 2
Xiachuan Dao 49 J 6
Xiaguan 48 G 5
Xiamen 49 K 6

Xi'an 49 H 4
Xiangfan 49 J 4
Xiangtan 49 J 5
Xianju 49 L 5
Xianyang 49 H 4
Xiaogan 49 J 4
Xiaojin 49 G 4
Xiapu 49 L 5
Xiawa 50 D 4
Xichang 49 G 5
Xicoténcati 20 E 3
Xigaze 48 D 5
Ximiao 48 G 2
Xin Barag Youqi 50 C 3
Xin'anjiang Shuiku 49 K 5
Xinchang 49 L 5
Xing Xian 49 J 3
Xinghai 48 F 3
Xinghe 49 J 2
Xinging 54 A 1
Xingren 49 H 5
Xingtai 49 J 3
Xingyi 49 G 5
Xinhua 49 J 5
Xinhui 49 J 6
Xining 49 G 3
Xinjiang Uygur Zizhiqu 48 C 3
Xinjin 49 L 3
Xinmin 54 A 1
Xinning 49 J 5
Xinwen 49 K 3
Xinxiang 49 J 3
Xinyang 49 J 4
Xiqing Shan 49 G 3
Xiushui 49 J 5
Xiuwu 49 J 3
Xiuyan 50 D 4
Xixiang 49 H 4
Xizang Zizhiqu 48 C 4
Xo'jayli 45 J 4
Xouhil 20 G 4
Xuanhan 49 H 4
Xuanhua 50 C 4
Xuanwei 49 G 5
Xuchang 49 J 4
Xuguit Qi 50 D 3
Xupu 49 J 5
Xuwen 49 J 6
Xuyong 49 H 5
Xuzhou 49 K 4
Ya'an 49 G 4
Yablonovyy Khrebet 42 F 6
Yabuli 54 A 2
Yadgir 46 D 5
Yahyalı 35 F 5
Yailang 48 G 4
Yakima 18 B 2
Yakumo 54 D 2
Yaku-Shima 50 E 6
Yaku-shima 54 A 4

Yakutal 10 P 7
Yakutsk 42 J 4
Yala 52 C 4
Yalatorovsk 40 P 6
Yalong Jiang 49 G 4
Yalta 44 D 4
Yalta (Ukraine) 35 F 2
Yamagata 54 D 3
Yamaguchi 54 B 4
Yamal, Poluostrov 40 P 3
Yam-Alin', Khrebet 42 K 6
Yambo 22 G 7
Yambol 34 F 2
Yamdena 52 J 7
Yamethin 47 H 4
Yamma Yamma, Lake 60 G 5
Yamoussoukro 56 C 4
Yamzho Yumco 48 E 5
Yana 42 L 2
Yan'an 49 H 3
Yancheng 49 L 4
Yang Xian 49 H 4
Yangchun 49 J 6
Yanggao 49 J 2
Yangiyo'l 45 L 4
Yangjiang 49 J 6
Yangliuqing 49 K 3
Yangôn 47 H 5
Yangquan 49 J 3
Yangtze Kiang 48 F 4
Yangxin 49 K 5
Yangzhou 49 K 4
Yanji 54 A 2
Yankton 16 D 3
Yano-Indigirskaya Nizmennost' 42 M 3
Yanov Stan 41 S 4
Yanqing 50 C 4
Yanshou 50 E 3
Yantai 49 L 3
Yanyuan 49 G 5
Yanzhou 49 K 3
Yaoundé 56 E 4
Yap Islands 59 C 3
Yapen 53 K 6
Yaqui, Río 20 C 2
Yaransk 40 L 6
Yardimei Burnu 44 D 5
Yaren 59 F 4
Yarensk 40 L 5
Yarlung Zangbo Jiang 47 F 3
Yarmouth 14 F 2
Yaroslavl' 40 J 6
Yartsevo (Russia) 41 U 5

Yasawa Group 59 G 5
Yashkul' 44 G 3
Yasun Burnu 35 G 4
Yathkyed Lake 8 R 6
Yatsushiro 54 B 4
Yavatmāl 46 D 4
Yawata-hama 54 B 4
Yaxchilán 20 F 4
Yaxian 47 K 5
Yaya 41 T 6
Yazd 45 H 6
Yazoo City 16 E 5
Yazoo River 16 E 5
Ye 47 H 5
Yecheng 48 B 3
Yedinka 54 C 1
Yefremov 44 E 2
Yegor'yevsk 40 J 6
Yekaterinburg 40 O 6
Yelabuga 40 M 6
Yelan' 44 F 2
Yelets 44 E 2
Yelizarovo 40 P 5
Yelizovo 43 P 6
Yell 30 D 1
Yellow Sea 49 L 3
Yellowhead Pass 10 T 8
Yellowknife 10 U 6
Yellowstone Lake 18 D 3
Yellowstone National Park 18 D 3
Yellowstone River 16 C 2
Yelöten 45 K 5
Yel'sk 36 F 2
Yenangyaung 47 G 4
Yenisey 41 T 5
Yeniseysk 41 U 6
Yeniseyskiy Kryazh 41 T 5
Yeniseyskiy Zaliv 41 R 3
Yeo Lake 60 C 5
Yeovil 28 C 4
Yerbogachen 41 X 5
Yerevan 44 F 4
Yerköy 44 D 5
Yermitsa 40 M 4
Yermo 20 D 2
Yerofei-Pavlovich 42 H 6
Yershov 44 G 2
Yertsevo 40 K 5
Yeşilhisar 35 F 5
Yeşilırmak 35 G 4
Yessey 41 W 4
Yeu, Île d' 32 B 2
Yevpatoriya 35 E 2
Yevreyska Avtonom-naya Oblast' 54 B

Yeysk 35 H 1
Yi'an 50 E 3
Yibin 49 G 5
Yibug Caka 48 D 4
Yichang 49 J 4
Yichun (Heilongjiang, China) 50 E 3
Yichun (Jiangxi, China) 49 J 5
Yidu (Hubei, China) 49 J 4
Yidu (Shandong, China) 49 K 3
Yilan 50 E 3
Yıldızeli 35 G 5
Yin Shan 49 H 2
Yinchuan 49 H 3
Yingkou 50 D 4
Yining 48 C 2
Yirshi 50 C 3
Yishan 49 H 6
Yitong 50 E 4
Yitulihe 50 D 2
Yixian 50 D 4
Yiyang (Hunan, China) 49 J 5
Yiyang (Jiangxi, China) 49 K 5
Yizhang 49 J 5
Ymer Ø 8 Gg 4
Yogyakarta 52 E 7
Yokohama 54 C 3
Yokosuka 54 C 3
Yokote 54 D 3
Yonago 54 B 3
Yonaguni-shima 49 L 6
Yonezawa 54 D 3
Yongchang 49 G 3
Yongchuan 49 H 5
Yongdeng 49 G 3
Yonghung 54 A 3
Yŏngju 50 E 5
Yongxiu 49 K 5
Yonkers 14 E 2
York (Nebraska, U.S.) 16 D 3
York (Pennsylvania, U.S.) 14 D 3
York (U.K.) 28 D 3
York Factory 8 S 7
York, Cape 60 G 2
Yorke Peninsula 60 F 6
Yorkshire Wolds 28 D 3
Yorkton 10 W 8
Yoro 20 G 4
Yosemite National Park 18 B 4
Yoshkar-Ola 40 L 6
Yŏsu 50 E 6
Youngstown 14 C 2
Youyi Feng 41 T 8

Yozgat 35 F 5
Yreka 18 B 3
Yrghyz 45 K 3
Ysyk-Köl 45 N 4
Ytterhogdal 38 H 3
Ytyk-Kyuyel' 42 K 4
Yü Shan 49 L 6
Yüanlin 49 L 6
Yuanping 49 J 3
Yuanqu 49 J 3
Yübari 54 D 2
Yucatán 20 G 3
Yucatan Peninsula 20 G 3
Yucatán, Canal de 20 G 3
Yuci 49 J 3
Yueqing 49 L 5
Yuexi 49 G 5
Yueyang 49 J 5
Yugorskiy Poluostrov 40 O 4
Yugo-Tal 43 O 3
Yukhnov 44 E 2
Yukogirokoyo Plosko-gor'ye 43 O 3
Yukon 10 P 5
Yukon Flats 10 N 5
Yukon Flats National Monument 10 N 5
Yukon Plateau 10 P 6
Yukon River (Canada) 10 P 6
Yukon River (U.S.) 43 X 4
Yukon Territory 10 P 5
Yuli 48 D 2
Yulin (Guangxi, China) 49 J 6
Yulin (Shaanxi, China) 49 H 3
Yuma (Arizona, U.S.) 18 D 5
Yuma (Colorado, U.S.) 16 C 3
Yumen 48 F 3
Yumenzhen 48 F 2
Yun Xian 49 J 4
Yunaska Island 43 V 6
Yuncheng 49 J 3
Yunkai Dashan 49 J 6
Yunnan 49 G 6
Yunxiao 49 K 6
Yurga 41 S 6
Yushan 49 K 5
Yushkozero 40 H 5
Yushu 50 E 4
Yutian 48 C 3
Yuxi 49 G 6
Yuxian 49 J 3
Yuyao 49 L 4

Yuzhno Muyskiy Khrebet 42 F 5
Yuzhno-Aleksandrovka 41 V 6
Yuzhno-Sakhalinsk 54 D 1
Yuzhnyy Anyuyskiy Khrebet 43 Q 3
Zabol 45 K 6
Zabrze 36 D 2
Zabūrün'e 44 H 3
Zacapa 20 G 5
Zacápu 20 D 4
Zacatecas (Mexico) 20 D 3
Zacatecas (State, Mexico) 20 D 3
Zacatepec 20 E 4
Zachodnyaya Dzvina 38 L 4
Zadar 34 D 2
Zafra 33 A 2
Zagreb 36 D 3
Zahlah 44 E 6
Zakamensk 41 W 7
Zakopane 36 D 3
Zakynthos 34 E 3
Zalaegerszeg 36 D 3
Zalari 41 W 7
Zambeze 58 C 3
Zambezi 58 B 3
Zambia 58 B 3
Zamboanga 52 G 4

Zambonga Peninsula 52 G 4
Zambrów 36 E 2
Zamora 33 A 1
Zamora de Hidalgo 20 D 4
Zanesville 14 C 3
Zanjän 44 G 5
Zanul'ye 40 L 5
Zanzibar 58 C 2
Zanzibar Island 58 C 2
Zaoyang 49 J 4
Zaozhuang 49 K 4
Zapadno-Sibirskaya Ravnina 40 O 5
Zapadnyy Sayan 41 T 7
Zapala 24 D 6
Zaporizhzhya 44 E 3
Zara 35 G 5
Zaragoza 32 B 3
Zaragoza (Mexico) 20 D 2
Zarasai 38 L 4
Zárate 24 F 6
Zarghūn Shahr 45 L 6
Zaria 56 D 3
Żary 36 D 2
Zäskär Mountains 45 N 6
Zatoka Gdańska 38 J 4

Zatoka Pomorska 36 C 2
Zavitinsk 42 J 6
Zavodoukovsk 40 P 6
Zav'yalova, Ostrov 43 N 5
Zaysan 45 O 3
Zduńska Wola 36 D 2
Zeitz 36 C 2
Zelenodol'sk 40 L 6
Zelenogorsk 38 L 3
Zelenokumsk 44 F 4
Zenica 34 D 2
Žepa 34 D 2
Zestap'oni 35 K 3
Zeya 42 J 6
Zeya (River) 42 J 6
Zeyskoye Vodokhranilishche 42 J 6
Zgorzelec 36 D 2
Zhalaghash 45 K 3
Zhalpaqtal 44 G 3
Zhangaözen 44 H 4
Zhangaqala 44 G 3
Zhangatas 45 L 4
Zhangbei 49 J 2
Zhangguangcai Ling 50 E 4
Zhangjiakou 49 J 2
Zhangpu 49 K 6

Zhangwu 50 D 4
Zhangye 48 G 3
Zhangzhou 49 K 6
Zhänibek 44 G 3
Zhanjiang 49 J 6
Zhaoan 49 K 6
Zhaodong 54 A 1
Zhaodong Hulan 50 E 3
Zhaoguang 54 A 1
Zhaojue 49 G 5
Zhaoqing 49 J 6
Zhaotong 49 G 5
Zhaoxing 54 B 1
Zhaoyuan 50 E 3
Zhaozhou 54 A 1
Zharkent 45 N 4
Zhashkiv 44 D 3
Zhaysang Köli 45 O 3
Zhayylma 45 K 2
Zhayyq 44 H 3
Zhejiang 49 L 5
Zhelezïnka 45 N 2
Zheleznogorsk 44 E 2
Zheleznogorsk-Ilimskiy 41 W 6
Zhenghe 49 K 5
Zhengzhou 49 J 4
Zhenjiang 49 K 4
Zhenlai 50 D 3
Zhenning 49 H 5

Zhenxiong 49 G 5
Zhenyuan 49 H 5
Zherdevka 44 F 2
Zhetiqara 45 K 2
Zhezkazgan 45 L 3
Zhigalovo 41 W 7
Zhigansk 42 H 3
Zhigulevsk 44 G 2
Zhijiang 49 H 5
Zhmerynka 36 F 3
Zhob 46 B 2
Zhodzina 36 F 2
Zholymbet 45 M 2
Zhong Xian 49 H 4
Zhongshan 49 J 6
Zhongwei 49 H 3
Zhongxiang 49 J 4
Zhosaly 45 K 3
Zhou Shan Dao 49 L 4
Zhou Shan Quandao 49 L 4
Zhoukouzhen 49 J 4
Zhovtnevoye 44 D 3
Zhujiang Kou 49 J 6
Zhukovka 36 G 2
Zhumadian 49 J 4
Zhuolu 50 C 4
Zhuoxian 49 K 3
Zhushan 49 J 4
Zhuzhou 49 J 5
Zhytomyr 36 F 2
Zibo 49 K 3

Zielona Góra 36 D 2
Zigong 49 G 5
Zihuatanejo 20 D 4
Zile 44 E 4
Žilina 36 D 3
Zima 41 W 7
Zimatlán de Alvaréz 20 E 4
Zimbabwe 58 B 3
Zinder 56 D 3
Zitácuaro 20 D 4
Ziyang 49 G 4
Zlatoust 40 N 6
Zlín 36 D 3
Zmeinogorsk 45 O 2
Znamenka (Kazakhstan) 45 N 2
Znamenka (Ukraine) 44 D 3
Znojmo 36 D 3
Zonguldak 35 D 4
Zrenjanin 36 E 3
Zuera 32 B 3
Zugdidi 44 F 4
Zujevka 40 M 6
Zunyi 49 H 5
Zürich 36 B 3
Zvolen 36 D 3
Zwickau 36 C 2
Zwolle 36 B 2
Zyryanka 43 O 3
Zyryanovsk 45 O 3
Żywiec 36 E 3

This edition published 2006 by Geddes & Grosset, David Dale House, New Lanark, ML11 9DJ, Scotland
First published 2005, reprinted 2006 (twice)

Copyright © 2005 Geddes & Grosset

World maps created and supplied by Lovell Johns Limited, Oxfordshire, England

ISBN 10: 1 84205 496 1
ISBN 13: 978 1 84205 496 3

Printed and bound in India